BILINGUAL GRAMMAR O ENGLISH-SPANISH SYNTAX

With Exercises and Glossary of Grammatical Terms

THIRD EDITION

Sam Hill
María Mayberry
Edward Baranowski

University Press of America,® Inc.
Lanham · Boulder · New York · Toronto · Plymouth, UK

Copyright © 2014 by
University Press of America,® Inc.
4501 Forbes Boulevard
Suite 200
Lanham, Maryland 20706
UPA Acquisitions Department (301) 459-3366

10 Thornbury Road
Plymouth PL6 7PP
United Kingdom

All rights reserved
Printed in the United States of America
British Library Cataloging in Publication Information Available

Library of Congress Control Number: 2014936148
ISBN: 978-0-7618-6375-5 (clothbound : alk. paper)
ISBN: 978-0-7618-6376-2 (paperback : alk. paper)
eISBN: 978-0-7618-6377-9

Table Of Contents

Introduction		v

CHAPTERS

1	Basic Word Order in English and Spanish	1
2	English Verb Morphology	7
3	Spanish Regular Verb Morphology	17
4	Spanish Irregular Verb Morphology	31
5	The Comparative Syntax of Statements and Questions	47
6	A Question of Aspect: The Spanish Imperfect-Preterite Contrast	63
7	The Spanish Indicative and Subjunctive Moods	75
8	English Modal Auxiliaries and Their Spanish Equivalents	105
9	English Phrasal Verbs	127
10	English *To Be* vs. Spanish *Ser, Estar* and *Haber*	135
11	English and Spanish Personal Pronouns	147
12	*Gustar, Hacer, Tener* and *Dar*	167
13	Transitivity, Pronominal Verbs and Indefinite Subjects	175
14	The English and Spanish Imperative Systems	191
15	The Present Participle (Gerund) and the Infinitive	201
16	Passive Constructions	209
17	Conditional Sentences and Unreal Comparison	221
18	Spanish and English Verb + Preposition Constructions	229
19	Nouns and Articles; Possessive and Partitive Constructions	241
20	Descriptive and Limiting Adjectives	263
21	Possessive and Demonstrative Adjectives and Pronouns	275
22	Adverbs and Prepositions	283
23	Interrogatives, Admiratives, Ellipsis and Verification Tags	303
24	Spanish and English Contractions	317
25	Degrees of Comparison	321
26	Relative Words Used Between Clauses	331
27	Affirmative Words and their Negative Counterparts	341

Appendix I	351
Appendix II	357
Appendix III	359
Appendix IV	369
Glossary of Grammatical Terms	375
Bibliography	397
Index	401
About the Authors	411

Introduction to the Third Edition

The third edition of this text has an extensive history, dating back to the 1970's when Professor Hill developed a graduate level course in the comparative grammars of English and Spanish. Stockwell and Bowen had prepared their impressive inventory of the major inter-lingual contrasts with *The Grammatical Structures of English and Spanish* (1965), but although a brilliant contribution to comparative linguistics, the work was never useful in a truly pedagogical setting. In devising his course, Professor Hill strove to make the findings of these two scholars both accessible and helpful to advanced upper-division and graduate students, especially those planning on teaching careers. His materials first appeared as classroom handouts and then evolved into bound versions prepared by the campus bookstore. Students were enthusiastic about the new course and the embryonic teaching materials.

In the late '80's, Professor Bradford of the University of Puerto Rico, Río Piedras contacted Dr. Hill and, also concerned with the pedagogical validity of textbook writing, asked to co-author a published version of the original materials. As a professor of English linguistics, his contribution was to enhance the English component of the project. University Press of America published the text, and it appeared in two editions, the first in 1991 and the second (revised) in 2000. The third edition is a further revision and updating of the other two, but still dedicated to the concept that difficult and content-heavy linguistic courses can, through careful presentation, numerous examples and exercises be made friendly and practical to students working in and across the two languages. In preparing the third edition, the authors are particularly indebted to Stanley Whitley, Richard V. Teschner, Dale Koike and others too numerous to mention, whose relevant works appear in the bibliography.

Pedagogical Usefulness of the Text for Teachers and Translators

Two assumptions serve as the foundation for our comparative approach: (1) that we are all native speakers of one language and potentially successful learners of another, and (2) that we tend in our acquisition of a foreign or second language to carry over into it many of the linguistic features of our first language. The original materials for this book were prepared based on this Contrastive Analysis Hypotheses (CAH) originally formulated by Robert Lado in the late 1950's, and further developed by Bowen and Stockwell, and it remains true that many errors in the L2 (target language) are due to L1 (native language) transfer. In the late 60's and during the 70's, however, other studies (i.e., Error Analysis studies) have shown that errors/difficulties with the L2 are not always predicted by the contrast between the L1 and L2 (Corder, 1967). For instance, if the English speaker learning Spanish says, *Martha bonita*, the lack of a copula is not due to differences between the L1 and L2, since both languages use one. Today, then, any future language instructor must also be conversant with other hypotheses such as Input Hypothesis (Krashen, 1985), Interaction Hypothesis (Long, 1996), Noticing Hypothesis (Schmidt,1990), etc. as well as other developmental processes (i.e., *sobregeneralización*) that have been proposed to explain errors not accounted for by the CAH.

One of the most sought-after goals in the professional training of the foreign language or ESL/EFL/TOEFL instructors is total competency in both English and the target language. Yet even with this, teachers require a framework within which they can organize and categorize the host of seemingly disparate linguistic errors their students routinely make in the classroom Training in recognizing the areas of difference between the native language and the target language will help potential teachers to better comprehend and evaluate the linguistic behaviors of their students. Such understandings have become an essential component of the professional preparation of the foreign language or ESL/EFL/TOEFL instructor.

In recent years there has been much interest in language acquisition through actual communicative skill development, the well-researched so-called "direct approach." The errors learners make seem to be interferential primarily in the earliest phases of instruction. Developmental errors—those logically occurring as the learners attempt to expand their active skills patterned upon those they already dominate in the new language—soon became the focus of scholarly attention. The discipline of error analysis has become an area of considerable interest in linguistic studies. Discourse analysis, the examination of the context of utterances and the language strategies available to speakers, has also contributed to our overall knowledge of how languages actually function.

More recent research has placed lexical aspect alongside the traditional treatments of grammatical aspect in the Spanish rendering of past events. Likewise, the sequence of tenses in subjunctive sentences and the positioning of conjunctive (enclitic) pronouns with respect to various dependent infinitive constructions has been further clarified. The speaker's intentions as these affect indicative/subjunctive usage have also been demonstrated as a vital new insight into mood selection in Spanish. The fruits of such research appear in the third edition, but only to the extent that they serve the purpose of not only expanding but also further simplifying the original pedagogical mission of the text.

The comparative approach, then, to the extent that it promotes teachers' analytical skills, is clearly a necessary facet of any future language instructor's professional training. This text focuses upon the development of such skills by presenting the inter-lingual differences between English and Spanish as simply and directly as possible and by providing numerous exercises through which the nature of such differences become readily perceived and internalized.

Our Intended Audience

The third edition of the text will be useful to advanced upper-division or graduate students whose career plans include the teaching of Spanish to English speakers and *vice-versa*, and in the translation of both languages. Bilingual speakers whose professional goals do not include education or translation will find the manual useful if only as a reference work. Whether the student's native language is Spanish or English matters little provided one's four skills in both languages are essentially equal and well-developed. Ideally, students using the text will have taken previous coursework in advanced grammar and composition in both languages. A course in general linguistics providing an introductory study of phonology, phonetics, morphology and syntax would be very helpful, especially if it encompasses the vast array of topics included under the rubric of linguistics. Specific courses in both Spanish and English phonemics and phonetics would also be useful but not a requisite. Most important, however, is a solid knowledge of grammatical concepts and their terminology along with the realization that often a single phenomenon is designated by more than one technical term. Because terminology is a continually thorny problem in grammar studies, the authors have prepared an extensive glossary of grammatical terms for this third edition. It should prove invaluable to students.

Introduction to the Third Edition

Features of the Third Edition

The authors opted not to organize the new edition around the four major Parts encompassing the various Sections of the previous editions, but the newly designated "Chapters" do follow one another in a fairly logical sequence. Additionally, the original thirty-six Sections have morphed to twenty-seven Chapters, and some, especially old Sections 5 (Preterite/Imperfect), 20 (The Spanish Subjunctive) and 15/16 (Reflexives/Indefinite Subjects) appear as thoroughly revised and expanded in Chapters 6, 7 and 13, respectively. Chapter 8 (Modal Auxiliaries) and Chapter 19 (Nouns and Articles) show considerable reworking, with a greatly expanded treatment of noun gender in the latter. Necessary cosmetic changes and a careful re-combination of previously disparate Sections are additional highlights. We greatly expanded both the index and the bibliography for better access to a more extensive repository of materials. The Appendices were updated and better organized as well, with the omission of Appendix IV (Past Participles with Two Forms), and its replacement with a listing of verbal types and their usages. Last, the extensive glossary, mentioned earlier, is a novel feature of the third edition.

The re-combination of previous Sections is as follows: The new Chapter 23 (Short Structures) combines the previous Sections 24, 31, and 32 (Interrogatives, Admiratives and Ellipsis), respectively. Chapter 19 (Nouns and Articles) now includes Possessives and Partitives (former Sections 12 and 13). Chapter 22 (Adverbs and Prepositions) has added to it the original Sections 19 and 33 (Personal Accusative and the *por/para* contrast). Previous Sections 34 and 35 appear as Chapter 12, accounting for the peculiarities of verbs like *gustar* and locutions with *hacer, tener* and *dar*. Finally, we chose to exclude Section 36 (Miscellaneous Contrasts) of the first and second editions.

A salient feature of the text's second edition was the exercise key. The authors, after considerable classroom texting and input from colleagues at other institutions, took the decision to omit this feature in the third edition. We found to our surprise and dismay that the key produced more problems than it solved. The reason might be that the manual was never intended for students to work through independently, without a competent instructor and a group of classmates from various linguistic and dialectal backgrounds.

The Chapters, when taken as a whole, seek to represent an extensive inventory of the major grammatical differences between English and Spanish, but by no means has every possible contrast been covered. Aside from its presentation of the few essential phonetic items like the pronunciation of English plurals and the regular past tense, and of the morphological realities of gender/number inflections and the Spanish and English verbal systems, the text deals almost exclusively with syntax. We have taken into consideration the broad range of Spanish varieties viewed as standard and have consulted the opinions of linguistic authorities dealing with these. The relatively new *Gramática de la Real Academia Española* has been of great assistance as an authoritative source, one long awaited by all interested in the Spanish language. Another useful reference has been *Diccionario panhispánico de dudas*. As for the English component, standard American usage dominates, but common features of British English also appear. The lexicon of Spanish and its many regional varieties is often a problem for students; we advise that the instructor not become so concerned with it as to lose sight of the text's primary purpose—that of perceiving grammatical structure as a coherent system and a basis for inter-lingual structural comparisons. The authors have attempted throughout to maintain an even-handed balance between prescriptive and descriptive norms. The linguistic expectations of the highly educated language specialist and realities of daily spoken and written usage are often in needless conflict. We have sought a "happy medium" with annotations and explanations where appropriate.

Introduction to the Third Edition

The Exercises and a Notation Used in the New Edition

A major feature of the third edition, as was the case with former two versions of the text, is its exercises. We have retained them with only slight revision. Students seem to benefit most from the comparative analytical method when, after studying the nature of any given contrast, they perform exercises to consolidate their understandings and to discern clearly the applicable linguistic rule. The exercises are generally of two types: (l) translation from one language into the other as a means of perceiving and applying inter-lingual grammatical rules, and (2) restatement in the same language of a particular grammatical construction. The latter type proves particularly useful when either language has an alternate structure for conveying the same idea.

Many of the exercises have been framed bilingually, that is, alternating between the two languages on consecutive lines. We find this a unique approach to dual language comparison, and although some critics have voiced reservations about this format, the authors find that it aids students in developing complete bilingual competence. You should also note that students no longer have to provide any specific one of the five possible equivalents for English *you,* and are free to choose, with sporadic exception.

The symbol * (the asterisk) has various uses in the text:
1. In a grammar formula, it designates a possible contraction between one element, usually an auxiliary verb, and *not*: AUX *have* + not* > *have not* or *haven't*.
2. If doubled, the formula shows that the contraction is mandatory: AUX *do**+ not + S +* verbal remainder? > *Don't you know?*
3. It tags incorrect forms or non-grammatical utterances used only to make a point, such as, **truje, *vide* or **He don't got none*.
4. It may appear as usual to mark some item(s) which will be explained later in a note.

Finally, cross references within the text are marked for chapter and paragraph as, 16.4 (Chapter 16, paragraph 4).

Revised Edition Acknowledgements

We offer our special thanks to the many enthusiastic instructors who have used our former editions and communicated their constructive comments and suggestions, Additionally, we are greatly indebted to all learners who benefitted from our efforts and who subsequently informed us. We express further gratitude to our own Spanish M.A. candidates who, both as local Sacramento State students and as participants in the Department's Three-Summer M.A. Program in Guatemala, Mexico, Peru and Spain, have taken a special interest in our texts. Special acknowledgement is due to J. Alberto Santos Morales, who proofed and prepared the camera-ready manuscript, and for his many contributions through the old but trustworthy *"¿Te suena o no te suena?"* process.

Sam Hill (Emeritus, 2002)
María Mayberry
Edward Baranowski

California State University, Sacramento
March, 2014

1
Basic Word Order In English and Spanish

1.1
INTRODUCTION

In our study of syntactic structures, we compare the grammars of two major world languages—English and Spanish. English, it has been said, is the world's most widely used language for international communication and business, and Spanish is either the first or second language of many peoples throughout the Western Hemisphere. Spanish is spoken in Spain, Africa, the United States, Latin America and areas of the Pacific.

The linguistic origins of the two languages are quite different, both coming from essentially diverse backgrounds, but with some convergence in certain areas. The Latinized elements of English and its heavy Romance borrowings illustrate some of these. English belongs to the Germanic family of languages and in its evolution has experienced a reduction and in many cases a complete loss of the grammatical inflections characterizing other members of the family. A more rigidly structured word order has been the compensatory result of this morphological attrition. Spanish is a Romance language evolved from Latin, a highly inflected language with an extremely flexible word order. Modern Spanish retains many of those categories of inflection and variable syntax.

1.2
ELEMENTS OF PREDICATION

Traditionally, both English and Spanish sentences consist of predications, that is, one states (predicates) something about the subject. It follows that the main grammatical divisions of a sentence are the subject and the predicate, although in Spanish the subject may not always be as overtly discernible as in English. Since every finite verb form in Spanish implies a subject, the verb form alone can constitute a complete sentence. The predicate embraces units called elements of sentence structure, each named for the function it performs in the overall predication.

These elements consist of single or multi-word units, which further divide into parts-of-speech categories.

Because Spanish comes from Latin and its verbal forms are so clearly marked for person, number, tense, aspect, and mood, it allows considerable flexibility in the ordering of its sentence elements. English, however, exhibits less variation with respect to word order. This general observation is particularly important when we consider the positioning of the English subject and its verb.

1.3
BASIC WORD ORDER IN ENGLISH

English generally organizes the elements of its sentence structure with the subject (S) first and then follows it with the verb (V). The verb, the main component of the predicate, may take other elements, either singularly or in combinations. These are usually called complements (C): the direct object (DO), the indirect object (IO), adverbs (A), prepositional phrases (PP), in addition to others. In the examples given, the predicate appears in bold and its structural elements are in parenthesis.

Several men **came**. (S+V)
The lion **killed a person**. (S+V+DO)
I **sent a copy to my friend**. (S+V+DO+IO)
Few students **came into the classroom today**. (S+V+PP+A)

English does deviate more often than commonly thought from its usual subject + verb word order, as in these examples:

There are three of them. (existential *there*)
Am I ever bored! (emphatic statement)
"Ha, ha," **said** the clown. (direct quotation)

1.4
BASIC WORD ORDER IN SPANISH

Spanish routinely positions the subject after the verb as often as before it. Spanish may even suppress an overt subject since the various verbal endings clearly imply one. This is commonly referred to as the "null subject" and about this point, the *Real Academia Española* in its *Gramática* states (§202) that the inflected verb "contains in itself the subject, be it definite or indefinite, and is equivalent [the inflected verb] on its own to a complete sentence." Examine the following pairs of Spanish sentences, both renditions meaning the same, but with a somewhat different emphasis, as explained in 1.6.

La maestra **vino**. (S+V)
Vino la maestra. (V+S)

El hombre **nos dijo la verdad**. (S+IO+V+DO)
Nos dijo la verdad el hombre. (IO+V+DO+S)

Tus amigos te **esperaban ayer.** (S+DO+V+A)
Te esperaban ayer tus amigos. (DO+V+A+S)

Subject not overtly expressed:

Llegó en 1970. (V+PP)
En 1970 llegó. (PP+V)

1.5
COMPARISON

English speakers are often baffled by the word order V+S of Spanish since it occurs so rarely in English. Spanish instructors need caution English speakers about the frequency of the Spanish V+S word order and, although unusual in English, it is normal and of very high frequency in Spanish. The most common instance where the V+S word order occurs in English is in certain interrogative sentences where it is required (Chapter 5). All or part of the predicate shifts (is fronted, i.e., moved to the beginning of the sentence) also in assertive and common or folk expressions.

Who is that? (interrogative)
There standing before me was my accuser. (assertive)
Gone are the good old days. (common expression)

The one structure in which English parallels Spanish in not overtly expressing a subject is that of the imperative:

Stand in front of them! (V+PP)

Exercise 1

Write original English and Spanish sentences patterned after the syntactical (structural) types below:

LANGUAGE	STRUCTURAL TYPE	LANGUAGE	STRUCTURAL TYPE
1. Eng.	(S+V)	10. Span.	(IO+V+DO+S)
2. Eng.	(S+V+DO)	11. Span.	(S+V+DO)
3. Eng.	(S+V+DO+IO)	12. Span.	(V+DO+S)
4. Eng.	(S+V+PP+A)	13. Span.	(V+PP)
5. Eng.	(existential *there*)	14. Span.	(PP+V)
6. Eng.	(direct quotation)	15. Eng.	(interrogative)
7. Span.	(V+S)	16. Eng.	(assertive)
8. Span.	(S+V)	17. Eng.	(common expression)
9. Span.	(S+IO+V+DO)	18. Eng.	(imperative) (V+PP)

Exercise 2

Translate the following sentences placing the subject after the predicate. Then rewrite each translation, using the S+V+Complement word order.

1. Juan will do the job.
2. Four of my friends left the bus.
3. The guests didn't arrive until after ten (o'clock).
4. Freddy has my book and his parents know it.
5. Your papers are on the desk.
6. A salesman with a loud voice showed me the house.
7. Joseph didn't see anyone at the station this morning.
8. The birds were singing, but the deaf girl couldn't hear them.

1.6
WORD ORDER AND EMPHATIC USAGE IN ENGLISH AND SPANISH

When an English speaker wishes to place particular emphasis on a certain element of a sentence, he/she uses vocal stress (phonic intensification). In the written language, the stressed element is often italicized, as in the following examples.

The woman bought an orange. (i.e., not the man)
The woman **bought** an orange. (i.e., she didn't just take one)
The woman bought **an orange**. (i.e., not an apple)

The use of vocal stress for the purpose of placing special emphasis on a particular element of a sentence occurs in Spanish also, and usually combines with strategically placed pauses. Pauses may appear between the subject and predicate or between the S+V element and a complement.

La mujer | compró la naranja.
La mujer compró | *la naranja*.

In the first example vocal stress accompanies the first element of the sentence, *la mujer*, and in the second it appears with the last element, *la naranja*. In addition to vocal stress, and perhaps more frequently employed in Spanish, is a syntactic device used for emphasis. Spanish prosody helps put emphasis on the final element of a sentence, the place Spanish reserves for new and important information. The flexibility of Spanish word ordering allows this, and it has an emphatic effect wherever grammatically possible. Therefore, when the subject of the verb is the new or emphasized information, Spanish places it in the post-verbal position (Bolinger, 1954):

¿Quién compró una naranja?
La niña. or Compró una naranja **la niña**. (V+DO+S) = **The girl** bought an orange.

¿La niña compró una naranja?
No, la compró **su mamá**. (DO Pronoun + V + S) = No, **her mother** bought one.

¿Dónde estabas?
Se me perdió **la tarea.**

> **Note:** The verb does not appear in final position in any of these examples of conversational or normal usage. Final positioning of a finite verb is for classical poetry or archaic literary styles. For example: *La niña una naranja compró.*

These same formulas are possible when the predicate contains a complement of circumstance (i.e., A or PP).

¿Cuándo vendrá la mujer?
La mujer vendrá **inmediatamente/dentro de poco**. (S+V+C)
Vendrá la mujer **inmediatamente/dentro de poco**. (V+S+C)

¿Quién vendrá inmediatamente/dentro de poco?
La mujer. or Vendrá inmediatamente/dentro de poco **la mujer.** (V+C+S)

Spanish concurs with English in permitting the interchanging of direct object with indirect object complements in the predicate: *He gave me his car = He gave his car to me.* However, when the indirect object is a prepositional pronoun and not a pronominal phrase, certain restrictions apply in both languages (See 11.13).

¿Para quién trajo un libro?
Trajo un libro **para mí**. (V+DO+IO)

¿Qué trajo para ti?
Trajo para mí **un libro**. (V+IO+DO)

¿Qué nos trajo?
A mí me trajo un **libro**; a ti, **un CD.**

Sentences like the last two above are presented in Chapter 11 where we take up two topics showing that certain syntactic rearrangements are possible for stressing or contrasting direct and indirect objects. Nominal and pronominal reduplication appear in 11.13 followed by Topicalization in 11.14

Exercise 3

Translate the following sentences, showing that the bold elements are stressed or new information by placing them as close to the end of the sentence as grammatically possible.

1. **Many people** rent houses.
2. Many people **rent** houses.
3. Our daughter left **last night**.
4. My father isn't in **his office**.
5. I brought **a letter** for you.
6. I bring this gift **for all of you.**
7. **Many people** bought that book.

8. Many people **bought** that book.
9. Classes end **next week**.
10. The boys are **at home**.
11. They showed **the examples** to the teacher.
12. They showed the examples **to the teacher.**

2
English Verb Morphology

2.1

The most characteristic aspect of the English verbal system is its very limited number of verb forms and its heavy reliance upon auxiliary verbs. In classifying verbs according to their function, we distinguish lexical verbs (LV) from the closed system of auxiliary verbs (AUX). English verbs normally have five forms: the base form, also called the lexical verb (LV), the -s form, the past, the present participle, and the past participle. Variations occur within this system: some verbs have less than five forms and others have more. Examples are the eight-form verb *be*, which is over-differentiated (has an unusually large number of forms for English), and the modal verb *must*, classified as defective since it has but one form.

One form	must
Two forms	shall, should
Three forms	let, lets, letting
Four forms	call, calls, calling, called
Five forms	show, shows, showed, showing, shown
Eight forms	be, am, is, are, was, were, being, been

There are many irregular verbs in the English inventory, and these are often difficult to classify. Some irregular verbs will follow consistent phonological patterns, and others must simply be memorized since their patterns are so varied. The correct spelling of many forms is also problematic, not only for non-native but for native speakers of English as well. We shall begin by giving examples of the standard verbal forms found in the verb phrase (VP). Later we present examples of a regular verb and various irregular verbs used in sentences. The irregularities include both morphologic and orthographic variations.

LEXICAL VERB FORMS

FORM	EXAMPLE	USE
BASE/LEXICAL VERB	call drink put	(a) All persons, except 3rd person singular, present tense. (b) With all auxiliaries except *have* and *be* to form verb compounds. (c) Infinitive, either alone or in combination with the prepositional verbal particle *to*. (d) Imperative. (e) Subjunctive.
-s FORM	calls drinks puts	3rd person singular present tense.
PAST	called drank put	Past tense.
PRESENT PARTICIPLE	calling drinking putting	(a) Progressive aspect (*be* + base *-ing*). (b) Non-finite *-ing* clauses.
PAST PARTICIPLE	called drunk put	(a) Perfective aspect (*have* + past participle). (b) Passive voice (*be* + past participle). (c) Non-finite *-ed* clauses.

2.2
THE REGULAR VERB

An English verb is considered **regular** if its **past tense** and **past participle are identical** and **end in -ed**. A regular verb has only four distinct forms. Taking the regular verb *to walk* as an example, we find the following forms:

FORM	EXAMPLE	USE
BASE/LEXICAL VERB	walk	(a) I/You/We/They walk to school. (present tense) (b) You can walk now. (with auxiliary) (c) I made them walk/I want to walk. (infinitive) (d) Walk straight ahead. (imperative) (e) They require that he walk a lot. (subjunctive)

-s FORM	walks	She walks beautifully. (*3rd person singular, present*)
PAST	walked	They walked past us.
PRESENT PARTICIPLE	walking	(a) We are walking too fast. (*progressive aspect*) (b) Walking is good for you. (*non-finite -ing clause*)
PAST PARTICIPLE	walked	(a) They have walked a lot. (*perfective aspect*) (b) The dog is walked each day for exercise. (*passive voice*) (c) Walked to exhaustion, she went home. (*non-finite -ed clause*)

2.3
THE MORPHOLOGICALLY IRREGULAR VERB

An English verb is morphologically irregular if it has any one of the following characteristics:

a. its past and past participle forms are different (*came/come*),
b. its past and past participle forms are the same but do not end in –ed (*cut/cut*),
c. its present tense form does not use -s in the third person singular (*must*).

An irregular verb will usually demonstrate all five different forms, with some very common exceptions. Taking the irregular verb *go*, for example, the forms are:

FORM	EXAMPLE	USE
BASE/LEXICAL VERB	go	(a) I/You/We/They go to school. (*present tense*) (b) You may go. (*with auxiliary*) (c) I saw them go/I want to go. (*infinitive*) (d) Go straight home! (*imperative*) (e) The law requires that he go to school. (*subjunctive*)
-s FORM	goes	He goes to work early. (*3rd person singular, present*)
PAST	went	She went past us.
PRESENT PARTICIPLE	going	(a) We are going too fast. (*progressive aspect*) (b) Going by way of downtown, you save time. (*non-finite clause*)
PAST PARTICIPLE	gone	(a) They have gone two blocks. (*perfective aspect*) (b) It was gone when we came. (*passive voice*) (c) Our funds gone, we declared bankruptcy. (*non-finite clause*)

2.4

The verb *be* is particularly irregular since it has three forms in the present and two in the past. Furthermore, its past forms are different from its past participle. The verb *be*, either as a LV or an AUX has a total of eight distinct forms, most of which are suppletive (Chapter 4.14) *Be* is the most differentiated verb in English and its peculiarities follow:

FORM	EXAMPLE	USE
BASE	be	(a) You may be late to school. (with auxiliary) (b) I let them be here/I want to be a lawyer. (infinitive) (c) Be on time! (imperative) (d) They asked that we be on time. (subjunctive)
PRESENT	am is are	I am a student I He/She/It is at work. You/We/They are at school.
PAST	was were	I/He/She/It was on time. You/We/They were late.
PRESENT PARTICIPLE	being	(a) You are being difficult again. (progressive aspect) (b) Being well prepared, we knew all of the answers. (non-finite clause)
PAST PARTICIPLE	been	They have been here twice. (Note: *be* is not used in the passive voice nor in an *-ed* clause.)

A fairly complete listing of contemporary English irregular verbs appears in Appendix I.

2.5
THE ENGLISH AUXILIARY VERBS

The English auxiliary verbs are divided into two classes—primary and modal.

Primary Auxiliaries

The primary English auxiliary verbs (*do, have,* and *be*) carry no lexical or dictionary meaning of their own but are inflected for person, number, and tense. Do not be confused; they can occur as lexical verbs also where they have meaning. Thus we have *do, have, be* as LV and *do, have, be* as primary AUX. These three verbs are the only irregular verbs in the English present tense

Chapter 2 English Verb Morphology

DO ~ HAVE ~ BE

Used as lexical verbs:

We were in Spain.
They had five children.
He does his best work alone.

Used as primary auxiliaries:

We weren't living abroad.
They had left for Acapulco.
Does he know our names?

Do (primary AUX) is used to form negative statements or questions in the English present and past tenses. It combines with the base form/LV as follows:

PRESENT: *do/does*

I don't go often.
Do they go every day?
Doesn't he go every day?
When does she go?

PAST: *did*

I didn't go often.
Did they go every day?
Didn't he go every day?
When did she go?

As a lexical verb, *do* translates into Spanish as *hacer*. English *make* is also *hacer* in Spanish. This presents a difficult problem for the Spanish speaker learning English.

They do their homework in the library.
Hacen la tarea en la biblioteca.

The make a lot of noise playing.
Hacen mucho ruido jugando.

Have (primary AUX) plus the past participle of a LV forms the perfect tenses. These express both anteriority to other actions and the completion (perfection) of an action. As a lexical verb it expresses possession: *They have a new car.*

PRESENT PERFECT: *has/have*

He has left.
Have you done everything?
Haven't they arrived?
Where has he gone?

PAST PERFECT: *had*

He had gone earlier.
Had you done everything last week?
Hadn't they arrived already?
Where had he gone when you called?

Be (primary AUX) joins with the present participle (gerund/LV ending in –*ing*) to form the progressive tenses, which, as the name suggests, express ongoing actions in progress. *Be* also occurs with the past participle in producing the passive voice. (See Chapter 16). *Be* as a lexical verb uses Spanish *ser*, *estar* or *haber*, a major learning challenge for the English speaker.

PROGRESSIVE TENSES

I am telling you a story.
We aren't singing.
Are you bringing him?

PASSIVE VOICE

I am told many lies.
The tune is rarely sung.
He was brought by his sister.

Isn't he/she/it running?	It had been run incompetently.
Where are they keeping it?	It will be kept in a safe place.
I was eating.	It was eaten by the coyote.
They weren't showing it.	The movie wasn't shown.
Were you holding it?	The party was held here.
Wasn't he/she/it seeing well?	Have you been seen by anyone?
Why were we losing money?	Why was the money lost?

> **Note:** *Will* and *would* are also primary auxiliaries when occurring with lexical verbs to express futurity (*He will go later*) and conditionality (*He would go if he had the time*). They also appear as modal auxiliaries with a variety of meanings. (See Chapter 8)

Modal Auxiliaries

The modal auxiliaries verbs carry a dictionary or true lexical meaning of their own. Listed below are the most commonly cited ones. They are not inflected for person or number and regularly combine with the base form/LV; the last two usually require an infinitive (*to* + base form/LV = INF). Modal auxiliaries are taken up in detail in Chapter 8.

AFFIRMATIVE	NEGATIVE
can	cannot/can not/can't
could	could not/couldn't
may	may not
might	might not/mightn't
shall	shall not/shan't
should	should not/shouldn't
will/ 'll	will not/ 'll not/won't
would/'d	would not/ 'd not/wouldn't
must	must not/mustn't
need	need not/needn't
dare	dare not/daren't
ought (to)	ought not/oughtn't
used to	used to not/used not to/didn't used to

2.6
VERBS WITH ORTHOGRAPHIC IRREGULARITIES

There are verbs whose only irregularity involves the spelling of their present and past participles. They appear under five major categories.

1. With verbs ending in a single consonant preceded by a single accented vowel, before adding *-ing* or *-ed*, you double the consonant.

BASE FORM	PRESENT PARTICIPLE	PAST PARTICIPLE
commit	committing	committed
control	controlling	controlled
prefer	preferring	preferred
wed	wedding	wedded

Chapter 2 English Verb Morphology

2. With verbs ending in -*l*, -*m*, and a few in -*p*, even though the preceding vowel is unstressed, you double the consonant in the present participle and in the past participle in British English but not in the American variety (except in computer and technological usage).

BASE FORM	PRESENT PARTICIPLE	PAST PARTICIPLE
cancel	(Br) cancelling (Am) canceling	(Br) cancelled (Am) canceled
program	(Br) programming (Am) programing	(Br) programmed (Am) programed
worship	(Br) worshipping (Am) worshiping	Br) worshipped (Am) worshiped

Note: This same differentiation also applies to the nouns formed from such verbs: (Br) traveller, (Am) traveler.

3. Verbs ending in the letter -*c* change this to -*ck*- before adding the -*ing*/-*ed* endings.

BASE FORM	PRESENT PARTICIPLE	PAST PARTICIPLE
traffic	trafficking	trafficked
picnic	picnicking	picnicked

4. If a verb ends in silent -*e*, the vowel is dropped before adding the -*ing*/-*ed* inflections.

BASE FORM	PRESENT PARTICIPLE	PAST PARTICIPLE
accuse	accusing	accused
compare	comparing	compared
excite	exciting	excited
prove	proving	proved
smile	smiling	smiled

You retain the silent -*e* before -*ing*, however, in a few verbs like *dye* and *singe* and the few that end in -*oe*: *dyeing, singeing, hoeing*.

5. If a verb ends in a consonant + *y*, change the -*y* to -*ied* in the past and past participle forms. The rule also applies to the third person singular present tense forms (*apply* > *applies*) and to the regular formation of plural nouns (*ruby* > *rubies*).

BASE FORM	PAST	PAST PARTICIPLE
apply	applied	applied
carry	carried	carried

With the past participle forms of *lay, pay,* and *say*, which end in a vowel + *y*, you drop the -*y* after the vowel and add -*id*; the -*ing* form is unaltered.

BASE FORM	PAST PARTICIPLE	PRESENT PARTICIPLE
lay	laid	laying
pay	paid	paying
say	said	saying

On the other hand, in monosyllabic verbs such as *die* and *lie*, you change the *-ie* to *-y* before adding the *-ing* ending: *dying, lying*.

Exercise 1
Select ten regular English verbs other than those already mentioned and give all of their forms.

Exercise 2
Give the present participle and past participle forms of the following verbs:

1. prove
2. control
3. dye
4. commit
5. try
6. travel
7. worry
8. prefer
9. lie
10. compare
11. traffic
12. lay
13. program
14. say
15. worship

2.7
RULES OF PRONUNCIATION FOR CERTAIN ENGLISH VERBS

The present tense, third person singular verb form consistently ends in *-s*, but it may have three different pronunciations, depending on the final sound of the lexical verb.

Rules:
a. If the lexical verb ends in a **voiceless consonant sound** <u>other than</u> **[s], [ʃ],** or **[tʃ]**, *-s* is added with the value of **[s]**: *hit/hits* [hɪts], *kick/kicks* [kɪks], *step/steps* [stɛps], *laugh/laughs* [læfs]. Those voiceless consonant sounds that this applies to are **[p, t, k, f, θ]**.

b. If the lexical verb ends in **a vowel sound** or a **voiced consonant sound** <u>other than</u> **[z, ʒ, dʒ]**, *-s* is added with the value of **[z]**: *know/knows* [nouz], *see/sees* [siiz], *rain/rains* [reinz], *give/gives* [gɪvz]. The voiced consonant sounds that this applies to are **[b, d, g, m, n, ŋ, v, ð, l, r]**.

c. If the lexical verb ends in **the sibilants [s, z, ʃ, tʃ, ʒ, dʒ]**, the third-person singular marker *-s* has the value of **[-ɪz]** pronounced as an extra syllable and written in most instances as *-es*: *race/races* [reisɪz], *lose/loses* [luuzɪz], *wish/wishes* [wɪʃɪz], *enrich/enriches* [ɪnrɪtʃɪz], *pledge/pledges* [plɛdʒɪz].

Note: It should be mentioned here that exactly the same rules apply to the plural of most English nouns, as presented in Chapter 19.

2.8

The pronunciation of the **regular** past and past participial forms (those ending in *-ed*) is a follows:

Rules:

a. If the lexical verb ends in a **voiceless consonant sound** <u>other than</u> **[t]**, *-ed* is added with the value of **[t]**: *peep/peeped* [piipt], *kick/kicked* [kɪkt], *pass/passed* [pæst], *laugh/laughed* [læft]. The voiceless consonants occurring in final position in verbs are **[p, t, k, f, θ, s, ʃ, tʃ]**.

b. If the lexical verb ends in **a vowel sound** or in **a voiced consonant sound** <u>other than</u> **[d]**, *-ed* is added with the value of **[d]**: *sew/sewed* [soud], *tease teased* [tiizd], *blame/blamed* [bleimd], *stab/stabbed* [stæbd], *tag/tagged* [tægd]. The voiced consonants found in final position in verbs are **[b, g, v, ð, z, ʒ, dʒ, m, n, ŋ, l, r]**.

c. If the lexical verb ends in <u>either the sound of</u> **[t]** or **[d]**, then *-ed* is added with the value of **[ɪd]** pronounced as an extra syllable: *seat/seated* [siitɪd] *wade/waded* [weidɪd].

Exercise 3

Give the third person singular present tense form of the verbs in group A and the past/past participle form of the verbs in group B. Carefully pronounce each form and cite the applicable rules.

A.
1. sneeze	5. cry	9. go	13. cough	17. push
2. swim	6. strive	10. skate	14. sing	18. call
3. cook	7. search	11. judge	15. sew	19. start
4. prefer	8. slap	12. pass	16. hate	20. burp

B.
1. test	5. cash	9. convey	13. try	17. end
2. live	6. seem	10. crack	14. drag	18. rush
3. sob	7. precede	11. pay	15. breathe	19. stab
4. learn	8. raise	12. guarantee	16. grunt	20. hate

3

Spanish Regular Verb Morphology

3.1

An impressive characteristic of the Spanish verbal system is its numerous forms of the same verb, each normally marked morphologically for person, number, tense, aspect, and mood. Person and number refer to the three grammatical persons in both the singular and the plural that are reflected in the conjugation of Spanish verbs. This subject/verb relationship is called agreement.

PERSON	SINGULAR	PLURAL
1st	yo	nosotros/as
2nd	tú, usted, (vos)	vosotros/as, ustedes
3rd	él, ella	ellos, ellas

In addition to person and number agreement, there is the additional dimension of formal vs. familiar address, often called register. The pronouns *usted* (*Ud./Vd.*) 'you' singular (*vos* in some dialectal areas) and *ustedes* (*Uds./Vds.*) 'you' plural are in complementary distribution with *tú* and *vosotros/vosotras,* and this shows in the verbal inflections. Since these forms, *usted* and *ustedes*, were probably derived from *vuestra merced (Your Grace)*, Spanish uses the verb form which corresponds to the third person, not the second. Something similar occurs in English: We say, *You know...*, but *Your Honor knows...*, using the third person singular form to indicate deference to the addressee.

By tense we mean the three general time frames in which verbs are cast: present, past, and future. These may occur as a simple verb form or as a compound verb form using an auxiliary. Aspect tells us how one chooses to view an event: is it viewed as punctual, progressive, durative, repetitive, completed or incomplete? A Spanish verbal form, with few exceptions, expresses a variety of grammatical features through morphological inflection: the different persons, the two numbers, the various tenses and aspects, in addition to mood.

Mood in the verb form is a broader classification which describes the speakers' attitude towards what they are saying (for example, a statement, an opinion, a wish, etc.). Spanish has three moods: indicative, subjunctive, and imperative, although some authorities reject the imperative as a true mood. The indicative mood expresses factual statements. The subjunctive mood denotes a subjective idea. For example, in *Sé que el juego es a las seis,* there is a statement of fact. However, in *Me alegra que el juego sea a las seis,* the game is still a reality, but we are venturing an opinion on or reaction to that fact. A subjunctive verb form is almost always subordinate to another verb or expression conveying opinions, feelings, wishes, doubts, etc., or it occurs to soften a command, as in, *Quiero que estudies.* The imperative mood expresses commands, requests, and advice, and in all but two cases its forms are those of the subjunctive mood.

3.2
MORPHEMES OF THE SPANISH VERB AND THE COMPONENTS OF VERBAL PARADIGMS

In morphological terms the Spanish verb consists of four elements: a stem (root) morpheme (*morfema lexemático*), a thematic morpheme (*vocal temática*), a tense/aspect morpheme (*morfema auxiliar*), and a person/number morpheme (*morfema concordante*). We describe the verb in a slightly different manner for sound pedagogical reasons. Elements two and three (thematic morpheme and tense/aspect morpheme) combine into one (mood/tense/aspect), thereby lessening the learner's memorization burden. In certain conjugations, some morphemes are absent. These are marked ø.

The model regular verbs *amar, temer,* and *vivir* illustrate these three morphemic elements as follows:

VERB FORM	STEM	MOOD/TENSE ASPECT	PERSON/ NUMBER
(2nd s.) amabas	am-	-a ba-	-s
(1st pl.) tememos	tem-	-e re-	-mos
(3rd pl.) vivieron	viv-	-ie ro-	-n

Based on the vowel of the infinitive ending, regular Spanish verbs are classified in three groups. The first conjugation has an *-ar* ending, the second conjugation, an *-er* ending and the third conjugation, an *-ir* ending. The *-r* in each case is the infinitive marker. The infinitive is the nominal (noun) form of the verb—the name of the action or state of being. Each conjugation appears in two moods, the indicative and the subjunctive. Some add a third mood, the imperative. Under indicative and subjunctive headings you find the various tenses of each mood which include both the simple and the compound tenses. The three morphemes involved perform their specialized grammatical functions through the numerous tenses and forms of both moods.

Falling outside the above classifications is another group of verbal forms which are of a non-finite, non-personal character, that is, they remain largely uninflected. These are the so-called verbids, composed of the infinitive (*decir*), the present participle (gerund), *diciendo* and the past participle (*dicho*).

Traditional Spanish grammars show a regular Spanish verb paradigm to have a total of 62 simple verb forms and 56 compound verb forms, making the grand total of 118 conjugated forms in a complete regular verb paradigm.

Chapter 3 Spanish Regular Verb Morphology

SIMPLE TENSES OF THREE MODEL REGULAR VERBS

3.3

	FIRST CONJUGATION	SECOND CONJUGATION	THIRD CONJUGATION
INFINITIVE	am a r	tem e r	viv i r
PRESENT PARTICIPLE	am a ndo	tem ie ndo	viv ie ndo
PAST PARTICIPLE	am a do	tem i do	viv i do

INDICATIVE MOOD

PRESENT
- (1 s.) am o / tem o / viv o
- (2 s.) am a s / tem e s / viv e s
- (3 s.) am a / tem e / viv e
- (1 pl.) am a mos / tem e mos / viv i mos
- (2 pl.) am á is / tem é is / viv í s
- (3 pl.) am a n / tem e n / viv e n

IMPERFECT
- (1 s.) am aba / tem ía / viv ía
- (2 s.) am aba s / tem ía s / viv ía s
- (3 s.) am aba / tem ía / viv ía
- (1 pl.) am ába mos / tem ía mos / viv ía mos
- (2 pl.) am aba is / tem ía is / viv ía is
- (3 pl.) am aba n / tem ía n / viv ía n

PRETERITE
- (1 s.) am é / tem í / viv í
- (2 s.) am aste Ø / tem iste Ø / viv iste Ø
- (3 s.) am ó / tem ió / viv ió
- (1 pl.) am a mos / tem i mos / viv i mos
- (2 pl.) am aste is / tem iste is / viv iste is
- (3 pl.) am aro n / tem iero n / viv iero n

FUTURE
- (1 s.) am aré / tem eré / viv iré
- (2 s.) am ará s / tem erá s / viv irá s
- (3 s.) am ará / tem erá / viv irá
- (1 pl.) am are mos / tem ere mos / viv ire mos
- (2 pl.) am aré is / tem eré is / viv iré is
- (3 pl.) am ará n / tem erá n / viv irá n

CONDITIONAL
- (1 s.) am aría / tem ería / viv iría
- (2 s.) am aría s / tem ería s / viv iría s
- (3 s.) am aría / tem ería / viv iría
- (1 pl.) am aría mos / tem ería mos / viv iría mos
- (2 pl.) am aría is / tem ería is / viv iría is
- (3 pl.) am aría n / tem ería n / viv iría n

SUBJUNCTIVE MOOD

PRESENT
- (1 s.) am e / tem a / viv a
- (2 s.) am e s / tem a s / viv a s
- (3 s.) am e / tem a / viv a

	(1 pl.)	am	e	mos	tem	a	mos	viv	a	mos
	(2 pl.)	am	é	is	tem	á	is	viv	á	is
	(3 pl.)	am	e	n	tem	a	n	viv	a	n
	(1 s.)	am	ara/ase		tem	iera/iese		viv	iera/iese	
	(2 s.)	am	ara/ase	s	tem	iera/iese	s	viv	iera/iese	s
	(3 s.)	am	ara/ase		tem	iera/iese		viv	iera/iese	
PAST	(1 pl.)	am	ára/áse	mos	tem	iéra/iése	mos	viv	iéra/iése	mos
	(2 pl.)	am	ara/ase	is	tem	iera/iese	is	viv	iera/iese	is
	(3 pl.)	am	ara/ase	n	tem	iera/iese	n	viv	iera/iese	n
	(1 s.)	am	are		tem	iere		viv	iere	
	(2 s.)	am	are	s	tem	iere	s	viv	iere	s
FUTURE	(3 s.)	am	are		tem	iere		viv	iere	
	(1 pl.)	am	áre	mos	tem	iére	mos	viv	iére	mos
	(2 pl.)	am	are	is	tem	iere	is	viv	iere	is
	(3 pl.)	am	are	n	tem	iere	n	viv	iere	n

IMPERATIVE MOOD*

(1 s.)	No form			No form			No form		
(2 s.)	am	a		tem	e		viv	e	
(3 s.)	am	e		tem	a		viv	a	
(1 pl.)	am	e	mos	tem	a	mos	viv	a	mos
(2 pl.)	am	a	d	tem	e	d	viv	i	d
(3 pl.)	am	e	n	tem	a	n	viv	a	n

* Negative forms are not included since these are all forms of the present subjunctive, preceded by *no*, for example, *no ames, no améis*. (See Chapter 14).

THE PERFECT TENSES

3.4

The Spanish and English perfect tenses are formed by using the conjugated auxiliary (*haber/have*) before the uninflected past participle.

	AUXILIARY	FIRST CONJUGATION	SECOND CONJUGATION	THIRD CONJUGATION
PERFECT INFINITIVE	hab e r	amado	temido	vivido

INDICATIVE MOOD

	(1 s.)	h	e		amado	temido	vivido
	(2 s.)	ha	∅	s	amado	temido	vivido
PRESENT	(3 s.)	ha	∅		amado	temido	vivido
PERFECT	(1 pl.)	h	e	mos	amado	temido	vivido
	(2 pl.)	hab	é	is	amado	temido	vivido
	(3 pl.)	ha	∅	n	amado	temido	vivido

Chapter 3 Spanish Regular Verb Morphology

> **Note:** The present perfect tense is logically referred to in some Spanish textbooks as the *antepresente*. Frequently used is the term, *pretérito perfecto (compuesto)*, and this inter-lingual conflict in terminology is a major source of confusion. The English term stems from the fact that the auxiliary (*haber*) is conjugated in the present tense. The Spanish name shows that the tense expresses a recent past time. (See Appendix II)

PLUPERFECT	(1 s.)	hab	ía	amado	temido	vivido
	(2 s.)	hab	ía s	amado	temido	vivido
	(3 s.)	hab	ía	amado	temido	vivido
	(1 pl.)	hab	ía mos	amado	temido	vivido
	(2 pl.)	hab	ía is	amado	temido	vivido
	(3 pl.)	hab	ía n	amado	temido	vivido
PRETERITE PERFECT	(1 s.)	hub	e	amado	temido	vivido
	(2 s.)	hub	iste Ø	amado	temido	vivido
	(3 s.)	hub	o	amado	temido	vivido
	(1 pl.)	hub	i mos	amado	temido	vivido
	(2 pl.)	hub	iste is	amado	temido	vivido
	(3 pl.)	hub	iero n	amado	temido	vivido
FUTURE PERFECT	(1 s.)	hab	ré	amado	temido	vivido
	(2 s.)	hab	rá s	amado	temido	vivido
	(3 s.)	hab	rá	amado	temido	vivido
	(1 pl.)	hab	re mos	amado	temido	vivido
	(2 pl.)	hab	ré is	amado	temido	vivido
	(3 pl.)	hab	rá n	amado	temido	vivido
CONDITIONAL PERFECT	(1 s.)	hab	ría	amado	temido	vivido
	(2 s.)	hab	ría s	amado	temido	vivido
	(3 s.)	hab	ría	amado	temido	vivido
	(1 pl.)	hab	ría mos	amado	temido	vivido
	(2 pl.)	hab	ría is	amado	temido	vivido
	(3 pl.)	hab	ría n	amado	temido	vivido

SUBJUNCTIVE MOOD

PRESENT PERFECT	(1 s.)	ha	ya	amado	temido	vivido
	(2 s.)	ha	ya s	amado	temido	vivido
	(3 s.)	ha	ya	amado	temido	vivido
	(1 pl.)	ha	ya mos	amado	temido	vivido
	(2 pl.)	ha	yá is	amado	temido	vivido
	(3 pl.)	ha	ya n	amado	temido	vivido
PLUPERFECT	(1 s.)	hub	iera/iese	amado	temido	vivido
	(2 s.)	hub	iera/iese s	amado	temido	vivido
	(3 s.)	hub	iera/iese	amado	temido	vivido
	(1 pl.)	hub	iéra/iése mos	amado	temido	vivido
	(2 pl.)	hub	iera/iese is	amado	temido	vivido
	(3 pl.)	hub	iera/iese n	amado	temido	vivido

	(1 s.)	hub	iere		amado	temido	vivido
	(2 s.)	hub	iere	s	amado	temido	vivido
FUTURE	(3 s.)	hub	iere		amado	temido	vivido
PERFECT	(1 pl.)	hub	iére	mos	amado	temido	vivido
	(2 pl.)	hub	iere	is	amado	temido	vivido
	(3 pl.)	hub	iere	n	amado	temido	vivido

Students often seem confused as to exactly how the perfect tenses operate. First, observe that these tenses show time relationships relative to the simple tenses, whether past (preterite/imperfect), present or future. What the perfect tenses do is express anteriority to and completion of acts relative to the three simple temporal frames. They show that an action was completed (perfected) prior to a past (pluperfect), present (present perfect) or future (future perfect) point of reference. The following graph will show these time relationships between the perfect and simple tenses in past, present and future time frames, and a discussion with examples then follows.

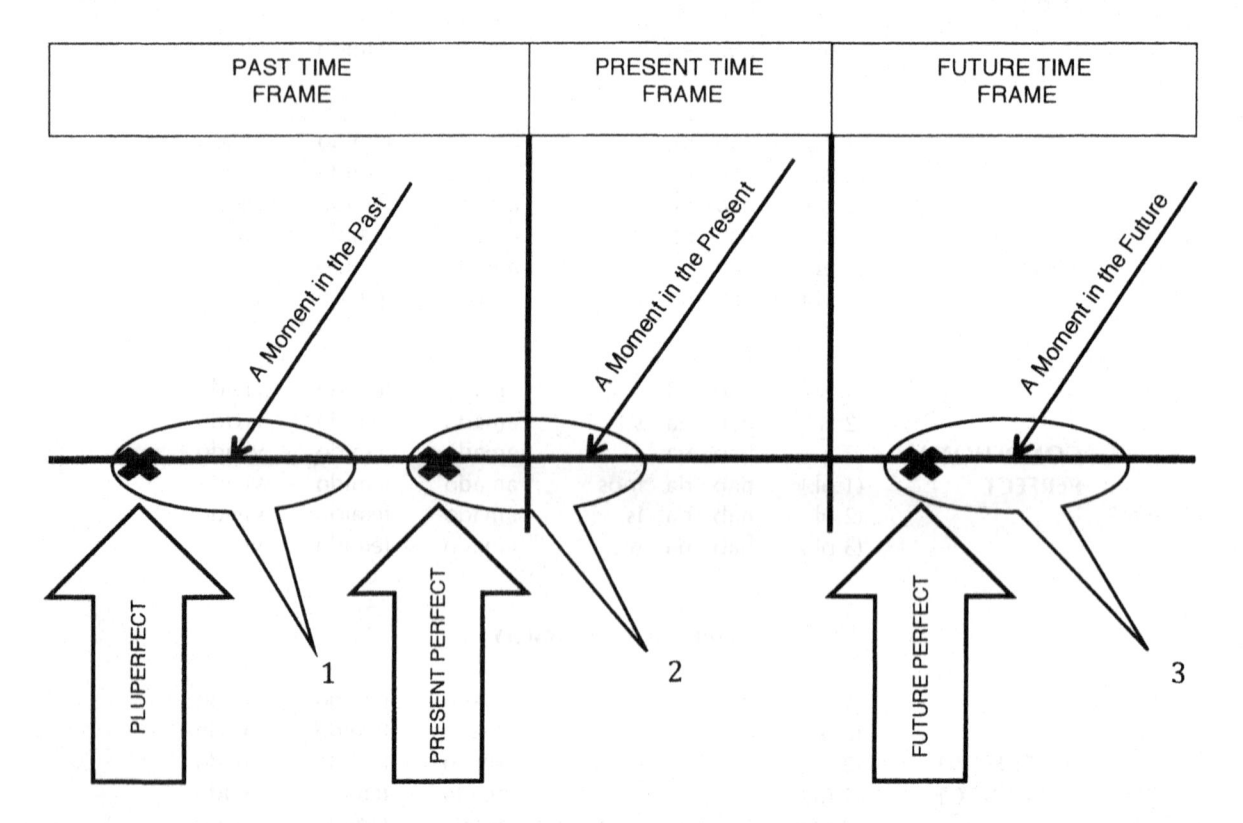

Bubble #1. The pluperfect shows an event that occurred prior to another point of reference in the past. That point of reference might be another action or a mere reference to time.

> He had suffered a great deal and finally decided to see a doctor.
> Había sufrido mucho y por fin se decidió a ver al médico.
> By six o'clock everyone had already eaten.
> Para las seis, ya habíamos cenado todos.

> **Note:** Often, more than one event occurred in the past prior to the main event. In such cases, the pluperfect always expresses the action that took place the earliest.
>
> Anoche soñé con el perro que había comprado antes de casarme.
> Last night I dreamt about the dog (that) I had bought before getting married.

Bubble # 2: There are two actions, one in the present and one in the recent past, and so close to the present as to, as one student said, *"Dejar huellas en el presente."* Again ask, "Which action occurred in the immediate past to produce the present result?"

Estás en la cárcel porque has cometido un delito mayor.
You're in jail because you've committed a felony.

El niño tiene un fuerte dolor de estómago, porque ha comido fruta verde.
The kid has an awful stomachache, since he's eaten unripe fruit.

> **Note:** In Latin America, the preterite occurs more frequently than the present perfect in expressing events in the recent past. For example, the model sentences above would be: *Estás en la cárcel porque cometiste un delito mayor,* and *El niño tiene un fuerte dolor de estómago porque comió fruta verde.*
>
> Also, English uses the present perfect with the adverbs *ever/never* to relate that in one's total experience something has or has not taken place. Spanish uses the tense similarly:
>
> Have you ever seen a flying saucer?
> Has visto alguna vez un platillo volador?
>
> We've never been to Argentina.
> Nunca hemos ido a/estado en Argentina.

Bubble #3: Two separate times are projected into the future. One is to occur before to the other.

Para las 5 de la tarde mañana, ya habremos llegado.
By 5 pm tomorrow, we will have already arrived.

Como siempre, estará furiosa porque se nos habrá olvidado (de) llamar.
As always, she'll be furious because we will have forgotten to call.

Exercise 1

Write original sentences as instructed below using the perfect tenses. Then, translate each sentence into the other language:

1. Two sentences showing a past prior to another past.
2. Two sentences showing a recent past with its continuing effects on the present.
3. Two sentences showing a future prior to another future.

3.5
THE PROGRESSIVE TENSES

Contrary to the custom in English grammar of including the progressive tenses as part of the verbal paradigms, Spanish treats the auxiliary + -*ndo* forms as verbal phrases, and generally excludes them from the usual conjugational paradigms. Furthermore, unlike English, the progressive aspect in Spanish is not restricted to using only one auxiliary as in English, the *be* auxiliary. In addition to *estar*, Spanish can employ any of the following auxiliaries to convey the aspect of progression: *ir, venir, andar, seguir* and *llegar*, as exemplified:

Está trabajando en la fábrica.
Iba diciéndole toda índole de mentiras.
Vinieron pidiendo limosna.
Anda quejándose de su mala suerte
Seguirán haciendo las mismas estupideces.
Llegamos trayendo las noticias más maravillosas.

The English progressive aspect occurs with far greater frequency than is the case with Spanish. Much to the dismay of Spanish grammarians and under the influence of certain business correspondence manuals translated from English, the progressive aspect is gradually creeping into more common usage in some regions. Gili Gaya (1980) gives an example where *Estamos enviando esta carta para comunicarle...* replaces the grammatically correct form, *Le enviamos esta carta...* (§98). The verb *enviar* 'send' describes a punctual action, and its usage in the progressive aspect is inconceivable.

Since this text is in English, the authors have opted to present the progressive and perfect progressive paradigms in their entirety. For each, both the indicative and subjunctive moods are shown, but only the first person singular forms appear for the sake of brevity. The auxiliaries *estar* and *haber* are not broken down morphologically.

PROGRESSIVE TENSES
(*estar* + LV-*ndo*)

INDICATIVE	Present Progressive:	estoy + -ndo
MOOD	Preterite Progressive	estuve + -ndo
	Imperfect Progressive:	estaba + -ndo
	Future Progressive:	estaré + -ndo
	Conditional Progressive:	estaría + -ndo
SUBJUNCTIVE	Present Progressive:	esté + -ndo
MOOD	Past Progressive:	estuviera/-se + -ndo

PERFECT PROGRESSIVE TENSES
(*haber* + *estado* + LV-*ndo*)

INDICATIVE	Present Perfect Progressive:	he estado + -ndo
MOOD	Preterite Perfect Progressive :	hube estado + -ndo
	Pluperfect Progressive:	había estado + -ndo
	Future Perfect Progressive:	habré estado + -ndo
	Conditional Perfect Progressive:	habría estado + -ndo

SUBJUNCTIVE	Present perfect progressive:	haya estado + -ndo
MOOD	Pluperfect progressive:	hubiera/-se estado + -ndo

As stated above, any of the several verbs listed could serve as progressive auxiliaries: *voy hablando, vendrá diciendo, había seguido tratando, habría llegado quejándose*, etc. We selected *estar* for the above progressive tense lay-outs since it corresponds to the English auxiliary *to be*.

Exercise 2

Find at least one each regular Spanish *-ar*, *-er*, and *-ir* verbs, other than *amar*, *temer*, and *vivir*. For each example give the following forms:

1. Preterite indicative, 1st person plural.
2. Present indicative, 2nd person plural.
3. Imperfect indicative, 1st person singular.
4. Conditional indicative, 3rd person singular.
5. Future indicative, 2nd person singular.
6. Imperative, formal plural.
7. Present subjunctive, 3rd person singular.
8. Past subjunctive, 1st person plural.
9. Future subjunctive, 2nd person plural.
10. Past subjunctive, 3rd person plural.
11. Present perfect indicative, 1st person singular.
12. Pluperfect indicative, 2nd person singular.
13. Preterite perfect indicative, 3rd person singular
14. Future perfect indicative, 3rd person plural.
15. Present perfect subjunctive, 2nd person plural.
16. Future perfect subjunctive, 1st person plural.
17. Pluperfect subjunctive, 1st person singular.
18. Imperative, 1st person plural.
19. Pluperfect subjunctive, 1st person singular.
20. Imperative, 2nd person singular.
21. Future progressive, 3rd person plural
22. Pluperfect progressive, 2nd person singular subjunctive

Exercise 3

Give the person, number, tense and mood for each of the following regular verb forms:

1. vendió
2. pasamos
3. insistirán
4. vendiéramos
5. pasarías
6. hemos insistido
7. venda
8. habrían pasado
9. insistimos
10. habrás vendido
11. están pasando
12. hubiera insistido
13. venden
14. estaremos pasando
15. hayan insistido
16. vendiste
17. pasábamos
18. hubiesen insistido
19. habría vendido
20. hubiera pasado
21. estuviera insistiendo
22. habrían estado vendiendo
23. siga pasando
24. haya venido insistiendo

3.6

Some general observations concerning the Spanish verbal system:

1. The first and third person, singular forms are identical in a number of tenses. One avoids confusion on the basis of context or by using the appropriate subject pronoun, if necessary. The tenses are: a) the imperfect indicative (*cantaba/vendía/vivía*), b) the conditional (*cantaría/vendería/viviría*), c) the present subjunctive (*cante/venda/viva*), and d) the past subjunctive (*cantara-se/vendiera-se/viviera-se*).

2. The person/number morpheme for the second person singular is always –s, with one exception, that of the preterite: *cantaste, vendiste, abriste*. The force of analogy is so strong that such non-standard forms as **cantastes, *vendistes* and **abristes* are often heard. In the plural, the person/number morphemes are always –mos, -is, and –n, respectively.

3. The past subjunctives in –ra (*cantara/vendiera*) and –se (*cantase/vendiese*) are totally interchangeable, except in the conclusion clause of past counter-factual sentences. (**Si la hubiese visto, la hubiese matado.*) The only accepted forms here are either *habría* or *hubiera matado*). The –se form is rare in Spanish American usage, but is not unknown. On rare occasion, especially in oral narratives of a historical nature, the –ra form appears as an equivalent of the preterite, a throwback to its origins as an indicative form. "*Cuando la Division del Norte llegara a la capital y percibiera la destrucción causada por....*" Occasionally, in historical narratives and even in news broadcasts, the –ra form substitutes for the pluperfect indicative, again, due its original meaning in Latin and especially in subordinate clauses: *El dictador tomó medidas drásticas para eliminar a la oposición que, como traidores, se rebelara (= se había rebelado) en su contra*. Without exception, the past subjunctive derives from the third person plural, preterite (hablar > *habla-ron* > *habla-ra/se*; traer > *traje-ron* > *trajera/se*). This applies to all verbs, regular or irregular.

4. The present subjunctive derives from the present indicative. Without exception, if the first person singular present indicative ends in -o, that root is the stem/root for all forms of the present subjunctive. For example, *hablar* > *habl-o* > *habl-e/habl-es*. etc. The rule applies to irregular verbs as well: *tener* > *teng-o* > *teng-a/teng-as*, etc. The only verbs whose first person present indicative ends in other than –o follow. Their present subjunctive forms cannot be derived and must simply be memorized: *dar (doy)* > *dé, estar (estoy)* > *esté, haber (he)* > *haya, ir (voy)* > *vaya, saber (sé)* > *sepa, ser (soy)* > *sea*.

5. From the English point of view, the simple imperfect (*cantaba*), the preterite progressive (*estuve cantando*) and the imperfect progressive (*estaba cantando*) are all translated as "I was singing." We take up this matter is in Chapters 6 and 15.

6. The present perfect (*he cantado*) is translated as "I have sung" and the pluperfect (*había cantado*) and preterite perfect (*hube cantado*) as "I had sung." The latter tense is now rare in writing and virtually extinct in spoken Spanish.

7. The future subjunctive (*cantare*) is no longer actively used in either spoken or written Spanish, and appears today only in sayings (aphorisms) like, *Adonde fueres haz lo que vieres*, and the occasional legal document.

3.7
VERBS WITH ORTHOGRAPHIC CHANGES

Spanish has a fairly large number of verbs which, although generally regular, exhibit changes in spelling at the end of their stems when various vowel endings are added. Such verbs are referred to as orthographically changing verbs. Some of these verbs are also radically changing (stem-changing) verbs which are irregular, for example, *empezar* and *seguir*. However, radical changes (vowel or consonant changes in the stem of the verb, treated in the next chapter) and orthographic changes (consonant spelling changes at the end of the stem) are completely unrelated and independent phenomena.

The following bracketed phonetic symbols, which appear again in the boxed charts below, represent the consonant sounds of Spanish having more than one spelling. Each symbol appears with various Spanish words whose bold type spellings represent the symbol's sound when the words are pronounced.

1. [k] as in **ca**ma, **co**ma, **cu**na, **que**so, **qui**so
2. [g] as in **ga**ta, **go**ta, **gu**sta, **gue**rra, **guí**a
3. [x] as in **ja**la, **jo**ta, **ju**ra, **je**fe/**ge**ma, **ji**rafa/**gi**ma.
4. [s] as in **sa**nto, **so**mos, **su**ma, **se**so, **si**lla,
5. [ṣ] as in **za**nca, **zo**na, **zu**mo, **ce**dro, **ci**fra
   (This sound [ṣ] in the Americas is pronounced as [s].
   In the Spanish of the Castilian variety, the sound is pronounced [θ]).
6. [gu̯]+ vowel, as in **Gua**temala, anti**guo**, a**güe**ro, lin**güi**sta

You will see the application of the spelling chart to various Spanish verb forms below. We give four forms for each infinitive listed under each consonant sound symbol. They are (1) the first person singular, present indicative; (2) the second person singular, present indicative; (3) the first person singular, present subjunctive; and (4) the first person singular, preterite. Observe how the consonant spelling changes manifested in the verb forms operate in accordance with the spelling chart. They are highlighted in bold type.

SYMBOL	INFINITIVE	1st SGL. PRES. IND.	2nd SGL. PRES. IND.	1st SGL. PRES. SUBJ	1st SGL PRETERITE
[k]	sa**c**ar	sa**c**o	sa**c**as	sa**qu**e	sa**qu**é
	delin**qu**ir	delin**c**o	delin**qu**es	delin**c**a	delin**qu**í
[g]	lle**g**ar	lle**g**o	lle**g**as	lle**gu**e	lle**gu**é
	se**gu**ir	si**g**o	si**gu**es	si**g**a	se**gu**í
[x]	reco**g**er	reco**j**o	reco**g**es	reco**j**a	reco**g**í
		Verbs whose infinitive roots end in *-ger* or *-gir* must use *g* whenever that spelling is possible. Where *g* is not permissible to represent the [x] sound before a Spanish vowel, the spelling must change to *j*.			
	de**j**ar	de**j**o	de**j**as	de**j**e	de**j**é

Chapter 3 Spanish Regular Verb Morphology

	Verbs whose infinitive roots end in *j* use that spelling in all forms since, as can be seen in the chart, *j* represents the [x] sound before any Spanish vowel.				
[s]	pasar	paso	pasas	pase	pasé
[ṣ]	rezar	rezo	rezas	rece	recé
	vencer	venzo	vences	venza	vencí
	This symbol is an invention of the authors. In the Americas, it is pronounced as [s], while in the Castilian areas of Spain, the [θ] sound is heard.				
[gu̯]+ vowel	averiguar	averiguo	averiguas	averigüe	averigüé

In the following chart, the Spanish consonant sounds from the above paragraph appear top to bottom at the left. You find the Spanish vowels listed across the top of the chart. In the squares you see the correct spellings for each consonant sound when it occurs before each Spanish vowel. The chart represents the spelling "convention," of modern Spanish, that is the agreement among contemporary authorities concerning how Spanish is to be correctly spelled and punctuated, regardless of whether the variety is Peninsular or American. The other Romance languages each have their own spelling conventions.

SOUND CONSONANT	a	o	u	e	i
[k]	ca	co	cu	que	qui
[g]	ga	go	gu	gue	gui
[x]	ja	jo	ju	je/ge	ji/gi
[s]	sa	so	su	se	si
[ṣ]	za	zo	zu	ce	ci
[gu̯]+ vowel	gua	guo	---	güi	güe

Exercise 4

Certain consonant sounds appear bracketed in the following Spanish verb forms. Show how the given verb form would be spelled. Also, write the infinitive from which the form derives.

1. con[s]e[g]imos
2. se[k]an
3. es[k]o[x]a
4. apa[ṣ]i[gu̯]emos
5. ar[gu̯]í
6. lle[g]a
7. [ṣ]ur[ṣ]iste
8. e[s]co[x]en
9. apa[g]ó
10. reco[x]í
11. traba[x]o
12. men[gu̯]a
13. averi[gu̯]es
14. sa[k]o
15. [k]onven[ṣ]es
16. pro[s]e[g]í
17. [s]e[k]emos
18. ven[ṣ]a
19. [k]o[x]es
20. to[k]é
21. si[g]e
22. amorti[gu̯]o
23. [ṣ]an[x]a
24. re[ṣ]o
25. [k]a[s]ar
26. [k]a[s]é
28. empe[ṣ]é
29. [k]o[ṣ]er
29. [k]a[ṣ]ar
30. [k]o[s]er

3.8

In addition to the five orthographic changes listed above, there are several additional ones that reflect Spanish phonological processes operating in the verbal system:

(a)	d > ø	*levantad + os > levantaos*
(b)	s > ø	*volvamos + nos > volvámonos*
(c)	i > y	In certain verbs, the endings *-ió,- ieron,- iera, -iese,-iendo* become *oyó, oyeron, oyera, oyese, oyendo* since Spanish spelling conventions do not permit an unstressed *i* between vowels, eg.,*oieron > oyeron*.
(d)	i > ø	When the verb stem ends in a palatal sound, the *i* of all the endings is lost (assimilated): *reír* becomes *rió/rieron/riera-se/riendo*, *bullir* becomes *bulló/bullendo*, etc., *tañer* becomes *tañó/tañendo*, etc.

Exercise 5

Write the indicated forms of the following Spanish verbs, paying special attention to spelling.

1. **arrancar**: 1st person singular, preterite indicative.
2. **distinguir**: 3rd person singular, present subjunctive.
3. **colgar**: 1st person plural, present subjunctive.
4. **escoger**: 1st person plural, present subjunctive.
5. **esparcir**: 3rd person singular, present subjunctive.
6. **averiguar**: 1st person plural, present subjunctive.
7. **freír**: 1st person singular, preterite indicative.
8. **pagar**: 1st person singular, present subjunctive.
9. **remolcar**: 3rd person plural, preterite indicative.
10. **bruñir**: gerund/present participle/-*ndo* form.
11. **conseguir**: 1st person plural, present subjunctive.
12. **sentarse**: 2nd person plural, imperative .
13. **oír**: 3rd person plural, preterite indicative.
14. **volverse**: 1st person plural, imperative.
15. **refreír**: gerund/present participle/-*ndo* form.

3.9

A final note on differences in verbal nomenclature in Spanish and English is necessary. Spanish grammarians do not always use the grammatical terms the *Real Academia* designates, and many renowned authorities in Spanish grammar have devised their own terminology through the years. This is much like what has happened among modern linguists in contrast with conventional grammarians in describing English. Moreover, the Spanish and English terminologies don't always have a one-to-one correspondence. The English *present perfect* in contrast with Spanish *pretérito perfecto* is a prime example, since both designate *he cantado*.

Language students must realize that various different terms can denote one specific grammatical phenomenon. Some say that *ate* is the **simple past**, others, **the perfect**, and still others, **the aorist**. The problem is no less vexing with grammar terms outside the verbal system. Some say **determiners** while others call these **limiting adjectives**. Other investigative and analytic fields, especially the physical sciences, have long since standardized their technical terminology, but the field of linguistic science has yet to do so and most likely never will. The sad fact is that a highly challenging field is made all the more difficult by this persistent lack of agreement on terminology. With respect to the varieties of nomenclature used for the Spanish verbal system, Appendix II should prove helpful.

Exercise 6

A. Examine Appendix II, and find the technical vocabulary used by *La Real Academia* for these terms used in our text:

1. present participle (*hablando*)
2. past participle (*hablado*)
3. imperfect indicative (*hablaba*)
4. preterite (*hablé*)
5. conditional (*hablaría*)
6. present perfect (*he hablado*)
7. preterite perfect (*hube hablado*)
8. past subjunctive (*hablara/hablase*)

B. In Appendix II, the terms listed under "other Spanish grammarians" come primarily from the works of Andrés Bello, a noted Colombian scholar from the late 19th century. He uses the concept of relative time references as the basis for his Spanish tense terminology. Write the English name for the following terms used by Bello, and explain the rationale behind his tense designations:

1. copretérito (*hablaba*)
2. postpretérito (*hablaría*)
3. antepresente (*he hablado*)
4. antecopretérito (*había hablado*)
5. antefuturo (*habré hablado*)
6. ante-postpreterito (*habría hablado*)

4
Spanish Irregular Verb Morphology

4.1

Spanish grammar traditionally describes irregular verbs as those having forms that depart from the conjugations established for the three regular verb patterns (See previous chapter). The vast majority of these "irregularities" take the forms of allomorphic variations on the stem (radical/root) morpheme or of the mood-tense-aspect morpheme and are the result of phonological laws affecting the whole system of the Spanish language. The person/number morpheme is constant with but one exception, the second person singular form of the preterite tense explained in the previous Chapter (3.6, #2). Some few verbs have suppletive stems (4.14).

For the sake of better organization, we divide the irregular verbal examples into two major groups: verbs with vowel irregularities and those with consonantal ones. Since many verbs exhibit a combination of both types of irregularities and, strictly speaking, fall outside the two systematic categories designated, an exhaustive analysis of these would be overly complicated and perhaps even counter-productive. With this in mind, the most important of the multivariable verbs appear in Appendix III.

Larousse, Conjugación (2007), a well-known publication frequently consulted as a reference for over 10,000 verbs, lists just under seventy different types of irregular verb conjugations in Spanish, and an additional twenty different types of verbs which undergo orthographic and prosodic modifications. We introduced several of these in Chapter 3.7-8.

VOWEL CHANGES IN THE RADICAL
(Radically or Stem-Changing Verbs)

4.2

Irregular verbs of the radically-changing type exhibit predictable vocalic changes in the verb stem/root. Since the root vowel nearest the infinitive *-r* ending is the one receiving syllable stress in many of the forms, stress is the determining factor in these changes. The vowel alterations take the form of vowel diphthongization (*e > ie* and *o > ue*) or of vowel raising by the substitution of a semi-close (mid) vowel (*e* or *o*) with a close (high) vowel (*i* or u). When the vowel *e* occurs in the infinitive, it is subject to change in the verb forms to *ie* or to *i*: *sentir* becomes *siento* and *sintió*. The vowel *o* of the infinitive changes to *ue* and in exceptional cases to *u*: *dormir* becomes *duermo* and *durmió*. Such changes in the radical obey specific rules involving whether the vowel of the root is stressed or not, or whether certain phonetic factors (stressed *ie*, *io* or *a*) are present in the endings of the conjugated verb forms.

A verb's infinitive does not reveal whether it is radically irregular or not. For example, *comer > como* is not a stem-changing verb, whereas *mover > muevo* is. A better indicator of whether a verb belongs to the radically-changing category is its first person singular, present indicative form. If the root vowel is diphthongized or is raised in this form, then the verb is clearly a radically-changing verb, and its forms obey several consistent rules.

We illustrate the two types of vowel changes below:

DIPHTHONGIZATION	RAISING
sentir: e > ie siento	pedir: e > i pido
dormir: o > ue duermo	morir: o > u murió

It should be noted that if a verb is radically-changing, the radical vowel of the root will always be the one nearest the infinitive ending. In the verb *preferir*, for example, the second *e* is the affected vowel. In verbs such as *resolver*, it is the *o* that is diphthongized. Radically-changing verbs fall under three classifications, and the verbs in each of these categories obey rules applicable to their specific class. Radical verbs of the first and second conjugations (i.e., those whose infinitives end in -*ar* like *pensar* and *volar* and those ending in -*er* like *perder* and *volver*) show fewer complexities in their changes than do those of the third conjugation (-*ir* verbs like *sentir, dormir* and *pedir*).

RADICALLY-CHANGING VERB CLASSES AND GOVERNING RULES
4.3
CLASS I verbs *(e > ie/ o > ue)*

To Class I belong verbs drawn from the first two conjugations only, **the -*ar* and -*er* verbs**. Such verbs have two possible roots: a diphthongized root which is stressed and an atonic one with the vowel unaltered. Representative members of Class I are,

- *pensar* with the roots *pens-* (unstressed vowel) and *piens-* (stressed vowel > diphthong). Other examples like *pensar* are *acertar, cerrar, comenzar, despertar, empezar, sentar*, etc.

- *volar* with the roots *vol-* (unstressed) and *vuel-* (stressed > diphthong). Like *volar* are *acordar, acostar, almorzar, apostar, colgar, contar, costar, encontrar, mostrar, probar, recordar, rogar, sonar*, etc.

- *perder* with the roots *perd-* (unstressed) and *pierd-* (stressed > diphthong). Like *perder* are *ascender, condescender, entender, defender*, etc.

- *volver* with the roots *volv-* (unstressed) and *vuelv-* (stressed > diphthong). Like *volver* are *doler, mover, soler,* etc.

Rule: (Class I Radically-Changing Verbs)

When the verbal root is stressed, its vowel is diphthongized (*e > ie/ o > ue*): otherwise, no change occurs in the root vowel.

A survey of all tenses reveals that the diphthongized root of Class I radically-changing verbs occurs only in the following tenses, persons and numbers:

1. present indicative/ 1st, 2nd, and 3rd persons singular; 3rd person plural.

   pienso, piensas, piensa/ piensan
   vuelo, vuelas, vuela/ vuelan
   pierdo, pierdes, pierde/ pierden
   vuelvo, vuelves, vuelve/ vuelven

2. present subjunctive/ 1st, 2nd, and 3rd persons singular; 3rd person plural.

   piense, pienses, piense/ piensen
   vuele, vueles, vuele/ vuelen
   pierda, pierdas, pierda/ pierdan
   vuelva, vuelvas, vuelva/ vuelvan

3. All **regularly** formed imperatives, affirmative and negative, familiar and formal, since these are forms of the present indicative or present subjunctive (*piensa, no pienses*). The eight irregular *tú* imperatives (*di, haz, ve, pon, sal, sé, ten, ven*) and all *vosotros* affirmative command forms (*hablad, comed, venid*) are unaffected under the rule. (See Chapter 14)

The root vowel is unstressed in all the other tenses, so the non-diphthongized form of the radical remains.

   pensé, volaba, perdía, volví, etc.

Finally, if the radical vowel occurs as the first element in a word, the *e > ie* change is spelled, *ye-*, for example, *errar > yerro, yierre,* etc. When initial in a word, the *o > ue* dipthong is written *hue-*, as follows: *oler > huelo, huela.*

4.4
CLASS II *(e > ie/i ; o > ue/u)*

To class II belong assorted verbs of the **third conjugation only**, verbs with *-ir* endings in the infinitive. Verbs in this group will have three possible roots: the unaltered root, a root with a diphthongized stressed vowel, and a root showing vowel raising. Here are examples of Class II radically-changing verbs:

- *sentir* with the roots *sent-* (unstressed vowel), *sient-* (stressed vowel > diphthong), and *sint-* (raised vowel). Like *sentir* are *mentir, preferir, sugerir,* etc.
- *dormir* with the roots *dorm-* (unstressed), *duerm-* (stressed vowel > diphthong), and *durm-* (raised vowel). Like *dormir* are *adormir* and *morir.* The latter also has the irregular past participle *muerto.*

Three rules govern Class II verbs:

Rule 1: A diphthongized root occurs when the root is stressed. This is observed in the first, second, third persons singular and third person plural, present indicative and present subjunctive forms.

Indicative:	siento, sientes, siente/ sienten
	duermo, duermes, duerme/ duermen
Subjunctive:	sienta, sientas, sienta/ sientan
	duerma, duermas, duerma/ duerman

Rule 2: When the verbal root takes **an ending containing stressed *ie, io,* or *a*,** its vowels *o* and *e* raise to *u* and *i* respectively. Affected forms are:

(a) 3rd person singular and plural preterite and all forms of past subjunctive.

Preterite:	sintió, sintieron; durmió, durmieron
Past Subj.	sintiera/se sintieras, sintiera, sintiéramos, sintierais, sintieran
	durmiera/se, durmieras, durmiera, durmiéramos, durmierais, durmieran

(b) 1st and 2nd persons plural, present subjunctive.

Pres. Subj.:	sintamos, sintáis
	durmamos, durmáis

(c) Gerund (-*ndo*): sintiendo/ durmiendo

Rule 3: All other forms, those not covered by rules 1 and 2 carry the unaltered radical vowel of the infinitive: *sentí, sentido; morimos, morirán,* etc.

4.5
CLASS III *(e > i/i)*

As was the case with Class II verbs, **only verbs of the third conjugation** belong to Class III. These verbs also end in *-ir*, but have only two roots—one root with the unstressed vowel unaltered and the other with the radical stressed vowel raised, **but for two different reasons.**

An example of a Class III verb is *pedir*, which has *ped-* and *pid-*. Like *pedir* are *ceñir, elegir, reír, repetir, seguir, servir, vestir*, etc. Three rules condition the phonetic variations of Class III verbs:

Rule 1: If the root vowel *-e-* is stressed, it is raised to *-i-*. This occurs in the first, second and third persons singular, and the third person plural of the present indicative and the present subjunctive.

Indicative: pido, pides, pide/ piden
Subjunctive: pida, pidas, pida/ pidan

Rule 2: When **stressed ie, io,** or ***a*** occur in the syllable following the root, phonological conditioning **also** raises the root vowel to *-i-*. It affects the third person singular and plural preterite, all forms of the past subjunctive, the first and second persons plural of the present subjunctive, and the gerund *(-ndo)*.

Preterite: pidió, pidieron
Past Subjunctive: pidiera/se, pidieras, pidiera, pidiéramos, pidierais, pidieran
Present Subjunctive: pidamos, pidáis
Gerund (-ndo)   pidiendo

Rule 3: If the root *-e-* is either unstressed or if it is not followed by stressed *ie, io,* or *a*, it remains as *e* in all the forms since neither rule 1 nor 2 applies.

You must be especially careful not to include by analogy verbs which do not belong to the separate categories described above. By way of example, *defender* belongs to the *perder* class but *ofender* does not; *renovar* is of the *volar* class but not *innovar*.

4.6

Two additional vowel changes affect the tonic vowel of the radical in certain verbs. Since these variations apply only to a very limited number of verbs (one having but a single example), they appear in Appendix III.

CLASS I	CLASS II
u > ue jugar (only)	i > ie adquirir, inquirir, etc.

Exercise 1

Find the indicated forms for the following stem-changing verbs, and determine to which radical class (I, II, or III) each belongs. State why a stem vowel change does or does not occur.

1. cerrar, 2. acostar, 3. perder, 4. hervir, 5. seguir, 6. volver

  1. 1st person singular, present indicative.
  2. 3rd person singular, present indicative.

3. 1st person plural, present indicative.
4. 3rd person plural, present indicative.
5. 2nd person singular, present subjunctive.
6. 3rd person singular, present subjunctive.

Exercise 2

Give the indicated forms for these stem-changing verbs, and classify each as belonging to class II or III. State why a vowel change does or does not occur:

1. *sugerir*, 2. *morir*, 3. *mentir*, 4. *dormir* 5. *reír*, 6. *servir*.

1. 2nd person singular, present indicative.
2. 3rd person singular, preterite indicative.
3. 1st person plural, present subjunctive.
4. 3rd person plural, past subjunctive .
5. gerund (-*ndo*)
6. 2nd person plural, present subjunctive

Exercise 3

After carefully examining the following list of forms derived from radically-changing Spanish verbs, for each example determine, 1) the tense, person and number represented, 2) to which class the verb belongs (I, II, III) and 3) the conditions (rules) governing the form. Also say if no conditions apply in any given case. Also provide the infinitive of each verb form.

1. defienden	6. mueren	11. repitas
2. durmiendo	7. comencemos	12. prefiriéramos
3. suelen	8. sirvió	13. muestre
4. pidiendo	9. costó	14. cerré
5. sugiramos	10. sintieron	15. empezarán

4.7
CONSONANT CHANGES IN THE RADICAL

Like vowel changes in the radical of the irregular verb, consonant changes also occur. These are predictable in many of the registered instances; however, such verbs often demonstrate other variations which complicate classification. Three types of irregularities are manifest: 1) the substitution of one stem consonant for another, 2) the addition of a second consonant to the stem when it ends in a consonant or 3) the addition of a consonant or of a second vowel plus a consonant to a final vowel in the radical. These irregularities apply only to verbs of the second and third conjugations and affect primarily the present indicative (first person singular) and all forms of the present subjunctive.

4.8
CONSONANT SUBSTITUTION

There is only one productive consonant substitution process—the replacing of [ṣ], written c + e/i, or z, with g. This affects the first person singular present indicative and all forms of the present subjunctive.

z/c >g

hacer	Pres. Indicative:	**hago**, haces, hace, hacemos, hacéis, hacen
	Pres. Subjunctive:	**haga, hagas, haga, hagamos, hagáis, hagan**

Also belonging to the *hacer* group are *deshacer, rehacer, satisfacer*, etc.

decir	Pres. Indicative:	**digo**, dices, dice, decimos, decís, dicen
	Pres. Subjunctive:	**diga, digas, diga, digamos, digáis, digan**

Like *decir* are such verbs as *predecir, maldecir, bendecir*, etc.
Note that the root vowel change (e > i) in all the forms presented are those of a Class III radically-changing verb like *pedir*.

4.9
VELAR EXTENSION

The phenomenon of velar extension shows up in four different environments, each conditioned by a post positioned back vowel (*a/o*).

1. Verbs ending in –*cer* or –*cir*, **preceded by a vowel**, change -c- to -zc- before *a* and *o* (*hacer* and *decir* are exceptions to this rule). Phonetically the [ṣ] is extended to [ṣk].
   nacer V[ṣ] > V[ṣk] + a/o **nazco/a**

2. The nasal of the stem of a verb ending in -*oner*, -*ener*, or -*enir* extends to -*ng*.
   poner o/e + n > -ong-/-eng- + a/o **pongo/a**

3. The *l* of a stem when its infinitive is -*aler* or -*alir* extends to -*lg*-.
   salir   a + l > -alg- + a/o **salgo/a**

4. The *a* of the radical of verbs whose infinitives are -*aer* extends to -*aig*-.
   traer   a > -aig- + a/o **traigo/a**

Affected are the first person singular present indicative form and all of the present subjunctive. To the first category belong over two hundred Spanish verbs, which makes this the most productive of all irregular verb processes.

1. *c > zc*

   parecer   Pres. Ind.:   **parezco**, pareces, parece; parecemos, parecéis, parecen

             Pres. Subj.: **parezca, parezcas, parezca; parezcamos, parezcáis, parezcan**

   deducir   Pres. Ind.:   **deduzco**, deduces, deduce; deducimos, deducís, deducen

             Pres. Subj.: **deduzca, deduzcas, deduzca; deduzcamos, deduzcáis, deduzcan**

2. *n > ng*

   poner   Pres. Ind.:   **pongo**, pones, pone; ponemos, ponéis, ponen
            Pres. Subj.: **ponga, pongas, ponga; pongamos, pongáis, pongan**

   tener   Pres. Ind.:   **tengo**, tienes, tiene; tenemos, tenéis, tienen
            Pres. Subj.: **tenga, tengas, tenga; tengamos, tengáis, tengan**

   venir   Pres. Ind.:   **vengo**, vienes, viene; venimos, venís, vienen
            Pres. Subj.: **venga, vengas, venga; vengamos, vengáis, vengan**

3. *l > lg*

   valer   Pres. Ind.:   **valgo**, vales, vale; valemos, valéis, valen
            Pres. Subj.: **valga, valgas, valga; valgamos, valgáis, valgan**

   salir   Pres. Ind.:   **salgo**, sales, sale; salimos, salís, salen
            Pres. Subj.: **salga, salgas, salga; salgamos, salgáis, salgan**

4. *a > aig*

   caer   Pres. Ind.:   **caigo**, caes, cae; caemos, caéis, caen
            Pres. Subj.: **caiga, caigas, caiga; caigamos, caigáis, caigan**

   traer   Pres. Ind.:   **traigo**, traes, trae; traemos, traéis, traen
            Pres. Subj.: **traiga, traigas, traiga; traigamos, traigáis, traigan**

Included in the above categories are other verb examples showing like patterns, although some have other irregularities also.

Like *parecer* are *conocer, nacer,* and numerous other verbs.

Like *deducir* are *lucir* and its derived forms.
Like *poner* are *componer, disponer, imponer, oponer, posponer, reponer* and many other derived forms.
Like *tener* are *atenerse, contener, obtener, sostener*, etc.
Like *venir* are *convenir, intervener*, etc.
Like *valer* are *equivaler* and *prevaler*.
Like *salir* are *resalir* and *sobresalir*.
Like *caer* are *traer* and derived forms, *atraer, contraer*, etc.

4.10
VERBS WITH Y- EXTENSION

Y-extension, which is also called "yod-extension," is employed in all verbs whose infinitives end in *-uir*. This sizeable group adds a *-y* to the final *-u* of the stem in all but two persons (first and second plural) of the present indicative; however, all forms of the present subjunctive show the *–uy-* extension.

u > uy

| *huir* | Pres. Ind.: | **huyo, huyes, huye**; huimos, huís, **huyen** |
| | Pres. Subj.: | **huya, huyas, huya; huyamos, huyáis, huyan** |

Some other common verbs inflected like *huir* are *atribuir, concluir, construir, excluir, incluir, instruir, obstruir, sustituir*, etc.

4.11

Two additional consonant changes need mention. These variations apply to such a limited number of verbs that they appear with all their forms in Appendix III.

b > y   haber (hay)

ab > ep   caber (quepo/quepa), saber (sepa)

Exercise 4

Give, a) the first person singular present indicative and b) the first and second person plural forms for the present subjunctive of the following verbs.

1. satisfacer
2. nacer
3. relucir
4. oponer
5. atenerse
6. convenir
7. prevaler
8. sobresalir
9. caer
10. incluir

4.12
STRONG PAST TENSE FORMS

A legacy from Latin surfaces in various present-day Spanish verbs, the majority with a high frequency of occurrence. It manifests in verbs with "strong" past tense (preterite) forms. Similar to the so-called strong verbs of English with variable past forms (*teach-taught, sing-sang, get-got*, etc.), the Spanish strong verbs show irregularities in both the preterite indicative and the past subjunctive. These may appear in a variety of guises. Verb roots may show vowel substitution and/or consonant substitution and vowel extension and/or consonant extension. The strong past tense forms are classified under three categories.

STRONG FORM IN -a-
   traer: traje   trajera/se

STRONG FORM IN -i-
   decir: dije   dijera/se
   hacer: hice   hiciera/se
   querer: quise   quisiera/se
   venir: vine   viniera/se

STRONG FORM IN -u-
   andar: anduve   anduviera/se
   caber: cupe   cupiera/se
   conducir: conduje   condujera/se
   estar: estuve   estuviera/se
   haber: hube   hubiera/se
   poder: pude   pudiera/se
   poner: puse   pusiera/se
   saber: supe   supiera/se
   tener: tuve   tuviera/se

These strong preterites are distinguished from weak (regular) preterites in two ways:

First, the roots of their first and third person singular forms are stressed (rhizotonic); *TRAJ-e/o, VIN-e/o, PUD-e/o*. In the weak forms, stress is on the endings in all cases. Second, regarding the first and third persons singular forms, the endings differ from the weak preterites*. In their other forms, the strong preterite endings are those of *–er* and *–ir* regular preterite paradygms. The strong preterite endings follow:

		SINGULAR	PLURAL
1	traj vin pud	-e*	-imos

2	traj vin pud	-iste	-isteis
3	traj* vin pud	-o*	-ieron (-eron) (if root ends in *j*: *dijeron*)

4.13
FUTURE AND CONDITIONAL IRREGULARITIIES

Historically, the future and conditional tenses are closely related, and in the modern language they share the same irregularities. Both are synthetic tenses since they represent a fusion of the infinitive with the present and imperfect indicatives of *haber*, respectively. In modern speech we hear such periphrastic (using more than one word) future references such as, *Hemos de visitar ese sitio*, or *Han de cenar esta noche con los Pérez*. As it evolved, Spanish began to postpose (place after the infinitive) the present tense forms of *haber*, producing a synthetic (one word) rather than a periphrastic (more than one word) future form.

(h)e de ver > ver + (h)e > veré

In a parallel fashion, the synthetic conditional evolved from the periphrastic construction using the imperfect of *haber*:

(hab)ía de ver > ver + ía > vería.

In modern Spanish, irregularities in the synthetic future and conditional occur as contractions of the original infinitive before endings are added. Such contractions are of three types:

1. The infinitive vowel is lost, referred to as syncope (the loss of an inter-tonic vowel).

    caber > cabr-é/-ía

2. The infinitive vowel is not only lost but is replaced by –d- (called the intrusive or epenthetic -d-).

    tener >tendr-é/-ía

3. In two verbs, *decir* and *hacer*, the infinitive is highly contracted, both –c- and -e- being lost in each.

    decir > dir-é/-ía
    hacer > har-é/-ía

Appendix III lists all verbs irregular in the future and conditional tenses.

4.14
SUPPLETIVE VERB FORMS

There are two very important verbs in Spanish which transcend even the many irregularities already documented: *ser* and *ir*. Due to the fact that both have multiple verb stems which have neither vowel nor consonant changes exclusively, but show suppletion of the whole stem, they are classified in a separate category from other irregular verbs as suppletive verb forms. Both verbs have much in common with the over-differentiated *be* of English. *Ser* has four stems: s-, er-, fu-, and ø while *ir* has three: v- in the present, fu- in the preterite, past and future subjunctives, and ø in the imperfect. One example, *ser*, is given here, while the forms of *ir* are in Appendix III.

Ser

Present	soy, eres, es, somos, sois, son
Imperfect	era, eras, era, éramos, erais, eran
Preterite	fui, fuiste, fue, fuimos, fuisteis, fueron
Pres. Subj.	sea, seas, sea, seamos, seáis, sean
Past Subj.	fuera/se, fueras, fuera, fuéramos, fuerais, fueran

---

Exercise 5
Give the third person plural preterite and the first person plural past subjunctive for these verbs.

1. traer
2. decir
3. hacer
4. querer
5. venir
6. conducir
7. saber
8. haber
9. poder
10. poner
11. estar
12. tener

4.15
LEXICALLY CONDITIONED IRREGULARITIES
Irregular Participles

Another inheritance from Latin, like strong past tense forms but on a more limited scale, is a series of verbs with two grammatically acceptable past participles. One participle is usually regular and the other irregular, the latter coming more directly from Latin. This irregularity applies only to certain verbs of all three conjugations. The regular form is usually reserved for use in the perfect tenses (*haber* + past participle) while the irregular form more often functions as an adjective. The verbal form is invariable in –o while the adjectival form is fully inflected for gender and number.

	PAST PARTICIPLE AS VERB	PAST PARTICIPLE AS ADJECTIVE
atender	Ya me han **atendido**.	No estás **atento/a**.
bendecir	El Papa los había **bendecido**.	Esta **bendita** perra me mordió.
corregir	He **corregido** el examen.	Esa palabra no es **correcta**.

English has some verbal and adjectival past participle pairs, an example of which is *shaved* vs *shaven*: *He had <u>shaved</u> off his beard and arrived at the event clean <u>shaven</u>.*

A number of irregular past participles have not been listed in Appendix III because their verbs have mostly regular forms. Among these are, *abrir > abierto, cubrir > cubierto, escribir > escrito, morir > muerto,* and *soltar > suelto*.

There are also some irregular present participles (gerunds), such as *ir > yendo, poder > pudiendo, venir > viniendo*. All radically changing Class II and III verbs (verbs in *–ir*) have irregular present participles: *dormir > durmiendo, sentir > sintiendo, pedir > pidi*endo.

4.16
DEFECTIVE (Incomplete) AND UNIPERSONAL VERBS

Due to their inherent semantic properties, certain verbs cannot be conjugated in all three persons nor in all tenses. These verbs, which are semantically incompatible with certain given conditions and consequentially have incomplete conjugations, belong to a special group called defective verbs. Some thirty-odd verbs belong to this group.

Many syntactic structures will admit only non-personal subjects. Such structures exclude all but the third person forms of the verb. *Acontecer* is one such verb —people are not usually "happening." Other verbs with similar idiosyncrasies are *atañer* and *concernir*. Another defective verb is *soler*, with limited use in both the indicative and subjunctive moods.

In addition to the type of verb limited by syntactic or phonetic structures, there is another considerable list of verbs classified as unipersonal verbs. These all deal with phenomena of nature and are restricted to the third person form of the conjugation paradigm. *Larousse de la Conjugación* lists forty-five such verbs like *llover* 'rain', *tronar* 'thunder', *atardecer* 'get dark'. *Haber*, when expressing existence, (*Hay/Hubo/Ha habido unas huelgas*) is unipersonal, but only in these usages.

4.17
IN SUMMARY

Like many world languages, Spanish is no exception in having an abundance of verb forms that resist systematic classification. Some changes may be predictable, and others seem randomly applied. There are some morphophonemic features operating to the exclusion of others, in complementary distribution. There are others applied only in conjunction with other features, and some occur only as a consequence of other features. Take the common verb *tener* as an example, with its irregular forms in bold type, and compare it to the regular paradigm for *-er* verbs. To establish a comprehensible and systematic classification of this verb would incur more exceptions than concurrences with the regular conjugation pattern. Since this verb runs the gamut of possible irregularities, the task would be pedagogically futile.

Chapter 4 Spanish Irregular Verb Morphology

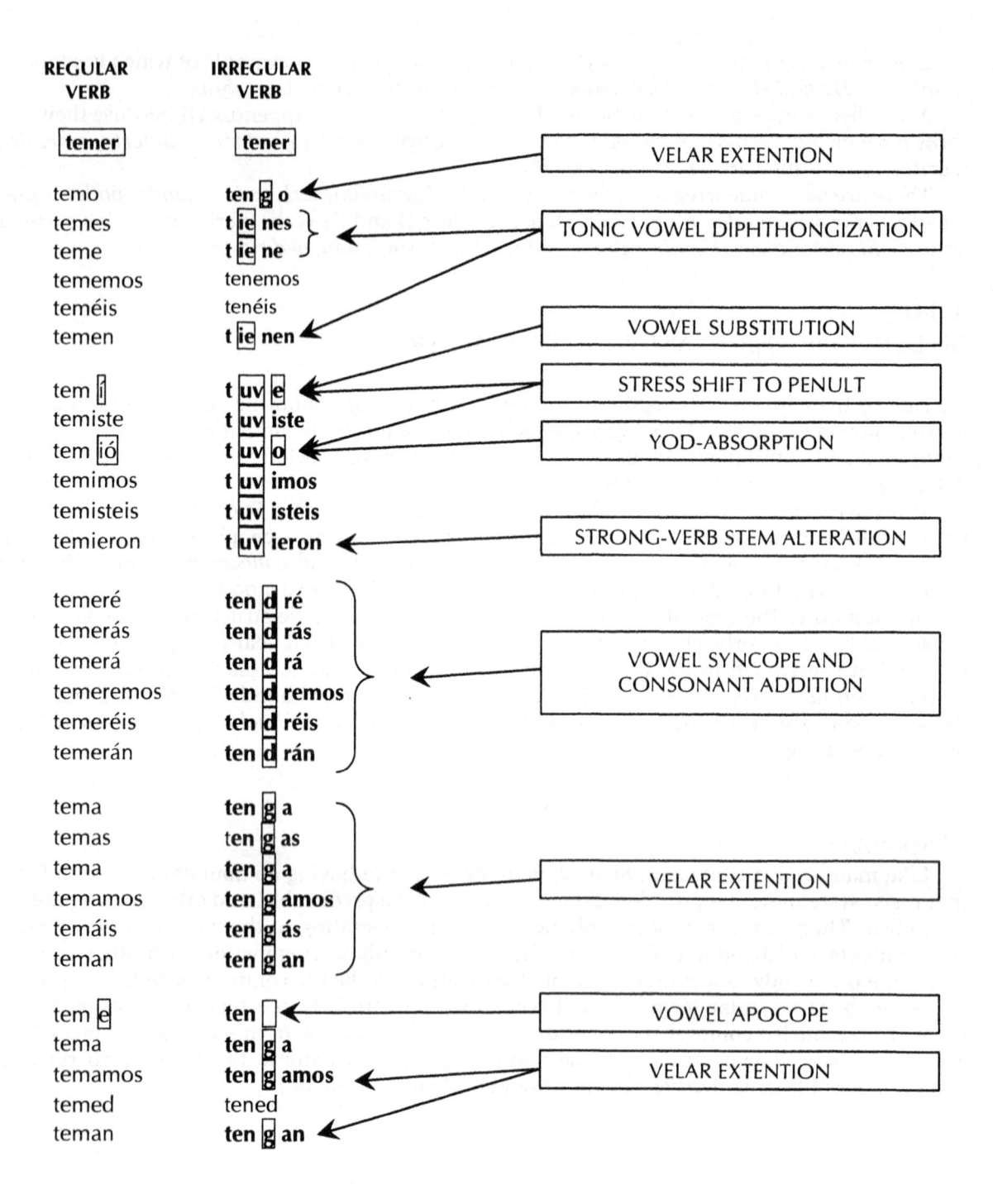

REGULAR VERB	IRREGULAR VERB	
temer	tener	→ VELAR EXTENTION
temo	ten**g**o	
temes	t**ie**nes	⎫
teme	t**ie**ne	⎬ → TONIC VOWEL DIPHTHONGIZATION
tememos	tenemos	
teméis	tenéis	
temen	t**ie**nen ←	VOWEL SUBSTITUTION
tem**í**	t**uv**e ←	STRESS SHIFT TO PENULT
temiste	t**uv**iste	
tem**ió**	t**uv**o ←	YOD-ABSORPTION
temimos	t**uv**imos	
temisteis	t**uv**isteis	
temieron	t**uv**ieron ←	STRONG-VERB STEM ALTERATION
temeré	ten**d**ré	
temerás	ten**d**rás	
temerá	ten**d**rá	⎫ → VOWEL SYNCOPE AND CONSONANT ADDITION
temeremos	ten**d**remos	⎬
temeréis	ten**d**réis	
temerán	ten**d**rán	
tema	ten**g**a	
temas	ten**g**as	
tema	ten**g**a	⎫ → VELAR EXTENTION
temamos	ten**g**amos	⎬
temáis	ten**g**ás	
teman	ten**g**an	
tem**e**	ten ←	VOWEL APOCOPE
tema	ten**g**a	
temamos	ten**g**amos ←	VELAR EXTENTION
temed	tened	
teman	ten**g**an ←	

The most common verbs demonstrating uniqueness in their morphology and those belonging to a specific class with a very reduced number of members have been grouped together in Appendix III. The listing represents a fairly complete inventory of many commonly used Spanish irregular verbs.

Exercise 6

Refer to Appendix III, and find all verbs whose first person singular, present indicative form ends in –o. Then, examine the present subjunctive of these verbs. What rule seems to be operating here? See also those verbs whose first person singular, present indicative does not end in –o. What can be said about their present subjunctive forms?

Exercise 7

The past and future subjunctive are derived from the preterite. What form of the preterite serves as the root for the these subjunctives, and are there any exceptions listed in Appendix III?

Exercise 8

For all future and conditional forms found in the list of irregular verbs in Appendix III, make a three-part classification based upon: a) forms which show only the loss of the infinitive vowel (syncope), b) forms where the infinitive vowel is replaced by –d– (epenthesis) and c) forms showing both the –c– and –e– as lost from the original infinitive root.

Exercise 9

For all the irregular strong preterite forms listed in Appendix III, classify them under three headings: a) those with a stem vowel of *u*, b) those with a stem vowel of *i*, and c) those with a stem vowel of *a*. How do the endings of these verbs differ from those of regular verbs in the preterite?

Exercise 10

Select all the first person singular present indicative forms from the list of irregular verbs in Appendix III and list them under headings which show identical irregularities. Example: u >uy in *construir, incluir*.

Exercise 11

From Appendix III, list the verbs which have, a) irregular –*ndo* (present participle/gerund forms), and, b) irregular past participles.

5

The Comparative Syntax of Statements and Questions

5.1

English and Spanish predications each have three families of tenses—the present, the past and the future/conditional. Four basic tenses appear in each of these three time frames:

	PRESENT	PAST
SIMPLE	He teaches here. Él enseña aquí.	He taught here. Él enseñaba aquí. Él enseñó aquí.
PROGRESSIVE	He is teaching here. Él está enseñando aquí	He was teaching here. Él estaba/estuvo enseñando aquí.
PERFECT	He has taught here. Él ha enseñado aquí.	He had taught here. Él había enseñado aquí.
PERFECT PROGRESSIVE	He has been teaching here. Él ha estado enseñando aquí.	He had been teaching here. Él había estado enseñando aquí.

FUTURE/CONDITIONAL

SIMPLE	He will/would teach here. Él enseñará/enseñaría aquí.
PROGRESSIVE	He will/would be teaching here. Él estará/estaría enseñando aquí.
PERFECT	He will/would have taught here for twenty years in May. En mayo, él habrá/habría enseñado aquí por veinte años.
PERFECT PROGRESSIVE	In May, he will/would have been teaching here for twenty years. En mayo, él habrá/habría estado enseñando aquí por veinte años.

5.2

Each of the English and Spanish tenses listed above may occur in sentences of five different structural types; only the simple present tense appears in the examples.

AFFIRMATIVE STATEMENT	John wants an interview Juan desea una entrevista.
NEGATIVE STATEMENT	John doesn't want an interview. Juan no desea una entrevista.
AFFIRM. YES/NO QUESTION	Does John want an interview? ¿Desea Juan una entrevista?
NEGATIVE YES/NO QUESTION	Doesn't John want an interview? ¿No desea Juan una entrevista?
CONTENT QUESTION	What does John want? ¿Qué desea Juan?

5.3

The verbal constituents of the three tense families follow. For each tense sentence examples are provided in both languages for affirmative and negative statements, affirmative and negative *Yes/No* questions and content questions. A brief discussion then follows.

The Present Tense Family

SIMPLE PRESENT

Sara writes a book.   (Sara) escribe un libro.
Sara doesn't write a book.   (Sara) no escribe un libro.

Chapter 5 The Comparative Syntax of Statements and Questions

Does Sara write a book?	¿Escribe (Sara) un libro?
Doesn't Sara write a book?	¿No escribe (Sara) un libro?
Why does Sara write a book?	¿Por qué escribe (Sara) un libro?[2]

ENGLISH: The lexical verb (LV) is inflected (two forms) in the affirmative structure only. In all the other structures, the AUX-do [inflected *do/does*] must be introduced, followed by the base form/LV. The interrogative structures have subject/AUX inversion, that is, they switch position.

SPANISH: The lexical verb (LV) is consistently inflected in all six forms (first, second, third persons, singular and plural). The interrogative structures have subject/verb inversion if an expressed subject appears. No auxiliaries occur.

Note: The following observations apply to all Spanish tenses:
1) Concerning the Spanish subject, it is optional in all cases when context makes its identity clear. It is stated generally only for contrast or clarification.
2) Concerning subject/verb inversion in Spanish Yes/No questions, we cite the following authorities: Rutten, 1995; Torrego, 1984; King and Suñer 2004; Olsen, 2010; Zagona, K., 2002.

Generally yes/no questions are acceptable with or without subject/verb inversion:

¿Miguel tiene una computadora? (Olsen, 2010)
¿Tiene Miguel una computadora?
¿Tiene una computadora Miguel?

3) Concerning content questions, the interrogative *¿por qué?* allows a stated subject either to precede or follow the verb (King and Suñer, 2004).

a. ¿Por qué **Juan** arregló esta bicicleta?   a. ¿Por qué **el senador** no ha llegado?
b. ¿Por qué arregló **Juan** esta bicicleta?   b. ¿Por qué no ha llegado **el senador**?

But with other interrogatives the subject/verb inversion is obligatory:

a. ¿Qué *ha comprado* Juan?
b. *¿Qué Juan *ha comprado*? (Rutten, N. 1995)
which would make A. Machado's line, *¿Adónde el camino irá?...* acceptable only on the basis of poetic license. (Torrego, E. 1984)

PRESENT PROGRESSIVE

Sarah is writing a book.	Sara está escribiendo un libro.
Sarah isn't writing a book.	Sara no está escribiendo un libro.
Is Sarah writing a book?	¿Está escribiendo (Sara) un libro?
Isn't Sarah writing a book?	¿No está escribiendo (Sara) un libro?
What is Sarah writing?	¿Qué está escribiendo Sara?

ENGLISH: The LV is in *-ing* form. The inflected AUX-*be* (*am, is, are*) is essential. The interrogative structures have subject/AUX-*be* inversion.

SPANISH: The LV is in *-ndo* form. Inflected AUX-*estar* (present tense) appears. The interrogative structures have subject/VP inversion where there is an expressed subject. VP means "verb phrase," consisting of the main verbal unit conjugated in any of its simple or compound tenses

PRESENT PERFECT

Sara has written a book.	Sara ha escrito un libro.
Sara hasn't written a book.	Sara no ha escrito un libro.
Has Sara written a book?	¿Ha escrito (Sara) un libro.
Hasn't Sara written a book	¿No ha escrito (Sara) un libro?
What has Sara written?	¿Qué ha escrito Sara?

ENGLISH: The LV is in the past participle form. The inflected AUX is *have* (*has/have*) The interrogative structures show subject/AUX-*have* inversion.

SPANISH: The LV is in the past participle form. The AUX is *haber* [inflected] in the present tense. The interrogative structures have subject/VP inversion where there is an expressed subject.

PRESENT PERFECT PROGRESSIVE

Since last year... **Desde el año pasado...**

Sara has been writing a book.	Sara ha estado escribiendo un libro.
Sara hasn't been writing a book.	Sara no ha estado escribiendo un libro.
Has Sara been writing a book?	¿Ha estado escribiendo (Sara) un libro?
Hasn't Sara been writing a book?	¿No ha estado escribiendo (Sara) un libro?
How much has Sara been writing?	¿Cuánto ha estado escribiendo Sara?

ENGLISH: The lexical verb is in -*ing* form. Two auxiliaries occur; the first, *have*, is inflected, and the second, *be*, is in the past participle form. The interrogative structures have subject/AUX-*have* inversion.

SPANISH: Two auxiliaries occur; the first, *haber*, is inflected, and the second, *estar*, is in the past participle form. The LV is in the -*ndo* form. The interrogative structures have subject/VP inversion in the case of an expressed subject.

5.4

The Past Tense Family

SIMPLE PAST

Sara wrote a book.	Sara escribió/escribía un libro.
Sara didn't write a book	Sara no escribió/escribía un libro.
Did Sara write a book?	¿Escribió/Escribía (Sara) un libro?
Didn't Sara write a book?	¿No escribió/escribía (Sara) un libro?
What did Sara write?	¿Qué escribió/escribía Sara?

Chapter 5 The Comparative Syntax of Statements and Questions

ENGLISH: The verb (LV) is in the past in the affirmative structure only. In all other structures, AUX-*do* [past *did*] occurs with the LV. The interrogative structures have subject/AUX-*do* inversion.

> **Note:** Teachers often comment on how challenging English past tense verbal forms are for Spanish natives. There are two reasons. First, the English past tense is rife with irregular forms, most of which defy any helpful classification (See Appendix I). Second, the English past tense forms occur with relatively little frequency, that is, only in the past tense + structure, as shown, but not in the other four. Its only other appearance is in subordinate clauses: Where did they go? > I don't know where they went (See 5.11).

SPANISH: Since in Spanish the simple past may use either the preterite or the imperfect, the verb may be in either tense (See Chapter 6). No auxiliaries occur. The interrogative structures have subject/VP inversion with an expressed subject.

PAST PROGRESSIVE

Sara was writing a book.	Sara estaba/estuvo escribiendo un libro.
Sara wasn't writing a book.	Sara no estaba/estuvo escribiendo un libro.
Was Sara writing a book?	¿Estaba/Estuvo escribiendo (Sara) un libro?
Wasn't Sara writing a book?	¿No estaba/estuvo escribiendo (Sara) un libro?
Why was Sara writing?	¿Por qué estaba/estuvo escribiendo Sara?

ENGLISH: The main verb (LV) is in *-ing* form. The AUX is *be* [inflected *was/were*] in the past. The interrogative structures have subject/AUX-*be* inversion.
SPANISH: The main verb is in *-ndo* form. The AUX-*estar* is either in the preterite or imperfect tenses. The interrogative structures have subject/VP inversion where there is an expressed subject.

PAST PERFECT

Before finishing her studies...   **Antes de terminar sus estudios...**

Sara had written a book.	Sara había escrito un libro.
Sara hadn't written a book.	Sara no había escrito un libro.
Had Sara written a book?	¿Había escrito (Sara) un libro?
Hadn't Sara written a book?	¿No había escrito (Sara) un libro?
What had Sara written?	¿Qué había escrito Sara?

ENGLISH: The main verb (LV) is in past participle form. The AUX is *have*, [past tense *had*]. The interrogative structures have subject/AUX-*have* inversion.
SPANISH: The main verb (LV) is in past participle form. The AUX is *haber* [usually imperfect], although the preterite auxiliary (*hube hablado*) occasionally appears in writing. The interrogative structures have subject/VP inversion where there is an expressed subject..

PAST PERFECT PROGRESSIVE

All that morning...   **Toda esa mañana...**

Sara had been writing a book.	Sara había estado escribiendo un libro.
Sara hadn't been writing a book.	Sara no había estado escribiendo un libro.
Had Sara been writing a book?	¿Había estado escribiendo (Sara) un libro?
Hadn't Sara been writing a book?	¿No había estado escribiendo (Sara) un libro?
Where had Helen been writing?	¿Dónde había estado escribiendo Sara.

ENGLISH: The main verb (LV) is in *-ing* form. Two auxiliaries occur: the first, *have* [past], and the second, *be* [past participle]. The interrogative structures have subject/AUX-*have* inversion.

SPANISH: The main verb is in *-ndo* form. Two auxiliaries occur: the first, *haber* [most commonly in the imperfect], and the second, *estar* [past participle]. The interrogative structures have subject/VP inversion if an expressed subject occurs

5.5 The Future/Conditional Family

> **Note:** When discussing either the future or conditional, one must bear in mind that aside from their usual meanings of pure futurity or conditionality, these tenses can in certain contexts express probability or conjecture, in present or past time, respectively:
> *¿Qué pensarán de nosotros?* = What must they think of us?
> *¿Dónde estaría?* = Where could he have been? (See Chapter 8)

SIMPLE FUTURE/CONDITIONAL

Sara will/would write a book.	Sara escribirá/escribiría un libro.
Sara won't/wouldn't write a book.	Sara no escribirá/escribiría un libro.
Will/Would Sara write a book?	¿Escribirá/Escribiría (Sara) un libro?
Won't/Wouldn't Sara write a book?	¿No escribirá/escribiría (Sara) un libro?
What will/would Sara write?	¿Qué escribirá/escribiría Sara?

ENGLISH: The main verb is the LV i.e., the base form. The AUX-*will* or *would* must be used. The interrogative structures have inversion of the subject/AUX-*will/would*.

SPANISH: The lexical verb is in the future or conditional tense. No auxiliaries occur. The interrogative structures have subject/verb inversion with an expressed subject.

PROGRESSIVE FUTURE/CONDITIONAL

Sara will/would be writing a book.	Sara estará/estaría escribiendo un libro.
Sara won't/wouldn't be writing a book.	Sara no estará/estaría escribiendo un libro.
Will/Would Sara be writing a book?	¿Estará/Estaría escribiendo (Sara) un libro?
Won't/Wouldn't Sara be writing a book?	¿No estará/estaría escribiendo (Sara) un libro?
What will/would Sara be writing?	¿Qué estará/estaría escribiendo Sara?

ENGLISH: The main verb is in *-ing* form. Two auxiliaries are used: the first, *will/would*, and the second, *be* [base form]. The interrogative structures have subject/AUX-*will/would* inversion.

Chapter 5 The Comparative Syntax of Statements and Questions

SPANISH: The main verb is in *-ndo* form. *Estar* [future or conditional] is the only auxiliary used. The interrogative structures have subject/VP inversion when an expressed subject appears.

PERFECT FUTURE/CONDITIONAL

Sara will/would have written a book.	Sara habrá/habría escrito un libro.
Sara won't/wouldn't have written a book.	Sara no habrá/habría escrito un libro.
Will/Would Sara have written a book?	¿Habrá/Habría escrito (Sara) un libro?
Won't/Wouldn't Sara have written a book?	¿No habrá/habría escrito (Sara) un libro?
When will/would Sara have written a book?	¿Cuándo habrá/habría escrito (Sara) un libro?

ENGLISH: The main verb is in past participle form. Two auxiliaries occur; the first is *will/would* and the second is *have* [base form]. The interrogative structures have subject/AUX-*will/would* inversion.

SPANISH: The main verb is in past participle form. *Haber* [future or conditional] is the only auxiliary used. The interrogative structures have subject/VP inversion where there is an expressed subject.

PERFECT PROGRESSIVE FUTURE/CONDITIONAL

Sara will/would have been writing a book.	Sara habrá/habría estado escribiendo un libro.
Sara won't/wouldn't have been writing a book.	Sara no habrá/habría estado escribiendo un libro.
Will/Would Sara have been writing a book?	¿Habrá/Habría estado escribiendo (Sara) un libro?
Won't/Wouldn't Sara have been writing a book?	¿No habrá/habría estado escribiendo (Sara) un libro?
What will/would Sara have been writing?	¿Qué habrá/habría estado escribiendo Sara?

> **Note:** The Spanish sentences under perfect progressive future/conditional would probably be construed as having the meaning of probability: *I wonder if/Do you suppose that/Could it be that Sara has/had been writing a book?* Again, see Chapter 8.

ENGLISH: The main verb is in *-ing* form. Three auxiliaries occur: the first, *will/would*, the second, *have* [base form], and the third, *be* [past participle]. The interrogative structures have subject/AUX-*will/would* inversion.

SPANISH: The main verb is in *-ndo* form. Two auxiliaries are used, the first being *haber* [future or conditional] and the second, *estar* [past particple]. The interrogative structures have subject/VP inversion where one finds an expressed subject.

Exercise 1

Examine the following sentences. For each, determine the structural type (affirmative or negative statement, affirmative or negative question, or content question) and the tense of the verb units. Then translate each sentence and determine the nature of all the verbal constituents.

1. Mis padres no vieron esa película.
2. When did he ask you for the money?
3. ¿No habías estado estudiando en la biblioteca?
4. Don't they need help with their work?
5. Almorzaremos hoy en un lugar cercano.
6. What are they doing right now?
7. ¿Viajarán Uds. pronto al extranjero?
8. We hadn't used very much gasoline.
9. ¿No lo estuvieron ayudando ellos ayer hasta muy tarde?
10. Why have you been waiting for the bus?

Exercise 2

Write original English (EN) or Spanish (SP) sentences of the structural types and in the tenses called for. Be able to account for the nature of every lexical and auxiliary verb in all the sentences.

1. EN affirmative statement, present progressive.
2. SP negative statement, preterite.
3. EN affirmative Yes/No question, present perfect progressive.
4. SP content question, past progressive.
5. EN content question, present.
6. SP affirmative statement, future perfect.
7. EN negative Yes/No question, present perfect.
8. SP negative Yes/No question, future perfect progressive.
9. EN negative statement, past progressive.
10. SP affirmative Yes/No question, past perfect progressive.

5.6
BASIC SENTENCE TYPES AND THEIR STRUCTURAL FORMULAS

Here is a listing of the structural formulas for the five basic sentence types of English and Spanish. A detailed description, several examples, and a contrastive analysis of each formula and sentence type then follows. Each formula accounts only for the subject, question elements (whether as words or as intonation), negative elements, auxiliaries and lexical verbs. The structural symbols we use follow:

LEGEND

AUX	auxiliary verb
INTERROG	interrogative word or phrase
LV	lexical verb (main verb in base form = the infinitive without *to*)
S	mandatory subject
(S)	exclusively optional (null) subject
VP	verb phrase, consisting of the main verbal unit conjugated in any of its simple or compound tenses; verbal elements not separated
VR	verbal remainder, that is, the portion of the verbal unit remaining

Chapter 5 The Comparative Syntax of Statements and Questions 55

	intact after the first auxiliary is separated from it by some non-verbal element. The VR appears underlined in the following examples: *What has he <u>been doing</u>? Where will she <u>be</u> going? They don't <u>know</u> him.*
↑	rising terminal intonation when spoken
↓	falling terminal intonation when spoken
*	indicates that a contraction between AUX and *not* is optional
**	indicates that a contraction between AUX and *not* is mandatory

SENTENCE TYPE	ENGLISH STRUCTURE	SPANISH STRUCTURE
Affirmative Statement	S + VP↓	(S) + VP + (S) ↓
Negative Statement	S + AUX* + not + VR↓	(S) + no + VP + (S) ↓
Affirmative Yes/No Question	AUX + S + VR↑	(S) + VP + (S)↑
Negative Yes/No Question	AUX** + not + S + VR↑	(S) + no + VP + (S)↑
Content Question	INTERROG+AUX+S+VR↓	INTERROG+VP+(S) ↓

5.7
THE AFFIRMATIVE STATEMENT

ENGLISH: S + VP↓
  a. The subject must be expressed either as a noun, a pronoun, or an equivalent form.
  b. The entire verb phrase unit follows the subject.
    Examples:
      She lives here.
      My boss likes his new car.
      They would have done anything for you.
      We have been working very hard.

SPANISH: (S) + VP + (S)↓
  a. The subject may be optionally expressed depending on circumstances.
  b. If stated, the subject may either precede or follow the entire verb phrase, never in both positions.
  c. As in English, the verb phrase is kept intact.
    Examples:
      Mi padre trabaja. (Subject expressed and stated first.)
      Han estado corriendo. (No subject expressed.)
      Había llegado una señora. (Subject expressed last.)

CONTRASTIVE ANALYSIS:
   a. The affirmative structures of both languages are virtually the same, except that,
   b. In English the subject must be expressed and precedes the verb phrase.
   c. In Spanish the subject is frequently optional, but if stated, may either precede or follow the verb phrase.

5.8
THE NEGATIVE STATEMENT

ENGLISH: S + AUX* + not + VR↓
   a. The subject in English must appear.
   b. An auxiliary follows the subject. It may be *do, have, be, will, would,* or a modal auxiliary plus *not*.
   c. An optional contraction occurs between the auxiliary (AUX*) and *not*.
   d. The verbal remainder (VR) comes last and is what remains of the verbal unit after the first AUX separates from it.
      Examples:
         You have not read the newspaper as yet.
         My brother isn't going to Colombia next summer.
         They didn't understand your questions.
         My students would not be studying this late.

Note: The indication that a contraction between AUX and *not* may or may not occur is a bit misleading. Usually there is a choice, as in *will not > won't, does not > doesn't, are not > aren't,* etc. There are cases, however, in which contractions involving the modal auxiliaries are not possible. For example, usually no contraction occurs between *may* or *might* and *not*. *Shall + not* can be *shan't*, but the form seems archaic.

SPANISH: (S) + no + VP + (S)↓
   a. As always, the subject is optional and may precede or follow the verb phrase.
   b. *No* before the entire VP produces the negation.
   c. The verb phrase (VP) is integrated (kept intact), regardless of the number of its elements.
      Examples:
         El autor no ha escrito nada esta semana.
         No ha estado haciendo mucho frío.
         Los jóvenes no están aquí en este momento.

CONTRASTIVE ANALYSIS
   a. English and Spanish negative structures are very different.
   b. The mandatory English subject occurs first, while the Spanish subject is optional, but when expressed, can either precede or follow the verb phrase.
   c. English breaks up its verbal unit, removing the first auxiliary. A contraction may or may not appear between this auxiliary and *not*.
   d. Spanish, as always, integrates the verb phrase, allowing nothing to intervene between or among its elements.

5.9
THE AFFIRMATIVE YES/NO QUESTION STRUCTURE

ENGLISH: AUX + S + VR↑
 a. An auxiliary comes first, followed by the mandatory subject and then the verbal remainder (VR).
 b. When rendered orally, there is terminally rising intonation (↑). A question mark (?) accompanies the question in writing.
    Examples:
       Have you been eating too much?
       Did your parents see the movie?
       Are the Russians planning a new system?
       May I have a little more wine, please?

SPANISH: (S) + VP + (S)↑
 a. The Spanish affirmative Yes/No question and affirmative statement structures are virtually identical.
 b. There is, however, a terminally rising oral intonation in the question structure, and in writing, the double question marks (¿?) are mandatory.
 c. Almost always the subject, if stated at all, occurs after the verb phrase in these questions, but it may appear before as well as mentioned earlier.
    Examples:
       ¿Ha estado manteniendo (él) a sus padres?
       ¿Estás peinándote?
       ¿Su hijo tiene novia?

CONTRASTIVE ANALYSIS
 a. The Spanish and English Yes/No question structures are quite different.
 b. English states the first auxiliary initially, follows it with the mandatory subject, and leaves the verbal remainder (VR) for last.
 c. Spanish uses the same structure it employs for affirmative statements, but the subject tends to appear after the verb phrase. Written Spanish requires the double question marks (¿?).
 d. In both languages, the affirmative Yes/No question structures coincide in using rising terminal oral intonation.

5.10
THE NEGATIVE YES/NO QUESTION STRUCTURE

ENGLISH: AUX** + not + S + VR↑
 a. A mandatory contraction occurs between the first auxiliary AUX** and *not*.
 b. Then comes the required subject, which in turn is followed by the verbal remainder (VR).
 c. Rising terminal intonation characterizes this type of question in oral rendition. In written English, a question mark (?) appears.
    Examples:
       Didn't you visit your friends in Peru?
       Can't your friend find his car?

Won't he have been complaining excessively by then?
Weren't your problems causing you trouble?

> **Note:** English has an alternate structure for negative Yes/No questions; it is common in British English but rare in the American variety. It is, AUX + S + not + LV↑
>
> Does he not recognize us?
> Had they not arrived?
> Are you not going home?
> Should we not stop talking?

SPANISH: (S) + no + VP + (S)↑
  a. The Spanish negative Yes/No question structure is virtually identical to the syntax of its negative statements.
  b. The subject, if stated, usually occurs after the verb phrase, but the option of using it before still remains; *no* precedes the verb phrase.
  c. Rising terminal intonation occurs in speech, and in writing, (¿?) is obligatory.
     Examples:
       ¿No se está preocupando mucho tu abuela?
       ¿No vienes mañana?
       ¿Su hijo no ha llegado todavía?

CONTRASTIVE ANALYSIS
  a. The English and Spanish negative Yes/No question structures differ considerably.
  b. In English, the first AUX and *not* function as a mandatorily contracted unit and the subject and verbal remainder (VR) then follow.
  c. In Spanish, the verb phrase is kept intact, *no* precedes it for negation, and the subject, if stated at all, usually occurs after the VP. The subject, as usual, may appear before the VP as well.
  d. The structures are similar, nevertheless, in their requiring a terminally rising oral intonation.

5.11
THE CONTENT QUESTION STRUCTURE

ENGLISH: INTERROG + AUX + S + VR↓
  a. The INTERROG (interrogative element) is stated first. It consists of either a word (*When?*) or a phrase (*At what time?*).
  b. Then comes the first auxiliary.
  c. Third is the mandatory subject--a noun, a pronoun, or an equivalent form.
  d. The verbal remainder (VR) appears last.
  e. Although the content question, when written, requires a question mark in English, a falling terminal oral intonation is the rule.
     Examples:
       Where have you been studying?
       At what time will your friends arrive?
       How much did they spend?
       What can you see?

Chapter 5 The Comparative Syntax of Statements and Questions

SPANISH: INTERROG + VP + (S)↓
  a. As in English, the interrogative element (word [¿Adónde?] or phrase [¿A qué hora?]) appears first.
  b. Then comes the entire VP, nothing appearing between or among its elements.
  c. The subject is optional; if stated, it appears after the VP, with one exception, that of ¿Por qué? as noted earlier: ¿Por qué ha salido Edna? = ¿Por qué Edna ha salido?
  d. The written language requires (¿?), but in oral renditions, as in English, there is falling intonation.
  Examples:
   ¿Adónde van tus amigos?
   ¿A qué hora vienes?
   ¿Con quién has estado comentando el asunto?
   ¿Qué han resuelto los senadores?
   ¿Por qué venden drogas tus amigos? = ¿Por qué tus amigos venden drogas?

CONTRASTIVE ANALYSIS
  a. The English and Spanish content question structures show numerous differences.
  b. Both languages state the interrogative element first, but in Spanish, the following verb phrase is integrated. In English, the subject intervenes between the first AUX and the VR..
  c. The English subject is mandatory, the Spanish one optional and usually stated after the VP.
  d. Both languages use falling oral intonation.

Note: The content question structure assumes a different syntax when appearing as a subordinate clause, usually a noun clause. It converts to the affirmative (+) structure introduced by the interrogative word or phrase.

Question:	Answer:
What did they say?	I don't know *what he said*.
	* I don't know *what did he say?*
How can they see that far?	We can't tell *how they can see that far*.
Where has she gone?	Who cares *where she's gone*.
Why are you talking?	Don't worry about *why we're talking*.

No such syntactical changes occur in Spanish, but the question word in the subordinate clause retains its orthographic accent since it remains interrogative and thus stressed even in the "indirect question."

¿Cómo logró hacerlo? Nadie sabe *cómo logró hacerlo*.
¿Dónde vas a vivir? No te digo *dónde voy a vivir*.

Exercise 3

For each of the following sentences, (a) name the tense used, (b) cite the basic sentence type represented (affirmative or negative statement, affirmative or negative Yes/No question, or content question), and (c) write the structural formula for each sentence, accounting for only the S, AUX, negative element, interrogative element and verbal unit.

1. ¿A qué has estado jugando en tu tiempo libre?
2. They didn't tell their story to anyone.
3. ¿No tiene esa ley un propósito muy importante?
4. Will your parents be giving a lot of parties?
5. Los jóvenes de esta generación no están haciendo nada de importancia.
6. This summer hasn't been as hot as the one before.
7. Muchos viajeros visitan las ruinas antiguas.
8. When would you have told them the truth?
9. ¿Saben tus amistades tu número de teléfono?
10. Didn't you do all the assigned exercises?

Exercise 4

Examine the following list of structural formulas, each marked EN for English and SP for Spanish. Determine the basic sentence type represented—affirmative or negative statement, affirmative or negative Yes/No question or content question. Then, write an original sentence in the language indicated which fits the specifications of the structural formula. Use any subject and any tense.

1. EN: INTERROG + AUX + S + VR↓
2. SP: (S) + VP + (S)↑
3. EN: S + AUX* + not + VR↓
4. SP: (S) + VP + (S)↓
5. EN: AUX** + not + S + VR↑
6. SP: INTERROG + VP + (S)↓
7. EN: AUX + S + VR↑
8. SP: (S) + no + VP + (S)↓
9. EN: S + VP↓
10. SP: (S) + no + VP + (S)↑

Exercise 5

Examine the following sentences. For each determine the tense and the structural type and write the structural formula. In writing the formulas, you need account only for S, negative element, INTERROG, AUX, VP or VR, and terminal intonation.

1. John was here yesterday.
2. ¿No habían calculado los daños causados por la marea alta?
3. Had your father seen a doctor?
4. ¿Estás leyendo algo interesante?
5. Won't you have been living there by then?
6. La criatura habrá cumplido un año para el verano.
7. Would you give him that much money?
8. El gobierno no había estado realizando cabalmente sus obligaciones.
9. Where have you been living during the past few months?
10. ¿Cuánto dinero habían gastado tus amigos en Chile?
11. Has your mother met my friends?
12. ¿Iba tu abogado a corte con frecuencia?
13. What language had they been speaking in the restaurant?

Chapter 5 The Comparative Syntax of Statements and Questions

14. Un señor estaba dándole instrucciones a mi esposa.
15. The secretary didn't know my name.
16. ¿Adónde han ido todos los guardias?
17. Hadn't your brother seen any of them before?
18. ¿Qué novela estabas leyendo antes?
19. She hadn't been doing any work at all at school.
20. ¿No vendieron nada las muchachas en la feria?

6

A Question of Aspect: The Spanish Imperfect-Preterite Contrast

6.1

Spanish expresses past time through two different simple past tenses, the imperfect and the preterite. However, because both forms express past events, the difference between the two is better understood as an aspectual rather than as a temporal contrast. For instance, the forms *escribió* 'she/he wrote' [perfective] and *escribía* 'she/he was writing' [imperfective] in the sentences below both relate past events.

> *Martha **escribió** un correo electrónico.*
> Martha wrote an e-mail. (perfective aspect)
>
> *Martha **escribía** un correo electrónico cuando sonó el teléfono.*
> Martha was writing an e-mail (imperfective aspect) when the phone rang.

These two tenses record past events, states or conditions from distinct points of view, that is, from two different aspects. Aspectual differences come from the speakers' ways of conceptualizing the events they are describing. One must ask certain pertinent questions before determining which of the two tenses is applicable. Is the event being described specific to one point in time and thus instantaneous, or is it recurrent or lasting over an extended period? What part of the event is relevant in the description— the beginning, the middle or the end, or the overall happening including beginning, middle and end? Also, is there an implied result to an action, and is that the primary focus?

English distinguishes less clearly between these different points of view concerning past events, but when pressed to do so, it can render past time from two distinct viewpoints as does

Spanish. English, however, has to use verbal periphrases (i.e., constructions involving more than one verbal form) to accomplish what Spanish does with a single form.

The grammatical category that defines this aspectual distinction between the preterite and imperfect is "grammatical" or "viewpoint" aspect (Smith 1991), because it indicates whether the speaker views an event as perfective (completed) or not. However, grammatical aspect is different from "lexical aspect," which refers to the semantic features of verbal predicates as determined by the specific nature of the event described. For instance, a verb such as *correr* conveys an inherent durative property, whereas *entrar* is by nature instantaneous. Lexical aspect will be addressed in 6.6.

6.2
DESCRIPTION OF THE IMPERFECT TENSE

The Spanish imperfect verb form describes an event, state, or condition in terms of a recalled moment in the middle of a single event in the past or of a series of repeated events. The description is reasonably free of boundaries or references to a beginning or end. The imperfect is useful in describing scenes in the past or the reliving of experiences. Unlike the preterite, described below, an imperfect action is ongoing in relation to the moment of recollection. Its use is statistically less frequent for some verbs than others than the preterite, as demonstrated when we take up "lexical aspect." English renders the Spanish imperfect in a variety of ways since the tense may express either past description or past habitual (repeated) events. The aspectual concept held by the speaker is instrumental in choosing the English mode of expression.

Past Description

The Spanish imperfect expresses past description. English uses the past progressive tense to express this concept: AUX-*be*[PAST] + LV-*ing*.

> *Caía* la lluvia y el viento *soplaba*.
> The rain *was falling* and the wind *was blowing*.

> *Aprendían* sus tablas de multiplicación cuando llegó el maestro.
> They *were learning* their multiplication tables when the professor arrived.

> *Estudiábamos* en México en la Universidad Autónoma.
> We *were studying* in Mexico at the Autonomous University.

Past Habitual Events (Repetition of Past Events)

The Spanish imperfect expresses habitual events in the past. English uses any of the following three structures to show the past repetition of actions.

1. MODAL AUX*used to* + LV

   > Juan *buscaba* toda clase de excusas antes, pero ya no.
   > John *used to look for* all kinds of excuses before, but not now.

   > Yo *comía* de vez en cuando en ese lugar.

Chapter 6 A Question of Aspect: The Spanish Imperfect-Preterite Contrast

I *used to eat* occasionally in that place.

Pedro *trabajaba* con el gobierno.
Peter *used to work* for the government.

2. MODAL AUX*would* + LV

Ella *jugaba* con sus compañeras todas las tardes.
She *would play* with her playmates every afternoon.

Yo de niño *comía* demasiado, y por eso *me enfermaba* frecuentemente.
As a child I *would eat* too much, and that's why *I would* frequently *get sick*.

Él *asistía* a las actividades solo para impresionarnos.
He *would attend* the activities only to impress us.

> **Note:** This usage of AUX-*would* in the expression of past repetition (*When I was younger, I would exercise more* =... *I used to exercise more*) must not be confused with its function as the conditional tense of English where AUX-*would* operates either in the conclusion clause of conditional sentences (*If I had the time, I would do it*), or as a future to past time (*Yesterday, she promised (that) she would go with me*).

3. PAST TENSE + ADV [indefinite time] placed initially, medially, or finally; eg., *sometimes, once in a while, occasionally, always, now and then, never*, etc. Such adverbs accompany repeated actions.

Yo <u>nunca</u> *llegaba* a tiempo.
I <u>never</u> arrived on time.

<u>A veces</u> yo *comía* en la cafetería de la escuela.
<u>Sometimes</u> I ate in/at the school cafeteria.

Ella *salía* temprano <u>de vez en cuando.</u>
She left early on <u>occasion/occasionally/once in a while.</u>

6.3
DESCRIPTION OF PRETERITE TENSE

The Spanish preterite expresses a completed past event, state, or condition viewed at the moment of speaking as over and done with in its entirety. It covers all aspects except the middle part of the description, that is, either the beginning or the end. The preterite indicates an event initiated or culminated at a specific, recalled moment, or an event seen as a point in the past or an event continued during a certain past time period but now viewed has ended. The meaning of the preterite covers a broader expanse than that of the imperfect; consequently, it is used more frequently. English generally uses its simple past tense to render the Spanish preterite.

Pensé que no venías, pero me da gusto que hayas cambiado de opinión.
I thought that you weren't coming, but I'm glad you changed your mind.

Era temprano cuando *entré* a la tienda.
It was early when I entered the store.

Salieron de la función a las seis.
They came out of/left the performance at six (o'clock).

Exercise 1

Translate the following sentences, being mindful of the contexts in which they might occur. In your choice of tenses, follow the general guidelines just presented.

1. I was waiting for you until they closed the building.
2. Según su costumbre, apenas ella salía de casa se ponía sus lentes oscuros.
3. We weren't watching the road when a truck crossed in front of us.
4. Unos comían mientras otros hablaban de los eventos del día.
5. It never snowed, but it was always very cold.
6. Ángela cantaba antes en ese club nocturno.
7. When we were younger, my brother would tease me a lot.
8. No hacían nada cuando los vi.
9. More people used to travel by train than by airplane before.
10. Para cuando llegué a clase a las ocho, ya estaban allí los otros.

6.4
TWO PERSPECTIVES ON SIMPLE PAST TENSE USAGES IN SPANISH

We contrast here the two simple Spanish past tenses according to their most common usages by providing an extended explanation of the comparative conditions under which each tense occurs, followed by illustrative sentences. Close examination of these examples will benefit the English speaker in deciding which tense most appropriately conveys the aspectual situation described in past time.

IMPERFECT	PRETERITE
Contrast 1	
The imperfect expresses a repeated or continued past activity upon which no limitation of time is imposed.	**The preterite, in contrast, expresses a repeated or ongoing past activity that came to a end at a specific point prior to the moment of speaking.**
Íbamos al río a menudo. We used to go to the river frequently.	Fuimos al río a menudo el año pasado. We went to the river frequently last year.
De vez en cuando visitábamos ese lugar. We would occasionally visit that place.	Visitamos ese lugar varias veces hasta que encontramos otro mejor. We visited that place several times until we found a better one.
Contrast 2	
The imperfect describes an action, state or situation in the past as a continuum in time with-	**The preterite expresses the resolution, outcome, end or result of an action, state or situa-**

Chapter 6 A Question of Aspect: The Spanish Imperfect-Preterite Contrast

out reference either to the beginning or end. Neither is there any reference made to the outcome or the resolution of that action, state, or condition.

Teníamos que trabajar por la tarde (y por eso decidimos no ir a la fiesta).
We had to (felt obliged to) work in the afternoon. (It's not clear that we did.)

Había un concurso de belleza (que quería ver en la televisión).
There was (scheduled to be or taking place at that moment in the past) a beauty contest.

Contrast 3: The Preterite and Imperfect in Narrations.

The imperfect tense describes a scene in the past.

Llovía fuerte y yo andaba sin paraguas.
It was raining hard, and I was without an umbrella.

Mientras ellos dormían yo leía.
While they were sleeping, I read.

Era una misa inolvidable ya que todos llegaban a la catedral con flores.
It was a memorable mass since everyone was showing up with flowers.

tion in the past. It may also express the beginning of a state of mind or a state of affairs, both transpiring prior to the moment of speaking.

Tuvimos que trabajar por la tarde (así que llegamos a casa completamente rendidos).
We had to work the afternoon. (We not only had to but did work.)

Hubo un concurso de belleza (que se transmitió en todos los canales).
There was (scheduled and took place) a beauty contest.

The preterite, on the other hand, advances the action of a narration.

Llovió, salió el sol y me fui.
It rained, the sun came out, and I left.

Anoche todos durmieron en el patio.
Last night everyone slept in the patio.

Colón llegó a América en 1492 y regresó en 1493, en 1498 y en 1502.
Columbus arrived in America in 1492 and returned in 1493, 1498, and 1502.

While the middle part of the narration shows the contrast between preterite as foreground material and imperfect as background information, the start and end of the narration can be expressed with the preterite to provide a summary of it:

(Starting) **Tuve un día horrible**. Primero, cuando salía para al trabajo, no podía encontrar las llaves. Por fin las encontré y salí tan pronto como pude. Hacía mucho frío pero, por las prisas, se me olvidó ponerme el abrigo. Ya en el trabajo.....etc, etc.; ...y justo antes de terminar mi turno, tuve una discusión con mi jefe. Y claro, al salir y llegar al carro, batallé para prenderlo. Por fin llegué a casa cansado y con mucho frío. Me dolía la cabeza pues me estaba resfriando, así que me fui a dormir. (Ending)**En fin, mi día fue un desastre total**.

The aspectual structure Spanish uses in narrations is outlined below as it applies to a narrative which follows:

1. The beginning of the narrative=preterite: The speaker still sees events from the point of view of the present (detached viewpoint from the past). [in italics in the narrative below]

2. The middle of the narrative. The speaker is reliving the past and, in doing so, uses the preterite and imperfect as follows:
   a) Preterite=foreground events (advance the action, etc.)
   b) Imperfect=background events (scenario, two events happening at the same time, etc.).

3. The end of the narrative=preterite. Since the speaker mentally returns to the present, s/he may use the preterite again. [in italics in the narrative below]

> *Cristóbal Colón* **fue** *uno de los navegantes más talentosos y atrevidos de su época. Sus tres viajes a las Américas* **cambiaron** *totalmente el concepto prevaleciente de la geografía mundial.* Cuando Colón **llegó** al nuevo mundo por primera vez, **le cambió** el nombre que **tenía** y lo **llamó** "Juana,"porque una de las hijas de Fernando e Isabel **se llamaba** así. Colón **pensaba** que **iba a llegar** a la India, pero no **fue** así. Cuando **ocupó** la primera isla, **observó** que los indios **vivían** en aldeas pequeñas y pobres, y aún así todo **era** simple y tranquilo. La tierra misma **era** muy hermosa, pero no **tenía** las riquezas que los españoles **andaban buscando**. Aunque el navegante no **estaba** nada satisfecho con su logro, **sabía** que **tenía que impresionar** a su benefactora, La Reina Isabel *La Católica*. Así que cuando **le escribió** su primera carta a La Reina para contarle su hallazgo, **exageró** bastante lo que le **describió**. **Pudo** hacerlo porque **sabía** que la monarca nunca **iba a ver** esas tierras. Colón ya **estaba** cansado y algo enfermo después de su viaje por el Atlántico; y aunque **descansó** en la primera isla a la que **llegó**, **salió** a continuar sus expediciones en busca de oro. *En fin, el famoso capitán* **hizo** *cuatro viajes al Nuevo Mundo, pero en ninguno de ellos* **encontró** *el tan buscado tesoro.* **Murió** *solo y desilusionado a principios del sigo XVI sin riquezas ni gloria.*

6.5
IMPERFECT PROGRESSIVE VS. PRETERITE PROGRESSIVE

The Spanish imperfect progressive tense (*estaba tomando*) describes a continuing, progressing past activity without any time limit imposed on the ongoing event. It is a substitute for the simple imperfect indicative and is used simply to intensify the notion of durative action or action in progress. As explained earlier, a simple imperfect verbal form already conveys the durative aspect. To express the same ongoing event in the past, English uses the past progressive tense.

Estábamos tomando (tomábamos) café en aquel restaurante.
We were having coffee in that restaurant over there.

Estaban viajando (viajaban) por México para conocer más de la cultura.
They were traveling through Mexico to know more of its culture.

When we wish to express a continuing, progressing past action which ended at a specific point in the past, we use the preterite progressive (*estuve tomando*). The English past progressive (*was drinking*) does not imply, in contrast to the Spanish preterite version, the termination of an action. Since the Spanish preterite progressive denotes perfectivity and English denotes only progression, the two tenses cannot be equivalents. English translates the Spanish preterite progressive as the past perfect progressive (*had been drinking*) or as the simple preterite (*drank*).

Chapter 6 A Question of Aspect: The Spanish Imperfect-Preterite Contrast

Both the preterite progressive and the imperfect progressive tenses of Spanish depend strongly on the inherent semantic qualities of the verb involved. We examine this further when we take up "lexical aspect," but for now, consider Gili Gaya's example of an ungrammatical usage: **El soldado estuvo disparando un tiro* (§97).

Estuvimos tomando café hasta que cerraron el restaurante.
We had been drinking coffee until they closed the restaurant.
We drank coffee until they closed the restaurant.
We were drinking coffee until they closed the restaurant.

Estuve viajando por Argentina hasta que tuve el accidente.
I had been traveling through Argentina until I had the accident.
I traveled through Argentina until I had the accident.
I was traveling through Argentina until I had the accident.

Estuvieron pasando esa película en el Cine Numancia.
They had been showing that movie at the Numancia Cinema.
They showed that movie at the Numancia Cinema.
They were showing that movie at the Numancia Cinema.

6.6
LEXICAL ASPECT

Whether one expresses an event as perfective or not (i.e., grammatical aspect), the internal temporal structure (inherent properties) of a verbal predicate do not change. For instance, a phrase such as *escribir un correo electrónico* possesses an inherent "durative" property that does not change by the selection of preterite or imperfect. That is, whether the speaker focuses on the completion (preterite) or on the evolving nature of the situation (imperfect), the event of *writing an e-mail* is durative because it takes time to realize. As such, this event contrasts with a verb such as *meter un pastel al horno*, which is inherently instantaneous or punctual (non-durative). Thus, we distinguish grammatical aspect from lexical aspect by the fact that the latter refers to the semantic features inherently expressed by verbal predicates: punctuality, dynamism, and telicity.

Punctuality is a semantic property that distinguishes durative vs. punctual events. Durative events, such as *comer*, as in *comer una manzana*, *escribir* as in *escribir una carta* take time to execute. Conversely, punctual events are instantaneous (e.g., *entrar*, as in *entrar a casa*, or *sacar* as in *sacar un pastel del horno*).

Dynamism is a semantic feature that contrasts dynamic events with statives. While dynamic events require energy to be mantained (e.g., *comer*, as in *comer una manzana*, etc.), statives do not require energy to be initiated or sustained (e.g., *ser, estar, querer, creer*).

Telicity is the semantic property that distinguishes between events with concrete or abstract initial and final end-points. Examples of telic events are *comer una manzana* or *correr de las 2 a las 3 pm*, which have concrete beginnings and endings. Atelic events such as *comer* (*comer* *manzanas*), *correr* (*correr para la salud*), *mirar* (*mirar la televisión*), are so called because their initial and final points are abstract.

Following Vendler's analysis (1957), one can use the previous three semantic features involving verbal predicates to classify the following situational types: states, activities, accomplishments, and achievements.

States: These are situations with the following inherent properties: durative, non-dynamic, and atelic (i.e., they do not have concrete initial nor final end-points). Examples of states are *ser, estar, querer, creer, conocer*.

Activities: These are durative, dynamic, atelic situations. Examples are *comer* (*comer manzanas*), *correr* (*correr en el parque*).

Accomplishments: These are durative, dynamic, telic situations (i.e., they have concrete initial and final end-points). Examples are *comer una manzana, comer 100 manzanas, correr 3 millas, correr una hora, correr de las 3 a las 4 pm*.

Achievements. These are punctual (i.e., non-durative), dynamic, and telic situations. Examples are, *meter el pastel al horno, salir, llegar, reconocer a alguien*.

REVIEW OF LEXICAL ASPECT FEATURES

	Dynamic	Telic	Punctual	Examples
States	−	−	−	tener, querer, creer, ser, estar
Activities	+	−	−	caminar, jugar fútbol, comer
Accomplishments	+	+	−	caminar una milla, jugar un partido de fútbol, comer una manzana
Achivements	+	+	+	tirar el anzuelo, meter el pastel al horno, salir, cerrar el baúl

Familiarity with both grammatical and lexical aspects are basic to one's understanding of the expression of past time in Spanish, particularly in the context of discourse that goes beyond simple sentences, as in the narrative below:

> Esta mañana **llegué** a mi oficina a las 9 de la mañana; **abrí** la puerta y **me senté**. **Estaba cansada** y la oficina **se sentía** fría. No **tenía ganas** de hacer nada. Aún así, **prendí** la computadora y **comencé** a leer mi correo electrónico. **Contesté** todos los mensajes importantes y después **me puse** a preparar mis clases. **Tenía que** preparar dos clases y corregir tareas. Mientras **preparaba** la primera clase, **sonó** el teléfono. **Era** mi esposo. **Se oía** muy contento. Me **llamaba** para decirme que ya **había** comprado los boletos para nuestro viaje a Monterrey. Me **dio** tanto gusto oír esa noticia. Después **colgué** y **seguí** preparando mis clases con una actitud mucho más positiva.

Chapter 6 A Question of Aspect: The Spanish Imperfect-Preterite Contrast 71

In the extended narrative discourse above, atelic situations (statives such as *estaba cansada* and activities such as *me llamaba*) tend to be viewed as imperfective and occur to provide the background of a story. Conversely, telic situations (achievements such as *llegué a la oficina* and accomplishments like *contesté todos los mensajes importantes*) usually take the preterite and are related to foreground material in that they advance the plot line of a story. The telic feature of achievements and accomplishments is what allows the sequential ordering of natural events in the foreground; that is, each new event mentioned serves to provide the end-point for the previous event. However, as the example shows, the use of the imperfect with telic situation types emphasizes the focus on the middle part of a situation (e.g., *mientras preparaba la primera clase*) and sees the situation as background information. Conversely, the use of the preterite with statives expresses a change of state as in *me dio tanto gusto* and serves to advance the plot (i.e., foreground information) as in the example above.

Other considerations regarding lexical and grammatical aspect relate to the use of adverbials. Adverbs such as *durante dos días, ese día, de las tres a las cuatro* provide concrete initial and final end-points to atelic events. For example, a stative such as *estar enferma* and an activity like *caminar en el parque* are rendered as telic events using the preterite: *Estuve enferma durante dos días* and *Ayer caminamos en el parque de la una a las dos de la tarde*. Adverbs of frequency such as *todos los días, siempre, frecuentemente* make possible the use of the imperfect with achievements such as *llegar* and *salir* and accomplishments such *comer una manzana* as in the following examples: *Siempre llegaba tarde a clase* and *todos los días comía una manzana*. Frequency adverbs and the imperfect indicate the habitual nature of actions.

6.7
LEXICAL VARIETY USED TO EXPRESS ASPECTUAL DIFFERENCES

Statives such as *creer, saber, ser, estar, querer, gustar, poder* are usually expressed by the imperfect because of their atelic property, that is, they do not have concrete initial or final endpoints. The change of state, however, is conveyed with these verbs through the preterite. For example, in a sentence such as, *No conocía a Juan antes de la fiesta. Lo conocí cuando Pedro me lo presentó,* the imperfect conveys a state of mind that held for an extended period of time, while the preterite expresses the moment in which a change of state occurred: The subject goes from not being familiar with someone to being familiar with them.

There are a limited number of verbs which, because of their particular semantic qualities *vis-à-vis* differences in Spanish-oriented and English-oriented cultures, cannot be translated literally from one language to the other by following the equivalencies outlined in the previous sections. Reality, as interpreted through different logic and different frames of reference in Spanish and English, varies considerably when these particular verbs are placed in a durative, imperfect time frame or an initiative (inchoative) or terminal preterite one. Often, in order to express equivalent conditions of knowledge, perception and being, a different verb from the Spanish lexical verb must be used in English. The classic example of this semantic difference is found in the verb *saber: Supe que estabas enfermo = I learned/heard/found out (that) you were ill. Sabía que estabas enfermo = I knew (all along) (that) you were ill.*

With stative verbs, the imperfect tense describes the middle of a continuing physical state, a state of affairs, or a state of mind that has already begun and is in effect. The preterite tense emphasizes the beginning of a state of being or the end, outcome, or resolution of that state. It tells more about the past than does the imperfect.

conocía	I knew or was acquainted with someone.
conocí	I met/got to know/became acquainted with...

costaba	It was priced at …
costó	It was bought for …
creía	I thought/believed/was under the impression that…
creí	I got the impression that…
estaba allí	I was (already) there.
estuve allí	I got there (arrived)
me gustaba	I liked it.
me gustó	It pleased me (right then).
quería	I wanted to/was willing to/loved…
quise	I tried to/once loved (but don't anymore)…
no quise	I refused to…
podía	I was able to (latent ability, yet to be demonstrated)…
pude	I could/managed to (ability put to test successfully)…
no pude	I tried (but failed).
sabía	I knew/had the knowledge…
supe	I learned/found out/heard/discovered…
tenía la noticia	I had the news (already).
tuve la noticia	I received/got the news.

We should reiterate that, despite what many grammars say, these are not verbs that "change meaning" in the preterite. That would be a distinctly English oriented point of view. Indeed, native Spanish speakers do not identify *conocí* and *conocía* as verb forms belonging to two distinct verbs or having two separate meanings. What is actually occurring here is that English, at times, needs to resort to different lexical forms, e.g., *to meet* and *to know*. These express what in Spanish is an aspectual distinction between the preterite and imperfect, where the former conveys the beginning or end of a state and the latter, its middle part. Equally important is that the English translations commonly given for *supe, (no) quise, pude*, etc. are not always correct. *Quise*, for example, can have other meanings, as seen below.

Te quise por mucho años.
I loved you for many years. (past activity which ended and no longer affects me)

Quise decírtelo en cuanto me enteré de la noticia.
I wanted/tried to tell you as soon as I learned the news. (that very day)

Whitley (2002: 120) gives the following example and translation of *supe*:

Después de pensarlo bien, supe el motivo.
After thinking it through, I knew [came to know/finally understood] the motive. (not "found out")

Exercise 2

Translate the following sentences into the other language. Keep in mind the possible contexts in which each sentence might occur as you use the imperfect and preterite tenses in Spanish or their equivalents in English.

1. Last night we went to the theater.
2. Había muchas personas inocentes que no sabían el peligro que corrían.
3. She studied for the exam until at least ten o'clock.
4. Se me acercaron, me saludaron y se fueron sin decir nada.
5. I never knew (found out) her name.
6. La joven quería comprar la cadena, pero costaba mucho.
7. It was raining and no one was walking along the streets.
8. Tuve que trabajar todo el día para poder obtener mis beneficios.
9. My brother knew them well; he met them in Bogotá.
10. A Isabel le dio mucho miedo ver todos esos animales sueltos.
11. I wasn't wearing a shirt, and later it got cold.
12. Guillermo tenía náuseas y por eso no quiso comer nada.
13. I couldn't hear you because there was lots of noise.
14. Hubo una huelga en la compañía porque el administrador no había querido pagarle a nadie lo suficiente.

From your readings or experiences, cite other verbal examples like those listed above where Spanish and English semantic ranges differ with regard to the preterite/imperfect contrast.

Exercise 3

Translate the following narratives into Spanish, and be able to explain your choices between preterite and imperfect.

A. Last semester was long and difficult. I couldn't get all the classes I needed, lost my job, and got sick with pneumonia. But one class I took was an inspiration, and I learned a lot of Spanish in it. It was winter and was always cold in my room when I woke up. I wasn't usually hungry, so I rarely had breakfast. One Friday, I got up a little late, didn't shower, got dressed, picked up my books and left for the University. When I got to class, nobody was there. Then on the chalkboard I saw some words that said that the class was getting together at The Pub, a rather intimate place that was near the main cafeteria. I remembered that the professor always had to have his coffee, so he had the habit of taking the class to converse at The Pub while everybody drank coffee. I liked the idea because we could practice Spanish in a relaxed atmosphere. As I walked toward the Student Union, I began to get a little hungry, and that day I not only drank coffee but ate several pastries. It was a great class, and Dr. Blanc was unforgettable. I didn't converse a lot but I surely ate well. I liked that Spanish class more than any other.

B. Last night, Ada slept very little. She worked hard all day, got home late, fixed dinner, then had to study. She was barely able to wash the dishes and finally got to bed around midnight. She went to sleep right away. It was three o'clock when suddenly Ada woke up and took a look at the clock. She heard the sounds of people who were talking loudly and of someone who was playing a saxophone. Then, someone jumped or fell into the swimming pool, and the others started laughing. Clearly, they all were drunk. And all this was going on at three a.m. and poor Ada was exhausted and only wanted to sleep. It was the *&%#@ neighbors who worked nights and sometimes forgot that others were asleep when they got home. In vain, Ada covered her head with a pillow and tried to employ her yoga techniques. She had no success with that, so she finally got up and screamed "Shut up!" out the window. Incredible! They all got quiet and then went to bed. And Ada, at last, managed to go back to sleep.

Exercise 4

Rewrite the following paragraphs changing the present tense verbs, when appropriate, to either the imperfect or the preterite.

Por la mañana, a mediodía y al ocaso, **resuenan** leves pisadas en las estancias del piso bajo. **Hablan** un hidalgo y un mozuelo. El hidalgo **se halla** sentado en un pozo del patio; el mozuelo, frente a él, **va comiendo** unos mendrugos de pan que **ha sacado** del seno. Tanta **es** la avidez con que el rapaz **yanta**, que el hidalgo **sonríe** y le **pregunta** si tan sabroso, tan exquisito **es** el pan que **come**. **Asegura** el muchacho que de veras tales mendrugos **son** excelentes, y entonces el hidalgo, sonriendo como por broma—mientras **hay** una inenarrable amargura allá en lo más íntimo de su ser—**le toma** un mendrugo al muchachito y **comienza** a comer. (Excerpt from "Lo Fatal" in *Castilla* by Azorín [José Martínez Ruíz]).

Exercise 5

Translate the following narrative excerpt into Spanish, attempting to interpret the verbal forms correctly in the imperfect or the preterite tenses. Be prepared to explain why you chose either tense. Remember that the imperfect presents background information whereas the preterite advances the action. Also, keep in mind that statives tend to be expressed in the imperfect, unless a change of state occurs.

The room in which I found myself was very large. The windows were long and narrow, and at so vast a distance from the floor as to be altogether inaccessible from within. Feeble gleams of light made their way through the panes, and served to render sufficiently distinct the more prominent objects around; the eye struggled in vain to reach the remoter angles of the chamber, or the recesses of the vaulted ceiling. Dark draperies hung upon the walls. The general furniture was profuse, antique, and tattered. Many books and musical instruments lay scattered about, but failed to give any vitality to the scene. I felt that I breathed an atmosphere of sorrow. An air of deep and irredeemable gloom hung over all.

Upon my entrance, Usher arose from a sofa on which he had been lying, and greeted me with warmth which had much in it, I thought at first, of an overdone cordiality. A glance, however, at his countenance, convinced me of his sincerity. We sat down; and for some moments, while he spoke not, I gazed upon him with a feeling half of pity, half of awe. It was with difficulty that I could bring myself to admit the identity of the being before me with the companion of my early boyhood. (Adapted from *The Fall of the House of Usher* by Edgar Allan Poe.)

7

The Spanish Indicative and Subjunctive Moods

7.1

In order for English speakers to understand the contrast between the Spanish subjunctive and indicative, they must first be aware of the structural conditions that govern this opposition. The subjunctive usually appears in subordinate clauses, although it also occurs in a few independent ones such as those introduced by *ojalá, quizá(s)* and *tal vez*.

A subordinate clause is a group of words with the following grammatical characteristics:

1. It has minimally its own subject and verb. Since every Spanish verb form implies a subject, a simple finite verb can constitute a clause.

2. It makes little sense alone, its meaning depending at least partially upon a main clause to which it is attached.

Both the indicative and the subjunctive are possible in subordinate clauses. English speakers must be able to identify subordinate clauses and then analyze them as (1) noun (nominal) clauses, (2) adjective (adjectival) clauses or (3) adverb (adverbial) clauses. In the following sentences, the subordinate clauses are in italics but not as yet classified.

[Yo] No quiero *que [tú] cometas una injusticia.*
Él se da cuenta de *que tienes mucho talento.*
Ramón va a buscar a un señor *que le arregle el programa.*
Conozco al profesor *que te dio esa excelente calificación.*
Voy a seguir llamando *hasta que contesten.*

Martha siempre llora *cuando oye esa canción.*

7.2

A subordinate **noun clause** functions as a noun, that is, it takes the place of a noun; when the noun represents "something", it answers the question **¿Qué?/What?** A subordinate noun clause most commonly appears as a direct object, but it may also assume the function of a subject or object of a preposition. In the following discussion, the noun clause, which is italicized, will be shown to represent "a something" and to answer the question **¿Qué?/What?**

Yo quiero un triunfo
  (**Un triunfo** is a noun phrase in the position of a direct object. It is the thing I want and answers the question **¿Qué quieres?**)

Yo quiero triunfar
  (In this case, **triunfar** is an infinitive, the noun (nominal) form of a verb. It functions as a noun and is in the position of the direct object. **Triunfar** answers the question **¿Qué quieres?**)

Yo quiero *que tú triunfes*
  (Here, ***que tú triunfes*** is a subordinate clause in the position of the direct object. Since it functions as a noun, it is called a *noun clause*, and answers the question, **¿Qué quieres?**)

Creo *que no va a hacer tanto calor este verano*
  (*...**que no va a hacer tanto calor este verano*** is a noun clause in the position of the direct object, and it too answers the question **¿Qué crees?**)

Es importante *que triunfes*
  (This may be restated as **Que triunfes es importante**, with the noun clause *...**que triunfes*** in the canonical position of the subject of the sentence, that is, the clause goes before the verb. As a noun clause, **que triunfes** represents "a something" and answers the question **¿Qué es importante?** Again, notice that the noun clause is in the position of the subject rather than that of a direct object as in the previous examples.)

Me gusta *que no haga tanto calor en el verano*
  (*...**que no haga tanto calor en el verano*** is a noun clause in the position of the subject of this sentence, and it answers the question **¿Qué te gusta?**)

Me alegro *de que estés aquí.*
  (Here, *...**que estés aquí*** is a noun clause functioning as the object of a preposition, in this case, **de**.)

The following are examples of Spanish sentences with subordinate noun clauses, all of which are italicized. Note that some of the noun clauses use indicative verbal forms, others, subjunctives.

Supongo *que va a ser muy amoroso con ella.*
Aseguraron *que van a estar en la fábrica.*
No creo *que tengas tanta edad como yo.*
Mi padre se alegró de *que estuviéramos en el baile.*
Me di cuenta de *que tenías fe en la juventud.*
Insisto en *que dejes todo ese romanticismo.*
Me sorprende *que no hayan llegado.*
Es práctico *que empleen más personal de seguridad.*
Que empleen más personal de seguridad es práctico.

7.3

A subordinate **adjective/adjectival clause**, also known as a relative clause, functions as an adjective, that is, it describes or somehow modifies a noun or a pronoun referred to as the antecedent of the clause. In the following examples, we have italicized the adjective clauses.

Voy a construir una villa típica.
(**Típica** is a one-word adjective modifying the noun antecedent **villa.**

Voy a construir una villa *que sea típica*.
(...*que sea típica* is a clause replacing the adjective; its antecedent is **villa**. In other words, ...*que sea típica* is a subordinate adjective clause, and **villa** is its antecedent (modified word).

The following are examples of Spanish sentences containing subordinate adjective clauses. Again, these appear in italics. Notice that some of the subordinate adjective clauses have indicative verb forms while others use subjunctives.

Busco a alguien *que me atienda el negocio*.
Lo encerraron en una torre *que se hallaba en la colonia*.
Quiero comprar un perro *que no ladre mucho*.
El año pasado compraron un perro *que ladra mucho*.
Haz lo *que te pido*, por favor.
No debes confiar en él. No hagas lo *que te pida*.
(In the previous two cases, the adjectival clauses modify the neuter pronoun *lo*, the antecent.)
Necesitamos a alguien *que se encargue de la disciplina*.
Conocemos a la persona *que se encarga de la disciplina*.

7.4

The subordinate **adverbial clause** functions as an adverb since it answers such questions as **When?, Where?, How?,** etc. The adverbial clauses are italicized.

Alfredo viene mañana.
(**Mañana** is a one-word adverb telling **when**.)
Alfredo siempre viene *cuando tiene tiempo*.
Alfredo va a venir *cuando tenga tiempo*.
(In both sentences, the clause following **cuando** is adverbial since it tells **when**.)

Further illustrative examples follow:

Roberto va a repararlo con cuidado.
(**Con cuidado** is an adverbial phrase telling **how**.)
Roberto va a repararlo *según/como tú le digas*.
(The italicized clause ...*según/como tú le digas* is an adverbial clause, again telling **how**.)
Pondré el cuadro aquí.
(**Aquí** is a one-word adverb telling **where**.)
Está bien. Pondré el cuadro *donde me dices*.
(...*donde me dices* is an adverbial clause telling **where**.)
Estoy lista. Pondré el cuadro *donde me digas*.
(...*donde me digas* is an adverbial clause also telling **where**.)

78 *Chapter 7 The Spanish Indicative and Subjunctive Moods*

The following are examples of Spanish sentences which contain subordinate adverbial clauses, shown in italics. Some have subjunctive forms while others use indicatives.

Daré un paseo *mientras estés haciendo tus ejercicios.*
Lo midieron *según tú les señalaste.*
Junto dinero *para que mis hijos puedan asistir a la universidad.*
Me lo pagó *antes (de) que aumentara el precio.*
Nicolás me dijo la verdad *cuando lo vi.*
Nicolás me va a decir la verdad *cuando lo vea.*
Lo comprobaron *sin que nadie presentara pruebas.*

Exercise 1

Examine the following sentences and identify the subordinate noun, adjective, or adverbial clauses in each. Name the clause type, and in each case identify the mood, indicative or subjunctive.

1. Siempre lo noto nervioso cuando habla con ella.
2. Creo que las tijeras están encima del escritorio.
3. La tienda que está en la esquina está a la venta.
4. Vamos a retirarnos para que puedas descansar un poco.
5. Es verdad que su reacción fue violenta.
6. Quiero emprender un negocio que responda a las necesidades ambientales del mundo.
7. Anoche soñé con el éxito hasta que me desperté.
8. No conocemos a nadie que haya encontrado la solución a ese problema.
9. Es increíble que la ley no requiera un castigo más fuerte.
10. Van a insistir en que registremos toda la propiedad.
11. Te lo voy a agradecer mucho cuando cambies ese temperamento.
12. Allá está el buque nacional que vimos ayer en el puerto.

Sometimes the verbal form used in the three types of clauses above (noun, adjective and adverbial) must be a subjunctive. The problem for the English speaker learning Spanish is that of using the Spanish subjunctive actively and correctly. On the other hand, the Spanish-speaker learning English will discover that the lack of overt marking of the subjunctive in English is a problem.

English uses the lexical verb as its present subjunctive form, even in the third person singular, unlike the present indicative. So, the subjunctive of *to work* is *work/not work* for all persons: *His boss insists that he work/not work at night.* English uses a large array of different structures to express concepts Spanish conveys through the subjunctive in subordinate clauses: *She wants us to leave* follows a different pattern from *Ella quiere que salgamos.* In fact, the English subjunctive in subordinate clauses is relatively rare, its forms now being confined largely to expressions such as, *be that as it may* or *Thy kingdom come, Thy will be done.* However, it often appears in sentences parallel with Spanish: *We advise that your son be here/not be here with a lawyer/Aconsejamos que su hijo esté/no esté aquí con un abogado.*

7.5
THE TWO MOODS OF SPANISH:
THE INDICATIVE AND THE SUBJUNCTIVE.

Of the five simple tenses of Spanish, two (the present and past subjunctives (*tenga* and *tuviera/se*, respectively) belong to the subjunctive mood. The other three are indicative tenses, the present (*tengo*), the preterite (*tuve*) and the imperfect (*tenía*). We do not include the future (*tendré*) and conditional (*tendría*) among the simple indicative tenses since they are synthetic forms, both evolved over time from a fusion of verbal units. Some specialists do, however, include them among the simple tenses.

The indicative tenses occur in both independent (main) and dependent (subordinate) clauses. They express the world of facts, that is, what happened or was happening (preterite/imperfect), what is happening or occurs in a general sense (present), or what will happen in an expected future. Examples follow:

Mi hija estudiaba cuando alguien tocó a la puerta.
Estudio química porque es una de las ciencias físicas que me gusta.
Van a ir a misa mañana, ya que va a ser domingo.

In dependent clauses, the indicative tenses express what the speaker considers to be facts, whether they are known (*Sabemos que enseña inglés en Perú*) or perceived (*Vimos que habían entrado por la ventana*), or whether they communicate information (*Dicen que los rebeldes van a poder más; Tengo un par de gatos que se pelean a menudo; Descanso mucho cuando tengo gripe; Nadie sabe adónde fueron; No me quieren decir cómo hacerlo*).

The subjunctive tenses occur in various different contexts. They are confined essentially to subordinate clauses, but Spanish uses present subjunctive forms to serve as imperatives (commands) for all persons except the second person singular (*tú*) and plural (*vosotros/-as*) affirmative. This brings us to one of the most common functions of the subjunctive, that of expressing the idea of something yet to happen; this idea is also expressed by the imperative. For example, when someone gives the command, *¡Venga Ud!* or *¡No vengas!*, the event ordered exists only in the mind of the one issuing the command and not yet in his/her experienced reality. Similarly, in, *Queremos que nos ayude con este problema*, the help we hope to receive has yet to be granted. In, *Busquemos un lugar que sea más tranquilo*, the place referred to is, at the moment of speech, only a figment of our imagination. Finally, in *Van a seguir trabajando hasta que resuelvan el misterio*, the mystery has yet to be discovered, and for that matter, may never be.

Far more difficult for the English speaker are the cases in which either mood can be used. For example, verbs or expressions of comment and reaction (*no gustarle a uno/alegrarse de/molestarle* [See 7.10]) may take subordinate noun clauses reflecting facts, whether these facts are in the past or not. For the Spanish learner it is easy to understand the use of the subjunctive if the subordinate clause includes an event projected into a future which may or may not ever take place, as in the following sentence: *Pedro se alegra de que María venga mañana*. However, the complement of some comment clauses may also appear in the indicative: *Pedro se sorprende de que María viene mañana*. In the following example, either mood is acceptable: *A Ana le molesta mucho que sus hijos no quieran/quieren hablar español con sus abuelos*.

King and Suñer (2004) explain that the use of the indicative serves to emphasize the veracity of the event expressed in the subordinate clause while mitigating the subjective qualities that would usually entail the subjunctive. Mejías-Bikandi (1994, 1998) advances the notion of the speaker's intention in a pragmatically based approach to the distribution of mood in noun clauses following expression of comment or reaction. Following Lavandera's (1983) and Lunn's

(1989) analyses regarding a relationship between mood selection and relevance, Mejías-Bikandi's account suggests that the use of the indicative in the subordinate clause is a discourse strategy used when a speaker intends to 'foreground' information (i.e., to make it more salient) "if s/he regards that information as particularly relevant." (1998, p. 946) Consequently, in a situation in which the speaker has a personal connection to that which is expressed in the subordinate clause, s/he will use the indicative to make it stand out. For instance, one can imagine the following sentence spoken between siblings about the death of their father: *¡Es una pena que papá murió tan joven!* The use of the indicative here serves to emphasize the pain associated with the memory of the event being described. However, if the conversation were about the assassination of John F. Kennedy Jr. instead, the subjunctive would be the rule since the speaker intends not to convey any personal connection to the information expressed in the subordinate clause: *¡Es una pena que John F. Kennedy muriera tan joven!*

The previous explanation holds up well with mood selection in adjective clauses (See 7.19-20). In, *Voy a comprar un modelo que sea deportivo*, the speaker is only making reference to the existence of many sporty models on the market, but with the indicative (*...que es deportivo*), the speaker implies that he/she has seen and is focused on a particular sporty model and is thus foregrounding that information.

Pragmatic analysis can also be generalized to certain adverbial clauses, particularly temporal ones (See 7.21). According to prescriptive grammar, the indicative mood is mandatorily selected in temporal clauses introduced by the adverbial conjunction *hasta que* when the event of the main clause refers to present or past habitual situations. Current research, however, has shown that native speakers accept both the indicative and the subjunctive with such clauses (Mayberry, 2000). Thus, when a speaker referring to a habitual occurrence (*Yo siempre te espero hasta que llegas*) intends to foreground the event in the subordinate clause (*...hasta que llegas*) as relevant information, s/he uses the indicative. With the subjunctive (*...hasta que llegues*), however, the speaker is presenting the event as less relevant information.

A more in-depth analysis of this topic—including such notions as relevance, pragmatic presupposition, and pragmatic assertion (as opposed to the semantically defined notion proposed by Terrell and Hooper [1974])—is beyond the scope of this text. The reader is referred to Mejías-Bikandi's research, (1994, 1998) and that of others mentioned in the previous paragraphs, for further reading.

In Chapter 17, we present both the past (*tuviera*) and pluperfect (*hubiera/se tenido*) subjunctives in a special function, not as past sequence versions of the present (*tenga*) or present perfect (*haya tenido*) subjunctives, but as the tenses used in conditional sentences. These convey ideas that run contrary-to-fact. *Si tuviera/hubiera tenido el dinero...* implies that I don't/didn't, in fact, have the money.

7.6
THE SPANISH SUBJUNCTIVE IN THE NOUN CLAUSE

A subjunctive verbal form is mandatory in the Spanish noun clause under the following two conditions, both of which apply to the same sentence.

1. There is a different subject between the main clause and the subordinate noun clause.

   Yo quiero que **tú** vayas.
   Yolanda sugiere que **nosotros** salgamos.
   Ella insiste en que **ellos** traigan los resultados.

Chapter 7 The Spanish Indicative and Subjunctive Moods 81

Es (= **it** is) imposible que los **políticos** ya hayan llegado.

If there is no change of subject between clauses, then an infinitive occurs: *Nosotros queremos ir*. We are the ones who want to go, and we are the ones who will eventually go.

2. There is a verb in the main clause classifiable under one of the following three semantic categories:

    a. A verb or an impersonal phrase of influence or volition, sometimes referred to as "will over will," that is, a verb which brings pressure upon the subject of the subordinate noun clause to do or not to do something, (eg., **querer, insistir en, prohibir, preferir, decir** [= tell], **ser importante, ser necesario**).

    b. A verb or an impersonal phrase of doubt or denial (eg., **dudar, no creer, negar, ser dudoso, ser imposible**).

    c. A verb of comment or personal reaction (eg., **temer, alegrarse de, sentir** [=regret], **esperar, gustar**).

The indicative verbal form can also occur in the Spanish noun clause even if there is a different subject between the main clause and the subordinate noun clause.

Yo sé que **tú** estás diciendo la verdad.
Yolanda cree que **nosotros** salimos poco los fines de semana.
Ella asegura que **ellos** mienten.
Es cierto que **los políticos** ya han llegado.

If the indicative verbal form does occur, the verb in the main clause falls under one of the following semantic categories that convey affirmation of an event:

   a. A verb or phrase of belief or knowledge (eg., **acordarse de, creer, descubrir, pensar, recordar, saber, ser cierto, ser evidente, ser obvio, ser seguro, estar convencido de, estar seguro de**).

   b. A verb or a phrase of communication (eg., **avisar, confirmar, comunicar, decir** [=say], **escribir, informar, mencionar, estar confirmado, estar escrito**).

   c. A verb of perception or sensation (eg., **escuchar, mirar, notar, oír, observar, sentir** [=feel/sense], **ver**).

7.7
MAIN EXPRESSIONS OF INFLUENCE OR VOLITION

The following is a fairly complete listing of the main Spanish expressions of influence or volition. Note that each expression has a meaning which places pressure upon the subject of the subordinate noun clause to do or not to do something. The pressure may be quite intense (eg., *mandar*), or it may be relatively light (eg., *preferir*). Observe also that the following formula consistently applies to sentences with subordinate noun clauses.

Chapter 7 The Spanish Indicative and Subjunctive Moods

$$(S)_1 + V_1[\text{indicative}] + que + (S)_2 + V_2[\text{subjunctive}]$$

The wide variety of English structures used to render the Spanish subjunctive will be presented later.

aconsejar:	Te aconsejo que no cedas tu título.
aprobar:	No apruebe que destruyas tu matrimonio.
decir (= tell):	Me dijo que estudiara más.
dejar:	No dejes que te amenacen.
desear:	Deseo que te diviertas en Mérida.
hacer:	Me hizo que aprobara lo decidido.
impedir:	No voy a impedir que lo publiquen en la prensa.
insistir en:	Ella insiste en que nos ayudemos en clase.
mandar:	El capataz mandó que cortáramos ese árbol.
necesitar:	Necesito que me ayudes a planificar el estudio.
oponerse a:	La gerencia se opuso a que organizáramos una unión laboral.
pedir:	Piden que se establezca un área verde en nuestro vecindario.
permitir:	Las circunstancias no permitirán que olvidemos el futuro.
preferir:	Prefieren que compres el pastel de queso.
prohibir:	Él prohibe que jueguen en su jardín.
querer:	No querían que las tropas ocupasen el edificio.
rogar:	Te rogamos que no participes en la manifestación.
ser acosejable:	Es aconsejable que respetemos la tradición.
ser importante:	Era importante que instalaran un régimen justo.
ser necesario:	Es necesario que terminemos esta discusión.
ser preciso:	Será preciso que le adviertas de las consecuencias.
ser preferible:	Sería preferible que no lo compraras este mes.

> **Note:** Frequently on signs, written instructions or admonitions, the subordinating *que* is omitted. This usage is rare in speech: *Rogamos bajen las maletas antes de desayunar; Se pide no llevar las toallas del hotel a la playa.*

Several of the main verbs just presented may also use an infinitive construction. All of them are verbs that take indirect objects, that is, each one may be accompanied by *le a uno*. The most common of these verbs are *dejar, hacer, mandar, ordenar, permitir* and *prohibir*. Each appears below with both a permissible infinitive construction and with a full noun clause subjunctive one.

dejar(le) a uno:
　Mi madre no me deja fumar.
　Mi madre no (me) deja que fume.

hacer(le) a uno:
　Nos hace sonreír a cada paso.
　Hace que nos sonriamos a cada paso.

mandar(le) a uno:
　Su majestad le mandó salir.
　Su majestad le mandó que saliera.

ordenar(le) a uno:
El director le ordenó preparar un reporte completo.
El director le ordenó que preparara un reporte completo.

permitir(le) a uno:
No te permito tender la ropa en el patio.
No te permito que tiendas la ropa en el patio.

prohibir(le) a uno:
Te voy a prohibir renunciar a la herencia.
Voy a prohibirte que renuncies a la herencia.

7.8
ENGLISH STRUCTURES FOR SPANISH VERBS OF INFLUENCE OR VOLITION

Whereas Spanish consistently uses the structure $(S)_1 + V_1$[indicative] + *que* + $(S)_2 + V_2$[subjunctive], English has a number of formulas that translate sentences with Spanish verbs of influence or volition. Several of the verbs may take more than one structure, there being no difference in meaning, but merely a change in level of formality.

(1) **S + V + DO + INF:** used with main verbs *advise (aconsejar), allow (dejar), ask (pedir), beg (rogar), command (mandar), forbid (prohibir), like (gustar), need (necesitar), order (odenar), permit (permitir) tell (decir),* and *want (querer/desear).*

advise	I advise you to leave immediately.
allow	They won't allow me to speak now.
ask	I ask you to try a little harder.
beg	She begged us to help her that fateful night.
command	They commanded us to shoot.
forbid	I forbid you to see that boy.
like	I don't like you to smoke in the house.
need	We needed them to carry the groceries.
order	He ordered him to write a complete report.
permit	She won't permit us to work here.
tell	They told them to get out of town.
want	We want you to be successful.

(2) **S + V + DO + LV:** used with main verbs *have [=cause] (hacer), let (dejar),* and *make (hacer).*

have	He had me bring several examples.
let	They won't let us see the puppies.
make	She made us stay in class an extra hour.

(3) **S + V + *for* + IO + INF:** used with main verbs like *ask (pedir), like (gustar), prefer (preferir), say (decir),* or impersonal verbal phrases like *be advisable (ser aconsejable, be im-*

potant (ser importante), be necessary (ser necesario/preciso), be preferable (ser preferible).

ask	He asked for us to try harder.
be advisable	It is advisable for them not to leave so soon.
be important	It's important for you to get to work on time.
be necessary	It is necessary for them to do all the exercises in the book.
be preferable	It was preferable for us to go by train rather than by bus.
like	I don't like for you to drink so much.
prefer	We prefer for them to stay here.

(4) **S + V + DO +** *from* **+ LV-ing**: used with the main verbs *prevent (impedir), stop (impedir)*.

prevent	He prevented me from leaving on time.
stop	She stopped you from making a big mistake.

(5) **S + V + POSS ADJ** or **DO + LV-ing**: used with main verbs *forbid (prohibir), like (gustar), oppose (oponerse a), prevent (impedir), recommend (recomendar/aconsejar)*.

forbid	I forbid your/you smoking in the house.
like	They don't like my/me working at night.
oppose	We oppose your/you becoming governor.
prevent	They prevented his/him saying anything.
recommend	They recommended our/us seeing a good lawyer.

(6) **S + V + PREP + POSS ADJ** or **DO + LV-ing**: used with main verbal expressions *approve of (aprobar), be opposed to (oponerse a), insist on (insistir en)*.

approve of	They approved of our/us getting married.
be opposed to	She was opposed to his/him leaving.
insist on	I insist on your/you telling me.

(7) **S$_1$ + V$_1$ +** *that* **+ S$_2$ + V$_2$[subjunctive]**: used with the main verbal expressions *ask (pedir), command (mandar), demand (exigir), insist (insistir en), prefer (preferir), propose (proponer), recommend (recomendar/aconsejar), suggest (sugerir)*, or impersonal verbal phrases like *be advisable (ser aconsejable), be important (ser importante), be necessary (ser necesario), be preferable (ser preferible)*.

> **Note:** The above formula (7) is identical to the Spanish subjunctive structure, and all of the examples demonstrate occurrences of the true English subjunctive (shown in italics).

advise	We advised that he *not go* to Mexico.
ask	I ask that he *find* the time to do it.
be advisable	It is advisable that they *not be* here when he arrives.
be important	It's important that he *see* the professor right away.
be necessary	It is necessary that she *take* care of the children today.
be preferable	It's preferable that I *be* with my parents.

command	He commanded that she *open* the door.
demand	He demanded that she *open* the door.
insist	They insist that he *work* here.
prefer	I prefer that you *not be* here so early.
propose	We propose that he *be* hired now.
recommend	They recommend that she *decide* immediately.
suggest	We suggested that he *study* the problem more carefully.

Exercise 2

Translate the following sentences into the other language. Spanish will consistently use its special formula, while English will use one of the formulas under 7.8. If more than one English version is possible, provide all. For every translated sentence, show the structural formula.

1. Nos aconsejaron que no bajáramos del avión.
2. We forbid them to eat in that restaurant.
3. No van a dejar que él inicie la protesta.
4. They wanted us to bring the food for the party.
5. Es importante que examines tu conciencia antes de obrar.
6. They made him work with the prisoners.
7. Es preferible que no aluda al comentario.
8. We need you to help us with this project.
9. Mis padres insisten en que mi hermano estudie medicina.
10. They prevented us from seeing our relatives.
11. No le gusta que juguemos a los dados los domingos.
12. They forbid us to speak Spanish to the children.
13. Hicieron que lo invitara a la fiesta.
14. My father opposed my studying in a foreign country.
15. El presidente insiste en que todos tratemos de probar nuestra habilidad.
16. My parents don't approve of my getting married this year.
17. El general impidió que los soldados atacaran de inmediato.
18. She insists on our being on time for class.
19. Le piden que firme el manuscrito auténtico.
20. I advised them not to work there at night.
21. Mi abuela prefería que sus hijos le hablaran en alemán.
22. She proposes that we study the economic problems of Central America.
23. Querían que atravesáramos la aldea antes de que comenzara a caer nieve.
24. We suggest that they write a letter to the President.

7.9
MAIN VERBS AND OTHER EXPRESSIONS OF DOUBT OR DENIAL

The following is a relatively complete listing of the main verbs of doubt or denial. When we doubt or deny propositions, they are "put at issue" as the legal system phrases it, and we must await further information for our concerns to be allayed. Also involved is the element of politeness, as the subjunctive concedes that the other parties might have a legitimate opposing argument or point of view. But in the final analysis, either mood is possible in the subordinate noun clause depending upon the degree or intensity of the doubt expressed within any context in which doubt is an issue: the deeper the doubt, the more the tendency to use the subjunctive, and the reverse. Prescriptive grammar requires the subjunctive with all main verbs of doubt or denial.

no creer	No creemos que ellos falten a la exposición.
¿creer?	¿Crees que Wilfredo sepa/sabe dónde estamos?
	(Spain prefers the subjunctive, Spanish America the indicative with interrogative *creer*.)
dudar	Dudo que hayan hecho el trabajo completo.
no dudar	No dudamos que tenga las mejores intenciones.
	(Although no doubt is expressed, speakers tend to use the subjunctive here, for whatever reasons.)
negar	Niego que la fórmula tenga errores.
no saber	No sabemos dónde estén.
no ser cierto	No es cierto que hayan tenido tanta fama.
no ser evidente	No era evidente que la falla fuera mecánica.
no ser seguro	No es seguro que logren pronto la reforma en el sistema de fianzas.
no ser verdad	No es verdad que lo haya descubierto accidentalmente.
poder ser	Puede ser que este verano no llueva.
ser difícil	Es difícil que lleguen a tiempo para la boda.
ser imposible	Es imposible que hagan tanta labor.
ser improbable	Es improbable/poco probable que llueva esta noche.
ser posible	Es posible que nombre a un familiar para el puesto.
ser probable	Es probable que tropiecen con dificultades.

Non-verbal expressions (English *perhaps, maybe*)

acaso	Dime a qué hora vas a llegar, por si acaso pueda ir.
quizá(s)	Quizá(s) hayan olvidado tu apellido.
tal vez	Tal vez logren aprobar el proyecto de ley para la asistencia médica pública.

With these non-verbals of doubt and possibility, it is grammatical to use either the indicative or subjunctive. The subjunctive generally appears in these constructions if the adverb precedes the verb and is not separated from it by a pause.

Quizás escuchó/escuchara lo que dijimos.
Posiblemente es/sea un buen pronóstico.
Probablemente llegará/llegue temprano.

Again, when both the indicative and subjunctive are possible, how a speaker intends the information conveyed to be interpreted determines mood selection. The subjunctive appears when the speaker expects the listener to interpret the information as of little immediate importance, something said "in passing." The indicative alerts the listener to information that is foregrounded and therefore relevant: *Quizá(s)/Tal vez/Acaso haya/ha escuchado lo que dijimos.*

If the adverb of doubt or possibility follows the verb, the indicative is the only acceptable mood.

Escuchó quizás lo que dijimos
Es posiblemente un buen pronóstico.
Llegará tal vez temprano.

7.10
MAIN VERBS AND OTHER EXPRESSIONS OF COMMENT OR PERSONAL REACTION

A fairly complete listing of the Spanish main verbs and other expressions of comment or personal reaction follows. As was the case with both the main verbs and expressions of influence, volition, doubt or denial, Spanish consistently employs the formula **(S)$_1$ + V$_1$ + que + (S)$_2$ + V$_2$ [subjunctive]**. The subjunctive is the prescriptive norm, but the indicative also occurs to alert the listener to information brought forward as relevant and therefore important.

alegrarse	Me alegro (de) que logres tu ilusión de formar un hogar. (noun clause is DO)
	Me alegra que logres tu ilusión de formar un hogar. (noun clause is S)
doler	Me duele que se hayan involucrado en la política.
esperar	Espero que estés dispuesto a ejercer esa profesión.
estar contento	Están contentos de que no hayamos perdido el concierto.
estar encantado	Estoy encantado de que puedas lucirte en la recepción.
estar triste	Estoy triste de que hayas tomado esa decisión.
extrañar	Me extraña mucho que te expreses de esa manera.
gustar	(No) nos gusta que pases tanto tiempo con Alberto.
parecer mentira	Parece mentira que nadie sepa como arreglarlo.
sentir	Siento tanto que nadie haya evitado esa desgracia.
ser absurdo	Es absurdo que causen tanta confusión.
ser bueno	Es bueno que estés estudiando árabe.
ser curioso	Es curioso que haya llegado acompañado.
ser lamentable	Es lamentable que Ud. piense de esa manera.
ser malo	Es malo que piensen de esa manera tan negativa.
ser raro	Es raro que el marqués se exponga a la muerte.
ser ridículo	Es ridículo que gastes tanta energía en gritar.
ser triste	Es triste que no tengan mejor criterio.
ser una lástima	Es una lástima que ella no tenga más confianza en sí misma.
temer	Temía que se fuera sin comunicárnoslo.
tener miedo	Tiene miedo de que esa pesadilla que tuvo se convierta en realidad.

(non-verbal)

ojalá: ¡Ojalá (que) se haga un milagro!
¡Ojalá tuviera más tiempo para arreglarme y verme más bella!

7.11
MAIN EXPRESSIONS OF BELIEF AND KNOWLEDGE

The following is a fairly complete listing of the main Spanish expressions of belief and knowledge for declarative and interrogative sentences. Note that each expression has a meaning stating that an event is known or believed to be a fact. Interrogative sentences with these expressions ask for verification of what the speaker believes to be factual. Notice also that the following fomula consistently applies in Spanish sentences with subordinate noun clauses.

$$(S)_1 + V_1[\text{indicative}] + que + (S)_2 + V_2[\text{indicative}]$$

acordarse de	Ahora me acuerdo de que todavía tengo que pagar esa factura.
creer	Creo que te van a dar un aumento de sueldo.
descubrir	Descubrieron que esa medicina no era tan efectiva como decían.
estar convencido de	Estoy convencido de que la verdad saldrá a la luz.
estar seguro de	Estoy segura de que fumas en la habitación.
pensar	Ella piensa que regresarán mañana.
recordar	¿Recuerdas que hacíamos muchas travesuras de niñas?
saber	¿Sabes que tenemos un examen mañana?
ser cierto	¿Es cierto que tenemos un examen mañana?
ser evidente	Con tanto esfuerzo, es evidente que lograrán el triunfo.
ser obvio	Era obvio que no habían estudiado lo suficiente.
ser seguro	Es seguro que ganaremos las elecciones.

7.12
MAIN EXPRESSIONS OF COMMUNICATION

The following is a fairly complete listing of the main Spanish expressions of communication for declarative and interrogative sentences. Note that each expression conveys information. Interrogative sentences with these expressions ask for verification of what the speaker believes to be a fact. Once more, the following fixed formula consistently applies to Spanish sentences with subordinate noun clauses.

$$(S)_1 + V_1[\text{indicative}] + que + (S)_2 + V_2[\text{indicative}]$$

avisar	¿Ya te avisaron que cambiaron la hora del concierto?
comunicar	Hoy me comunicaron que me darán el ascenso que les pedí.
confirmar	Nos han confirmado que llegarán mañana antes del mediodía.
decir	Te dije que ya hice las reservaciones en el hotel.
escribir	Me han escrito que volverán a tiempo para la graduación.
estar confirmado	Ya está confirmado que te darán la beca para tus estudios.
estar escrito	Estaba escrito que lo nuestro duraría para siempre.
informar	¿Ya les han informado que todos los participantes calificaron para las pruebas preliminares?
mencionar	Me mencionaron que se canceló la boda por la lluvia.

7.13
MAIN EXPRESSIONS OF PERCEPTION OR SENSATION

The following is a fairly complete listing of the main Spanish expressions of perception or sensation for declarative and interrogative sentences. Note that each expression conveys information gained through the senses. As in the previous cases where the indicative occurs, interrogative sentences with expressions of perception asks for verification of what the speaker perceives to be a fact. The usual noun clause structure again applies:

$$(S)_1 + V_1[\text{indicative}] + que + (S)_2 + V_2[\text{indicative}]$$

escuchar	¿Alguna vez escuchaste que los insectos son una fuente de proteína en algunos países?
notar	Notaron que todos andábamos muy nerviosos por el examen.
observar	Hoy en día podemos observar que muchos jóvenes prefieren enviar un mensaje de texto que hablar por teléfono.
oír	¿Oíste que hay un restaurante panameño en Nueva York?
sentir	Sentí que el dolor se me extendía por toda la pierna.
ver	Ayer vimos que ya habían abierto la nueva discoteca.

7.14
INDICATIVE VS. SUBJUNCTIVE IN THE NOUN CLAUSE: THREE PROBLEMATIC CASES.

Three Spanish verbs deserve special attention, since their use with either mood determines their translation in English. The three verbs in question are *decir, insistir* and *sentir*.

Decir

***Decir* + indicative:** The English meaning is *to say*, a verb of communication:

Dicen que la evolución es la única teoría válida.
They say that evolution is the only valid theory.

***Decir* + subjunctive:** In English, the translation would be *to tell someone to do something*. Here *decir* is a verb of influence or volition:

Nos dijo que estuviéramos listos para salir con poca anticipación.
He told us to be ready to leave with very little warning.

Insistir

***Insistir* + indicative** : As a verb of opinion, *insistir* would be rendered in English as *to insist* in the sense of maintaining a point of view, possibly despite evidence to the contrary.

Hay quienes insisten en que el mundo fue creado en solo siete días.

There are those who insist that the world was created in a mere seven days.

***Insistir* + subjunctive:** Here the verb is one of influence or volition, and the translation is *to insist that someone do something*:

Sus padres insisten en que todos estén en casa a la hora de cenar.
Her parents insist that everybody be at home at the dinner hour.

Sentir

***Sentir* + indicative:** English has various translations for this verb of perception among which are *to sense, feel, hear, get the impression that*, etc.

Siento que en el fondo tienes mucho odio hacia tus familiares.
I sense/get the impression that you harbor a lot of hatred toward your relatives.

***Sentir* + subjunctive:** Here, the speaker expresses a personal reaction to or emotionally laden comment on some fact. Translation would include to *be sorry, to regret,* or even *to resent*.

Sienten que su hija se haya/ha casado con un drogadicto.
They are sorry/regret that their daughter has married a drug addict.

Exercise 3

Translate the following sentences. Remember that Spanish will use the structure $(S)_1$ + V[indicative] + ***que*** + $(S)_2$ + V_2[subjunctive], if you classify the verb or verbal phrase in the main clause as a verb of influence or volition, doubt or denial, comment or personal reaction. However, use the formula $(S)_1$ + V_1[indicative] + ***que*** + $(S)_2$ + V_2[indicative], if the verb or verbal phrase expresses belief or knowledge, communication, perception or sensation. If more than one English version of a model sentence is possible, provide all.

1. They believe that they will find a solution.
2. We allowed them to return home as soon as possible.
3. It was necessary for him to call them.
4. I know that you will visit him more often.
5. It was obvious that he took care of all of you.
6. He suggested that I close that chapter of my life forever.
7. The professor insists on my doing the homework every day.
8. Did you hear that tuition went up again?
9. I feel (sensation) that they have not accomplished their goals.
10. I regret/am sorry that they have not accomplished their goals.
11. I'm telling you that I don't want to go.
12. He told me to close the door.
13. They noticed that we get along very well.
14. They always advise their students to drive carefully.
15. She wrote him that she would not be coming back.

Chapter 7 The Spanish Indicative and Subjunctive Moods

16. It will be important that you read the instructions on the exam.
17. Are you sure that tomorrow it is going to rain?
18. She insists on our being on time for class.
19. The professor noticed that nobody was paying attention in class.
20. It was important for them to pay attention in class.
21. It has been confirmed that everyone passed the exam.
22. They asked her to forget that incident.
23. They knew she had forgotten that incident.
24. We insist that you come with us to the party.

7.15
SEQUENCE (CORRESPONDENCE) OF TENSES IN SPANISH SUBJUNCTIVE SENTENCES

Traditionally, the sequence (correspondence) of tenses in Spanish subjunctive sentences has been explained in terms of a temporal agreement between the verbal forms of the main and the subordinate clauses. That is, if the main verb of a Spanish sentence belongs to the present family, the subordinate subjunctive verb will generally be either the present or present perfect subjunctive (See 7.16). Likewise, if the main verb is of the past family, then the subordinate subjunctive verb will usually be either the past or the pluperfect subjunctive. However, the most recent studies of the Spanish subjunctive in subordinate clauses suggests that the sequence of tenses follows the same general principle found in the use of the indicative in subordinate clauses. We must consider when the event of the subordinate clause occurs with respect to the event of the main clause. Does the event occur before the main event or before another event in the past (relationship of anteriority), at the same time as the main event (simultaneous), or after the main event (subsequent)? Both indicative and subjunctive forms appear in the subordinate clauses in the following examples; regardless, the temporal relationships of those clauses to their main clauses become apparent.

Sé que vas al cine todos los días.
(simultaneous to main event)

Dudo que vayas al cine todos los días
(simultaneous to main event)

Sé que te irás mañana sin permiso.
(subsequent to main event)

Dudo que te vayas mañana sin permiso.
(subsequent to main event)

Sé que te fuiste al cine sin permiso.
(prior to main event)

Dudo que te fueras/hayas ido al cine sin permiso.
(prior to main event)

Sé que ya habías ido a ese cine antes de conocerme.
(prior to another event in the past)

Dudaba que ya hubieras ido a ese cine antes de conocerme.
(prior to another event in the past)

Sabía que siempre te ibas sin permiso.
(simultaneous to main event)

Dudaba que siempre te fueras sin permiso.
(simultaneous to main event)

Sabía que te ibas a ir (irías) sin permiso al día siguiente.
(subsequent to main event)

Dudaba que te fueras/te fueras a ir sin permiso al día siguiente.
(subsequent to main event)

Sabía que te habías ido sin permiso.
(prior to the main event)

Dudaba que te hubieras ido sin permiso.
(prior to the main event)

The principles of the sequence of tenses apply not only to sentences involving noun clauses but to some containing adjective and adverbial clauses. In general, however, mood selection in adjectival and adverbial clause is influenced by other factors to be discussed later in this chapter. For the present, here are some examples:

ADJECTIVE CLAUSES

Busco a la persona que arregló la tubería de mi casa ayer.
(prior to main event in the present)

Busco a una persona que ya haya trabajado con este tipo de problema.
(prior to main event in the present)

Busco a una persona que pueda arreglar la tubería de mi casa.
(subsequent to main event in the present)

Buscaba a una persona que ya hubiera trabajado con este tipo de trabajo.
(prior to main event in the past)

ADVERB CLAUSES

Siempre deja de tomar la medicina cuando se siente mejor.
(simultaneous to main event in the present)

Dejó de tomar la medicina cuando se sintió mejor.
(simultaneous to main event in the past)

Como siempre, dejará de tomar la medicina cuando se sienta mejor.

Chapter 7 The Spanish Indicative and Subjunctive Moods 93

(simultaneous to main event in the future)

Consulta al médico antes de que dejes de tomar la medicina.
(Here, the main event is supposed to occur before the event in the subordinate clause.)

7.16
THE TWO FAMILIES OF MAIN VERBS

The main verbs of the present tense family are:
Present indicative: *espero/veo*
Future indicative: *esperaré/veré, voy a esperar/voy a ver*
Any imperative (command): *¡dígale!, ¡no le diga!*
Present perfect: *he dicho/he visto*

The main verbs of the past tense family are:
Preterite: *esperé/vi*
Imperfect: *esperaba/veía*
Conditional: *esperaría/vería*
Pluperfect: *había esperado/había visto*

7.17
PRESENT TENSE FAMILY

When the main verb is of the present tense family, the subordinate verb may express a time subsequent to the main verb. Notice that the following examples include subordinates with the indicative and the subjunctive.

Espero (ahora) que vengas dentro de un par de días.
Creo (ahora) que viene dentro de un par de días.
Dudo (ahora) que tengan tiempo para hacerlo más tarde.
Sé (ahora) que no tendrán tiempo para hacerlo más tarde.
Es ridículo (ahora) que no vengan a visitarnos el mes que viene.
Es obvio (ahora) que pronto se va a enojar.

In structures where the main verb is of the present tense family, the subordinate verb may express a time simultaneous with that of the main verb.

Siento (ahora) que pienses de esa manera acerca de nosotros (ahora).
Estoy segura (ahora) que piensas de esa manera acerca de nosotros (ahora).
No creo (ahora) que estén en la facultad (ahora).
Es muy seguro (ahora) que están en la facultad (ahora).
Esta situación tan difícil exige (ahora) que examinemos otras opciones (ahora).
Creo (ahora) que nos disponemos de otras opciones (ahora).
Es una lástima (ahora) que ella no tenga buenos sentimientos (ahora).
Todos saben (ahora) que ella no tiene buenos sentimientos (ahora).

When the main verb is of the present tense family, the subordinate verb may express a time prior to that of the main verb.

Parece mentira (ahora) que hayas disfrutado de esa película tan tonta (antes).
Sé (ahora) que ya has visto esa película tan tonta (antes).
Es posible (ahora) que ya hayan llamado (antes).
Es obvio (ahora) que ya han llamado (antes).
¿Crees (ahora) que esas personas hayan/han influido en sus ideales (antes)?
Sí, creo (ahora) que esas personas han influido en sus ideales religiosos (antes).
Me extraña (ahora) que él no haya podido con ese examen (más temprano).
Creo (ahora) que él no ha podido con ese examen (más temprano).

When the main verb is of the present tense family, the subordinate verb may express a time prior to another event in the past. The pluperfect, whether indicative or subjunctive, is the tense expressing the most prior past possible in any temporal sequence.

Me extraña (ahora) que no hubiera llamado (evento antes del evento en el pasado) antes de venir (evento en el pasado).

Sé (ahora) que no había llamado (evento antes del evento en el pasado) antes de venir (evento en el pasado).

Es posible (ahora) que hubiera llamado (evento antes del evento en el pasado) antes de salir (evento en el pasado).

Es obvio (ahora) que había llamado (evento antes del evento en el pasado) antes de salir (evento en el pasado).

No creo (ahora) que hubiera faltado a clase (evento antes del evento en el pasado) el día antes del examen (evento en el pasado).

Creo (ahora) que había faltado a clase (evento antes del evento en el pasado) el día antes del examen (evento en el pasado).

7.18
PAST TENSE FAMILY

When the main verb is of the past tense family, the subordinate verb may express a time subsequent to the main verb. Notice that the following examples include subordinates with the indicative and the subjunctive.

Yo no creía (entonces) que Juan tuviera motivo de protestar (más tarde).
Yo sabía (entonces) que Juan tendría motivos para quejarse (más tarde).
Él temía (entonces) que destruyeran el local (más tarde).
Él estaba seguro que destruirían el local (más tarde).
Sería una lástima que ella fuera parte de la investigación (más tarde).
Era verdad que ella iba a ser parte de la investigación (más tarde).

Chapter 7 The Spanish Indicative and Subjunctive Moods

Yo quería (entonces) que él me hiciera los cálculos del presupuesto (luego).
Era cierto (entonces) que él me haría los cálculos del presupuesto (luego).

> **Note:** Sentences involving this time sequence are often troublesome for English speakers as they translate from English to Spanish. *He feared that they would destroy the building* uses the English conditional (*would destroy*) which the English native tends to translate as *destruiría*. Since the conditional expresses futurity to past time. However, the main verb of comment or reaction calls for a subjunctive, so *destruyera* (=*would destroy*) is obligatory.

When the main verb is of the past tense family, the subordinate verb may express a time simultaneous to that of the main verb.

El director no creía (entonces) que estuvieran en la conferencia (entonces).
El director sabía (entonces) que estaban en la conferencia (entonces).
Era raro (entonces) que la mayoría supiera lo que estaba ocurriendo (entonces).
Era seguro (entonces) que la mayoría lo apoyaba (entonces).
Confiaba (entonces) en que se estuvieran contentos (entonces).
Muchos creían (entonces) que se estaba formando un escándalo (entonces).
Era increíble (entonces) que ella se sintiera bien (entonces).
Era cierto (entonces) que ella ya no pensaba de la misma manera (entonces).

When the main verb is of the past tense family, the subordinate verb may express a time prior to that of the main verb.

Me daba tristeza (entonces) que me hubiera transformado en espíritu (antes).
Sabía (entonces) que yo había tenido un cambio radical (antes).
No era verdad (entonces) que le hubiera sucedido esa tragedia a Ud. (antes).
Era verdad (entonces) que le había sucedido esa tragedia a Ud. (antes).
¿Te molestó (entonces) que yo te hubiera mentido (antes).
Creías (entonces) que yo te había mentido (antes).
Temí (entonces) que los niños hubieran pasado hambre (antes).
Era obvio (entonces) que los niños habían pasado hambre (antes).

The preceding guidelines for tense sequence in Spanish subjunctive sentences are by no means iron clad. Frequent variations occur, especially in the Spanish of the Americas, and particularly in broadcast journalism. If both the main verb and the subordinate one occur wholly within a past context, the standard rule holds up well: *El quería (el lunes) que viniéramos (el miércoles)*. The Monday and the Wednesday referred to were two days last week. But after the subordinate verb refers to a time future to now, and the main verb occurred in the past, the present subjunctive (rather than the past subjunctive) often appears: *En su presentación (anoche), el Presidente pidió que, (de aquí en adelante), todos nos esforcemos más para ahorrar energía*. Furthermore, it is quite common for Latin American speakers to use the past subjunctive instead of the present perfect subjunctive. This is related to their preference for the preterite indicative over the present perfect indicative. For example, rather than saying, *Sé que ya has comido*, a Latin American would say, *Sé que ya comiste*. A similar usage appears with the subjunctive. In place of, *Me extraña que él no haya cubierto la distancia*, some American speakers use, *Me extraña que él no cubriera la distancia*.

Exercise 4

Translate the following sentences and be certain to observe all the rules concerning the sequence of tenses. All when translated will contain noun clauses, but not all will require a subjunctive verbal form in the subordinate noun clause. Be able to state in each case why a subjunctive form is or is not required.

1. We don't believe that he has arrived yet.
2. I think that she has my keys.
3. He wanted me to bring my friends.
4. They insist on our being here early.
5. Perhaps your father had met the man in South America.
6. I know that he lives near the university.
7. He was sorry that they hadn't seen the film.
8. We believe that they understand all the questions.
9. He is going to make us read a long book in English.
10. Our parents never permitted us to smoke at home.
11. Tell him that his family has arrived.
12. She told me to open the door.
13. It seems to me that the boy is very ill.
14. It seemed a lie that he would say something like that.
15. My mother advised me to study Latin in school.
16. It's a pity that you haven't been able to work.
17. He denied that his children had stolen the money.
18. They said that you had bought a new car.
19. We hoped that you would tell us the truth.
20. I am opposed to your going to the party with them.

7.19
THE SPANISH SUBJUNCTIVE IN THE ADJECTIVE CLAUSE

Whether or not a subjunctive verbal form occurs mandatorily in a Spanish subordinate adjective clause depends entirely upon the nature of the antecedent of that clause. The antecedent is the noun or pronoun modified by the adjective clause. A subjunctive verbal form is required in the subordinate adjective clause under either of two possible conditions.

(1) The antecedent is imaginary or indefinite in the mind of the speaker at the moment referred to, that is the subject has yet to experience the antecedent of the adjective clause.

Buscamos una **casa** *que tenga jardín.*
(The house referred to by the adjective clause is in the speakers' minds only. They haven't yet experienced the house in reality. At the moment referred to, in this case the present, the house is an imaginary house.)

Chapter 7 The Spanish Indicative and Subjunctive Moods

Quiero enamorarme de **alguien** *que sepa estimar mis cualidades.*
(The someone referred to is in the speaker's mind, not in his/her experienced reality at the time the sentence is uttered. The person is, therefore, imaginary and indefinite.)

Vamos a buscar a **personas** *que sean más tranquilas.*
(The persons mentioned have yet to be found. They are imaginary, indefinite people in the mind of the speaker only, waiting to be found at some future time, if at all.)

But,

¿Ve Usted la **estrella** *a la que se refiere el texto?*
(This is a definite star. It is being experienced at the time referred to. It is not imaginary; therefore, an indicative form appears in the adjective clause describing this antecedent.)

Sometimes the choice of one mood over the other is a function of the context in which the sentence occurs or the relative degree of definiteness the speaker feels concerning the existence and identity of the antecedent.

Quiero comprar un **carro** que <u>sea</u> deportivo.
(The only requirement is that the car be sporty, but the speaker has no specific car in mind, nor has he/she even initiated the search let alone found such a car. The information is provided but not highlighted.)

Quiero comprar un **carro** que <u>es</u> deportivo.
(The speaker has probably seen a number of sporty cars and may be on the verge of selecting one of them or one very much like all of them. The information is deemed important and relevant, and thus brought to the foreground.

Note: Notice also that the speaker's attitude towards the existence of the antecedent is revealed through his/her use of definite or indefinite articles. While a definite article affirms the existence and identity of an entity and requires the indicative, the unconfirmed existence of an antecedent with an indefinite article would occasion the subjunctive:
Busco **al** estudiante que **habla** español. ¿Trabaja hoy?
Busco (a) **un** estudiante que **hable** español. ¿Conoce a alguno?

However, the following sentence pairs would seem to defy the rule concerning antecedents marked by either indefinite or definite articles:

Busco a **un** estudiante (= a certain student) que **habla** español. ¿Sabe si trabaja en esta oficina?

No compres el primero que veas.

(2) The antecedent is negated, that is, said not to exist.

No hay nadie que anime una actividad como él.
No hay mal que dure cien años.
No había persona que alzara la vista.

But,

Me indicó a alguien que podía repararlo.
(Antecedent is not negated nor is it imaginary or indefinite, so the indicative is used.)

7.20

Lo que (=English non-interrogative *what*) is another Spanish structure marking an adjective clause and taking the subjunctive only in certain instances. Although grammarians analyze *lo que* in various ways, for our purposes, *lo* is the antecedent of the adjective clause introduced by *que*.

1. If *lo* refers to a definite thing in the speaker's mind, then the indicative occurs in the subordinate adjective clause introduced by *que*.

    No percibo lo que pretendes haber logrado.
    No merece lo que recibe en este momento.
    No va a ser definitivo lo que prometen hacer.

2. If *lo* refers to something indefinite in the speaker's mind, to something which has yet to be experienced, a subjunctive form must appear in the subordinate adjective clause introduced by *que*.

    Voy a rechazar lo que me indiques.
      (I haven't yet been shown what to reject.)

    Tienes que escoger lo que te haga feliz.
      (I don't know what it is that makes you happy.)

But,

   Voy a rechazar lo que me indicas.
      (I have been shown what to reject.)

   Tienes que escoger lo que te hace feliz.
      (I know what it is that makes you happy.)

Exercise 5

Translate the following English sentences containing adjective clauses. Be mindful of the rules for the sequence of tenses. Some sentences will require a subjunctive, others will not, but in any case be able to state your choice of mood in the subordinate adjective clause.

1. I am looking for the man who wrote this book.
2. He was looking for a house that was comfortable.
3. You should do what he tells you. (He hasn't told you anything yet.)
4. You should do what he tells you. (You have already been told.)
5. There is someone in the hotel who can speak English.
6. There was no one in the hotel who could speak English.
7. Is there anyone in the hotel who can speak English?
8. I met a man who could drink a lot of wine.
9. My parents couldn't believe what they heard.
10. I know I'm not going to believe what I hear. (But, I have not heard anything as yet.)

11. I don't know anyone who can drink that much.
12. They want to buy a car that works well.
13. Last year we bought a car that didn't work well.
14. Did you see the lady who sold this dress?
15. I need to see a lady who sells dresses.
16. Do you want to see the lady who sells dresses?
17. They had a dog that barked a lot.
18. They want to buy a dog that barks a lot.
19. They didn't want to buy a dog that barked a lot.
20. He wanted to meet a girl who had a lot of charm.

7.21
THE SPANISH SUBJUNCTIVE IN THE ADVERBIAL CLAUSE

Spanish sentences which have subjunctive forms in the adverbial clause consistently use the formula:

$$(S)_1 + V_1 + ADV\ EXPRESSION + (S)_2 + V_2[subjunctive].$$

Certain adverbial expressions, primarily those which indicate future time, a condition or a final goal, always occasion a subjunctive in the adverbial clause.

1. **a menos que = unless**
   No cedo a menos que tú me convenzas.
   No quería obtenerlo a menos que a ti te interesara.

2. **antes (de) que = before**
   Establécelo definitivamente antes (de) que deje de ser oportuno.
   Verificamos la respuesta antes (de) que nos pudieran meter en serios problemas.

3. **con tal (de) que/siempre y cuando = provided that**
   Tomarán medidas firmes con tal (de) que cese la violencia.
   Felipe hace buen trabajo siempre y cuando le paguen bien.

4. **para que = so that**
   Dedujeron el impuesto para que no se aumentara el precio.
   Te di el dinero para que pudieras comprar la provisión.

5. **sin que = without**
   Transcurre el tiempo sin que haya ninguna esperanza.
   Abrieron la puerta sin que nadie los viera.

Other similar adverbials which always take the subjunctive are:

6. **a condición (de) que = on/with the condition that**
7. **a fin de que/con el fin de que = so that ; to the end that**

8. a no ser que = lest, unless
9. con la intención de que = with the intention that
10. con vistas a que = with the hope that
11. en caso de que = in case that
12. salvo que = unless

The remaining adverbial expressions may or may not require the subjunctive depending upon the time relationships between the main clause and the subordinate adverbial clause, or upon the speaker's knowledge of or feeling about the situation described.

7.22
ADVERBS OF TIME (temporal adverbs)

cuando = when

The indicative follows *cuando* when no futurity, either in relation to the present or to the past, is implied. *Cuando* + INDICATIVE expresses an already experienced occurrence or a routine activity.

Cuando Emilia viene, siempre la recibimos con alegría.
Mi familia se preocupa mucho cuando estoy fuera.
Cuando mi querida madre me llama, siempre salgo de prisa.
Cuando tengo dinero, compro la mar de cosas que no les doy uso.
Julia me llamó cuando había llegado a su destino.

The subjunctive is mandatory after *cuando* when the reference is to future time, either with respect to the present or the past.

Cuando Emilia venga, vamos a recibirla con alegría.
   (She has not yet arrived at the moment of speaking.)
¡Hijo mío!, cuando seas mayor, sabrás más de esos asuntos.
Vamos a cambiar el plan de ataque solo cuando sea debido.
Quiero viajar al exterior cuando estemos preparados.
Me dijo que me iba a escribir cuando llegara a Buenos Aires.

hasta que = until

The indicative follows *hasta que* when no futurity is implied. *Hasta que* + INDICATIVE, like *cuando* + INDICATIVE, expresses a usual or routine occurrence in either the present or the past.

Siempre toman la medicina hasta que se sienten mejor.
El Primer Ministro gobernó con afán hasta que perdió la salud.
La marcha duró hasta que llegaron al palacio.
El borrachón siempre consume hasta que no puede más.
Ella estudió su oficio hasta que lo dominó completamente.

When the subjunctive follows *hasta que*, the reference is always to future time, either with respect to the past or to the present.

Tienes que estudiar la lengua hasta que la asimiles bien.
No quiero disponer del comercio hasta que lo tengamos en completo orden.
No quería disponer del comercio hasta que no lo tuviéramos en completo orden.
¡Come, muchacho, hasta que no puedas comer más!

mientras = while

Mientras introduces events which are co-existent with another event. When such co-existence refers to present or past time, the indicative occurs.

Siempre viajamos por la provincia mientras mamá está aquí.
Mientras viajábamos por el continente, vimos muchas cosas de valor.
Me dedico a la pintura mientras ella practica la música.
Mientras sus hermanos se educaban, él andaba tras la fantasía.

The subjunctive occurs after *mientras* if co-existence refers to future time with respect to either the past or the present. In these contexts, *while* could in most cases be rendered as *for as long as*.

Vamos a viajar por la provincia mientras mamá esté aquí.
¿Qué piensas hacer mientras estés en EE.UU.?
Nos dijo que iba a estar ocupado mientras diéramos la vuelta.
¿Qué puedo yo hacer al respecto mientras estén meditando?
Ella pensaba desviarse a Burgos mientras yo siguiera directo a Madrid.

en cuanto/tan pronto como = as soon as

As is the case with the other adverbial expressions of time *en cuanto (tan pronto como)* takes the indicative when conveying usual or routine occurrences in any time sequence.

Ella siempre se pone en contacto conmigo en cuanto (tan pronto como) sabe algo distinto.
Alberto siempre gasta todo su dinero en cuanto (tan pronto como) recibe su jornal.
Me hiciste falta en cuanto (tan pronto como) te fuiste.
En cuanto (Tan pronto como) lo veo, me enojo.

However, this adverb of time takes the subjunctive whenever the reference is to the future.

Mi amiga se va a poner en contacto conmigo en cuanto (tan pronto como) sepa algo distinto.
Néstor me iba a decir la verdad en cuanto (tan pronto como) las circunstancias le dejaran hacerlo.
Sé que Alberto va a gastar todo su dinero en cuanto (tan pronto como) reciba su jornal.
En cuanto (Tan pronto como) lo veas, dile que quisiera hablar con él.

7.23
CONCESSIVE ADVERBS (These concede that something may or may not be true).

> **aunque = even though/although** (with the indicative), **even if** (with the subjunctive)

An indicative follows *aunque* when the speakers affirm their belief in the truth of what is stated or when they indicate that they know the beliefs held by the listener. English would render *aunque* + indicative as *even though/although*.

Es verdad, aunque tú no lo crees.
(The speaker asserts that the listener does not believe what the speaker holds to be true.)

Aunque puede tratarlo con desdén, él no se atreve a hacerlo ahora.
(The speaker knows the person can, indeed, treat someone disdainfully.)

Aunque trajeron los productos, no repartieron ninguno.
Aunque ella quiere pagarnos, no va a poder hacerlo.
Aunque tenía conocimiento de la industria, no lo nombraron para el cargo.

Aunque takes the subjunctive when the speaker is unsure of the truth of what is stated, or when there is uncertainty about what the listener might believe. English *even if* would be used in the translation.

Es verdad, aunque no lo creas.
(The speaker is saying "Despite your disbelief, this is true." In other words, whether the listener believes it or not is inconsequential..)

Aunque pueda/pudiera hacerlo, él no va a tratarlo con desdén.
(The person discussed may or may not be able to treat someone disdainfully; the speaker simply does not know.)

No van a poder repartir ningun producto aunque los traigan.
(The bringing of the product may or may not occur; in either case the bringing is inconsequential to the fact that no distribution will take place.)

Aunque tenga conocimiento del trabajo, no lo van a nombrar para el cargo.
(Whether or not the individual has knowledge about the work will not change the outcome.)

> **Note:** It is not uncommon for speakers to use *aunque* + the subjunctive even when there is certainty: *Aunque seas mi hermano, no me fío de ti.* = Even if you are my brother, I don't trust you. Here, there can be no doubt about what is presented in the subordinate clause.

> **a pesar de que/pese a que = In spite of the fact that**

The indicative follows these concessive adverbials when "the fact" is asserted. .

A pesar de que/Pese a que el sol representa el núcleo de nuestro sistema solar...
In spite of the fact that the sun represents the nucleus of our solar system...

They take the subjunctive when the issue at hand has yet to be resolved or when an indefinite future resolution is anticipated. The information presented is deemed inconsequential and therefore not highlighted.

A pesar de que /Pese a que sus creencias científicas sean erróneas...
In spite of the fact that their scientific views may be/may turn out to be erroneous...

7.24
ADVERBS OF MANNER (These show how something is done).

según/como = according to/how

The indicative follows *según/como* when expressing some definite or already experienced idea.

Voy a hacerlo según/como me dices. (The speaker has already been told how to do it.)
No pude hacerlo exclusivamente según/como el maestro me lo explicó.
No quiero ponerlo en el último puesto según/como tú me explicas.
No pueden creer tu historia de locura según/como se la cuentas.

Según/como takes the subjunctive when stating an indefinite concept or something projected for future time.

Voy a hacerlo según/como me digas. (The speaker is not certain how to do it but is willing to do it as later instructed.)
Sé que podré hacerlo según/como me lo expliques.
Pensaban componerlo según/como el maestro se lo explicara.
Ya sé que no voy a creer la historia según/como me la cuentes.

7.25
A LOCATIVE ADVERB (an adverb of place)
[For another point of view on *donde* see Chapter 26.4 and 26.12]

donde = where

Donde takes the indicative when the place referred to is known to exist and can be identified.

Piensan comprarlo todo donde vieron que la mercancía está en oferta.
Vamos a ir adonde uno se puede andar con traje de baño todo el año.

The subjunctive follows *donde* when the place described is uncertain or has yet to be found.

Cómpralo todo donde la mercancía esté en oferta.
No queremos vivir donde no haya cuatro temporadas del año distintas.

7.26
AN ADVERB OF EXTENT

> por más/mucho que = however/no matter how/regardless of how much

These expressions take the indicative if the extent has been experienced or is known. The example asserts that the individual did try hard; that information is highlighted.

Por más que trató, no pudo resolver el problema.
However/No matter how/Regardless of how hard he tried, he couldn't (=failed to) solve the problem.

These adverbials take the subjunctive if the extent expressed is unknown or yet to be determined. There is no new information; the speaker knows the listener tends to complain.

Te digo que no cambiará de parecer por mucho que te quejes.
I'm telling you he won't change his mind however/no matter how/regardless of how much you complain.

Exercise 6

Translate the following sentences. Although all of them contain adverbial clauses, some will require subjunctives and others will not. Be careful with tense sequence and be able to state your reasons for mood choice in each case

1. He left before we could speak to him.
2. They worked hard until they finished the job.
3. Do you plan to work until you finish the job?
4. His family spent a lot of money so that he could become a doctor.
5. We weren't going to see them unless they came on time.
6. What did you say when you saw him?
7. What are you going to say when you see him?
8. He was reading a book while she was washing clothes.
9. She said she would bring her husband provided you brought yours.
10. The horse always escapes without anyone seeing it.
11. He used to drink without his girlfriend's knowing it.
12. What are you going to study before we go to class?
13. Although his wife may not know it, he has a girlfriend.
14. Please explain it to me according to how he explained it to you.
15. Although he arrived late, we all went to the party.
16. I was going to write it according to how he wanted it. (I hadn't yet been told how to write it.)
17. I'm going to read that book as soon as I buy it.
18. She went shopping as soon as she received her salary.
19. They built the factory where there was an oil field.
20. Your children will be happier where they have more opportunities.
21. Regardless of how hard you work, you'll always be poor.
22. No matter how little he ate, he continued to gain weight.

8
English Modal Auxiliaries and Their Spanish Equivalents

8.1

Nothing so characterizes the English verbal system as its dependence upon auxiliary verbs. The least complicated of the English auxiliaries are the non-modals, also called primary auxiliaries, which carry no true lexical meaning but serve the purely grammatical functions of expressing progression (*be*), present and past tense (*do*), or perfectiveness (*have*). The position these non-modals take in the five basic sentence types of English is predictable. The modal auxiliaries, in spite of their other intricacies, assume the same positions as the non-modals in basic English syntax. Grammarians disagree on the exact number of English modal auxiliaries (See 2.5, modals aux's), and any discussion of this facet of English grammar is challenging to organize, particularly since most such verbs have more than one meaning and often do not function in all structures, tenses, and/or persons.

Context often determines the exact meaning of many modals, as can be seen when *He must work very hard to always look so tired*, expressing probability or conjecture, is contrasted with, *He must work very hard to accomplish his goal*, conveying obligation. The social connections between speakers often determines the exact nature of modal usages, and the affective domain of linguistic performance (register, emotion, emphasis, speech strategy) comes into play influencing the selection of one modal over another with only slight changes of meaning or overtone. Thus, each modal usages requires individual consideration, with context and dialectal variation always kept in mind.

Unlike English, Spanish makes much less use of modal auxiliary verbs; three frequently cited ones are treated in this chapter. In order to translate English modal usages accurately, Spanish often relies on intonation, special verbal tenses, or verbal periphrases. Often an exact translation of an English modal sentence is problematic; occasionally such translation borders upon the impossible. Nevertheless, we have made an effort throughout this chapter to present the most common meanings of the various interlingual modals.

8.2
MODAL SYNTAX IN ENGLISH

We noted previously that the syntax of English sentences containing modal auxiliaries is identical to that of those with non-modals (primary auxiliaries). Compare, for example, the positions occupied by the non-modal and the modal auxiliaries in the following sets of sentences. Observe that the modal auxiliaries *must* and *can* take the same syntactical ordering as do the non-modals *do* and *have*.

POSITION OF MODALS

SENTENCE TYPE	NON-MODAL AUX-*do* [past]	MODAL AUX-*should*
Affirmative	They **did** go. (emphatic)	They should go.
Negative	They didn't go.	They should not/shouldn't go.
Yes/No Quest	Did they go?	Should they go?
Neg. Quest.	Didn't they go?	Shouldn't they go?
Content Quest.	Where did they go?	Where should they go?

SENTENCE TYPE	NON-MODAL AUX-*have* [present perfect]	MODAL AUX-*can*
Affirmative	They have eaten	They can eat.
Negative	They haven't eaten	They can't eat.
Yes/No Quest.	Have they eaten?	Can they eat?
Neg. Quest.	Haven't they eaten?	Can't they eat?
Content Quest	What have they eaten?	What can they eat?

8.3
MODAL FUNCTION AND CLASSIFICATION

Listed below is our order of presentation of the English modal auxiliary system with Spanish equivalents. The paragraph number for each entry is also indicated. You will find the English modals grouped under assorted semantic categories. A few problematic Spanish modals are also included. As noted before, many modals can convey various different meanings depending on context, speaker and dialect.

> PHYSICAL AND/OR MENTAL ABILITY (8.4)
>   *can/could/be able to = poder/saber/ser capaz de*
>   *can* (8.5)
>   *could* (8.6)

Chapter 8 English Modal Auxiliaries and Their Spanish Equivalents

PERMISSION GRANTING (8.7)
can/could/may/will/would = *poder*

MAKING OF REQUESTS (8.8)
can/could/will/would = *poder/querer*

DEBER vs. *DEBER DE* IN PRESENT DAY SPANISH (8.9)

CONJECTURE/PROBABILITY (8.10)
must with MULTIPLE SPANISH EQUIVALENTS (8.11)

POSSIBILITY (8.12)
could/may/might with MULTIPLE SPANISH EQUIVALENTS (8.13)

SUPPOSITION (8.14)
should = *deber (de)*

WISHES (8.15)
may = **que + present subjunctive**

DETERMINATION/REFUSAL (8.16)
will = **future indicative**/*would* = ***no querer*** **(preterite)**

MODALS EXPRESSING REPEATED ACTIONS (8.17)
would **(past)** = **imperfect indicative**/*soler*; *will* **(present)** = **present indicative**/*soler*

INEVITABILITY (8.18)
must = *tener que/deber*

SOLICITATION OF OPINION (8.19)
shall/should = *deber (de)*/ **present indicative**

THREE SETS OF ENGLISH MODALS OF OBLIGATION AND THEIR SPANISH EQUIVALENTS

ADVISED OBLIGATION (8.20)
should, ought (to) = *deber (de)* **in the tenses of attenuation: imperfect indicative** *(debía)*, **conditional** *(debería)*, **past subjunctive in** *–ra (debiera)*; *might/could* **(as a suggestion)** = *poder* **(attenuated)**

POTENTIAL CONSEQUENCE OBLIGATION (8.21)
had better, be supposed to = *deber (de)* **in the tenses of attenuation: imperfect indicative** *(debía)*, **conditional** *(debería)*, **past subjunctive in** *–ra (debiera)*

STRONG OBLIGATION (8.22)
must, have to, have got to = *tener que, deber* **(present indicative)**

TWO SETS OF SPANISH MODALS OF OBLIGATION AND THEIR ENGLISH EQUIVALENTS

PERSONAL OBLIGATION (8.23)
haber de/tener que + inf = *to be* + inf/*to have to*

IMPERSONAL OBLIGATION (8.24)
haber que + inf = three English equivalents.

8.4
PHYSICAL AND/OR MENTAL ABILITY
can/could/be able to

The modals expressing physical and/or mental ability are *can*, *could* and *be able to*. *Can* and *could* have a periphrastic equivalent in the phrasal *be able to*. Whenever the English modals *can* and *could* occur expressing either physical or mental abilities, the phrasal modal *be able to* can replace them.

PRESENT	They can solve the problem	They are able to solve the problem.
FUTURE	They can work tomorrow.	They will be able to work tomorrow.
PAST	They could do it yesterday.	They were able to do it yesterday.
CONDITIONAL	They could accomplish it if they tried.	They would be able to accomplish it if they tried.

However, when one expresses physical or mental ability in a tense other than the four listed above, *can* and *could* do not occur. The only possibility is the phrasal *be able to*. This restriction applies to all the perfect tenses.

PRESENT PERFECT	They haven't been able to work every day. (*can/could* not possible)
PAST PERFECT	They hadn't been able to go. (*can/could* not possible)
FUTURE PERFECT	They will have been able to go, I'm sure. (*can/could* not possible)

Unlike the English modals, which do not readily differentiate between physical and mental abilities, Spanish makes a distinction, expressing it with different verbs, as seen in the following two paragraphs.

8.5
MODAL *CAN*

Can functions in all persons and structures for present time in the expression of physical or mental ability. The Spanish equivalent is *poder* when physical ability is intended, although mental ability may also be implied, as in *Pueden hacer esos problemas matemáticos mentalmente*. They are successful because, not only do they have the knowledge, but they are also disposed of the time, the strategies, etc. to solve the problems. *Saber* stresses knowledge: *Saben resolver ecuaciones cuadráticas muy difíciles*. The following sentences should help illustrate this difference: *Puede tocar el violín con los ojos cerrados/ Sabe tocar el violín, pero no la viola.* Spanish *ser capaz de* would translate English *can* for either type of ability.

8.6
MODAL COULD

Could renders ability, either physical or mental, for past time in all persons and structures. For Spanish, however, the *poder/saber* distinctions of the previous paragraph still apply, with the added proviso that one must consider the aspectual factor (imperfect vs. preterite) in all cases of *saber/poder* and *ser capaz de*.

SABER (imperfect) = *could*: *Mi mamá sabía preparar fabada asturiana.* (She knew how to and more: she had the knowledge plus the ingredients, recipe, time and everything else needed to be successful at the project)

PODER (imperfect) = *could*: *Mi mamá podía preparer fabada asturiana en poco tiempo.* (She had a special ability, one perhaps lacking in other cooks.)

PODER (preterite) = *could* (demonstrated ability): *El sábado pasado y con poca anticipación, ella pudo preparar en poco tiempo una fabada para veinte personas.*

SER CAPAZ DE (= *saber/poder*): *could*:
Imperfect: *Era capaz de preparar una fabada en poco tiempo.* (She had the ablility.)
Preterite: *Fue capaz de preparar una fabada en poco tiempo.* (She demonstrated that ability.)

Exercise 1
Whenever change is possible, rewrite these sentences expressing ability. Substitute *can/could* for *be able to* and vice versa. In each case, state why a second version is or is not possible.

1. I am able to help you.
2. She can't see you now.
3. They haven't been able to find the professor.
4. When will you be able to bring it?
5. Could you see the mountain from there?
6. The students can be here by nine o'clock.
7. We weren't able to read the message.
8. I could explain it to you before, but I can't now.

Exercise 2
Translate the following expressions of ability. The type of ability implied is in parenthesis.

1. I can't see you. (physical)
2. Could they read German when they were children? (mental)
3. They couldn't bring it. (demonstrated physical ability)

4. I didn't know what they could do to help. (possession of physical ability)
5. Are you able to write well? (mental)
6. Yes. I could have gone with you, but you didn't ask me. (physical)
7. They were able to leave early. (demonstrated physical ability)
8. Wasn't he able to say anything? (possession of physical ability)
9. He can't help us. (either type)
10. Who could do it? (either type)

8.7
PERMISSION GRANTING
can/could/may/will/would

A total of five modals occur in the requesting or granting of permission and in the making of requests. These are *can, could, may, will,* and *would*. In formal English *may* and in colloquial usage *can* appear in affirmative and negative statements to indicate that permission to act has or has not been granted. Only *can* functions in all three question structures, whereas *may* is defective, not occurring in the negative Yes/No question. All persons, singular or plural, may be involved in these structures. Spanish uses *poder* to render *can* or *may* when either expresses permission.

Affirmative:	You may/can leave.	Puedes salir.
Negative:	You may not/cannot/can't leave.	No puedes salir.
Yes/No Quest:	May/Can I leave?	¿Puedo salir?
Neg. Quest.:	Can't I leave?	¿No puedo salir?
	(*May* is not used in the negative question.)	
Content Q.:	When may/can I leave?	¿Cuándo puedo salir?

English uses *could* to give permission in past time. *Might* as the past of *may* does not occur in this context. Spanish uses *poder* in the imperfect.

He said that we could go home.   Dijo que podíamos ir a casa,
We were warned that we couldn't leave.   Nos avisaron que no podíamos salir.

Exercise 3

Translate the following sentences expressing permission. Use a variety of translations and the familiar form for *you*.

1. May/Can I visit her tomorrow?
2. You can't/may not go to Santiago this weekend.
3. Your brother can/may bring a friend if he wants to.
4. We were told that the children couldn't play outside.
5. When may/can we see your new car?
6. Can't I have a little more time to study?

7. The children may not/can't play in the street.
8. When may/can I paint the house?

8.8
MAKING OF REQUESTS
can/could/will/would

Can, could, will, and *would* appear interchangeably in English in making requests. Although one might maintain that *can* and *could* emphasize the physical abilities of the speaker while *will* and *would* stress one's intentions, most native speakers make no real distinction. It is true, nevertheless, that *can* and *will* render the request in a fairly direct fashion, while *could* and *would* soften it to some degree. Since requests usually assume interrogative form, these four modals function mostly in the question structures. We show as follows that Spanish has a variety of ways of translating requests.

• Use of the verb *querer* in one of three possible tenses, (a) the present indicative, (b) the conditional or (c) the past subjunctive usually in *–ra* form, all plus the infinitive. Theoretically, the request becomes increasingly more softened or attenuated as we proceed from tense (a) through tense (c).

Can/Could/Will/Would you (please) leave?   a. ¿Quiere(s) salir?
                                            b. ¿Querría (s) salir?
                                            c. ¿Quisiera(s) salir?

• Use of the verb *poder* in the same tenses and with the same degrees of politeness.

Can/Could/Will/Would you (please) help me?   a. ¿Me puede(s) ayudar?
                                             b. ¿Me podría(s) ayudar?
                                             c. ¿Me pudiera(s) ayudar?

• Use of the simple present indicative in question form.

Can/Could/Will/Would you (please) bring it to me?   ¿Me lo trae(s)?
Can/Could/Will/Would you (please) read it for me?   ¿Me lo lee(s)?

• Several periphrastic expressions appear to make attenuated requests.

Can/Could/Will/Would you (please)   a. ¿Me hace el favor de no fumar?
not smoke?   b. ¿Tendría la bondad de no fumar?
                                    c. ¿Sería tan amable de no fumar?

8.9
MODERN SPANISH EQUIVALENCY of *deber/deber de* + inf

Semantic readings of verb forms in English expressing conjecture/probability and possibility/supposition include the auxiliaries *can, could, may, might, must*, and *should*. Spanish uses *deber* and *deber de* as well as a variety of specific verbal tense forms. Much disagreement exists among native Spanish speakers on both sides of the Atlantic on the usage of *deber de* + INF vs. *deber* + INF as modals of supposition, conjecture, and probability as well as of obligation. The lack of agreement seems to stem from many sources—dialectal, idiolectal, societal, educational, etc. In its *Esbozo* the *Real Academia Española* (1979) made the following observation and suggestion:

> En la lengua clásica se encuentran ya ejemplos de confusión entre *deber de* y *deber* seguido del infinitivo sin preposición; en la actualidad la confusión es muy frecuente en el habla corriente oral y escrita. En la lengua literaria se mantiene más clara la diferencia entre *deber de* (suposición) y *deber* (estar obligado): *Deben de volver* significa *supongo, creo que vuelven*, en tanto que *Deben volver* equivale a *tienen obligación de volver*. La diferencia es muy expresiva y la Academia recomienda mantenerla (*Esbozo*, §3.12.4. h).

Note: According to the *Diccionario Panhispánico de Dudas*, Primera edición (octubre 2005), any formal distinction between supposition and obligation with *deber* continues to be blurred, to wit:

> [El verbo] *deber* [f]unciona como auxiliar en perífrasis de infinitivo que denotan obligación y suposición o probabilidad: a) *deber* + infinitivo [d]enota obligación: «Debo cumplir con mi misión» (Mendoza Satanás [Col. 2002]). Con este sentido, la norma culta rechaza hoy el uso de la preposición *de* ante el infinitivo: «Debería de haber [should be] más sitios donde aparcar sin tener que pagar por ello» (Mundo [Esp.] 3.4.94). b) *deber de* + infinitivo: Denota probabilidad o suposición: «No se oye nada de ruido en la casa. Los viejos deben de haber salido» (Mañas Kronen [Esp. 1994]). No obstante, con este sentido, la lengua culta admite también el uso sin preposición: «Marianita, su hija, debe tener unos veinte años» (V. Llosa *Fiesta* [Perú 2000]).

8.10
CONJECTURE/PROBABILITY
Must

The English expression of conjecture and probability appears only as affirmative and negative statements. The times referred to are either present or past, and the expressions can include all persons. *Must* (orally unstressed) is the modal used in the expression of conjecture/probability. It functions as follows:

PRESENT AFFIRMATIVE:	*must* + LV
PRESENT NEGATIVE:	*must* + not + LV (optional contraction [*mustn't*] rarely used))
PAST AFFIRMATIVE:	*must* + *have* + PAST PARTICIPLE
PAST NEGATIVE:	*must* + *not have* + PAST PARTICIPLE (optional contraction [*mustn't*] rarely used)

The test for an English sentence conveying conjecture or probability is the substitution of the word *probably* for the modal in the sentence. Observe the following sentence equivalencies.

He must be a doctor.	He probably is a doctor.
He must not be a doctor.	He probably isn't a doctor.
She must have been sick.	She probably was sick.
She must not have been sick.	She probably wasn't sick.

8.11
SPANISH EQUIVALENTS OF CONJECTURAL *must*

The English modal *must* for conjecture or probability has a number of Spanish equivalents.

- *A lo mejor* occurs frequently for conjecture/probability. Although it conveys some doubt, the indicative routinely follows it.

- With verbs expressing states or actions, the present indicative of *deber (de)* + INF is used. *Haber de* + INF, although less common, also appears, and since it is the periphrasis from which the synthetic future (*ha de ser* > *será*) is derived, the one word future also occurs for probability in the present. Likewise, the conditional, periphrastic or synthetic, (*había de ser* or *sería*) express probability in past time.

He must be sick.	A lo mejor está enfermo.
	Debe (de) estar enfermo.
	Ha de estar enfermo.
	Estará enfermo.
Mary must have a problem.	A lo mejor María tiene un problema.
	María debe (de) tener un problema.
	María ha de tener un problema.
	María tendrá un problema.
Victor must have lived here.	Víctor debía (de) vivir aquí.
	Víctor había de vivir aquí.
	Víctor habría vivido aquí.
She must have read a lot.	Ella debía (de) leer mucho.
	Ella había de leer mucho.
	Ella habría leído mucho.

Note: English occasionally uses its future (*will*) and conditional (*would*) to express present and past conjecture/probability, respectively, as in the following examples:

Present probability: "Someone's at the door."
                              "Oh, That will be (probably is) the mailman."
Past probability: "Something woke me up in the middle of the night."
                          "Oh, that would have been (probably was) the train passing."

The Spanish future and conditional of probability are frequently difficult of translate into English. Inguina and Dozier provide these interlingual equivalencies, with some English speculative expressions (*I guess...*, *I suppose...I wonder..., Maybe...*etc.) not provided in previous paragraphs. The question/answer examples are ours:

1. Spanish future > English probability in the present:
   - ¿Dónde estará Edna? (I wonder where Edna is.)
   - Estará en clase. (She probabily is in class/She must be in class/I guess she is in class/She'll be in class.)

2. Spanish future perfect > English probability in the past or the present perfect:
   - ¿Adónde habrá ido Eva? (I wonder where she went/has gone.)
   - Habrá ido a casa. (She probably went/has probabily gone home/She must have gone home/I guess she went/has gone home/She'll have gone home.)

3. Spanish conditional > English probability in the imperfect aspect of the past:
   - ¿Dónde estaría la secretaria? (I wonder where the secretary was.)
   - Estaría en el cine. (She probably was at the movies/She must have been at the movies/I guess she was at the movies.)

4. Spanish conditional perfect > English probability in the pluperfect:
   - ¿Dónde lo habría hallado? (I wonder were he had found it.)
   - Lo habría hallado en la playa. (He had probabily found it on the beach/He must have found it on the beach/I guess he had found it on the beach.)

The future and conditional progressives translate similarly:

5. Spanish future progressive > English present progressive
   - ¿Qué estarán leyendo los niños? (I wonder what the kids are reading.)
   - Estarán leyendo las tiras cómicas. (They are probably reading the comics/They must be reading the comics/I guess they are reading the comics/They'll be reading the comics.)

6. Spanish conditional progressive > English past progressive
   - ¿Qué estaría comiendo el zorrillo? (I wonder what the skunk was eating.)
   - Estaría comiendo gusanos. (It was probably eating worms/It must have been eating worms/I guess it was eating worms.)

Exercise 5

Rewrite the following sentences, using the other possible formulations to express conjecture/probability

1. Ese señor debe (de) ser un arquitecto famoso.
2. ¿Cómo serían los indígenas de este valle?
3. Esa anciana ha de tener mucho dinero.
4. El asesino debe (de) haber estado en este mismo sitio.
5. ¿Dónde habrá un teléfono?
6. Mi padre no debe (de) estar en su oficina después del día doce.

7. No tendrían suficiente gasolina para llegar.
8. Ese joven se ve muy fuerte; levantará pesas.

Exercise 6
Translate the following sentences involving conjecture/probability. Give assorted renditions.

1. You must be very tired.
2. Llegaron muy tarde. Tendrían problemas con su coche viejo.
3. They must have brought very little money.
4. Juanita debe de pronunciar muy bien el ruso porque tiene buen oído.
5. He must not have many friends here.
6. ¿Por qué no habrán llegado? ¿Habrían te nido un accidente?
7. That boy must not know the answer.
8. ¡Qué contento estará ese señor!
9. The tribe must have been very small.
10. Debe de haber sido la señora Méndez quien llamó.

8.12
POSSIBILITY
could/may/might

It is often difficult to distinguish clearly between the semantic concepts of probability and possibility in English. When English uses the word *possibly* with a verb as a substitute for a true modal, possibility rather than probability is the intended meaning. English sentences expressing possibility may refer to the past, the present or the future and occur in all five basic structures and in all persons. Sentences referring to the future are indistinguishable from those whose reference is to the present. English uses the perfective auxiliary *have* in sentences of possibility for past time. The following examples on the left containing modals are equivalent to those on the right without them, substituting *possibly*. All examples refer to the present.

Affirmative	He could/may/might work here.	He possibly works here.
Negative	He may not/might not work here. (*could* restricted)	He possibly doesn't work here.
Yes/No question	Could he/Might he work here? (*may* restricted)	Does he possibly work here?
Negative question	Couldn't he work here? (*may, might* restricted)	Doesn't he possibly work here?
Content question	Where can/could/might he work?	Where does he possibly work?

> **Note:** The adverbs *maybe* and *perhaps* followed by the simple present tense also express possibility: **Maybe/Perhaps he works here; Maybe/Perhaps he doesn't work here**.

8.13
POSSIBILITY
Spanish equivalents

Spanish uses a wide variety of expressions to translate the English modals of possibility. *Poder* works well in all structures. Since a measure of doubt is present, the following periphrastic phrases also occur: *poder ser que, ser posible que, tal vez, quizá(s)* and *acaso*. These routinely take either the subjunctive or indicative moods. (See Chapter 7.9) In question structures, the future tense with conjectural force appears. In the content question structure particularly, the future tense of the main verb or the verb *poder* as an auxiliary seem to be the only means of expressing possibility. *A lo mejor* with the indicative occurs with both meanings—probability and possibility.

AFFIRMATIVE
He could/may/might work here.
Puede ser que él trabaje/trabaja aquí.
Es posible que él trabaje/trabaja aquí.
Tal vez él trabaje/trabaja aquí.
Quizá(s) él trabaje/trabaja aquí.
Acaso él trabaje/trabaja aquí.
A lo mejor él trabaja aquí.

NEGATIVE
He may/might not work here.
Puede ser que él no trabaje/trabaja aquí.
Es posible que él no trabaje/trabaja aquí.
Tal vez él no trabaje/trabaja aquí.
Quizá(s) él no trabaje/trabaja aquí.
Acaso él no trabaje/trabaja aquí.
A lo mejor él no trabaja aquí.

YES/NO QUESTION
Could he/Might he work here?
¿Puede ser que él trabaje/trabaja aquí?
¿Es posible que él trabaje/trabaja aquí?

NEGATIVE QUESTION
Couldn't he work here?
¿No puede ser que él trabaje/trabaja aquí?
¿No es posible que él trabaje/trabaja aquí?

CONTENT QUESTION
Where can/could/might he work?
¿Dónde trabajará él?
¿Dónde podrá trabajar él?
¿Dónde podría trabajar él?

Exercise 7

Translate the following sentences, all of which express possibility. Give various versions.

1. Tal vez la mujer sepa/sabe hablar chino.
2. Where could he be at this late hour?
3. Puede ser que no tenga/tiene bastante dinero.
4. Could he be the new Spanish professor?
5. ¿No es posible que surja/surge una crisis?
6. My nephew may leave tomorrow night.
7. Es posible que no te conozcan/conocen.
8. He might not be as intelligent as you are?

8.14
SUPPOSITION
should

Should is the English modal auxiliary most frequently used to express suppositions. All persons can appear, but apparently only the affirmative statement, negative statement, and content question structures are involved. Spanish most appropriately translates the *should* of supposition with *deber (de)* + INF. and uses the conditional and past subjunctive *-ra* forms interchangeably with no apparent difference in meaning.

I should finish soon.	Yo debería (de)/debiera (de) terminar pronto.
She shouldn't be late.	Ella no debería (de)/no debiera (de) tardar
When should he have arrived?	¿Cuándo debería (de)/debiera (de) haber llegado él?
We should have fun.	Deberíamos (de)/Debiéramos (de) divertirnos.
They shouldn't have problems.	No deberían (de)/debieran (de) tener problemas.
How much should I earn?	¿Cuánto debería (de)/debiera (de) ganar?

Exercise 8

Translate the following sentences expressing supposition.

1. A estas horas mi prima debería (de) estar ya en casa.
2. He shouldn't need any help.
3. No debiéramos (de) encontrar a nadie en el centro esta noche.
4. When should the train leave?
5. Deberían (de) llegar muy cansados.
6. You should know all of your students within a few days.

8.15
WISHES
may

English *may* is the modal used to express wishes. This usage of *may*, often referred to as the optative mood (expressions of hope) in Latin grammar, is confined to affirmative and negative statements. In slogans *may* is omitted; only the LV appears. Spanish renders the optative with *que* + PRES. SUBJUNCTIVE. *Que* is absent in slogans.

May you live forever!	¡Que vivas para siempre!
May you never have problems!	¡Que nunca tengas problemas!
May they know the truth!	¡Que sepan la verdad!
(slogan) Long live the Revolution!	¡Viva la Revolución!

8.16
DETERMINATION/REFUSAL
will/would

In addition to its use as a future auxiliary, the modal *will* expresses volition or determination. Vocal stress accompanies the usage, and it occurs only in the first person singular and plural of the affirmative. Spanish generally employs a periphrastic expression to communicate strong determination towards an action.

I will win!	¡Yo sí que ganaré! ¡Voy a ganar!.
We will overcome!	¡Sí que venceremos! ¡Vamos a vencer!

In the negative *will* (*will not/won't*) renders **refusal** to act. Spanish uses *no querer*.

He needs to see a psychiatrist, but he won't do it.
Necesita ver a un psiquiatra, pero no quiere hacerlo.

English expresses refusal in the past with negative *would* (*would not/wouldn't*). Spanish often denotes past refusal with *no querer* or the more vehement *negarse a*, both in the preterite.

They owed us money, but wouldn't pay us.
Nos debían dinero, pero no nos quisieron pagar/se negaron a pagarnos.

Exercise 9
Translate the following sentences which express wishes and/or volition.

1. ¡Que nunca oigas lo que me han dicho!
2. May you always have enough money.
3. ¡Que no estén aquí cuando llegue yo!

4. May you live in peace.
5. ¡Que te cases con una bruja!
6. May we never see them again.
7. ¡Lograré lo imposible!
8. We will reach our goal!
9. El señor no quiso cooperar.
10. I won't stand for insults!
11. Le dije que se callara, pero no quiso hacerlo.
12. He needs a heart transplant, but he won't consider it.

8.17
MODALS EXPRESSING REPEATED/HABITUAL ACTIONS:
would (past)/*will* (present)

In Chapter 6, *would* + LV was shown to be roughly equivalent to *used to* + LV in expressing the past repetition of actions, rendered in Spanish by the imperfect indicative. *Soler* (imperfect) + INF is another possibility.

He would/used to tell us stories about the olden days. (Spanish: *contaba/solía contar*)
My father would/used to bring rabbits home to cook. (Spanish: *traía/solía traer*)

English uses *will* to express the repetition of actions, but in these cases, the reference is to the present. Spanish uses *soler* with similar effect. The simple present will often suffice.

My dog will sit by the door for hours waiting for me to come home.
Mi perro suele pasar horas sentado a la puerta esperando a que regrese a casa.

He'll drink until very late and then (will) go to sleep on the floor.
Bebe hasta muy tarde y luego se duerme en el piso.

8.18
INEVITABILITY

must

In addition to expressing probability, *must* conveys the idea of inevitability. This is an example of the multifaceted nature of so many of the English modals. Spanish uses *tener que* + INF to express inevitability. *Deber* is another possibility.

All things must die.	Todo tiene que/debe morir.
The sun must rise.	El sol tiene que/debe salir.
The months must pass.	Los meses tienen que/deben pasar.
Birds must leave the nest.	Los pájaros tienen que/deben dejar el nido.

8.19
SOLICITATION OF OPINION
shall/should

First Persons

In the affirmative Yes/No question structure, both *shall* and *should* occur with first person subjects (singular and plural) to solicit opinions concerning intended future actions. However, with these persons, *should* is the only modal possible in the negative Yes/No interrogative. Spanish commonly uses attenuated *deber* (imperfect, conditional or past subjunctive in *-ra*) in the translation. For the first person plural, Spanish can also employ a simple present: ¿(No)Entramos? = *Shall we enter/Shouldn't we enter?*

Shall I help them?	¿(No) debía/debería/debiera (de) ayudarlos?
Should(n't) I help them?	¿(No) los ayudo?
Shall we inform them?	¿(No) les debíamos/deberíamos/debiéramos (de) avisar?
Should(n't) we inform them?	¿(No) les informamos?

Second And Third Persons

Should, however, is the only allowable modal for soliciting opinions concerning second or third persons. Again, it is confined to the question structures—Yes/No and content. *Deber (de)* in any of its three softened/attenuated forms is the Spanish equivalent.

Should you be here?	¿Debías/deberías/debieras (de) estar aquí?
Shouldn't he work?	¿No debía/debería/debiera (de) trabajar?
When should they go?	¿Cuándo debían/deberían/debieran (de) irse?

Exercise 10

Translate the following sentences; all express the solicitation of opinions. Give a variety of translations.

1. Shall I bring my relatives?
2. ¿No deberíamos (de) regresar antes de que llegue ella?
3. Should we tell him the truth?
4. ¿Bailamos?
5. Shall we write him a letter?
6. ¿No debiera (de) negarle el permiso?
7. Should they be playing in the street?
8. ¿Debíamos (de) pasar la noche en un hotel?
9. When should we arrive?
10. ¿Compramos un modelo nuevo?

THREE SETS OF ENGLISH MODALS OF OBLIGATION AND THEIR SPANISH EQUIVALENTS

We have divided the English modals of obligation into three separate groupings: advised obligation, obligation based on potential consequences and strong obligation.

8.20
ADVISED OBLIGATION:
should, ought (to)

The modals *should* and *ought (to)* express a weak type of obligation which some grammarians refer to as "moral obligation," although the term "advised obligation" is found in various ESL texts. Speakers or listeners under this type of pressure often have been advised to perform in a certain way, but may feel no immediate or strong compulsion to act. These modals do, however, convey a sense of some urgency, often internally generated, to do or not to do something.

Should functions in all persons and in all structures. Spanish best renders the concept with *deber (de)* + INF, *deber* conjugated in one of the so-called "tenses of attenuation:" (a) imperfect indicative, (b) the conditional, or (c) the past subjunctive in *-ra*. In most varieties of Spanish, *deber* in the present indicative is simply too strong to convey the sense of advised obligation for *should* and *ought (to)*. The present tense of *deber* means *must*.

I should leave now.	Yo debía/debería/debiera (de) salir ahora.
You shouldn't go.	No debías/deberías/debieras (de) irte.
What should she do?	¿Qué debía/debería/debiera (de) hacer ella?

Ought (to) expresses a type of advised obligation roughly equivalent to *should*. However, it is a defective modal since it does not appear in all structures. *Ought (to)* functions:

- In the affirmative structure in conjunction with the English infinitive.

    I ought to go.
    She ought to work more.

- In the negative structure, *not* in non-contracted form appears between *ought* and the LV.

    They ought not go.
    We ought not mention it.

- *Ought* rarely appears in question structures, where it is replaced by *should*.

    Should they go?   Ought they go? (rare in Am. Eng.)
    Shouldn't they go?
    Where should they go?

Ought (to), like *should*, is translated into Spanish with *deber (de)* in the attenuated forms previously mentioned.

You ought to leave.	Debías/Deberías/Debieras (de) irte.
I ought to remain here.	Yo debía/debería/debiera (de) quedarme aquí.
You ought not go.	No debía/debería/debiera (de) irse usted.
They ought not stop.	No debían/deberían/debieran (de) parar.

Suggestions expressing mild obligation use *might* or *could*: *You might drop by to see if she's better; We might give them a call.* Spanish would use attenuated *poder* as an appropriate equivalent: *Podías pasar a ver si está mejor; Pudiéramos llamarlos.*

Exercise 11

Translate the following expressions of advised obligation giving a variety of versions.

1. You ought to see that film.
2. Usted debía (de) ir a verlo a su despacho.
3. We shouldn't drink so much beer.
4. ¿A qué hora deberían (de) llegar?
5. He ought not spend so much money.
6. No deberías (de) prestarles tanta importancia.
7. I should buy a new car this year.
8. ¿No debiéramos (de) invitarlos a la fiesta?
9. We might/could visit the museum before dinner.
10. Pudieran invitar a sus primos a cenar cuando lleguen.

8.21
POTENTIAL CONSEQUENCE OBLIGATION:
had better, be supposed to

Had better and *be supposed to* express a type of obligation intermediary between *should* or *ought (to)* and *must/have to/have got to*, these latter three showing strong obligation. The type of obligation conveyed by *had better* and *be supposed (to)* often seems imposed from the outside or to be the product of the speakers' inner rationalizations, both focusing on the potential consequences of taking or not taking some action. It seems clear that the speaker senses a more intense need to act with these auxiliaries than when using *should* or *ought (to)*.

Had better functions for all persons and occurs primarily in the affirmative and negative statement structures. It takes the LV and is restricted to a present time frame. Spanish translates *had better* with *deber (de)* in the appropriately attenuated tenses.

We had better leave.	Debíamos/Deberíamos/Debiéramos (de) irnos.
You had better eat.	Usted debía/debería/debiera (de) comer.
I had better not drink that.	Yo no debía/debería/debiera (de) beber eso.
He had better not run.	Él no debía/debería/debiera (de) correr.

Be supposed to carries roughly the same obligatory force as *had better*. Again, you render it in Spanish by *deber (de)*. Aside from *have to*, which is discussed later as a modal of strong obligation, *be supposed to* is the only modal of obligation expressing a time frame other than the present. Since it can function in all persons, tenses, and structures, it is considerably less defective than its semantic equivalent *had better*.

I was supposed to do it.	Yo debía/debería/debiera (de) hacerlo.
You're not supposed to go.	Ud. no debía/debería/debiera (de) irse.
Isn't he supposed to work?	¿No debía/debería/debiera (de) trabajar él?
Are you supposed to speak?	¿Debías/Deberías/Debieras (de) hablar?
When are we supposed to go?	¿Cuándo debíamos/deberíamos/debiéramos (de) irnos?

The following example of how freely English can accumulate its modals comes from an overheard conversation: *I don't want to have to keep on being supposed to support you.*

Exercise 12

Translate the following sentences of consequence-based obligation and provide a variety of versions.

1. You had better see a doctor.
2. Debiéramos (de) complacer a nuestros padres.
3. Are they supposed to help you with the project?
4. ¿Dónde deberían (de) vivir durante el invierno?
5. I'm not supposed to say anything about it.
6. Debieras (de) ir pensando en lo que vas a contestar.
7. Aren't we supposed to be working now?
8. Debías (de) vender ese cuadro viejo.

8.22
STRONG OBLIGATION:
must, have to, have got to

These three modals express strong, compulsory obligation with which the speaker feels there can be no compromise. Compliance is absolutely necessary or consequences will result. *Must* operates in all persons and in all structures, with the exception of negative Yes/No questions. Spanish best translates *must* with *tener que* + INF, except in the negative structure where it requires negative *deber (de)* in the present indicative. This is because the negative structure (*no tener que*) expresses the "absence of obligation" as does English *I don't have to.*

I must leave now.	Tengo que salir ahora.
Must we stay here?	¿Tenemos que quedarnos aquí?
When must we arrive?	¿Cuándo tenemos que llegar?

But,

| You mustn't leave. | No debes (de) irte |

Have to functions in all persons and structures and, unlike a great majority of obligation modals, in all tenses. In all structures except the affirmative statement, it uses one of the non-modal (primary) auxiliaries *do, have, will/would*. When occurring in the negative structure, *have to* expresses the "absence of obligation" (*I don't have to*) rather than the obligation "not to do" a certain thing. *Must* is mandatory in expressing the latter idea (*I must not/mustn't*).

He has to work.	Él tiene que trabajar.
I don't have to work.	No tengo que trabajar. (absence of obligation)
You mustn't work.	No debes trabajar. (obligation *not to*)
Will you have to leave?	¿Tendrás que salir?
Haven't they had to agree?	¿No han tenido que consentir?
When do we have to arrive?	¿Cuándo tenemos que legar?

Have got to belongs more to the colloquial idiom than do either *must* or *have to* and is most common in British English. It functions well in all persons and in all structures to express strong obligation with one exception: In the negative statement structure, as was the case with *have to*, it expresses the absence of obligation. Unlike *have to*, however, *have got to* (like *must*) refers to present or future time only and uses no other auxiliaries in the five basic structures. You use *tener que* + INF to depict the Spanish idea of strong, compulsory obligation in all structures except negative statements. In those, *no deber* + INF occurs.

He has got to work.	Él tiene que trabajar.
He hasn't got to work. (absence of obligation)	Él no tiene que trabajar.
He must not/mustn't work. (obligation not to)	Él no debe trabajar.
Has he got to work? (Br.Eng.)	¿Tiene que trabajar él?
Hasn't he got to work? (Br.Eng.)	¿No tiene que trabajar él?
When has he got to work? (Br.Eng.)	¿Cuándo tiene que trabajar él?

Exercise 13

Translate the following expressions of strong obligation into the other language. Give various renditions and make certain that you distinguish between the absence of obligation and the obligation "not to do" something.

1. No debes (de) fumar.
2. My father mustn't work so hard.
3. Mi hijo no tiene que trabajar mucho.
4. You don't have to smoke.
5. ¿Cuándo tenemos que salir del hotel?
6. Haven't you got to speak French with her? (Br. Eng.)
7. Tienes que visitar a tus compañeros.
8. We must write to the children.
9. No debemos (de) contemplar más eso.
10. When have we got to be there? (Br. Eng.)

Chapter 8 English Modal Auxiliaries and Their Spanish Equivalents 125

SPANISH MODALS OF OBLIGATION, PERSONAL AND IMPERSONAL

There are three modals of personal obligation in modern Spanish. These are *haber de, haber que*, and *tener que*, all followed by the infinitive. *Haber de* is the oldest of these and today seems literary, even archaic; *tener que* has been substituted for it and is the preferred expression in all Spanish-speaking regions.

8.23
PERSONAL OBLIGATION
haber de/tener que + inf

The so-called personal modals of obligation assign obligation to particular individuals such as the speaker, the addressee, third persons, etc. They can convey obligation in essentially any time frame.

Haber de translates into English as *to be* + INF. This is a less intimidating obligation, one that we ourselves have imposed, as if noting an upcoming event on the calendar: *No te olvides de que hemos de recoger a los chicos en el cine* = *Don't forget that we are to pick up the kids at the movies.*

Tener que is rendered as *have to* + LV. The obligation here seems stronger, more intense--an obligation put upon us by factors outside our sphere of influence.

Había de hablar con mi padre.	I was to speak to my father.
Tenía que hablar con mi padre.	I had to speak to my father.
Hemos de llegar esta noche.	We are to arrive tonight.
Tenemos que llegar esta noche.	We have to arrive tonight.
Han de comprar unas cosas.	They are to buy some things.
Tienen que comprar unas cosas.	They have to buy some things.

8.24
IMPERSONAL OBLIGATION
haber que + inf

Haber que is a modal of impersonal obligation meaning that the obligation applies to all listeners in general, not just to particular individuals such as the addressee, third persons, and the like. Because it is impersonal, the verb *haber* always assumes third person singular form.

English best translates the expression in one of three ways when obligation in present time is intended: (a) *it is necessary to* + LV, (b) *one must* + LV and (c) *you* (impersonal) *should* + LV. *Haber que* in the past (preterite or imperfect) and future/conditional tenses translates as, *it was/will/would be necessary ...*

Hay que estudiar más.	It is necessary to study more.
	One must study more.
	You (impersonal) should study more.
Hubo que matarlo.	It was necessary to kill it.

Habrá que venderlo.   It will be necessary to sell it.

Habría que hablarle.   It would be necessary to speak to him.

Exercise 14

Translate the following sentences. Some express personal and others impersonal obligation. Give all versions.

1. Hemos de llamarlos cuando lleguemos.
2. One must see it to believe it.
3. Hay que darle cuerda para que funcione bien.
4. They are to bring several samples.
5. Este verano tengo que dar una clase sobre la filosofía clásica.
6. It's a horrible job because you have to get up so early.
7. Supongo que habrá que cuidarla, como siempre.
8. It was necessary to buy a house.
9. Tenías que confesármelo todo, pero no me dijiste nada.
10. It will be necessary to use force.

9
English Phrasal Verbs

9.1

Just as modern Spanish has its rich legacy from Latin, English shares an inheritance with other Germanic languages of a rich store of special verb forms. The product of this semantic-syntactic process has various names. Perhaps the simplest of these is the descriptive "two-word verbs"; some authorities call them "multi-word verbs," "two-part verbs" or "composite verbs." We use the term "phrasal verbs" in the sense of "two or more words conveying a single thought and functioning as a grammatical unit." You need make a clear distinction between verb phrase (VP) and phrasal verb.

9.2

Phrasal verbs add a particle, usually a preposition or an adverb, to a standard lexical verb. The verb + particle unit often has a meaning identical to or at least similar to the base form. Here are some examples: *eat* in contrast with *eat up*, *start* with *start up*, *burn* with *burn up/down*. In each of these examples the particle serves simply as an intensifier or an augmentative. In other cases—and these are the most prevalent—the phrasal verb differs considerably in meaning from the base form or even from the sum meaning of the base form plus the preposition/adverb. Observe these examples: *get*, meaning *obtain* in contrast with *get up*, meaning *rise*; *turn*, meaning *rotate*, with *turn off* meaning *stop*; *give*, in the sense of *bestow*, with *give in*, meaning *yield* or *give up* meaning *surrender*.

Since Spanish has nothing comparable in extended use to this English verbal system, these English verbs will be difficult for the majority of Spanish-speaking learners. Further complicating the problem is the fact that many of these multi-word verbs have various meanings. Compare, for example, *pass out* (intransitive) meaning *faint* with *pass out* (transitive) meaning *distribute*. The particles often appear in apparently inexplicable pairings. For example, you can *slow up* or *slow down* and *speed up*, but you cannot *speed down*. The system is highly productive in English, and the language continually creates new verbs on the basis of verb + particle, i.e., *count down, blast off, gross out,* etc. Many of the phrasal verb combinations have evolved into adjectives or even nouns, for example:

The engineers will *count down* beginning tonight.	(verb)
The *countdown* crew arrived early.	(adjective)
The astronauts were waiting for the *countdown*.	(noun)

9.3

When analyzing the syntactical behavior of the phrasal verb, one must consider some peculiarities.

- When a phrasal verb takes a direct object expressed as a noun, the noun may follow the entire verb + particle unit, or it may intervene between the lexical verb and its adjunct particle.

    He filled out the forms.
    He filled the forms out.

- However, when a phrasal verb takes a direct object pronoun, its position is invariable, always between the verb and the adjunct particle.

    She filled them out.
    *She filled out them.

9.4.
PEDAGOGICAL IMPLICATIONS

One way of introducing the Spanish speaker to the difficulties of the English phrasal verb system is to demonstrate that these verbs can often be expressed in an alternate way. Frequently the Spanish speaker who has studied English for any time at all and who has acquired some basic English vocabulary knows one-word verbal equivalents for the newly presented verb + particle units. For example, s/he may not know the meaning of the phrasal verb *pass out 'desmayarse'* but may be familiar with the meaning of the one-word English equivalent *faint*. Often the one-word equivalent for a phrasal verb will be cognate from Latin in both languages, a possibility facilitating the learning and manipulation of these structures. As an illustration, *put off* means *postpone*, which in Spanish is *posponer*; both words are Latin cognates. Taking this approach to acquiring phrasal verbs should greatly expedite the learning process.

The Spanish speaker should become aware early on that neat, one-word equivalencies for English phrasal verbs are relatively rare. In probably two-thirds or more of the total number of cases, s/he must simply learn the meaning of the verb + particle unit, with no aid whatsoever from another one-word verb having the same meaning. Therefore, we advise instructors to introduce the most common of these verb + particle units in context instead of just providing students with a long list of phrasal verbs to memorize. Also, advise students to use a modern dictionary as much as possible and to read all the definitions provided in order to become familiar with more verbal phrases and thus increase their vocabulary.

Exercise 1

Examine the following sentences, all of which contain phrasal verbs shown in bold. From the list at the right, find the one-word equivalent that best matches each verb + particle construction. Which of the one-word verbs are cognates with Spanish verbs? Give the Spanish cognate when possible.

1. We'd better **cut down** on what we spend.
2. Please **think** it **over** before tomorrow.
3. They **put up** that house in less than a week.
4. They plan to **tear down** the old theatre.
5. You can't believe how she **takes after** her mother.
6. I have to **look over** some papers right now.
7. I'm here, so please don't **cross out** my name.
8. It will **take up** too much time to do it now.
9. It rained, so we **called off** the picnic.
10. This project **calls for** a lot of planning.
11. You should **take back** what you said.
12. She **made up** a story to deceive them.
13. Try not to **leave out** any of the details.
14. I have to **turn in** my report before Christmas.
15. He **showed off** his muscles, which impressed us all.
16. As usual they **showed up** late and unprepared.
17. Let's **talk** it **over** after a good night's sleep.
18. The captain refused to **carry out** those orders.
19. The teacher **went over** the exam carefully.
20. I **came across** several mistakes in her paper.
21. The bad weather is **holding up** our project.
22. She **went on** talking and talking like a parrot.
23. **Cut** that **out**! You're not supposed to do that.
24. The "lone star" **stands for** the State of Texas.
25. I won't **stand for** arguing at the dinner table.

appear
cancel
consider
continue
delay
delete
demolish
discuss
display
encounter
erect
examine
execute
invent
occupy
omit
reduce
represent
require
resemble
retract
review
stop
submit
tolerate

Exercise 2

Below and to the right is a list of prepositions; to the left is a list of lexical verbs.
If you are a Spanish speaker, use a modern English dictionary to determine the meanings of as many verb + preposition combinations you can. If your native language is English, match each verb with each preposition and determine intuitively if a phrasal verb with meaning results. Use the following guidelines:

- If no meaning results from combining a base verb with a particle, make a note of it.

    Example: *sit off*

- If a meaning results, check to see if you can get more than one meaning.

Example: *run off* can be used transitively to mean *'prepare copies,'* but it can also be used intransitively meaning *'disappear suddenly'*.

- In cases like those described above, write an English sentence for each meaning and your best Spanish translation for each.

- When meaning results and English has a one-word verb matching it, give the one-word verbal cognate in Spanish. For example, *give back* has the meaning of *return* (*devolver/regresar*), but neither is cognate with *return*. However, *give in*, another phrasal combination, is equivalent to *assent*, and this verb is cognate with *asentir*.

VERB LIST	PREPOSITION LIST
back	around
get	away
give	down
hand	in
keep	off
look	on
make	out
pull	through
put	up
run	
take	
throw	

9.5 OTHER STRUCTURES WITH PHRASAL VERBS

Some phrasal verbs may occur both intransitively or transitively. Thus, we find in English, *I stood up* and *I stood it up*. In these two examples we are describing similar actions. The same phrasal intransitive verb *stand up* can become transitive when used in, *I stood her up*. Here the action described is that of failing to keep an engagement, which entails a totally different semantic reading.

A phrasal verb itself may take a preposition which links the verb + particle to the rest of the sentence as in, *I stood up before the audience*. Used in this way, a phrasal verb maintains the same meaning as in the intransitive verbal structure. However, the phenomenon becomes further complicated since a phrasal verb may call for a second particle, thus totally altering the original meaning: *I stood up for my rights*. Here, the verbal unit *stood up for*, called a "phrasal-prepositional verb," has the meaning of *defend*, which is different from all the other semantic possibilities.

Exercise 3

Try to find a Spanish translation for the following sentences containing a phrasal-prepositional verb. In which cases might the verb + particle(s) unit be expressed with only one English verb cognate with a Spanish verb?

1. Then I **caught on to** the funny aspect of the story.
2. May I please **look on with** you since I forgot my book?
3. I don't **go (in) for** wild parties at all.
4. I should **check up on** my mother since she has been ill.
5. My wife won't **put up with** my smoking.
6. We **dropped in on** them last Friday night.
7. You simply can't **run away from** your obligations.
8. My friends **get along with** my husband very well.
9. He tried to **get away from** the shark.
10. If you ran a little faster, you would **catch up with** me.
11. I **look back on** my childhood with fondness.
12. The President wants to **do away with** many regulatory agencies.
13. When will you ever **get through with** your homework?
14. Despite the problems, we **went ahead with** our plans.
15. The professor plans to **get together with** us tomorrow.
16. How will we ever **make up for** the lost time?
17. I don't **feel up to** going out today.
18. You won't pass the course unless you **keep up with** your classmates.
19. While you're in the mountains, you'd better **watch out for** bears.
20. How can I **get out of** going to Monterrey.

9.6
CONTRASTIVE ANALYSIS

Since Spanish has no verbal construction identical to the English phrasal verbs, we must base any contrastive analysis on a comparison of how Spanish expresses the same or similar actions. The syntactic examples we presented above are contrasted here.

	ENGLISH PHRASAL VERB	SPANISH EQUIVALENT
1.	I stood up.	Me puse de pie (or) Me paré.
2.	I stood it up	Lo enderecé.
3.	I stood her up.	La dejé plantada.
4.	I stood up before the audience.	Me puse de pie frente al público.
		Me paré frente al público.
5.	I stood up for my rights.	Defendí mis derechos.

In the first example, the English phrasal verb is intransitive, whereas the Spanish verb is reflexive. The second examples correspond favorably because both are transitive constructions. The third example in English represents a familiar usage as does the Spanish equivalent: a more formal translation might be, *Falté a una cita con ella. / Falté a la cita que tenía con ella.* = I *missed the appointment that I had with her.* The fourth example, a phrasal verb plus a preposition, again places an intransitive English verb in contrast with a Spanish reflexive construction. The last example, that of a phrasal-prepositional verb in English, uses a Latin cognate (*defender* 'defend') in the Spanish translation.

9.7
ENGLISH ADJECTIVES BASED UPON PHRASAL VERBS

Some of the many English phrasal verbs appear as adjectives. In some such instances, written English requires a hyphen between the verb and the particle to produce the verb-based adjective. Many of these are relatively new and represent terms now essential to technology, modern advertising, etc.

Exercise 4
Following is a list of phrasal verbs used as adjectives. Find acceptable Spanish translations.

1. trade-in allowance
2. pickup truck
3. cleanup campaign
4. tryout schedule
5. lookout post
6. closeout sale
7. playoff game
8. runoff election
9. takeoff time
10. slowdown strike
11. giveaway show
12. throwaway bottle
13. getaway car
14. takeout counter
15. makeup examination
16. layaway plan
17. run-on sentence
18. write-in vote
19. checkout time
20. touch-up work
21. dropout rate
22. warm up exercise
23. touchdown play
24. drive-in restaurant

9.8
ENGLISH NOUNS BASED UPON PHRASAL VERBS

Just as some adjectives evolved from the English verb + preposition (phrasal verb) system, many nouns have originated through the same process. Again, these nouns are often recent additions to the English lexicon; many come from the fields of computer technology, politics, advertising and so on.

The written language seems somewhat ambivalent in deciding how to represent these compound nouns orthographically—whether to write them as two separate elements, two hyphenated elements or two combined elements. This vacillation exists among the adjectival forms as well. Generally speaking, the older lexemes do not employ the hyphen and are written as one unit, while the more recent additions to the lexicon do use the hyphen since they are still in their formative stage.

The government of Bolivia had another big *shake-up*.
There is great danger from atomic *fallout*.
Hundreds of students participated in the *sit-in*.

Exercise 5

Translate the following sentences all of which have a verb-based noun.

1. William bought a brand new Ford *pickup*.
2. He did several *pushups* and then began his weight lifting.
3. There was a tremendous *pileup* on the freeway last night.
4. The professor always gives us helpful *handouts*.
5. The beggar was asking for a *handout*.
6. They gave her a big *send-off* before she left for Venezuela.
7. Paul is a real *show-off*, but he is still a fine person.
8. The government suffered a severe economic *setback*.
9. I need to have *feedback* from everyone before I continue.
10. She suffered a nervous *breakdown* and had to be hospitalized.
11. The movie was a terrible *letdown* for us all.
12. He was fired because he had a *run-in* with his boss.
13. That bank has had three *holdups* in the past month.
14. People like them have entirely too many *hang-ups*.
15. Most movie actors use *stand-ins* for dangerous scenes.
16. They anticipate a substantial *buildup* of funds.

10

English *To Be* vs. Spanish *Ser, Estar* and *Haber*

10.1
SER AND ESTAR

The important contrast between the uses of *ser* and *estar*, when English has but one verb *to be*, is of great significance to the English speaker. A different but excellent and thorough treatment of the topic appears in Gili Gaya's *Curso superior de sintaxis española* where he makes the following introductory comment:

> La finísima diferencia en el empleo de uno y otro verbo [*ser* y *estar*] es una de las cualidades más destacadas de la lengua española. Expresa un matiz de las oraciones atributivas difícil de percibir con precisión para los extranjeros cuya lengua no conoce más que un solo verbo copulativo (§44).

Generally speaking, Spanish *ser* and *estar* have mutually exclusive usages. There are two exceptions, however: 1) with the expression of certain types of locative concepts (i.e., locations) and 2) in constructions involving the predicate adjective. Most grammars limit their descriptions to the two most common Spanish copulas as attributing permanent or characteristic qualities to a complement with *ser*, and as expressing temporary or condition-related qualities when *estar* occurs. This is correct as far as it goes, but there are also other important factors involved in the selection between the two Spanish verbs. *Ser*, apart from its function as a copula (*Sus padres son abogados*), occurs alongside *estar* with past participles in passive sentences (See Chapter 16). So used, *ser* is an auxiliary with the past participle of transitive verbs, thus imparting an imperfective aspect to the description or mention of an action. There is no focus on the event's end point. *Ser* in this context could be termed an "actional auxiliary:" *La fruta es lavada antes de ser vendida*. Note that the sentence would be unusual simply because of the Spanish tendency to avoid the *ser* passive, but it is grammatically acceptable. The *estar* auxiliary has two distinct functions. When it occurs with a past participle, no action is involved, but instead, there is a description of the state of being or resultant condition of some action: *La fruta ya está lavada y lista para ir al mercado*. The perfective aspect is highlighted by the use of *estar*. The verb also accompanies the gerund (*-ndo*) to form the progressive aspect of verbal tenses: *Los trabajadores están lavando la fruta*.

10.2
THE EXCLUSIVE USAGES OF *SER*:

1. To express what something is made of.
    Mi reloj es de oro.
    Esta silla no es de madera; es de metal.
    Mi suéter es de lana, y no de algodón.

2. To express possession.
    La casa es de mis primos.
    Las flores son de mi abuela.
    Este auto es de Jaime.

3. With any predicate **noun**, thus identifying the subject.
    El señor Gómez es el nuevo **gerente**.
    Claudia es **mexicana**, pero su esposo es **italiano**.
    Berta es una **actriz** famosa.

4. To express the time of day.
    ¿Qué hora es?
    Son las ocho.
    Aún no eran las cuatro y media cuando llegamos.

5. To state most impersonal expressions.
    Es importante que estés aquí a tiempo.
    Es triste que te tengas que ir.
    Es obvio que te tienes que ir.
    Es imposible que salgas a estas horas.
    Es obvio que la diferencia entre *ser* y *estar* es difícil.

6. To express the origin of a person or thing.
    ¿De dónde son tus padres?
    La viuda es de Zaragoza, España.
    Esta chaqueta es de Argentina.

7. To form the actional (true) passive (see Chaper 16).
    El marqués fue bien recibido en Nueva Granada.
    Las puertas serán abiertas por el portero.
    El cuadro fue terminado por otro pintor.

8. To express the occurrence of events, the emphasis being upon their taking place rather than upon their precise location.
    La fiesta es a las siete y media.
    No sabemos dónde es la reunión.
    Mi cumpleaños es en noviembre.
    En Sudamérica, el invierno es en junio.
    El examen de español es a las cinco de la tarde.

10.3
THE EXCLUSIVE USAGES OF *ESTAR*:

1. To express the location of people, places or things, provided that a true location rather than a happening or event is involved.
    El examen está en el escritorio de la profesora.
    Puebla está cerca de México, D. F.
    Estábamos como a quince kilómetros al este de aquí.
    ¿Dónde están las columnas de que me hablaste?

2. To express the *estar* passive, a construction in which a past participle follows the verb and expresses the state or resultant condition of some previous action (see Chapter 16).
    La comida ya está preparada.
    La estructura estaba rodeada de flores.
    El suelo está todo cubierto de polvo.

3. To voice some impersonal expressions.
    ¿Está bien si doy un informe en relación al renacimiento?
    Está claro que nadie sabe quién es.

4. As an AUX to form progressive (or durative) tenses.
    Los abogados están juzgando la moral del ciudadano.
    ¿Qué estás haciendo ahí?
    La gente estaba saliendo de la iglesia.

5. *Estar* occurs in a number of useful expressions:
    estar de acuerdo (con)
    estar de buen/mal humor
    estar a dieta
    estar en huelga
    estar de luto
    estar de moda
    estar de pie
    estar de regreso/vuelta
    estar de rodillas
    estar de vacaciones
    estar de viaje

10.4
SER VS. ESTAR + PREDICATE ADJECTIVES

As we observed earlier, *ser* and *estar* generally have mutually exclusive usages. The most important of the two exceptions to this rule involves the predicate adjective. Either of the two copulas may occur here, but the meaning from the English viewpoint will always be different with each separate verb.

When *ser* occurs with a predicate adjective, the subject has the inherent quality of or is characterized by the adjective.

Mi padre es muy inteligente.
Humberto es más alto que su hermano mayor.
Su abuelo es viejo. (He is chronologically old.)
La sangre es roja. (Blood is usually a red substance.)
El cielo es azul. (The sky is usually thought of as blue.)

The use of *estar* plus a predicate adjective indicates that the subject is in the condition described by the adjective, and this condition may change. The subject may also appear as somewhat distinct or different on a certain occasion from our usual concept of it. It may have changed or become a certain way which, for us, is out of the ordinary. Often with *estar*, our sensual perception is emphasized, that is, the subject may seem to taste, look, feel, or appear a certain way, and our personal reactions (surprise, admiration, dismay, contempt) become highlighted. The immediacy of these reactions ("right now") also comes into play.

El agua está fría.
    (Describes the condition of the water which is subject to change.)

¡Qué gordo estás!
    (You've gained weight; you look fat. You've changed from my concept of your usual weight.)

Estoy muy aburrida.
    (Describes the condition in which I find myself.)

Ricardo está enfermo.
    (His condition.)

¡Qué linda está la casa!
    (It is all prettied up; it looks unusually nice. It's different.)

¡Qué sabrosa está esta manzana! ¡Pruébala!
    (The use of *estar* highlights an immediate (personal) reaction.)

Listed below are a number of Spanish adjectives which, when used predicatively with *ser* or *estar*, have different meanings, at least from the English viewpoint.

Chapter 10 English "To Be" vs. Spanish "Ser," "Estar" and "Haber"

With *ser*:		With *estar*:
	abierto	
open-minded		open (eg. A door, window, store)
	aburrido	
boring, tiresome		bored
	alto	
tall		located (way up there)
	amable (like *simpático*)	
kind, friendly by nature		behaving in a kind or friendly manner
	atento	
courteous		attentive
	bajo	
short (stature), low		located (way down there)
	bueno	
of good character or quality		healthy, tastes good (food)
	callado	
taciturn, introverted		silent, quiet (for the moment)
	cerrado	
closed-minded		closed (eg. a store, a book, a house)
	consciente	
knowing something or aware of something		conscious (not passed out)
	despierto	
alert and alive		awake (not asleep)
	enfermo	
sickly, invalid-like		sick, ill
	interesado	
self-seeking, selfish		interested
	limpio	
clean by nature (cats)		clean (i.e., as the result of washing, etc.)

ser		estar
	listo	
smart, bright, intelligent		ready
	loco	
silly, scatter-brained		insane, mentally ill
	malo	
mean, bad, evil		sick, ill, broken (machine)
	nuevo	
brand new		unused, as good as new, different
	orgulloso	
haughty, snobbish		proud (of someone or something)
	pesado	
annoying, a pest, boring, irritating		heavy
	preparado	
cultivated, educated		prepared, ready
	rico	
rich (financially)		delicious (food)/sexually appealing
	seguro	
safe, reliable		sure, certain, convinced
	simpático (like *amable*)	
kind, nice (by nature)		considerate, pleasant (in behavior)
	torpe	
dim-witted, awkward, clumsy (by nature)		slow, sluggish (observed behavior)
	triste	
deplorable		sad, depressed, gloomy
	verde	
green (in color)		unripe (fruit, etc.)
	vivo	
alert, keen, lively		alive (not dead)

10.5

The permanent or temporary characteristics of any element being described are tellingly evident in interrogative structures using *ser* and *estar*. The structure *¿Cómo + ser?*, whose English equivalent is *What is X like?*, asks the listener about the permanent characteristics of a person, place, or thing.

¿Cómo es tu madre?   (What is she like? tall? short? nice?)
¿Cómo es Ecuador?   (What is it like? large? rich? densely populated?)
¿Cómo es la clase?   (What is it like? hard? easy?)

On the other hand, the structure *¿Cómo + estar?*, whose English equivalent would be *How is X?*, requests information about the condition of the subject.

¿Cómo están tus padres?   (Are they well? sick?)
¿Cómo está el profesor?   (Is he happy? in a bad mood?)

Exercise 1

A predicate adjective is used in each of the following paired sentences. Provide the English meaning and the conditions under which each sentence might occur.

1. El profesor es aburrido.
2. El profesor está aburrido.

3. La manzana es verde.
4. La manzana está verde.

5. Mi hermana es lista.
6. Mi hermana está lista.

7. La comida italiana es muy sabrosa.
8. Esta comida italiana está muy sabrosa.

9. Ese hombre es muy entretenido.
10. Ese hombre está muy entretenido.

11. Mi madre es muy callada.
12. Mi madre está muy callada.

13. Mi tío es un enfermo mental.
14. Mi tío está enfermo.

15. El fumar es malo para la salud.
16. Nuestro hijo está malo.

17. La niña es triste.

18. La niña está triste.

19. La puerta fue cerrada por el portero.
20. La puerta estaba cerrada.

21. Los gatos son muy limpios.
22. Los gatos están muy limpios.

23. El profesor es un loco.
24. El profesor está loco.

Exercise 2
Why would the speaker choose one verb over the other in these cases?

1. ¡Qué azul está el cielo hoy!
2. ¡Qué viejo soy!
3. ¡Qué feo es ese carro!
4. ¡Qué roja está esta sangre, doctor!
5. ¡Qué viejo estoy! ¡No quiero mirarme en el espejo!
6. ¡Qué bonita está ella con el pelo así!
7. La leche estaba muy cara el mes pasado.
8. En mi país la leche es muy cara.
9. ¡Qué brillante está la luna esta noche!
10. La luna no es tan brillante como el sol.
11. Esos señores son muy amables.
12. ¡Qué amables estaban con los niños enfermos!
13. ¿Cómo son los profesores de esta facultad?
14. ¿Cómo están los profesores hoy después de la fiesta de anoche?

Exercise 3
Translate the following sentences and be able to justify your usage of *ser* and/or *estar*.

1. My class is large, but his is small.
2. She's sick today, but she says she will be here tomorrow.
3. How is your brother today?
4. What is your professor like?
5. All of our friends are from Bogotá.
6. Where are all of your friends?
7. My uncle is a lawyer, and his wife is a professor.
8. The carpet is (made of) nylon.
9. The windows were open when we arrived.
10. The door was opened by the little boy.
11. The party is going to be (take place) in my apartment.
12. My wristwatch is broken.
13. Roses are red and violets are blue.
14. It was already eleven o'clock, and I was tired.

15. That man is very stubborn.
16. I am bored simply because this class is boring.
17. His birthday is in the fall.
18. Elizabeth is furious because we are not ready.
19. Where are the tourists who are from Nicaragua?
20. What are they doing there?

EXISTENTIAL STRUCTURES

10.6

Spanish uses the verb *haber* (third person singular only) in its existential structures while the English formula is *there + to be* (third person, singular or plural). Both of these constructions state that something exists, but with no emphasis upon the exact location of the person or thing in question. When location is the issue, Spanish uses *estar* instead of *haber*, and English uses *be* without the "apparent subject" *there*.

The Spanish Construction with *haber*

There is no stated subject in Spanish constructions expressing mere existence and utilizing the verb *haber*. The affirmative and negative statement, affirmative and negative question, and content question structures freely occur just as they would with any other verb. Existential *haber* appears only in the **impersonal third person singular** form.

AFFIRMATIVE	Hay un castillo encima de la montaña.
NEGATIVE	No hay ningún castillo encima de la montaña.
YES/NO QUEST.	¿Hay un castillo encima de la montaña?
NEG. QUEST.	¿No hay un castillo encima de la montaña?
CONT. QUEST.	¿Qué hay encima de la montaña?

Haber, expressing mere existence, may also occur in tenses other than the present indicative, but again, only in the **impersonal third person singular** form.

IMPERFECT	había dos castillos ...
PRETERITE	hubo un accidente ...
FUTURE	habrá varias reuniones ...
CONDITIONAL	habría unas dificultades ...
PERFECT	haber habido: Ha habido/Había habido un problema.
MODALS	Puede/Debe/Tiene que haber un teléfono por aquí.

> **Note:** *Haber* expressing existence does not occur in the progressive tenses.

10.7

THE ENGLISH CONSTRUCTION

In the English structure, *there* operates as an "apparent subject." It has no real meaning, but serves only to occupy the subject position in the affirmative and negative statement, affirmative and negative question, and content question structures.

AFFIRMATIVE	There is a castle on the mountain.
NEGATIVE	There isn't a/is no/castle on the mountain.
YES/NO QUEST.	Is there a castle on the mountain?
NEG. QUEST.	Isn't there a castle on the mountain?
CONTENT QUEST.	What is there on the mountain?

In English tenses other than the present, the same structures occur, but the tenses of the verb *be* change.

PAST	There was/were a strike/strikes in Bolivia..
FUTURE	There will be a strike/strikes in Bolivia.
CONDITIONAL	There would be no use/no uses for that invention.
PERFECT	There has/have been a change/changes in our department.
MODALS	There can/could/must/should/etc. be objectivity in your decision.

Note: As is the case in Spanish, the English expressions of existence do not occur in the progressive tenses.

10.8

There is one major difference between the English and Spanish structures for expressing mere existence. English consistently distinguishes between a singular and a plural in the verbal forms and tenses using the locution.

There is a university in this territory.
There are some universities in this territory.

There was a university in this territory.
There were some universities in this territory.

There has been an agreement.
There have been some agreements.

Spanish, on the other hand, uses only the third person singular of the verb *haber*, regardless of whether the item in existence is singular or plural.

Hay una universidad/unas universidades en este territorio.
Había una universidad/unas universidades en este territorio.
Ha habido un acuerdo/unos acuerdos.

Heard frequently are such colloquial expressions as the following simply because subject/verb agreement is so characteristic of Spanish:

*Antes habían dos universidades en este territorio.

This usage of the third person plural of *haber* with plural entities is now so rooted in the spoken language virtually everywhere that, as one Guatemalan Spanish professor put it, "It's the way we now say it. No one even notices."

Exercise 4

Translate the following existential sentences:

1. There is a man in my room.
2. ¿Habrá un espectáculo cultural en la zona histórica?
3. Weren't there any oranges in the store?
4. Debe de haber un remolino de ideas en la cabeza de ese pobre infeliz.
5. There has been a terrible accident.
6. ¿Cuándo habrá más películas sobre el medio oriente?
7. There were several documents on the table.
8. Hay varios discípulos de la reforma cristiana.
9. Will there be another war?
10. ¿No es necesario que haya físicos en el laboratorio?
11. When was there a strike at the factory?
12. ¿Ha habido algún acontecimiento decisivo?
13. Can there be a bird in that cage?
14. Hay millares de militares concienzudos en el ejército.
15. There could be a problem with that generator.
16. Había habido un accidente en la fábrica.
17. There were various problems with his suggestions.
18. Tiene que haber un zorrillo por aquí.
19. There is going to be a demonstration tomorrow.
20. Hubo una tremenda explosión y luego un apagón.
21. There will be several congressmen at the meeting.
22. Habrá un ataque si no hay un ejército bien entrenado.
23. There is a solution to every problem.
24. En sus frecuentes pesadillas había personas malévolas que no conocía.
25. There used to be a gas station on this corner.
26. Había solo dos enfermeras en el hospital esa noche.

11

English and Spanish Personal Pronouns

11.1
GENERAL CLASSIFICATION

The Spanish personal pronouns are divided into two classes, the **disjunctives** and **conjunctives**. The disjunctive pronouns are so called because they may be separated from the verb. They include the **subject** pronouns and the **prepositional object** pronouns. The conjunctive pronouns are so termed because they must accompany the verb in the sentence, either directly preceding it or following and being attached to it. These include the **direct object** pronouns, the **indirect object** pronouns, and the **reflexive object** pronouns. We treat both types of disjunctive pronouns, the subject and prepositional object pronouns, in this section. We also present two sets of conjunctive ([en]clitic/"with verb") pronouns, the direct and indirect object pronouns. The reflexive object pronouns used with reflexive pronominal verbs appear in Chapter 13.

Grammarians divide the English personal pronouns into three classes. These are the **subject** pronouns, the **object(ive)** pronouns, and the **reflexive** pronouns. The objective (object) pronouns function as direct objects, indirect objects, or prepositional objects; their forms are identical for each of these various usages. The reflexive pronouns refer to the subject in the sentence and are formed by adding the English suffix *-self/-selves* to a pronoun base.

Note that with few exceptions and regardless of which set of pronouns in either language is involved, all show person (first, second and third) and number (singular or plural).

SPANISH DISJUNCTIVE PRONOUNS AND THEIR ENGLISH EQUIVALENTS

We have organized the following discussion around the Spanish classificational system.

11.2

The **subject pronouns** are those used as the subject of a sentence, that is, they represent the actors, the people or things about which the rest of the sentence is predicated.

	SINGULAR		PLURAL	
1st pers.	yo	I	nosotros, nosotras	we
2nd pers.	tú	you	vosotros, vosotras	you
	usted	you	ustedes	you
3rd pers.	él	he	ellos	they
	ella	she	ellas	they
	ello	it		

These Spanish pronouns are generally optional (See Chapter 1.4); they occur redundantly only to provide emphasis or contrast: *Yo hablo inglés, pero ella no*. They may also indicate that a new subject has been introduced into the discourse. The term discourse in its widest application is "language that communicates something in a coherent manner." (Celce-Muria and Olshtain, p. 4) *Cuando se conocieron, no se cayeron bien. Un día, **él** decidió romper el hielo y le habló por teléfono para invitarla a tomar un café. **Ella** se sorprendió mucho con la invitación.* In English, however, some expressed subject, either in noun phrase or in pronoun form, must accompany the verb. For this reason, the English subject pronouns will appear with far greater frequency than will the corresponding forms of Spanish.

One of the most difficult contrastive problems for the English speaker is that the English subject pronoun *you* has five different Spanish equivalents—*tú, usted, ustedes, vosotros/vosotras*. Each, with the exception of the last two listed, takes a different verbal form. In addition, the pronoun *vos*, with its various meanings and unusual verbal forms, requires comment since many speakers use it in southern Mexico, most of Central America, and a good part of South America (especially in Argentina, Chile and Uruguay). Called *voseo*, its usages are mainly colloquial and not usually seen in formal writing. Still, observers have commented upon its increasing usage in Central America, i.e., on a sign at the International Airport in Managua, Nicaragua and in the media in Honduras and El Salvador.

Spanish speakers acquiring English have a simple task—they simply learn to use *you* with any addressee, singular or plural, familiar or formal. There are a few exceptions, especially when addressing highly revered individuals, for example, *Your Honor, Your Majesty*, etc. The English speaker, on the other hand, must come to understand Spanish formal versus familiar register, as well as the concept of singular versus plural equivalents for English *you*. A more extensive treatment of this dilemma appeared in Chapter 3.

Spanish has no subject pronoun equivalent for English *it* when referring to a specific thing. This causes the Spanish speaker to render English *It's on the table* as **Is on the table*. The omission of *it* may be due to the Spanish speaker's problems with pronouncing the English consonant cluster [ts]. The Spanish neuter subject pronoun *ello* has limited use, and refers to abstract concepts or to whole ideas, never to concrete things. Speakers tend to replace it with *eso*: *No quisiera hablar de ~~ello~~ > eso*. Spanish shows gender distinctions in all its plural subject pronouns, except *ustedes*. In English, *we, you* (plural), and *they* do not show gender.

Exercise 1

Give all possible personal pronoun subjects for these Spanish verbal forms.

1. adelanté   4. calláis   7. fue
2. ascenderán 5. había crecido 8. asistimos
3. celebrabas 6. tuviera   9. habré

Exercise 2

Give all possible English personal pronoun subjects for these verbal forms.

1. goes   4. will go   7. is working
2. saw   5. would be   8. were
3. have done 6. am   9. are going

11.3
THE PREPOSITIONAL OBJECT PRONOUNS

The **prepositional object pronouns** are the those used as objects of prepositions such as *a, de, pero, por, sin*, etc. Those forms preceding the slash in the following chart are non-reflexive, whereas those following are reflexive. If no slash is used, then the forms are identical.

SINGULAR		PLURAL	
mí	me/myself	nosotros, -as	us/ourselves
ti	you/yourself	vosotros, -as	you/yourselves
usted/sí	you/yourself	ustedes/sí	you/yourselves
él/sí	him/himself	ellos, ellas, sí	them/themselves
ella/sí	her/herself		
él/sí	it/itself		
ella/sí	it/itself		
ello/sí	it/itself (abstract)		

In either language, the non-reflexive forms occur as objects of a preposition when the subject of the sentence and the object of the preposition are different entities. The reflexive forms are found when the subject and the object of the preposition are the same. In the Spanish reflexive usage of the prepositional object pronouns, *mismo* (fully inflected) generally accompanies the reflexive prepositional pronouns.

NON-REFLEXIVE EXAMPLES:

Esto es para mí.	This is for me.
Ese libro está cerca de él.	That book is near him.
Ella salió sin nosotras.	She left without us.
Yo sé nada de ello (> eso).	I know about it. (a concept)

REFLEXIVE EXAMPLES:

Lo hice para mí misma.	I did it for myself.
Él habló de sí mismo.	He spoke about himself.
Te mentiste a ti misma.	You lied to yourself.
Se apuntó la pistola a sí mismo.	He turned the gun against himself.

If the Spanish preposition *con* governs *mí, ti,* or *sí,* then new words are formed: *conmigo, contigo, consigo,* respectively: *Fueron al pueblo conmigo* = *They went to town with me.* Keep in mind that while *conmigo* means *with me* and *contigo* means *with you, consigo* has only a reflexive meaning, *with himself/herself.* In other words, *consigo* does not mean *with him/her.*

The **subject pronouns** and the **prepositional object pronouns** (non-reflexive) are **identical** in Spanish, **except in the first and second person singular**. The non-reflexive English prepositional object pronouns are the same as the English direct and indirect object pronouns (i.e., the object[ive] pronouns).

Spanish, as usual, distinguishes between formal and familiar address in both the singular and the plural prepositional object pronouns, while English does not. Gender distinctions are the norm in Spanish plural non-reflexive prepositional object pronoun usages, while in English no such distinctions are made.

The three Spanish prepositional object pronouns *ello/eso, él,* and *ella* may be translated as *it* with the following stipulations:

- When *it* refers to an idea in its entirety or to some abstract concept, then *ello/eso* is used: *No sé nada de ello/eso* = *I don't know anything about it.* Here, *it* might refer to what happened at the party last night or to some other event or occurrence.

- In *No sé nada de él/de ella* = *I don't know anything about it,* the *it* in translation refers to a specific gendered entity, for example *the book* (*él*) or *the idea* (*ella*). The authors suggest avoiding the prepositional object constructions when the reference is to things by using instead the null-subject option wherever possible: *Presentaron varias ideas, pero algunas (de ellas) fueron rechazadas.*

Finally, not every Spanish preposition governs the Spanish prepositional object pronouns. Some prepositions take the subject pronouns as their complements.

Entre tú y yo, no debe haber más discusión de este tipo.
Todos quieren ir, *menos yo*.
Nadie lo puede hacer, *excepto tú*.

In Chapter 11.11 and 11.13-14 we show how the non-reflexive prepositional object pronouns are used with the conjunctive pronouns for various grammatical and/or discourse related reasons.

Exercise 3

Translate the following sentences into Spanish. In each case, is the prepositional pronoun usage reflexive or non-reflexive?

1. There is a letter for you on the table.
2. I think you received a letter for me.
3. They don't know anything about us.
4. He wants to go with me.
5. Does your mother want to live with you?
6. She can't do anything for herself.
7. They weren't able to tell us anything about themselves.
8. The train was passing below them.

9. He showed me this poem. Do you know anything about it? (*it*= the writing of the poem)
10. He died in Puerto Rico. I don't know anything else about it.
11. Several teenagers had to appear before him (the judge).
12. My parents live near you.
13. He seemed very pleased with himself.
14. I would like to study with you.

Exercise 4

Translate the following sentences into English. In each case is the prepositional object usage reflexive or non-reflexive?

1. ¿No sabes nada de ella?
2. Nadie quiere compartir sus experiencias conmigo.
3. ¿Alguien quiere pintar con nosotros?
4. ¿Vive el matrimonio cerca o lejos de ti?
5. El árbol fue plantado por ellos.
6. Ese gobernador siempre habla de sí mismo.
7. Juana no va a decirme nada de ello.
8. Anunciaron que el premio era para mí.
9. Cecilia lo hace todo por sí misma.
10. El desconocido podría depender más de nosotros.
11. No puedo celebrar contigo esta ocasión.
12. No lo complazco por ella; lo hago por mí misma.
13. No van a dejar que salgamos sin ellos.
14. ¿Qué confianza le van a tener si lo oyen hablando consigo mismo?

11.4
SPANISH CONJUNCTIVE PRONOUNS AND THEIR ENGLISH EQUIVALENTS

Spanish has three sets of conjunctive pronouns. They are the direct object pronouns, the indirect object pronouns, and the object pronouns (direct or indirect) used with reflexive pronominal verbs. We discuss the last group in Chapter 13, as previously noted.

The following headings guide our discussion of the Spanish conjunctive pronouns and their English equivalents:

- Position(s) assumed by Spanish conjunctive pronouns with respect to the verb, and the English syntax of such pronouns.

- Spanish direct object pronouns.

- Spanish indirect object pronouns.

- Spanish direct and indirect object pronouns occurring in the same sentence, and the English equivalents.

- Spanish nominal and pronominal reduplication (redundancy) of direct and indirect object pronouns.

Conjunctive pronouns, also termed (en)clitic or "with-verb" pronouns, invariably appear in direct association with a verb form, positioned either directly before or after (and attached to) the verb. Nothing intervenes between these pronouns and the verb, not even the negating particle, *no*. The form of the verb itself conditions the placement of the conjunctive pronouns. Some verb forms require that the pronoun come before the verb (pre-positioning), others that it come after (post-positioning), and still others allow either arrangement. When the conjunctive pronouns occur with verbal forms, the usage is called "pronominal."

Here are the syntactical rules for conjunctive pronoun positioning with respect to the verb in modern Spanish. We include examples of the reflexive pronominal verbs, discussed later in Chapter 13, merely to illustrate the absolute consistency of the system:

- The conjunctive pronouns must **precede** the verb form if it is a **conjugated verb** showing person, number, tense, and mood, or if it is a **negative command** (imperative).

    Conjugated Verb Form:

DIRECT OBJECT	INDIRECT OBJECT	REFLEXIVE
Juan lo ve.	Juan nos habla.	Juan se viste.
Juan me verá.	Juan me escribe.	Ella se levantó.
Juan nos ha visto.	Él nos vendió comida.	Me había acostado.

    Negative Command (Imperative):

DIRECT OBJECT	INDIRECT OBJECT	REFLEXIVE
¡No lo mate!	¡No me escribas!	¡No se vista Ud.!
¡No me intimides!	¡No le digas eso!	¡No te levantes!
¡No los pongáis aquí!	¡No nos hable!	¡No os acostéis!

- The conjunctive pronouns must **follow** and be attached any **affirmative command** (imperative).

DIRECT OBJECT	INDIRECT OBJECT	REFLEXIVE
¡Mátalo!	¡Escríbeme!	¡Vístete!
¡Véame mañana!	¡Díganme la verdad!	¡Levántese!
¡Ponedlos aquí!	¡Tráeme tu libro!	¡Sentaos!

> **Note:** In *sentaos*, the *-d* of the *vosotros* imperative form falls when the reflexive pronoun is added. Theoretically, this allows a distinction between the command form and the plural past participle *sentados*. In spoken Peninsular Spanish, it is not unusual to hear *sentaros, probably because the infinitive can acquire imperative force, as in *No fumar*.

- The conjunctive pronouns may **either precede** the entire verbal unit **or follow** and attach to the last element of the verbal unit if the last element of this unit is either a dependent infinitive (i.e., an infinitive preceded by a conjugated verb) or a dependent *-ndo* form (i.e., an *-ndo* form preceded by a conjugated verb).

A dependent infinitive:

DIRECT OBJECT	INDIRECT OBJECT	REFLEXIVE
Me quiere matar.	Le voy a escribir.	Se tiene que vestir.
Quiere matarme.	Voy a escribirle.	Tiene que vestirse.

> **Note:** There are a few exceptions to this rule. In the expression *haber que + INF*, the pronoun must always follow and attach to the infinitive: *Hay que hacerlo mañana.* To express *We are going to see her*, either position is possible: *Vamos a verla* or *La vamos a ver*. But to say *Let's see her*, only *Vamos a verla* is possible. A topic of considerable scholarly interest over the past twenty years concerns the two theoretically permissible positions for conjunctive pronouns with dependent infinitives (Myhill, 1988; González López, 2008). At issue is the acceptability of both pre- and post-positioning of the conjunctive (clitic) pronouns in all instances of dependent infinitives (Nos va a visitar = Va a visitarnos.) and the relative frequency of each. The studies show, for instance, that *La insistimos en ver is questionable and that only *Insistimos en verla* seems correct. This is because the clitic (conjunctive) pronoun assumes the position nearest the element governing it, all within the syntactical norms of Spanish. However, in many cases, and more commonly in speech than in writing, the clitic pronoun appears attracted to the matrix verb, often an auxiliary in the most general sense of the word. The pronoun, then, seems to "climb" from a post-position to a pre-position; hence the term "clitic climbing." King and Suñer (2004) observe that the less truly lexical content the matrix verb has, the more likely it will permit clitic climbing. Some such verbal types follow. The examples are ours: 1) modal auxiliaries (*No quiero hacerlo > No lo quiero hacer*), 2) auxiliaries of motion (*Van a hacerlo hoy > Lo van a hacer hoy*). The topic has other interesting facets, but they fall outside the scope of this text.

A dependent -ndo form:

DIRECT OBJECT	INDIRECT OBJECT	REFLEXIVE
Me está matando.	Le estaba escribiendo.	Se está vistiendo.
Está matándome.	Estaba escribiéndole.	Está vistiéndose.

- The conjunctive pronouns must **follow** and attach to non-dependent infinitives and to non-dependent -ndo forms.

A non-dependent infinitive:

DIRECT OBJECT	INDIRECT OBJECT	REFLEXIVE
Al verlo así, me puse muy triste.	Después de escribirle, voy a visitar a su madre.	Tuvo que ir a trabajar sin afeitarse.

A non-dependent -ndo form:

DIRECT OBJECT	INDIRECT OBJECT	REFLEXIVE
Viéndola así, no sabía qué hacer.	Diciéndole la verdad, la convencerás.	Se pasa la vida quejándose.

> **Note:** In cases involving the perfect infinitive, the pronoun attaches to *haber*, for example, *Después de haberle hablado...; Antes de haberlos visitado....* Similarly, in the verbal construction, *habiendo* + past participle, conjunctive pronouns attach to the -ndo form, for example, *Habiéndonos abandonado en el desierto, regresaron a la ciudad.* Such constructions belong to the formal, written language and even there seem archaic to some native speakers.

Exercise 5

Examine the following sentences; the Spanish conjunctive pronouns are in bold. For now it's not important whether any given pronoun is a direct, an indirect, or a reflexive object pronoun. Simply state why the pronoun assumes the position it does. Some sentences may have more than one correct rendition.

1. Sé que no **me** van a decir nada.
2. **Lo** tienes que hacer cuando puedas.
3. No **te** acuestes tan tarde mañana.
4. Acosta**os** temprano, niños, pues tenemos mucho que aprovechar.
5. Levánte**se**, don Rafael.
6. Su esposo no **le** ha dicho nada.
7. No voy a permitir que **te** vayas en seguida.
8. Jorge no **me** está ayudando mucho con este proyecto.
9. ¿Quién estaba acompañándo**te** cuando **te** vi esta mañana?
10. Estudié alemán durante cinco años, pero no **lo** hablo muy bien.
11. Mi amada no **se** había peinado durante muchos días.
12. Ve**te**, hijo. No **te** puedo hablar en este momento.
13. No **te** alejes. No **te** he dicho todavía todo lo que **te** quiero decir.
14. Quería que **me lo** recordaras, pero no tenías mente para hacer**lo**.
15. Viéndo**la** así, cualquiera hubiera creído que **se** había enfermado.

11.5

The English equivalents for the Spanish conjunctive pronouns always follow the verb. The pronouns used are always the object(ive) forms:

She sees *me* every day.
She writes *to him* every month.
She needs to see *us* tomorrow.
She is dressing *herself* in the bedroom.
Help *her*!
Don't help *her*!

11.6

SPANISH DIRECT OBJECT PRONOUNS AND ENGLISH EQUIVALENTS

The Spanish **direct object pronouns** and their English equivalents function as the objects of transitive verbs.

SINGULAR		PLURAL	
me	me	nos	us
te (FAMILIAR)	you	**os** (FAMILIAR)	you
lo/le (FORMAL)	you	**los/les** (FORMAL)	you

la (FORMAL)	**you**	**las** (FORMAL)	**you**
lo/le	**him**	**los/les**	**them**
la	**her**	**las**	**them**
lo/la	**it**	**los** (INANIMATE)	**them**

There are virtually no important contrastive problems in the first and second persons singular or plural since there are one-to-one correspondences here. In the third persons singular and plural, however, numerous important contrasts occur, and even standard Spanish usage varies, depending upon the variety. Of these dialectal variations, the most important is the distinction between *loísmo* and *leísmo*.

11.7
LOÍSMO

Spanish speakers from Latin America are in the main *loísta* in their direct object pronoun usage; hence, the pronoun *lo(s)* is used for direct object pronouns that represent masculine nouns and *la(s)*, for those that represent feminine nouns, while *le/les* is reserved for indirect object nouns.

The *loísta* direct object pronoun system follows.

lo = you (masculine, formal)/*him*/*it* (masculine)
la = you (feminine, formal)/*her*/*it* (feminine)
los = you (plural, formal, if some males included)
los = them (people or things, one or more males included)
las = you (plural, feminine, formal)/*them* (feminine, people or things)

11.8
LEÍSMO

The *leísta* is generally from Spain and always uses *le* or *les* for the indirect object and also for direct objects representing masculine animate beings, especially in the singular.

The *leísta* direct object pronoun system follows.

le = you (masculine, singular, formal)/*him*
les = you (plural, formal, if some males included)/*them* (animate beings, some males included).
lo = it (masculine)
los = them (things only)
la = you (feminine, formal)/*her*/*it* (feminine)
las = you (feminine plural, formal)/*them* (feminine, people or things)

Both *loísmo* and *leísmo* are fully standard usages in modern Spanish. However, in teaching American Spanish to the English speaker, it is wise to present the *loísta* usage. In that way, the beginner will not become confused since *le/les* are reserved for indirect object use only and *lo*, *la*, *los*, and *las* remain the third person direct object pronouns. The *Real Academia Española* recommends this practice, but also includes the alternate use of *le* for the masculine direct object when referring to a male person. A Mexican informant observed that *leísmo* occurs, especially among people of little schooling when they address an individual of some status, be they male or female, as in, *Señor(a), le respeto mucho. Leísmo* in reference to inanimate objects can also be heard in colloquial parlance. Referring humorously to a moustache as if it were a living entity, someone said: *Hay que regarle para que crezca un poquito.*

Exercise 6

Translate the following sentences into Spanish, giving both the *loísta* and *leísta* version whenever they differ.

1. I see them. (the men)
2. I know her.
3. He sees them. (the books)
4. I don't know you. (fem. sgl., formal)
5. He knows you. (masc. sgl., formal)
6. He saw them. (the girls)
7. They know you. (masc. pl., formal)
8. We saw you. (fem. pl., formal)
9. I want it. (the letter)
10. She saw it. (the glass)
11. We don't know him.
12. They don't see her.

Exercise 7

Translate the following English sentences, all of which contain a direct object pronoun. Be consistently either *loísta* or *leísta*. Explain the positioning of the pronouns; some sentences may have more than one version.

1. I don't need to see you tomorrow.
2. He is studying it right now. (lección)
3. Where did you put it? (arma)
4. Bring it tomorrow! (dinero)
5. Don't put them there! (dulces) (familiar, plural)
6. When do we have to see him?
7. He is trying to call them. (Marta y Ofelia)
8. Don't eat it! (pan) (formal, plural)
9. Don't smoke them! (puros) (familiar, plural)
10. I know her well.
11. Where did he meet her?
12. Do they want to visit me in Spain?
13. Don't you want to use them? (datos)
14. He is attacking us.
15. Drink it! (vino) (familiar, singular)
16. I haven't seen her today.
17. Do we have to lead them? (ciegos)
18. Are they reading them? (revistas)
19. He doesn't want to write it. (párrafo)
20. Don't bother me! (familiar, plural)

11.9
SPANISH INDIRECT OBJECT PRONOUNS AND ENGLISH EQUIVALENTS

The **indirect objects** in both languages express "to whom" or "for whom" something is done. Their forms are outlined below.

SINGULAR		PLURAL	
me	(to/for) me	nos	(to/for) us
te, le	(to/for) you	os, les	(to/for) you
le	(to/for) him	les	(to/for) them
le	(to/for) her		
le	(to/for) it		

The English direct and indirect object pronouns are identical in form. English often, though not always, indicates the indirect object by preceding it with *to* or *for*. If not already knowledgeable in their usage, English speakers must learn to distinguish between direct and indirect objects in their native language. This insight is essential to their comprehending the relatively more complex Spanish system. The direct object (DO) receives the direct impact of the verb. The indirect object (IO) receives the benefit of that action, that is, the action is done *to* or *for* the indirect object. The objects, direct or indirect, may be pronouns or nouns, or any other type of noun phrase. Example: *They gave it (DO) to me (IO)* ; *Carlos bought the flowers (DO) for his sweetheart (IO)* ; *They sold her (IO) a new Chevrolet (DO)*. Notice that in the last example the indirect object is not introduced by *to/for*.

In Spanish the first and second person singular and plural use the same pronouns for both the direct and the indirect object. In the third person singular and plural, the following needs noting with regard to similarities and differences between direct and indirect object forms.

a. The *leísta* speaker uses *le(s)* for masculine animate beings occurring as direct objects and *le(s)* also for any third person indirect object. All other third person direct and indirect objects are distinct forms (*lo, la, los, las* vs. *le/les*).

b. As stated before, with the *loísta* speaker of Latin America, third person singular or plural direct and indirect object pronouns are always different in form: *lo(s)* for masculine nouns, *la(s)* for feminine nouns are direct objects regardless of whether the referent is animate or not, and *le(s)* is reserved for indirect objects exclusively.

> **Note:** The fact that no gender distinctions occur in the third persons singular or plural indirect object pronouns is rather uncharacteristic of Spanish,

---

Exercise 8

In the following English examples, which element is the direct and which is the indirect object?

1. He gave me the book.
2. They told everything to us.
3. She offered him some cigarettes.

4. We proposed some new plans to them.
5. They brought my mother some candy.
6. I think I owe you a couple of dollars.
7. The professor plans to teach her Portuguese.
8. The manager suggested a new approach to the employees.
9. She wrote them a very long letter.
10. Please introduce your friend to me.

Exercise 9

Translate the following sentences and give all possible word orders.

1. Bring me the cup! (familiar, singular)
2. He is going to give us the money.
3. Don't lend them your car! (formal, plural)
4. He is going to offer us a bribe.
5. You owe me a lot of money.
6. He paid them five dollars for the coat.
7. Read us the story. (familiar, singular)
8. He is selling all of his books to them.
9. Don't show her those papers. (formal, singular)
10. He has to teach us English.
11. Edward never tells her the truth.
12. I wrote them a long letter.
13. Explain the lesson to him. (familiar, plural)
14. He was mentioning his mother to me.
15. Don't return that copy to us. (familiar, singular)
16. We prefer to show them these articles.
17. When is he going to tell me where he lives?
18. The professor is teaching them Swahili now.
19. Write her a letter when you have the time. (familiar, plural)
20. Don't send us pesos; send us dollars! (formal, singular)
21. Lend me the money or don't ever speak to me again! (familiar, singular)
22. I am going to suggest something interesting to them.

11.10

Spanish sentences containing indirect object pronouns are often ambiguous to the English speaker, particularly when the context is unclear or lacking. The Spanish indirect object is therefore best viewed as a so-called "involved entity," that is, the individual affected in some way by the action expressed in the sentence. Older grammars often refer to the "involved entity" concept as "the dative of interest or separation," the last word in this definition referring to such sentences as, *Me quitaron los documentos* = *They took away my documents*.

Depending on context, *Me robó el dinero* can mean *He robbed the money from me*, or *He robbed the money for me*. Again, depending on the context, *Le vendieron la casa* can have three interpretations: *They sold the house to him*, *They sold the house for him*, or *They sold the house on him* (the selling of the house occurring unexpectedly, catching him unawares). Only context can aid in deciding whether, *Le tiré las llaves* could be interpreted as, *I threw the keys to him* or *at him.*

A further illustration of the importance of context appears in the following sentence: *Me chocaste el carro.* Possible meanings are, *You (in another car) crashed (into) my car,* or, *You (driving my car) crashed it.* Whitley, (137-8) cites further examples, collected from a variety of sources, demonstrating how generalized the "interests" of the involved entity (indirect object) can be:

Elena le preparó la comida a Juan. (= for Juan)
Elena le escondió la llave a Juan. (= from Juan)
Elena le puso otra sábana a Juan. (= on John's bed)
Elena le notó cierto desconcierto a Juan. (= in John)
Elena le sacó provecho a Juan. (= of John.)

In many cases, the involved entity is actually the possessor of the direct object:

Elena le apuntó el número a Juan. (= John's number)
Elena le levantó la cabeza a Juan . (= John's head)

See Chapter 13.5-6 for further discussion of this type of sentence.

Exercise 10

Translate the following sentences using a construction with *a* + noun (*a Elena*) or prepositional object pronoun (*a ella*) to indicate the indirect object as the "involved entity."

1. They broke his jaw in a fight,
2. Take that toy away from Adelina.
3. We detected many mental defects in that boy.
4. She made a Mexican meal for her roommates.
5. Hugo put a jacket on the little girl.
6. He always takes advantage of our family.
7. Elena hid her little girl from her husband.
8. I asked John for a loan.

11.11
BOTH DIRECT AND INDIRECT OBJECT PRONOUNS IN A SAME SENTENCE

When both direct and indirect object pronouns occur in the same sentence, Spanish and English show variances in their respective treatments. In Spanish, without exception, **the indirect object pronoun precedes the direct object pronoun.** As a unit, these two pronouns assume the same position with respect to any given verbal form that they would have if only one pronoun had been used. However, if a third person indirect object pronoun (*le/les*) precedes a third person direct object beginning with *l-* (*lo, le, la, los, les, las*), the indirect objects *le/les* must become *se*. Since this *se* substitute for indirect object *le/les* can be ambiguous in its reference, the speaker may clarify it by introducing a prepositional pronoun construction (*a él, a ella,* *a usted, a ellos, a ellas, a ustedes*). Note that *Se lo mostraron*, from the English point of view and without context, can have six different meanings: *to him/her/it/you/them/you* (plural).

We presented the syntax of conjunctive pronouns in 11.4, and it is reviewed here as it affects sentences with both indirect and direct object pronouns.

With conjugated verbal forms or negative commands, the pronoun unit (IO+DO) precedes the entire verbal form.

> Eugenio me lo entrega.
> Eugenio le > se lo entregó (a él).
>
> ¡Eugenio, no me lo entregues!
> ¡Eugenio, no le > se lo entregues (a ella)!

With affirmative commands, the pronoun unit (IO+DO) follows and attaches to the verbal form.

> ¡Entrégamelo!
> ¡Explíquele > selo (a ella)!
>
> ¡Explícanoslo!
> ¡Explícale > selo (a él)!

With dependent infinitives or dependent *-ndo* forms, the pronoun unit (IO+DO) may precede the entire verbal unit or follow and attach to the last element of the verbal unit.

> Alberto te lo va a entregar = Alberto va a entregártelo.
> Alberto le > se lo tiene que entregar (a ella) = Alberto tiene que entregárle > selo (a ella).
>
> Berta me lo está explicando = Berta está explicándomelo.
> Berta les > se lo está mostrando (a ellos) = Berta está mostrándoles > selo (a ellos).

With independent perfect infinitives and constructions like *estando + -ndo*, the unit attaches to the auxiliaries:

> Antes de habérmelo dicho...   La criada, estándotelo lavando...
> Antes de habérlelo > selo dicho... La criada, estándolelo > -selo lavando...

The previous two examples would be rare in modern written or spoken usage.

Exercise 11

Translate the following sentences and provide and explain all possible word orders.

1. He didn't tell it to me. (the joke)
2. She wants to bring them (the books) to me.
3. He is explaining them (the lessons) to her.
4. Don't bring it to her! (the glass)
5. Give them (the bottles) to him! (familiar)

6. He didn't offer it (the wine) to me.
7. She is going to read it (the story) to them.
8. They taught it (Spanish) to her.
9. Who sold them (the oranges) to you? (familiar)
10. Don't lend it (the pencil) to him!
11. Send it (the package) to her. (formal)
12. They returned them (the letters) to me.

11.12
THE ENGLISH SYSTEM

English generally allows two structures (both with the same meaning) when an indirect object and a direct object pronoun occur in the same sentence, although certain word-stress factors will restrict the use of some pronouns. Structure (a) below most closely resembles the Spanish system, since the indirect object precedes the direct object.

a. V + IO + DO	b. V + DO + to/for + IO
Lend me some money.	Lend some money to me.
Don't give them any.	Don't give any to them
He wants to tell you that.	He wants to tell that to you.
He is showing her one.	He is showing one to her.
She mailed us these.	She mailed these to us.

English clearly prefers structure (a) above when the direct object occurs as a noun, as in *He gave me the book*, and structure (b) above usually appears when both the indirect and the direct object are expressed as pronouns. *He gave it to me.* Moreover, in American English two personal pronouns do not generally occur together in an indirect-direct object combination making *He gave me it* of questionable acceptance, notwithstanding the fact that British English admits it.

Verbs which permit either structure (a) or (b) are, among others, **bring, give, lend, mail, offer, owe, pay, read, sell, send, show, teach, tell, throw, write**.

Verbs which allow only structure (b) include, among others, **apply, describe, explain, introduce, mention, present, prove, report, return, suggest**.

Exercise 12

Translate the following sentences; all have both an indirect and a direct object. If it is possible, give both structures (a) and (b) in the English translation.

1. Ella nos está leyendo un cuento ahora.
2. ¿No quieres devolverme el libro?
3. Susana se lo dará cuando lo vea (a Ud.).
4. Yo se lo presté el año pasado.
5. Efraín nunca nos la presentó.

6. No te voy a sugerir ningún plan nuevo.
7. ¿Cuándo puedo enseñarte francés?
8. No se lo puedo explicar a ellos.
9. Marianne me mostró su casa recién pintada.
10. Nunca te lo mandaron.
11. Díganos el resto del cuento.
12. No me arrojes esa bola.
13. Julio todavía no se lo ha apuntado.
14. ¿Quién te envió ese brillante tan lindo?

Exercise 13

Write original sentences in Spanish using the following conjunctive pronouns as indicated, placing each appropriately in the syntax as specified. (As noted, some sentences will have two possible renditions.) Then translate each sentence into English, and observe where the object pronouns always appear with respect to the verb. Here are two examples: #1: Specified is: *te* (IO), conjugated verb. Possible sentence(s) following the specification is: *Te dieron una camisa nueva.* > *They gave you a new shirt./They gave a new shirt to you.* (The object[ive] pronoun always follows the verb in English.) #2: Specified is: *nos las* (IO+DO) dependent infinitive (2) Possible sentences following the specification: *Nos las van a explicar/Van a explicárnoslas.* > *They're going to explain them to us.* (Again, the objective pronoun(s) always follow the verb in English).

1. me (IO), affirmative command
2. le (IO) , dependent infinitive (2)
3. me los (IO+DO), conjugated verb
4. nos (DO), negative command
5. lo (DO), dependent –ndo (2)
6. los (DO), conjugated verb.
7. la (DO), affirmative command
8. se la (IO+DO), conjugated verb
9. les (DO) [*leísmo*], conjugated verb
10. te los (IO+DO), dependent infinitive (2)
11. te (DO), dependent –ndo (2)
12. os (IO), conjugated verb

11.13

NOMINAL AND PRONOMINAL REDUPLICATION: The Use of Prepositional Nouns or Pronouns in Conjunction with Direct or Indirect Object Pronouns.

Reduplication, formerly called redundancy, is of two types: 1) pronominal reduplication, in which a conjunctive direct or indirect object pronoun occurs with a prepositional object pronoun, (DO) *A él lo necesito*; (IO) *A ellas les escribo,* and 2) nominal duplication, in which a conjunctive direct or indirect object pronoun works in conjunction with prepositional object noun, (DO) *A mi marido lo/le necesito*; (IO) *A mis sobrinas les escribo).* Such redundant Spanish usages affect English speakers as "saying things twice." The speaker may choose to keep the prepositional object as close to the conjunctive pronoun as possible (See Topicalization, 11.14) , as in the examples just provided, or to separate them, as in the following explanations, where some restrictions apply.

With direct objects, Spanish allows only pronominal reduplication (*La conoce a ella*), and rejects nominal reduplication (**La conoce a Elena*), except when the direct object noun has been topicalized as explained later (*A Elena, la conozco muy bien*).

PRONOMINAL REDUPLICATION	NOMINAL REDUPLICATION (ungrammatical)	WITHOUT REDUPLICATION
Lo conoce a él	* Lo conoce a Pedro	Conoce a Pedro
La conoce a ella	* La conoce a Elena	Conoce a Elena
Los conoce a ellos	* Los conoce a Pedro y a Juan	Conoce a Pedro y a Juan
Las conoce a ellas	* Las conoce a Elena y a Martha (all ungrammatical)	Conoce a Elena y a Martha

With indirect object pronouns, Spanish pronominal reduplication is obligatory, whether with pronominal prepositional constructions (*Le dio el regalo a él*) or nominal ones (*Le dio el regalo a Pedro*).

PRONOMINAL REDUPLICATION	NOMINAL REDUPLICATION	WITHOUT REDUPLICATION (ungrammatical)
Le dio el regalo a él/a ella	Le dio el regalo a Pedro	* Dio el regalo a Pedro
Les dio el regalo a ellos/a ellas	Les dio el regalo a Pedro y a Juan	* Dio el regalo a Pedro y a Juan

Exercise 14

Translate the following sentences into Spanish. Determine first if a direct or an indirect object is involved in each case. If possible, give two versions of each sentence, 1) in which the prepositional object and the direct or indirect conjunctive object occur together, and 2) in which the preposition and conjunctive objects are separated. In the second case, are nominal or pronominal reduplication always possible; why or why not?

1. We don't see them here.
2. I think he is writing his girlfriend a letter.
3. They don't know our mayor.
4. Aren't you going to bring your mother?
5. He always offers us tequila.
6. Don't they know your father?
7. I have to teach foreign languages to my students.
8. I don't see Norma.
9. Who showed them the new apartment.
10. Haven't we met your wife?
11. He is going to explain the incident to Bertha

12. Don't give Henry that much money!
13. They showed this book to their colleagues.
14. Everybody loves her.

11.14
TOPICALIZATION

Spanish has syntactical devices by which it identifies the topic of a sentence (who or what the sentence is about) without the topic's necessarily being the grammatical subject. By identifying the topic in this way, it is clearly identified, contrasted with other elements of the sentence, or emphasized. Examples are, 1) with a direct object noun: *El periódico, lo compra mi hijo a diario*, and 2) with an indirect object noun: *A Laura le han quitado el pasaporte*. English cannot accomplish such topicalization through syntactical maneuvers, but must rely on particularly heavy vocal stress on words or phrases to achieve the effect: *My boy buys the newspaper daily. / They've taken Laura's passport.*

Spanish slightly modifies the structures used nominally and pronominally with direct and indirect conjunctive pronouns (see the preceding paragraphs) to tropicalize items. The prepositional elements are "dislocated" from their usual position, and shifted to the left, usually to the beginning of the sentence. (Slabakova, et. al. p. 286)

SENTENCES WITH A DIRECT OBJECT PRONOUN:
A ella la conozco.	I know her.
A Julio no lo veo.	I don't see Julio.
A ti te amo, pero a Ada, no.	I love you, but not Ada.

SENTENCE WITH AN INDIRECT OBJECT PRONOUN:
A mí me gusta la estatua.	I like the statue.
A ti no te escribí.	I didn't write you.
A los perros no les hablo.	I don't speak to dogs.

Such topicalized sentences usually occur in contexts such as these in which emphasis or contrast is intended: *A tu hermano no le/lo he visto, pero a tu padre, sí; A Gilberto le presto dinero, pero a su hermano, no.* It could probably be argued with regard to another grammatical topic that the true (*ser*) passive in both languages is the topicalized rendition of an active sentence: *El oso fue fusilado por los cazadores < Los cazadores fusilaron (a)l oso.*

Exercise 15

Express the following sentences in Spanish tropicalizing the items in bold. Determine whether the prepositional construction appears in conjunction with a direct or indirect object.

1. **We** like him. (use *gustar*)
2. You didn't meet **Peter**; you met **Paul**.
3. You never saw **that cat** before.
4. I wrote to **them**, but not to **him**.
5. **Betty** doesn't care. (use *importar*)

6. He sent the flowers **to his mother-in-law**.
7. She never told **us** the truth.
8. The dog bit **my friend**, but it only barked **at me**.
9. He's going to sell **his roommate** everything.
10. We're about to visit **her** right now.

12

Gustar, Hacer, Tener and *Dar*

VERBS LIKE *GUSTAR*

12.1

Spanish syntax as concerns the usage of certain verbs, among which are *gustar* and *faltar*, is very difficult for the English speaker since it is so different from the English ways of expressing the same concepts.

Me gustas (tú).	I like you.
Me faltan cinco dólares.	I need five dollars.

Other Spanish verbs resembling *gustar* and *faltar* and used in the same structures are *doler, encantar, fascinar, importar, interesar, quedar, hacerle falta a uno*, etc. For the English speaker to best perceive the syntax required for these Spanish verbs, it is helpful to think of them as corresponding to English *to be* + LV *-ing* in the third person, singular or plural. A few Spanish verbs allow English translations using a syntax more similar to the Spanish construction, i.e., *That smell bothers me = Ese olor me molesta*. Here the English direct object *me* appears as an indirect object in Spanish.

disgustar = to be disgusting, to disgust
doler = to be hurting, to hurt
encantar = to be enchanting
faltar = to be lacking, to be missing
fascinar = to be fascinating
gustar = to be pleasing
hacerle falta a uno = to be lacking, to be needing/in need of
importar = to be important

interesar = to be interesting
molestar = to bother
quedar = to be remaining, to be left over
repugnar = to be disgusting/to disgust

The following diagram shows the syntax required with these Spanish verbs. We also provide literal English paraphrases using *to be* + LV-*ing*. These paraphrases are by no means grammatical; any native English speaker would find them meaningful, but they are not normal English. .

INDIRECT OBJECT (INDIVIDUAL AFFECTED)	VERB (3rd PERS. SGL. or PL.)	SUBJECT (SINGULAR or PLURAL)
me to me	duele it is hurting/painful	**la garganta** the throat
te to you	encanta it is enchanting	**la poesía** poetry
le to him/her/you	falta it is lacking	**dinero** money
nos to us	fascinan they are fascinating	**las películas francesas** French films
les to them/you (all)	gusta it is pleasing	**la casa** the house
me to me	hace falta it is lacking	**el tiempo** the time
te to you	importan they are important	**tus amigos** your friends
le to him/her/you	interesa it is interesting	**la literatura** literature
nos to us	queda it is remaining/left	**mucho por/que hacer** a lot to do

12.2

Acceptable English renditions of the paraphrases above follow; they deviate considerably from the Spanish syntactical specifications.

Me duele la garganta.   My throat hurts.
  My throat is sore.

	I have a sore throat.
Te encanta la poesía.	You love poetry. You are enchanted by poetry. Poetry captivates you.
Le falta dinero.	He/She needs/lacks money. You need/lack money.
Nos fascinan las películas francesas.	We love French films. We are fascinated by French films.
Les gusta la casa.	They like the house. They are pleased with/by the house.
Me hace falta el tiempo.	I lack the time. I don't have the time. I need the time.
Te importan tus amigos.	Your friends matter to you. You care about your friends. Your friends are important to you.
Le interesa la literatura.	Literature interests him/her/you. He/She is interested in literature. You are interested in literature.
Nos queda mucho por hacer.	We have a lot remaining/left to do.

12.3

A comparison of these English and Spanish constructions reveals that the English subject appears as the Spanish indirect object: *I like the house* = *Me gusta la casa*. Regarding the noun phrase (*the house/la casa*), it functions in English as a direct object whereas in Spanish, it is the subject: *I like the house* = *Me gusta la casa*. Note that the Spanish verbs involved in these constructions tend to be defective, that is they occur only in certain of their possible forms. In the examples given, they appear in the third persons singular and plural, depending upon the subject, which is stated last: *Me gusta la casa/Me gustan las casas*.

If the Spanish indirect object appears as a noun, a reduplicating/redundant disjunctive prepositional object construction also occurs, as in, *A mis padres les gusta bailar* (See 11.13-14). Indirect object pronouns follow the same pattern: *A ellos les gusta bailar y a ellas, cantar; A ellos les gusta bailar, pero a ellas no*. Reduplication is used to emphasize, to contrast or to disambiguate (as in the case of third person objects):

A mí me gusta la carne asada, no los mariscos. (emphasis)
A mí me gusta la carne asada y a ti, los mariscos. (contrast)
A Reinaldo le duele la garganta, no a Pedro. (disambiguation).

A mis padres les encanta la música clásica, no a mis tíos.
Al gobierno le faltan los fondos económicos para hacerlo.
A ti y a Delia os fascinan las flores azules, no las rojas.
A mí me gusta la clase de castellano y a ti, la de matemáticas.
¿Te hace falta dinero a ti, no a tu hermano?
A Ud. le importan los problemas del mundo pero a él, no.
A nosotros nos interesan tus planes para el futuro, pero a ti no te preocupan.
Nos molesta el humo a nosotros.
A ellos/ellas/Uds. les queda una hora para terminarlo.

Exercise 1

Translate the following sentences. Show first the "deformed" English which exemplifies the normal Spanish pattern. (*He cares about money > *To him is important the money > A él le importa el dinero*)

1. We don't like cats and dogs.
2. Do they need (lack) paper?
3. I don't care what you think about me.
4. They have sore feet.
5. I have twenty dollars left.
6. Do you like my car?
7. Isn't money important to your uncle?
8. What do we need (lack) now?
9. My friend has only one cigarette left.
10. My sister has a pain in her chest.
11. My brother doesn't like Hawaii.
12. The students don't matter to the teacher.
13. My elbow hurts.
14. We still have several questions (remaining) to be answered.
15. I'm not interested in your problems.
16. He's fascinated by the physical sciences.
17. Mexican movies captivate me.
18. Contemporary world problems interest them.

HACER IN EXPRESSIONS OF TIME DURATION.

12.4

Spanish and English structures expressing time duration are very different simply because of the point of view each language takes. Spanish tends to view such expressions as having current relevance, regardless of whether the points of view are present or past *Hace mucho tiempo que trabaja para nosotros* indicates that the individual continues to work for us. English, on the other hand, views the actions as existing in a period of time stretching backwards into some earlier time, a past with current relevance. *He has been working/has worked for us for a long time* does not imply that the individual works for us anymore.

Time duration beginning in the past and continuing up until and including the present employ distinct formulae in the two languages. Spanish uses the present tense of both the main verb and the verb *hacer*; English, the present perfect *(has/have worked)* or the present perfect progressive *(has/have been working)*, of the main verb.

hace + x-TIME + **que** + V[PRES]	S + V[PRES PERF]
or	or
V[PRES] + **desde hace** + x-TIME	[PRES PERF PROG] + **for** + x-TIME
Hace dos años que ella vive aquí.	She has lived/has been living here for two years.
Ella trabaja aquí desde hace seis meses.	She has been working/has worked here for six months.

For time duration beginning sometime in the past and also ending in the past (time wholly within the past), Spanish uses the imperfect of both the main verb and the verb *hacer*; English, the pluperfect *(had worked)* or the pluperfect progressive tense *(had been working)*.

hacía + x-TIME + **que** + V[IMPERF]	S + V[PLUPERF]
or	or
V[IMPERF] + **desde hacía** + x-TIME	[PLUPERF PROG] + **for** + x-TIME
Hacía cinco años que ella vivía aquí.	She had lived/had been living here for five years.
Ella trabajaba aquí desde hacía seis meses.	She had been working/had worked here for six months.

In order to convey the concept of x-TIME *ago*, Spanish uses the present tense of *hacer* and the preterite or imperfect of the main verb. English employs the past tense in conjunction with the adverb ***ago***.

hace + x-TIME + (**que**) + V[PRET] or [IMPERF]	S + V[PAST] + x-TIME + **ago**
or	
V[PRET] or [IMPERF] + **hace** + x-TIME	
Hace dos años (que) él vivió aquí.	He lived/worked here two years ago.
Él trabajó aquí hace dos años.	
Él vivía aquí hace dos años.	

Exercise 2

Translate the following sentences and give all possible versions:

1. We've been waiting for an hour
2. Hace dos semanas (que) estaba aquí mi hermano.
3. We visited them a month ago
4. ¿Cuánto tiempo hacía que estabas deprimida?
5. We have been studying here for five hours.
6. Eloísa tocaba el piano desde hacía mucho tiempo.

7. The firemen arrived ten minutes ago.
8. Fumo desde hace dieciocho años.
9. She's had emotional problems for several years.
10. Tuve que tomar ese examen hace un mes.
11. How long have you been studying Spanish?
12. Cuando te conocí hacía un año que estudiaba español.
13. We left Chile several weeks ago.
14. No hace mucho tiempo que ella cambió su apariencia por completo.
15. She was sick because she had been drinking for a long time.
16. Mi familia emigró de Portugal hace más de cien años.
17. I had been working in Bolivia for several years.
18. Hace quince años que tu padre está en Los Ángeles.
19. That boy has been eating only pizza for a long time.
20. Llegó el paquete hace una hora.

HACER IN EXPRESSION OF WEATHER PHENOMENA

12.5

Spanish uses *hacer* while English employs *to be* to express various weather conditions. *Hacer*, however, occurs only in the third person singular, and is followed by a noun. Any quantifiers (*mucho*) are adjectives. English uses *it* + the third person singular of *to be*, followed by an adjective. Here quantifiers must be adverbs (*very*). Not all possible weather phenomena use these formulae, but those that do follow:

hacer[3rd. pers. sgl.] + (quantifier ADJ) + NOUN	**it is** + (quantifier ADV) + ADJECTIVE
hace (mucho) calor	it is (very) hot
brisa	breezy
fresco	cool
frío	cold
sol	sunny
(muy) buen/mal tiempo	(very) nice/bad weather

EXPRESSIONS USING *TENER* AND *DAR*

12.6

The Spanish verb *tener* combines with many nouns to form common expressions in the language. Many of these seem purely idiomatic, but since English uses the verb *to be* to express identical ideas, the inter-lingual structures differ sufficiently to warrant attention here. As was the case with *hacer* vs. *it* + *be* in weather expressions, any quantifiers are adjectives in Spanish, but adverbs in English, since in the former nouns occur while in the latter, adjectives.

SPANISH **tener** + NOUN	ENGLISH **be** + ADJECTIVE
ansias de + INF	anxious/nervous + INF

x años (tener 8 años)	x years old (to be 8 years old)
la bondad de	kind enough + INF
(mucho) calor	(very) hot
celos	jealous
comezón	itchy
cuidado (de + INF/con + **noun**)	careful (+ INF/of + **noun**)
frío	cold
ganas de + INF	to feel like + V-*ing*
hambre	hungry
miedo (de + INF/de, a + noun)	afraid (+ INF/of + noun)
paciencia	patient
prisa (por/para + INF)	hurried/rushed (also, in a hurry + INF)
razón	right
no … razón	wrong
sed	thirsty
sueño	sleepy
(mucha) suerte	(very) lucky
valor	brave

12.7

Like *tener*, *dar* appears with many nouns to form expressions of common usage. Spanish often combines this verb with the indirect object pronoun plus a noun to express English, *to make one feel a certain way: Eso me da calor = That makes me feel warm.* Again, quantifiers in Spanish must be adjectives, since they modify nouns (*Me da muchos celos*), while in English, they are adverbs modifying adjectives (*It makes me very jealous*).

IO + **da(n)** + NOUN	**it makes/they make** DO + ADJECTIVE
ansias*	anxious/nervous
calor	hot
celos*	jealous
escalofríos	shiver
frío	cold
ganas de + INF*	feel like + V-*ing*
gusto + INF	happy (+ INF)
(mucha) hambre	(very) hungry
miedo (de + INF)*	afraid (+ INF)
(la) razón*	right
satisfacción (de + INF)*	pleased (+ INF)
sed	thirsty
sueño	sleepy

*These verbs, in addition to appearing in third person (singular or plural) form, may take any subject: *Nos das ansias de volver, Me dan ganas de escaparme, Le di miedo de nadar en el lago, No te damos la razón.*

Exercise 3

Translate the following sentences

1. Tu perro me da miedo.
2. He was hungry when he arrived.
3. El niño le tenía miedo a su abuelo.
4. The cold makes the children hungry.
5. ¿Tiene diez años tu hermano?
6. No hace sol hoy, pero tampoco hace frío.
7. Saying that doesn't make you right.
8. I don't like it when it is hot.
9. Ella no tiene ganas de ir al cine con nosotros.
10. We're fine; we're not hot nor cold.
11. It's always good weather in California.
12. El trabajar aquí bajo el sol me da sed.
13. This book on Mexico makes me feel like visiting that country.
14. I think it is windy there.
15. Hace fresco esta mañana, pero va a hacer calor esta tarde.

13
Transitivity, Pronominal Verbs and Indefinite Subjects

TRANSITIVITY

Both languages have verbs classified as either intransitive or transitive. Intransitive verbs do not take a grammatical object while transitive ones do, and the object may be direct, indirect or both.

13.1
INTRANSITIVE VERBS

Examples of these are, *ir/to go, venir/to come, llegar/to arrive, viajar/to travel. Ser* and *estar/to be* are intransitive since with *ser/to be* + a noun (nominal) predicate, the subject and the predicate noun are the same entities. *Estar/to be* does not take a grammatical object either. Proof of the intransitivity of these verbs is apparent as follows: *You can't 'travel' someone or something; You can't 'come' someone or something,* etc. An extensive list of Spanish intransitive verbs appears in Appendix IV, B.

13.2
TRANSITIVE VERBS

Unlike intransitives, transitive verbs do take a grammatical direct object. An indirect object may also appear, but rarely alone, since the direct object is either expressed or implied. Examples follow:

Direct object, inanimate:	He cut the apple. He cut it.
	Cortó la manzana. La cortó.
Direct object, animate:	We saw our relatives. We saw them.
	Vimos a nuestros parientes. Los/Les vimos.
Direct and indirect object:	They wrote us (a letter). = They wrote (a letter) to us.
	Nos escribieron (una carta).

Exercise 1
Determine if the verb is intransitive or transitive:

1. to encourage   4. jactarse   7. to build   10. traer
2. caer   5. to teach   8. parecer   11. to feel
3. to happen   6. leer   9. to worry   12. desaparecer

SPANISH PRONOMINAL USAGES

13.3

Before presenting this topic, some explanations of the notations used are in order. The formula **S = DO** means that the subject of any given sentence and the direct object are the same entities. Likewise, **S = IO** shows that the subject and the indirect object are identical. Conversely, **S ≠ DO** and **S ≠ IO** show that the subjects and the objects (direct or indirect) are different. In any of these four cases, if the direct or indirect objects are conjunctive/(en)clitic pronouns, we have a pronominal usage. In fact, any occurrence of a conjunctive/(en)clitic pronoun with a verbal form is pronominal. (Pronominal reduplication using prepositional pronouns for purposes of clarity, emphasis or contrast is presented in Chapter 11.13-11.14).

13.4
SPANISH "TRULY" PRONOMINAL VERBS
(traditionally called "reflexive verbs")

Spanish truly pronominal verbs are distinguished from other verbs by the identifying particle –se appended to the infinite form. Some examples are *vestirse, enojarse, caerse* and *burlarse*. Most pronominal verbs have non-pronominal counterparts such as *vestir, enojar,* and *caer*. In the simplest and most general of terms, "true reflexive" pronominal verbs, because they are transitive, express that the sentence subject and object (direct or indirect) are the same entities (**S = DO or IO**), *Yo me vestí/yo me corté las uñas*. In the case of other transitive pronominal usages, the subject and the objects are different (**S ≠ DO or IO**): *Yo lo conozco/Yo le envié dinero*. Truly "reflexive" pronominal verbs are but one type of the pronominal category; there are other groups as will be seen below.

The reflexive pronouns used pronominally are in the singular, *me, te, se,* and in the plural, *nos, os, se*. As they are true conjunctive/(en)clitic pronouns, their syntactical arrangements with respect to the verb are those of the other conjunctives (See Chapter 11.4) to wit, they precede conjugated verbs and negative commands (*Me vestí, ¡no te levantes!*), follow and attach to affirmative commands (*¡Vístete!*), and precede or follow dependent infinitives (*Se va a levantar/Va a levantarse*) and dependent –*ndo* forms (*Se estaba vistiendo/Estaba vistiéndose*).

Until recently, grammarians referred to truly pronominal verbs as "reflexive verbs." The fact is that although truly reflexive verbs are pronominal, the reverse is not the case. Consequently, we have organized the Spanish true pronominals into various groups which share commonalities: 1) True reflexive verbs, 2) Inner life/change of state pronominals, 3) Pronominals and non-pronominals of motion, 4) Pronominals and non-pronominals with a significant change in meaning and 5) Exclusively pronominal verbs.

13.5
TRUE REFLEXIVE PRONOMINAL VERBS

This class of pronominals expresses that the subject and object (direct or indirect) of a sentence are identical (**S = DO or IO**). The action expressed is usually observable, and such verbs generally describe daily routines (*levantarse, acostarse, vestirse, bañarse, cepillarse los dientes, ponerse un abrigo*, etc). Non-reflexively these verbs may occur as transitives in which the subject and the object are different entities: **S ≠ DO or IO**: *Nosotros los vestimos; Yo le puse el abrigo*.

REFLEXIVE AND TRANSITIVE	**NON-REFLEXIVE AND TRANSITIVE**
Direct Object, S = DO	**Direct Object, S ≠ DO**
vestirse: (Yo) Me vestí de negro. I dressed myself (got dressed) in black.	**vestir**: (Yo) Los vestí de negro. I dressed them in black.
bañarse: No te has bañado. You haven't bathed (yourself).	**bañar**: No la has bañado. You haven't bathed her.
pesarse: Se pesan todos los días. They weigh themselves daily.	**pesar**: Nos pesan todos los días. They weigh us daily.
Indirect Object, S = IO	**Indirect Object, S ≠ IO**
cepillarse: (Yo) Me cepillo los dientes. I brush my teeth.	**cepillar**: (Yo) Le cepillo los dientes. I brush his/her teeth (for him/her.)
ponerse: Se pusieron el abrigo. They put on their (own) coats.	**poner**: Le pusieron el abrigo They put his coat on ([for] him).

cortarse:
Te has cortado el dedo.
You've cut your finger.

cortar:
Me has cortado el dedo.
You've cut my finger.

13.6
PRONOUNS USED WITH REFLEXIVE AND OTHER TRUE PRONOMINAL VERBS

If there is a one-to-one correspondence between the Spanish and English true reflexive pronoun usages, which is not always the case, the forms are as follows:

Spanish and English Forms

SINGULAR		PLURAL	
me	myself	nos	ourselves
te, se	yourself	os, se	yourselves
se	himself	se	themselves
se	herself		
se	itself		

In the first and second persons singular and plural, the Spanish reflexive object pronouns are identical to the direct and indirect object pronouns. For example, *me* can function as a direct object as in *Carlos me atacó*, as an indirect object, *Carlos me escribió una carta*, or as a reflexive object, *No me levanté muy temprano*. In the third persons singular and plural, however, the reflexive object pronoun *se* is distinct from either the third person direct or indirect object forms.

The English reflexive object pronouns are the same as those used reflexively as objects of prepositions (*He likes to talk about himself*). The forms themselves are of some interest because they are compounds, some formed with possessives (eg., *myself, yourself, herself, ourselves*) and others based upon objective pronouns (eg., *himself, themselves*). The force of analogy has produced the colloquial **hisself* and **theirselves* for the last two.

It must be pointed out that English reflexive pronouns frequently occur, not as true reflexives, but as intensifiers, emphasizing the subject of a sentence. Spanish uses inflected *mismo* (inflected) in association with the subject to the same effect.

John did it himself, *or*
John himself did it.

Juan mismo lo hizo.

I myself saw her, *or*
I saw her myself.

Yo mismo/misma la vi.

They broke it themselves, *or*
They themselves broke it.

Ellos/Ellas mismos/-as lo rompieron.

13.7
A major problem in the comparison of English and Spanish true reflexive pronominal usages is that the two languages often fail to use parallel constructions, or they may select different lexi-

cal items to express ideas which are clearly reflexive in both languages. For example, *He goes to bed* cannot be rendered in English as **He beds himself*, and *We get up* cannot be translated as **We raise ourselves*, whereas in Spanish a true reflexive pronominal construction appropriately translates the same actions, *Él se acuesta* (literally, **He beds himself*) and *Nos levantamos* (literally, **We raise ourselves*).

Occasionally we find two different but related English verbs, one transitive and the other intransitive. English uses the intransitive form where Spanish employs a true reflexive verb. We provide three pairs of often confused English verbs which routinely confound even educated native speakers. They appear with their three principal parts:

TRANSITIVE (both languages) (S ≠ DO)	English: INTRANSITIVE Spanish: TRUE REFLEXIVE (S = DO)
raise, raised, raised/levantar He raised his hand. Él levantó la mano.	*(a)rise, (a)rose, (a)risen/levantarse* He (a)rises at nine. Él se levanta a las nueve.
set, set, set/poner She set it here. Ella lo puso aquí.	*sit, sat, sat (down)/sentarse* She sat down (seated herself) here. Ella se sentó aquí.
lay, laid, laid/poner They lay their books there. Ponen sus papeles allí.	*lie, lay, lain/acostarse* They lay (down) on the couch. Se acostaron en el sofá.

13.8

Because the English/Spanish grammatical contrast is so great, we provide further discussion here concerning sentences in which the Spanish pronominal form operates as an indirect object. Thus used, it functions as the "involved entity" presented in Chapter 11.10. The Spanish structure occurs most commonly when parts of the body or possessions (eg., articles of clothing) are the topic:

SPANISH	ENGLISH
S ≠ IO, *Me cortó el pelo. (non-reflexive)*, **S = IO**, and *Me corté el pelo (reflexive)*,	He cut my hair. I cut my (own) hair. (more usually rendered as, I went to get/I got a haircut.)
In either case the structure is,	In either case the structure is,
IO + V + article + DO[noun], literally, **To me he cut the hair.* **To myself I cut the hair.*	**S + V + poss. adj. + DO[noun]**,

This contrast frequently occurs in both the spoken and written language and is a source of persistent inter-language errors. Comparative examples follow:

	SPANISH	**ENGLISH**
TRANSITIVE : (**S ≠ IO**)	Te corté el labio.	I cut your lip. (literally, *I cut the lip to/for/on you)
REFLEXIVE : (**S = IO**)	Me corté el labio.	I cut my (own) lip (literally, *I cut the lip to/for/on myself)
TRANSITIVE :	Te afeitaré la barba.	I will shave your beard.
REFLEXIVE :	Me afeitaré la barba.	I will shave my (own) beard.
TRANSITIVE :	Me quitas la corbata.	You take off my tie (for me).
REFLEXIVE :	Te quitas la corbata.	You take off your (own) tie.
TRANSITIVE :	Ella me puso el sombrero.	She put my hat on me.
REFLEXIVE :	Ella se puso el sombrero.	She put on her (own) hat.

Exercise 2

Analyze the following Spanish sentences, and rewrite each as follows:

a. Are the subject and the object the same entities (reflexive [**S = DO or IO**] or are they different entities [**S ≠ DO or IO**])? In each case, can the sentence be analyzed as having a transitive verb?
b. Do the pronominal forms serve as direct or as indirect objects?
c. Finally, rewrite each sentence changing reflexive transitives (**S = DO or IO**) to non-reflexive transitives (**S ≠ DO or IO**), and *vice versa*.

1. Nos acostamos muy temprano en el invierno.
2. ¿Cuándo se quieren levantar?
3. ¡No los despiertes!
4. A los niños, los va a sentar en otro cuarto.
5. Nos vestimos, nos pusimos el abrigo y salimos.
6. Tenemos que levantarlos una hora antes.
7. Se quebró la pierna patinando.
8. No se baña ni se afeita la barba los domingos.
9. Les vamos a preparar arroz con pollo.
10. Mi amigo anda muy ebrio y lo tengo que acostar.
11. A sus cachorros, la zorra los escondió en una cueva.
12. Beto, lávate las manos antes de pasar a la mesa.
13. El pollo mal cocido les quitó el apetito.
14. Se rompió la blusa con una navaja.
15. Quítale el abrigo, pues se ha lastimado el brazo derecho.
16. ¿No vas a secarte el pelo antes de salir?

13.9
PRONOMINAL VERBS OF "INNER LIFE" / CHANGE OF STATE
(PHYSICAL, MENTAL, EMOTIONAL or SPIRITUAL)

"Inner life" verbs are those that describe mental, emotional and even spiritual states or feelings over which we have little conscious control and which can change, sometimes slowly, but more often rapidly. Changeable physical states also fall under this category.

This large class of verbs such as *enojarse, enfermarse, alegrarse* (See Appendix IV, A2) differs from the true reflexives just presented to the extent that their semantic content as expressions of inner life issues or changes of state stems from their pronominal use, with the grammatical subjects and objects appearing as the same entities (**S** = **DO**: *(Yo=Me) enojé; (Ellos=Se) enfermaron)*. The pronominal form is a "perfectivizing particle" since the verbs depict fully completed events. Some such verbs are inceptive (inchoative), stressing the onset of the state. A relatively large proportion occur as transitives, but with the subject and object being different entities (**S** ≠ **DO**), for example, *Los aburrí = I bored them, Me asombraron = They astonished me, Los/Les hemos calmado = We've calmed them (down)*.

In some Spanish varieties, many of these verbs occur not as true transitive expressions (**S** ≠ **DO**) [eg., *Los enojé (I angered them), La enfermaron (They made her sick/ill), Nos has alegrado (You've made us happy)*] buy as a periphrasis: *Los hice enojar, La hicieron enfermar, Nos hicieron alegrar*. English usually expresses the change of state concept with the verbs, *to get* or *to become* + adjective, i.e., *enojarse = to get angry, enfermarse = to get sick/to become ill, alegrarse = to become happy/glad, to rejoice*. Some inner life Spanish verbs occur in English as true reflexives (eg., *portarse = to conduct oneself, ajustarse = to adjust/adapt oneself, divertirse = to amuse/enjoy oneself/[have a good time]).*

Exercise 3
Translate the following sentences:

1. No nos acordamos del evento que has mencionado.
2. We felt very happy yesterday. (*sentirse*)
3. Se asustó al encontrarse perdida in el bosque.
4. Don't get angry! (*enojarse*)
5. Sus hijos no se comportan nada bien.
6. How does he feel? (*sentirse*)
7. Te has equivocado mucho en tu último examen de álgebra.
8. My mother is getting tired. (*cansarse*)
9. Nos exasperamos con la demora del vuelo a Buenos Aires.
10. I know I'm going to get bored in Nicaragua. (*aburrirse*)
11. Siempre me mareaba al tomar más de una bebida.
12. The child gets very excited and won't be quiet. (*emocionarse/callarse*)
13. Los padres siempre se preocupan por sus hijos.
14. They couldn't calm down after the accident. (*tranquilizarse*)
15. Anímate, que no es para tanto.
16. I don't want to get sick in Paraguay. (*enfermarse*)

17. Va a mejorarse con una medicina tradicional.
18. We got annoyed because she didn't write to us. (*enfadarse*)
19. Nos contentamos de comer solo en los restaurants étnicos.
20. He doesn't think he'll have fun in the mountains. (*divertirse*)

13.10
PRONOMINAL AND NON-PRONOMINAL VERBS OF MOTION

This class of verbs has such oppositions as, 1) transitive (**S ≠ DO**) vs. reflexive (**S = DO**), and 2) intransitive vs. reflexive (No object vs. reflexive pronoun used as an intensifier). These are listed and divided into two groups, as above, in Appendix V, A3(a-b).

Some comparative examples of the first type are:

S ≠ DO	**S = DO**
instalar "to install something"	instalarse "to move into someplace"
Instalaron el nuevo lavaplatos	Se instaló en un buen hotel
pasear "to walk [the dog]"	pasearse "to take a walk/stroll"
No me gusta pasear al perro.	Me paseé por el Río Americano.
dirigir "to direct"	dirigirse a "to head toward, to address"
Ese chico dirige la banda.	Me dirijo al correo
	Se va a dirigir al sindicato laboral.

The second group of these verbs of motion seems more problematic. Such oppositions as *ir/irse, venir/venirse, entrar/entrarse,* and *salir/salirse* are difficult to explain to the English speaker. *Ir/Irse* are distinguished in most varieties of Spanish as *to go* (with a goal in mind) vs. *to go away* (no specific goal), as in *¡vete!* As for the other verbs of motion above, and only in some Spanish varieties, one often hears such usages as *¡vente!* or *Se está saliendo el caballo.* Yet educated native speakers who utter such sentences will deny that the pronominal infinitive even exists. Since in terms of lexical aspect these verbs are punctual, the reflexive usage seems to introduce a particle with a perfectivizing effect.

Exercise 4.
Translate the following sentences:

1. He approached the house with extreme care. (*acercarse*)
2. Súbeme la guía telefónica, pues no hay en este piso.
3. She got off the bus on 20th Street. (*bajarse*)
4. Me metí en una calle en contra del tránsito.
5. They stood up and began shouting. (*pararse*)
6. Nos vamos a Costa Rica en el invierno.
7. Will you help us move it? (*mover*)

8. Tiene que irse, ya que lo está buscando la policía.
9. Don't move when you feel the change in pressure. (*moverse*)
10. Subámonos a ese árbol para ver mejor el desfile.

13.11
VERBS USED PRONOMINALLY AND NON-PRONOMINALLY WITH SIGNIFICANT CHANGES IN MEANING

Some Spanish verbs occur non-pronominally with one meaning and pronominally with another. Often the meaning change is very slight between one and the other usage, but with these verbs, the difference in meaning can be significant for the English speaker. Since the listing below is fairly complete, it will not appear in Appendix IV.

NON-PRONOMINAL	**PRONOMINAL**
caer = fall	caerse = fall (down)
Las hojas caen en el otoño.	Cuidado, que no te caigas.
casar = to marry one to another	casarse = to get married.
El cura los casó en Antigua.	Se casaron en una ceremonia civil.
comer = eat	comerse = eat up, skip over, omit
Hay que comer para vivir.	Él se comió una pera.
	El orador se comió palabras.
contentar = satisfy	contentarse = make up
Hay que contentar a los demás.	Se contentaron por fin los novios.
decidir = decide	decidirse = make up one's mind
Lo decidieron por votación.	No puedo decidirme entre tantos.
despedir = fire (an employee)	despedirse de = say good-bye/take one's leave
Tuvimos que despedir al portero.	Se van a despedir por última vez.
dormir = sleep	dormirse = go to sleep, fall asleep
El niño duerme en el piso.	No pude dormirme anoche.
fijar = fasten, fix	fijarse = pay attention, notice
Fija bien el eje a la sierra.	Fíjate bien en lo que te dicen.
llamar = to call	llamarse = to be called/named
Llamo a menudo a mi hermana.	Se llama José, pero su apodo es Pepe.
llevar = carry, manage	llevarse = take away, carry off, get along with

Él lleva encima una pistola.   El personal técnico se llevó el cadáver.
Ella lleva las cuentas del casino.   Me llevo bien con mis suegros.

morir = to die   morirse de = to die
Murió en una batalla.   Se murió de un ataque cardíaco.

negar = deny   negarse a = refuse (to do something)
Niega que su hijo sea ladrón.   Se negaron a asistir a la reunión.

ocupar = occupy   ocuparse con/de = to be/stay busy
Los Nazis ocuparon Grecia.   Se ocupa con las tareas de la casa.

parecer = seem   parecerse = resemble, look like
Parece que va a llover.   Te pareces a tu hermana.

poner = put   ponerse = put on, become
Voy a poner la figura ahí.   Me puse el traje. Se puso enferma.
    ponerse a + INF = begin, start
    Se puso a llorar.

probar = try/taste   probarse = try on (clothes)
Prueba la sopa; te va a gustar.   Se probó unos guantes de cuero.

resolver = solver   resolverse a = to decide to do something
Nunca resolvieron el problema.   Nos resolvimos a vender la casa.

> **Note:** To the previous listing might be added such oppositions as *aprender/aprenderse, saber/saberse, leer/leerse* and some others in which the pronominal usage seems to express perfection, with the meaning of *to learn, know, read thoroughly*.

Exercise 5

Translate the following English sentences:

1. I can't study because someone took away my books.
2. He can't make up his mind whether he can do it or not.
3. The children fell asleep in the living room.
4. They slept there all night.
5. I tried on a fur overcoat, but it was too heavy.
6. He resembles his father.
7. I don't want to eat that sandwich.
8. Don't put your feet on the table.
9. When I started (ponerse) to sing, everyone fell asleep.
10. He seemed to be sick before he fell down.
11. Pay careful attention (fijarse) to what I'm going to explain.
12. The law doesn't tolerate our carrying guns.
13. He made up his mind to lose weight.

14. They got married in April.
15. They fired him for drinking on the job.
16. Gravity makes both light and heavy things fall.

13.12
EXCLUSIVELY PRONOMINAL VERBS

See the listing in Appendix IV, A4 and complete Exercise 6 below.

Exercise 6

1. He remembered (brought to mind) the name of his first cat.
2. Religious fanatics believe that everyone needs to repent.
3. We dared to talk to our professor about our grades.
4. The boys were making fun of (poking fun at) the little girl.
5. They realized that they were in a dangerous situation.
6. She fainted because she had forgotten to take her medicine.
7. He fell in love with a gipsy girl from Romania.
8. I can't trust my thoughts.
9. The octopus can change its colors to avoid predators.
10. My grandparents complain about the musical tastes of their grand kids.
11. The students laughed at the professor's jokes.
12. Many religions teach that it is a sin to commit suicide.

13.13
RECIPROCAL ACTIONS

A reciprocal action is one in which at least two animate beings do the same thing to each other. Since all reciprocal actions involve two or more agents, the subject and its verb must be plural in both languages. Below are the reciprocal action formulas.

ENGLISH	SPANISH
S[plural] + V[plural] + each other/one another	(S)[plural] + PRON[reflexive] + V[plural] + clarifiers (if any)

They saw one another.	Ellos se vieron.
We greeted each other.	Nos saludamos.
The boys hit one another.	Los muchachos se golpearon.
They will kill each other.	Ellos se van a matar.

Spanish clarifies by gender and number who the participants are in a reciprocal action, tagging the constructions with such phrases as *unos a otros, el uno al otro, la una a la otra*, etc. English uses *each/one another*.

Ellos se dieron golpes unos a otros.   They hit each/one another.
Los muchachos se fiaron el un en el otro. The boys trusted each/one another.
Las mujeres se saludaron la una a la otra. The women greeted each/one another.

Note that Spanish reciprocal constructions, if not accompanied by their tags, are often ambiguous in meaning. A reciprocal usage could, without a meaningful context or a clarifying tag, have true reflexive meaning.

Ellos se vieron (en el mercado).   They saw each other... (reciprocal)
Ellos se vieron (como la gran garza).   They saw themselves... (reflexive)

Nos peinamos (para las fiestas formales). We do each other's hair... (reciprocal)
Nos peinamos (al levantarnos).   We comb our (own) hair...(reflexive)

Exercise 7

Translate the following sentences:

1. We greeted each other before the contest.
2. Los recién casados se aman muchísimo.
3. We didn't see one another in Panama.
4. Se besaron antes de despedirse.
5. They hated each other so much that they tried to kill one another.
6. Los perros comenzaron a ladrar cuando se vieron.

SENTENCES WITH INDEFINITE SUBJECTS

13.14

Both Spanish and English have ways of expressing ideas impersonally, that is, saying that an action affects everyone in general, not just me, you (to whom I am speaking), us or them (people we can identify). The subjects of such impersonal sentences are indefinite subjects.

English Indefinite Subjects

English uses the impersonal *you* (unstressed) or *one* as indefinite subjects.
The latter is the more formal option.

You forgive and forget.
One forgives and forgets.

You shouldn't cover that.
One shouldn't cover that.

You advance quickly at this institute.
One advances quickly at this institute.

You work hard, and what happens? You don't make enough money.
One works hard, and what happens? One doesn't make enough money.

Spanish Indefinite Subjects

Spanish uses the impersonal subject *se* (not to be confused with the reflexive *se*) or the indefinite subject *uno/-a* with the third person singular form of the verb. *Usted* also appears in such sentences, but with impersonal or indefinite force.

> **Note:** There is also the impersonal *ellos*: *Le dieron un aumento de sueldo.* Also the locution *hay que* + INF translates with an indefinite English subject: *Hay que perdonar y olvidar.* = One must forgive and forget; *No hay que cubrir eso* = You (impersonal) need not cover that.

Se perdona y se olvida.
Uno perdona y uno olvida.
Usted perdona y olvida.

No se debe cubrir eso.
Uno no debe cubrir eso.
Usted no debe cubrir eso.

Se avanza rápidamente en este instituto.
Uno avanza rápidamente en este instituto.
Usted avanza rápidamente en este instituto.
Avanzan rápidamente en este instituto.

Se trabaja duro y ¿qué pasa? Nunca se gana suficiente dinero.
Uno trabaja duro y ¿qué pasa? Uno nunca gana suficiente dinero.
Usted trabaja duro y ¿qué pasa? Nunca gana suficiente dinero.

13.15

A syntactic peculiarity of impersonal *se* is worth noting: When *se* is used as an impersonal subject, it assumes the position of a conjunctive ([en]clitic) pronoun, that is, it appears with the verb. In the first sentence of the second group above, if the subject were *él*, the sentence would be, *Él no debe cubrir eso. Él*, a subject pronoun, is a disjunctive pronoun, and *no* displaces it from the verb. *Se*, however, although it has the meaning of a subject, functions as a true conjunctive pronoun since in *No se debe cubrir eso*, *se* displaces the negative *no* from the verb.

13.16
APPARENTLY CAUSELESS EVENTS

Closely related to sentences with indefinite subjects are those which express actions as taking place in and of themselves with no apparent or explicitly expressed causative agent. Note the following English sentences expressing actions that have no apparent cause.

a. The fire didn't go out.
b. The train stopped.
c. The chant ended.
d. The door didn't open.
e. The windows got broken.
f. The meeting got organized.

Unlike English, Spanish does not show such actions as occurring in and of themselves. Instead, it conveys the apparently causeless English actions with a pronominal construction. English speakers find the Spanish rendition logical when animate beings are involved.

Ella se levantó.	(She got up, i.e., She raised herself.)
Él se acostó.	(He went to bed, i.e., *He bedded himself.)
El pájaro se bañó.	(The bird bathed itself.)

However, the English speaker may be baffled by the following sentences involving inanimate beings (things). Here, Spanish expresses the six English sentences (a) to (f) above with reflexive *se* as if the non-living entities were doing things to themselves.

a. No se apagó el fuego.
b. Se paró el tren.
c. Se acabó el canto.
d. No se abrió la puerta.
e. Se rompieron los cristales.
f. Se organizó la reunión.

Spanish uses the following formula to convey ideas where events seem to occur in and of themselves.

(S) + *se* + V [3rd pers. sgl. or pl.] + (S)

| El juego se terminó. | or | Se terminó el juego. |
| Los juegos se terminaron. | or | Se terminaron los juegos. |

Whichever version is chosen, the element expressed last is emphasized over the other sentence components because it is the new information:

-- ¿Qué pasó?
　-- El juego **se terminó**.

--¿Qué se terminó?
　-- (Se terminó) **el juego**.

13.17
UNPLANNED OR UNEXPECTED OCCURRENCES, SOMETIMES CALLED "NO-FAULT *SE*"

Spanish uses a special construction to convey the idea that someone is affected by an unplanned or an unexpected occurrence. The construction seems to remove the blame for the event from the person affected and to place it upon the thing involved. The structure occurs mostly with Spanish verbs like *escaparse (=escapársele a uno), morirse, ocurrirse, olvidarse,* and *romperse*, although other verbs employ the construction as well. The indirect object in such sentences is the "involved (affected) entity" explained in Chapter 11.10.

Chapter 13 Transitivity, Pronominal Verbs and Indefinite Subjects

Here is the Spanish formula for unplanned or unexpected occurrences.

se + IO + V[3rd pers. sgl. or pl.] + (S) [sing. or pl.]

Se me olvidó la foto.   Se me olvidaron las fotos.
   [literally: *to me it (they) forgot itself (themselves) the photo(s).]

Se te rompió una pieza del auto.   Se te rompieron unas piezas del auto.
¿Se le escapó el caballo?   ¿Se le escaparon los caballos?
¿Se nos murió la planta?   ¿Se nos murieron las plantas?
Se les ocurrió una idea.   Se les ocurrieron unas ideas.
Se me durmió el niño.   Se me durmieron los niños.

English expresses unplanned or unexpected occurrences with the following formula:

S + V + DO (or PREP OBJECT)

I forgot the picture.   I forgot the pictures.
You broke a part of the car.   You broke some parts of the car.
Did the horse escape from/on him?   Did the horses escape from/on him?
Did our plant die (on us)?   Did our plants die (on us)?
An idea occurred to them.   Some ideas occurred to them.
The kid went to sleep (on me).   The kids went to sleep (on me).

Exercise 8
Translate the following sentences and give all possible versions:

1. One can see my house from here.
2. Se acabó toda su angustia.
3. The children escaped from me.
4. De repente se detuvo la batalla.
5. You don't do that in my house.
6. ¿Cuándo se te rompió el paraguas?
7. A fantastic idea occurred to us last night.
8. Se nos murió el abuelo ese mismo año.
9. The class got organized very early.
10. No se aprende nada en este colegio.
11. He forgot to buy the soda.
12. Todas las luces se apagaron después de la catástrofe.
13. One has to think about money these days.
14. Se nos rompieron las cosas que habíamos comprado.
15. You can't concentrate with so much noise.
16. Se está muy bien aquí a la sombra de los árboles
17. The shutters opened and the doors closed in the wind.
18. A los soldados se les escapó el cabo.

19. One shouldn't drink the water in Malaga.
20. No se fuma durante la función.

14

The English and Spanish Imperative Systems

14.1

Both English and Spanish have ways of giving both direct and softened (attenuated) affirmative and negative commands. The major contrast between the two languages in this regard derives from the fact that English has only one pronoun for the addressee(s): *you* (singular and plural), while Spanish has four: two familiar, *tú* and *vosotros/-as* and two formal, *usted* and *ustedes*.

In addition to its direct commands, both affirmative and negative, English has a variety of other command structures used to soften or attenuate otherwise overly direct or brusque imperatives. Object(ive) pronouns always follow the English verbal form. Spanish, on the other hand, has specialized imperative forms for each of its four forms of address as well as polite or softened commands. Spanish further carries the notion of softening or attenuation into the making of requests, suggestions and criticisms. It places conjunctive pronouns after the verbal form only in affirmative commands. Unlike English, it positions such pronouns before the command form in negative commands.

14.2

The **English affirmative command** structure has two forms: the direct command and the less direct, more attenuated or polite command. The base form of the English lexical verb occurs for direct, affirmative commands:

Go! Come! Look! Study!
Work harder! Try it again! Eat all of it! Be here tomorrow!

The modals *can/could* and *will/would* appear periphrastically with *you,* along with optional *please,* to make these direct imperatives more polite. Since it assumes interrogative form, this structure requires a question mark in writing.

can/could/will/would + you + (please) + LV?

Can you (please) look?
Could you (please) come?
Will you (please) bring them?
Would you (please) eat?

14.3

The **English negative command** structure, like the affirmative one, takes two forms: a direct command and an attenuated one. The negative direct command uses AUX-*do* with an optionally-contracted negative marker (shown with *), and the lexical verb. As always, a object(ive) pronoun or any other complement follows the verb.

AUX-do* + not + LV

Don't go! Don't come! Don't look at me! Do not enter!
Don't work too hard! Don't eat it! Do not try that again!

A less direct and more polite negative command uses the modals *can, could, will* and *would* with *not.* Optionally, adding *please* will further soften the command. An object(ive) pronoun or other complement follows the verb, and a question mark ends the written sentence. We present more about indirect commands and attenuation later in this chapter.

MODAL AUX-*can/could/will/would* + you + (please) + not + LV?

Can you (please) not look?
Could you (please) not come?
Will you (please) not be here tomorrow?
Would you (please) not eat all of it?

Object(ive) pronouns, both direct and indirect, always follow English commands whether direct or softened.

Eat it!
Don't write to him!
Will you please bring them?
Would you please not give it to her?

> **Note:** As American culture becomes increasingly less authoritarian, other periphrases have appeared to replace preemptive, direct commands, for example, Affirmative: *Control your anger!* > *You need to control your anger*; Negative: *Don't do that!* > *You don't want to do that/Don't be doing that.*

14.4

The Spanish imperative system, like English, can form a less direct, attenuated or polite command equivalent to the English paraphrases, as follows: 1) *hacer el favor de* (no) + INF, 2) *ser tan amable de (no)* + INF or 3) *Tener la bondad de (no)* + INF.

¡Haz el favor de (no) entrar!
¡Sea tan amable de (no) decírmelo!
¡Tenga la bondad de (no) fumar!

> **Note:** *Hacer el favor de* + INF is in some dialects is reduced to, *Favor de (no)* + INF, a usage many speakers find outlandish. It does, however, appear on signs: *Favor de no fumar*.
>
> **Also used are** ¿*querer* + INF? or ¿*no querer* + INF?
>
> ¿Quieres entrar?   ¿No quieres entrar?
> ¿Queréis decírmelo?   ¿No queréis decírmelo?
> ¿Quiere(n) venir?   ¿No quiere(n) venir?
>
> But, according to Koike's (1995) pragmatic analysis of suggestions, the negative form communicates a suggestion; without negation, the speaker is asking only for information answerable with a simple *yes* or *no*.

Exercise 1

Translate the following. The level of formality and the elements of the structure appear in parentheses.

1. Could you please bring some friends? (plural familiar: *Tener la bondad*)
2. ¡Haz el favor de no actuar de esa manera! (*will/would*)
3. Will you please say something? (singular formal: *querer*)
4. ¿Quiere traer aquí la silla? (*can/could*)
5. Can you stop for a moment? (plural formal: *hacer el favor*)
6. Hagan el favor de adoptar la otra resolución. (*can/will*)
7. Would you not do that again? (singular familiar.(*ser tan amable*)
8. Por favor, ¿no quieres abrir la ventana? (*will*, negative)

14.5

Peripherally related to the Spanish attenuated commands is its system for making softened requests and criticisms. The verbs most typically involved are *querer, deber* and *poder*. With these verbs attenuation takes place by shifting tenses from the present indicative to the imperfect indicative, the conditional or the past subjunctive in *–ra*, all of which belong to the past tense family of verbs. Any subject is possible.

querer
¿Quieres irte?   Will you leave?

Attenuated:
¿Querías irte?   Can/Could/Will/Would you (please) leave?

¿Querrías irte?
¿Quisieras irte?

deber
No debemos hacerlo.   We must not do it.

Attenuated:
No debíamos (de) hacerlo.   We (really) shouldn't do it.
No deberíamos (de) hacerlo.
No debiéramos (de) hacerlo

poder
Podéis decir más.   You can (are expected to) say more.

Attenuated:
Podíais decir más.   You could say more.
Podríais decir más.
Pudierais decir más.

> **Note:** Most of the expressions just listed use verbal forms taken from the past tense family of verbs, but their reference is to the present. Both languages employ this so-called "step into the past" to produce an affective notion of politeness. When in Spanish one is ready for dessert at a restaurant, the server will approach saying, "¿Qué <u>deseaba</u> Usted de postre?", using the imperfect with reference to the present, for courtesy's sake. In English, when a salesperson approaches a confused customer, his/her question might be, "What <u>were</u> you looking for, sir/ma'am?" Were (past) is more polite than are (present) in this context.

Exercise 2
Give all possible Spanish renditions as indicated:

1. You could call a friend. (2 ways)
2. You can (and are expected to) do better on my examinations.
3. We would like to visit you.
4. Manuel shouldn't spend so much time there. (2 ways)
5. You must not send him the money.
6. They should buy a new car. (2 ways)
7. One must come to work on time daily.
8. Your pronunciation could be better. (2 ways)
9. I would like to write to your sister.
10. We could visit her in the hospital. (2 ways)

14.6

The Spanish direct commands are all forms of the present subjunctive with the exceptions of *tú* and *vosotros/-as* in the affirmative. The normal form for **the *tú* affirmative direct command** is the same as the **third person singular present indicative** of the verb.

Chapter 14 The English and Spanish Imperative Systems

¡Habla! ¡Come! ¡Vive!

There are, however, eight exceptions:

decir > di	salir > sal
hacer > haz	ser > sé
ir > ve	tener > ten
poner > pon	venir > ven

The form of **the negative *tú* command** uses the **second person singular present subjunctive** preceded by *no*. There are no exceptions.

¡No hables! ¡No comas! ¡No digas!
¡No vengas! ¡No vayas! ¡No seas conforme!

The form of **the affirmative *vosotros/-as* command is the infinitive form of the verb with a *-d* replacing the infinitive marker, *-r*.** There are no exceptions.

¡Hablad! ¡Comed! ¡Vivid! ¡Id! ¡Tened cuidado!

Note that the -d- is dropped with all reflexive verbs except *irse*: ¡Levantaos!, ¡Acostaos!, but ¡Idos! The loss of –d- in reflexive *vosotros* commands distinguishes the imperative from the plural past participles, *levantados* and *acostados*. Reflexive *vosotros* commands often appear as the infinitive + *os* (*sentaros, levantaros*) in colloquial usage in Spain.

The *vosotros/as* negative forms are the **second person plural present subjunctive** preceded by *no*. Here again, there are no exceptions.

¡No habléis! ¡No comáis! ¡No viváis!
¡No vayáis! ¡No vengáis! ¡No digáis!

The **formal *usted/ustedes* affirmative form** for direct commands is the **third person singular or plural of the present subjunctive**. There are no exceptions.

¡Hable! ¡Coman! ¡Viva feliz! ¡Sean prudentes! ¡Tenga cuidado!

The **negative form of the formal command (*usted/ustedes*)** is **the affirmative form**, only preceded by *no*.

¡No hablen! ¡No coma! ¡No me digan! ¡No sean tontos!

With respect to the Spanish formal direct commands, speakers routinely add *usted /ustedes* after the command form for additional politeness.

¡Venga usted!   ¡No salgan ustedes!

14.7

We review as follows the position of the Spanish conjunctive pronouns with respect to the direct command forms, either familiar or formal. (See 11.4)

- For any affirmative direct command, the pronouns follow and attach to the command form. When both pronouns occur, the order IO + DO is also attached after the verb.

	IO or DO	**IO+DO**	**Reflexive**
tú :	¡Háblame! ¡Cómelo!	¡Escríbeselo!	¡Báñate!
vosotros/-as:	¡Habladme! ¡Comedlo!	¡Escribídselo!	¡Bañaos!
usted:	¡Hábleme! ¡Cómalo!	¡Escríbaselo!	¡Báñese!
ustedes :	¡Háblenme! ¡Cómanlo!	¡Escríbanselo!	¡Báñense!

- For any negative direct command, the pronouns directly precede the verbal form, again in the order IO + DO, if both pronouns occur.

	IO or DO	**IO+DO**	**Reflexive**
tú:	¡No me hables! ¡No lo comas!	¡No se lo escribas!	¡No te bañes!
vosotras :	¡No me habléis! ¡No lo comáis!	¡No se lo escribáis!	¡No os bañéis!
usted :	¡No me hable! ¡No lo coma!	¡No se lo escriba!	¡No se bañe!
ustedes :	¡No me hablen! ¡No lo coman!	¡No se lo escriban!	¡No se bañen!

Exercise 3

After determining whether the Spanish commands given are *tú*, *vosotros/-as*, *usted* or *ustedes*, give the English direct command equivalents.

1. ¡No me lo diga!
2. ¡Háganselo inmediatamente!
3. ¡Tráiganosla en seguida!
4. ¡No lo abandonéis!
5. ¡Confírmelo pronto!
6. ¡Leedla de todos modos para mañana!
7. ¡Póngalo aquí en el comedor!
8. ¡Mándaselas aparte!
9. ¡Prepáramelos solamente para la fiesta!
10. ¡No me lo digas en ese tono de voz!

Exercise 4

Give Spanish direct command forms for the following infinitive constructions. The type of command, affirmative or negative, and the subjects *tú, vosotros/-as, usted* and *ustedes* are all indicated in parentheses.

1. dármelo (*vosotros/-as*, afirmativo)
2. decirle (*tú*, negativo)
3. estudiarlo (*usted*, afirmativo)
4. tenerlos (*tú*, afirmativo)
5. reunirlas (*ustedes*, negativo)
6. devolvérmela (*vosotros/-as*, negativo)
7. escribirle (*ustedes*, negative)
8. cargársela (*tú*, afirmativo)
9. ponerlo (*vosotros/-as*, negative)
10. explicármela (*ustedes*, afirmativo)
11. cantársela (*usted*, afirmativo)
12. decirlo (*tú*, afirmativo)
13. hacerlo (*usted*, negativo)
14. proponérsela (*tú*, afirmativo)

14.8

The English indirect command system uses the hortative auxiliaries *let/have* for third persons and *let us/let's* in the first person plural to form affirmative suggestions. Hortative is a grammatical term derived from Greek designating expressions calling individuals to action.

Let/Have + DO₁ + LV + DO₂ / *to* or *for* IO

Let/Have him do it!
Let/Her speak to him!
Let/Have your son bring it!
Let's visit your family!
Let/Have them eat cake!

Modern colloquial English has no regular system for converting an affirmative indirect command into a negative one. Note that if the affirmative command, *Let/Have him do it* is made negative, *Don't let him do it*, there is a change of meaning equivalent to *Don't permit him to do it*. This in Spanish would be *No le permitas hacerlo* or *No permitas que lo haga*. When the English subject is *we*, then English can directly change the indirect affirmative command into a negative version.

Let's go home. > Let's not go home.

For the other subjects, the best negative version English can provide uses the modal *may*, and the expression seems rhetorical, poetic, or even archaic.

***may* + S + *not/never* + LV**

May you never speak to her again.
May he always be young.
May it not keep you from leaving.

In chapter 8.23, *haber de* + *INF* = *to be* +*INF* were shown to express mild obligation similar to complying with an already scheduled event: *No te olvides de que esta noche hemos de cenar con los Dávila.* = *Don't forget that we're to have dinner with the Davila's this evening.* English also renders something akin to a direct command with its formula. A stern tone of voice accompanies the oral rendition.

| You're to sit down and shut up! | ¡Siéntate y cállate! |
| You're not to go out with that boy! | ¡No salgas con ese chico! |

For third persons, Spanish might use, *Que + present subjunctive*, as explained in the following paragraph.

| He's to be home by noon! | ¡Que esté en casa para mediodía! |
| They're not to leave their rooms! | ¡Que no salgan de sus cuartos! |

14.9

Spanish affirmative indirect commands use the present subjunctive, as was the case with most direct commands. Note, however, that the first-person plural has a different syntactic ordering for indirect commands and an alternate expression using the present indicative.

que + IO/DO +V[PRES SUBJ] + (S)

(for *nosotros/-as*) V[PRES SUBJ] + IO/DO, **or** *vamos a* + INF + IO/DO

él/Ariel	Que lo haga él/Ariel.
ella/Ana	Que lo haga ella/Ana.
ellos/ellas/noun (pl.)	Que lo hagan ellos/-as /los muchachos.
nosotros/-as	Hagámoslo or Vamos a hacerlo.

> **Note:** If a reflexive pronoun appears with the one-word option, the final *–s* of the verb is dropped: **Hagámosnos > Hagámonos*, as in *Hagámonos las disimuladas* = *Let's pretend not to notice.*

The negative indirect command uses the formula:

que + no + IO/DO + V[PRES SUBJ] + (S)

(for *nosotros/-as*) **no + IO/DO + V[PRES SUBJ]**

> **Note:** *No vamos a* + INF is not possible as a negative indirect command; Its meaning is *We're not going* + INF, grammatically a periphrastic future construction.

él/Ariel	Que no lo haga él/Ariel.
ella/Ana	Que no lo haga ella/Ana.
ellos/ellas/noun (pl.)	Que no lo hagan ellos/-as/las muchachas.
nosotros/-as	No lo hagamos.

Exercise 5

Translate the following indirect commands:

1. Let/Have them read it tomorrow!
2. ¡Que me lo diga mi padre!
3. Let's go to the movies!
4. ¡Que me lo preste Felícita!
5. Let/Have them bring it to us!
6. ¡No les escribamos!
7. Let's not give it to her.
8. ¡Vamos a decírselo!
9. Let/Have him send it!
10. ¡Que nos lo explique el oficial de policía!

15

The Present Participle (Gerund) and the Infinitive

15.1
THE PRESENT PARTICIPLE

The present progressive tenses in English and Spanish, although formed in corresponding ways (AUX-*be* + LV-*ing* / AUX-*estar* + LV-*ndo*), differ considerably in their usages. Spanish uses the present progressive to refer only to the moment of speech, while English, in addition to employing it for that purpose, also uses it to express future time. English also uses the simple present, the future or the future progressive to render the future. Compare these contrastive examples.

REFERENCE TO THE MOMENT OF SPEECH	REFERENCE TO THE MOMENT OF SPEECH AS WELL AS THE FUTURE
Estamos trabajando (ahora).	We are working (now). (present) We are working (= will work) tonight. (future)
Están comiendo (ahora).	They are eating (now). (present) They are eating (later) in that restaurant. (future)
¿Estás viviendo aquí (ahora)?	Are you living here (now)? (present) Are you living/Will you be living here next semester? (future)

Ella está hablando (ahora).	She is speaking (now). (present)
	She is speaking/will speak at a conference next month. (future)
No estoy leyendo nada (ahora).	I'm not reading anything (now). (present)
	I am not reading/won't be reading anything during my vacation. (future)

Spanish uses the present participles of the verb *ir* and *venir* in their progressive tenses, including the present progressive, only under limited conditions. For example, *¿Cómo te está yendo?* appears in colloquial usage. In translating the English progressives, *I'm going/coming*, Spanish uses the simple present indicative tense *Voy/Vengo* in their place*. If the English progressive construction has future reference, then Spanish selects from one of three options: (1) the simple present indicative with an adverb of futurity, *Voy/Vengo la semana próxima*, (2) the synthetic future tense, *Iré/Vendré* or, (3) the periphrastic future, *Voy a ir/ Voy a venir*.

> * **Note:** *Ir* and *venir* function differently from English *to go* and *to come*. Spanish uses both from the subject's viewpoint. When someone is called to the phone, Spanish says, *Ya voy*, English renders this as *I'm coming*. Spanish says *No olvides que voy a tu casa a estudiar*. English uses, *Don't forget, I'm coming over to your house to study*.

As noted above, the limited use of Spanish verbs *ir* and *venir* in the progressive tense does not exclude them from serving as auxiliaries in progressive constructions. Examples include *Voy hablando mejor* and *Vengo trayendo libros*. Several other verbs also occur as auxiliaries in progressive constructions, among them *andar* and *seguir*: *Ando trabajando mucho* and *Sigo estudiando idiomas*. (See Chapter 3.5) The present participle can also have an adverbial function as in, *Salió cantando y volvió silbando*.

Exercise 1

Translate the following English sentences. Provide all possible versions for each:

1. He is working in the factory now.
2. Are they having dinner with us tomorrow?
3. Where is she studying next semester?
4. They are coming to my house tomorrow night.
5. Is anyone looking at us right now?
6. What is she doing tomorrow morning?
7. Who(m) are you bringing to my party Saturday night?
8. Are their parents living in New York?
9. When are the students leaving for Peru?
10. What is he doing with the computer?
11. Where are we going after the game?
12. What language are they writing?
13. Is that man speaking Spanish or English?
14. If it's agreeable to you, I'm using your car tonight.
15. He's studying for an exam now.
16. She's not going to class today.

15.2
THE SPANISH INFINITIVE VS. THE ENGLISH PRESENT PARTICIPLE

After prepositions, Spanish consistently uses the infinitive while English uses the present participle. This contrast is very difficult for both the English speaker and the Spanish speaker to master in the target language.

¿Adónde vas después de comer?	Where are you going after eating?
Ella salió sin explicar sus motivos.	She left without explaining her motives.
Tomo leche antes de acostarme.	I drink milk before going to bed.
Sirve para tratar metal.	It's for treating metal.

The expression *al* + INF is equivalent to English *upon* + LV-*ing*.

Al abrir la puerta, lo oí todo.	Upon opening the door, I heard everything.
Al salir, vi a mi amiga.	Upon leaving, I saw my friend.
Siempre me salían las lágrimas al pensar en ello.	I always shed tears upon thinking about it.

Exercise 2

Translate the following sentences:

1. I never go there without buying something.
2. Upon entering, I saw that there was no one there.
3. After seeing her, he realized that she was his sister.
4. One needs a key for opening that safe.
5. You deserve that for being so stupid.
6. What did you see upon opening the window?
7. I dreamed about being a famous athlete.
8. She always worries about gaining weight.
9. Before buying it, we should have examined it.
10. I want to work instead of studying mathematics.
11. I didn't count on losing so much money.
12. He'll never learn to speak Spanish without studying more.

Exercise 3

Translate the following sentences:

1. ¿Qué vas a hacer después de terminar tus estudios?
2. Al verla, me escondí debajo de la escalera.
3. No sé qué van a hacer al recibir las noticias.
4. Para ser tan pequeño, tu hermano tiene mucha fuerza.
5. Me preocupa morir de cáncer; por eso voy a dejar de fumar.
6. Pensamos abrir una tienda con las últimas novedades en artículos de vestir.
7. ¿Qué definición puedo usar para explicar ese término literario?

8. No quiero llegar a la fiesta sin llevar algo nuevo.
9. No vas a creer lo que oí al escuchar su interpretación del suceso.
10. Debes buscar un plan determinado en vez de empezar sin nada.
11. Algunos hombres sueñan con alcanzar la gloria.
12. Antes de demostrarle nuestra satisfacción, averigüemos lo que opina él.

15.3

Certain main verbs of English are followed by the infinitive, while others take the present participle. There is no infallible way of determining which main verbs govern which type of dependent verbal form. Since both lists of main verbs are only representative, it is clear that the Spanish speaker will have to master an extensive system. An * marks the verbs taking either the infinitive or the present participle.

MAIN VERBS TAKING THE INFINITIVE	MAIN VERBS TAKING THE PRESENT PARTICIPLE
agree (I agree to take it.)	admit (I admit taking it.)
*begin	advise
claim	appreciate
demand	avoid
expect	cease
fail	consider
forget	delay
*hate	deny
hesitate	enjoy
hope	finish
intend	dislike
*like	imagine
long	keep
*love	mind
need	plan on
offer	postpone
plan	practice
pretend	recall
promise	recollect
refuse	resent
resolve	risk
seem	stop
*start	suggest
tend	
want	

15.4
NOMINALIZATION OF VERBS

The nominalization of verbs in the two languages occurs through totally different processes. To nominalize (make a noun out of) a Spanish verb, you usually place the masculine singular definite article *el* before the infinitive. English almost always uses the present participle.

(El) quejarse no vale nada.	Complaining isn't worth anything.
(El) renunciar no resuelve nada.	Resigning doesn't solve anything.
No me gusta nadar.	I don't like swimming/to swim.

Note: The use of the Spanish article *el* + INF for nominalizing a verb often occurs for purposes of specification. Compare, *No me gustar nadar* with *No me gusta el nadar de ese chico*. Another example is, *No me gusta el constante llorar de ese niño*. Solé and Solé observe that like other nouns, nominalized verbs can be modified by adjectives, demonstratives and possessives, as in, *El triste lamentar de los pastores...* (Garcilazo de la Vega), *Este constante roer del hambre..., Nuestro cantar en la iglesia....*The use of the infinitive article *un* also has a nominalizing function as in, *La noche transcurría entre un constante ir y venir de ambulancias*. Finally, the nominalized infinite, when operating as a subject, does not necessarily appear in the canonical position (i.e. first in the sentence) of a subject, as in *Me encanta el frío amanecer de los otoños*. It can also be a prepositional object: *Mi vida se ha convertido en un constante ir y venir*.

Exercise 4
Translate the following sentences:

1. They don't like waiting for us.
2. (El) verte así feliz es un encanto.
3. Hiding in your room isn't going to solve a thing.
4. (El) fumar marijuana está prohibido en este país.
5. Drinking wine is customary in Spain.
6. (El) mirar así tu reloj no hará pasar el tiempo con más rapidez.
7. Running stimulates the heart.
8. (El) querer tanto a tu amado podría resultar muy peligroso.
9. Losing weight is not easy in my family.
10. (El) saber que triunfaste me sirve verdaderamente de estímulo.

15.5

English regularly uses its present participle as an adjective, placing it directly after the noun it modifies, as in *the girl watching TV ..., the man eating the apple ..., the birds singing in the trees ....* Spanish, on the other hand, avoids the construction and instead requires an adjective clause introduced by *que*.

The man looking for the secretary is our professor.	El hombre que busca a el/la secretario/a es nuestro profesor.
He died from a shot penetrating his heart.	Él murió de un tiro que le penetró el corazón.

| Who is that girl looking through the window? | ¿Quién es esa chica que mira por la ventana? |

Spanish does, however, occasionally use the present participle with adverbial force as seen in 15.1, as in, *Mi hermano lo encontró barriendo; El niño se cayó corriendo por la playa; Entró cantando como si nada.*

Exercise 5
Translate the following sentences:

1. Do you know that boy swimming in the river?
2. The people eating in the restaurant were Chileans.
3. Who is that man smoking a cigar?
4. The students studying Spanish are in my classes.
5. All the professors teaching here earn a lot of money.
6. You have to meet the girl renting my apartment.
7. I have to say something to the children playing in my yard.
8. The black cat climbing the tree isn't mine.
9. The people praying are members of our church.
10. Don't say anything to that girl chewing gum.

15.6

Whenever Spanish expresses an action as perceived and there is a stated object, you may use either an infinitive construction or the present participle. The English constructions for perceived actions closely parallel the Spanish; both the LV and the present participle are possible. The same verbs of perception occur in both languages, including *observer/mirar* = *watch/see*, *oír* = *hear*, *sentir* = *feel*.

Lo observé abrir/abriendo la puerta.	I watched him open/opening the door.
Él me oyó salir/saliendo con prisa.	He heard me leave/leaving in a hurry.
Te sentí tocarme/tocándome.	I felt you touch/touching me.
Los vimos escapar/escapando.	We saw them escape/escaping.
Vi a Jorge cortar/cortando el árbol.	I saw George cut/cutting down the tree.

Exercise 6
Translate the following perceived action sentences, providing two versions for each:

1. When did you see them talking with us?
2. ¿No oíste al maestro hacer la comparación?
3. He felt her touching his face.
4. No te oí llamarme en el hospital.
5. In India we saw many people die on the streets.

6. Nos despertamos cuando oímos al perro ladrando.
7. Where were you when you saw the car burning?
8. Vi al hombre abrir la puerta con una llave.

15.7

Some English present participial usages, particularly those expressing physical postures or specific conditions of people or things, use Spanish *estar* + past participle. The Spanish structure is identical to the one used for the "apparent passive." (See Chapter 16.7)

She was standing on the corner.	Ella estaba parada en la esquina.
I was sitting in the living room.	Yo estaba sentado/a en la sala.
He is lying down in his room.	Él está acostado en su recámara.
They were sleeping.	Estaban dormidos/Estaban durmiendo.
The dog was hiding under my bed.	El perro estaba escondido debajo de mi cama.

Exercise 7

Translate the following sentences:

1. He didn't see me hiding in the corner.
2. Quiero que le digas al juez donde estaba parado usted.
3. Were you just lying down, or were you asleep?
4. El gato está dormido sobre mi cama.
5. Where were you sitting?
6. No me vio aunque estaba parado cerca de él.
7. Was she standing next to you or was she sitting down/seated?
8. David estaba escondido en su recámara.

16

Passive Constructions

ACTIVE *VS.* PASSIVE CONSTRUCTIONS

16.1

When we analyze a sentence grammatically, the nouns can function as subjects, direct objects, indirect objects or objects of a preposition. In a sentence such as *Martha paints landscapes*, the grammatical subject of the sentence is *Martha*, while *landscapes* is the direct object noun. The verb *paints* is inflected for the third person singular, present tense, to show agreement with its grammatical subject *Martha*. Conversely, in the sentence *Martha and her husband paint landscapes*, we inflect the verb *paint* in the third person plural to show agreement with its plural grammatical subject, *Martha and her husband*.

We can also analyze a sentence semantically. In that case, the nouns can be agents (the doers of an action) or patients (the receivers of an action or entities acted upon). In the example above, then, *Martha* is the agent, while *landscapes* is the patient.

When the grammatical subject of a sentence corresponds to the agent of the action, the verb is in the active voice, such as in the example *Martha paints landscapes*, where the agent *Martha* corresponds to the grammatical subject of the sentence. In a sentence such as *Those landscapes were pained by Martha*, however, the doer of the action (the agent, *Martha*) does not correspond to the grammatical subject (*Those landscapes*). Remember that the subject must show agreement with the verb phrase, in this case, *were painted*. This sentence is now in the passive voice. In its simplest form, an English passive sentence is one in which the grammatical subject (person or thing being discussed) is also the receiver of the action (the patient). The subject does not act but rather receives the action performed by the agent (doer) of the action, expressed or merely implied from the context. It could be argued that the entity expressed first in a passive sentence has been topicalized. (See Chapter 11.14)

ENGLISH PASSIVE CONSTRUCTIONS

16.2

The basic parts of an English passive sentence are (1) the "patient," in the position of the subject, (2) the verb phrase, which always includes a form of AUX-*be* used in any tense, plus the past participle and (3) the "agent," which can be optionally omitted or expressed as the object of the preposition *by*.

SUBJECT	VERB PHRASE	AGENT
My father	was elected	(by a majority)
His students	are tested	(by him)
The rebels	will be executed	(by the firing squad)
No problems	have been encountered	(---)
They	are being attacked	(---)

Only transitive verbs may occur in passive voice structures. Such constructions are not possible when there is co-reference between subject and object in the active voice sentence (i.e., reflexive, reciprocal or possessive pronouns in the object noun phrase).

reflexive:
  She could see herself in the mirror > *Herself could be seen in the mirror.
reciprocal:
  We saw each other faintly in the rain > *Each other was seen faintly in the rain.
possessive:
  In answer to the question, the student shook his head > *His head was shaken by the student in answer to the question.

16.3

In Chapter 11.12 we explained the syntax of English indirect objects in active sentences. Reviewing this, two structures may be used:

1) S + V + DO + to/for + IO (*He gave the book to her.*)
2) S + V + IO + DO (*He gave her the book.*)

An indirect object may appear in an English passive sentence if the verb allows one in the equivalent active one. Verbs using structure 1 above are, among others, *apply, describe, explain, introduce, mention, present, prove, report, return, suggest*. Such verbs permit only one passive version as can be seen in the following active to passive conversions. Note that the active direct object becomes the passive subject.

active: Someone described the book to me.
passive: The book was described to me. (not, *I was described the book.*)

active: Someone will explain the procedure to us
passive: The procedure will be explained to us. (*We will be explained the procedure.*)

active: No-one had reported the incident to her
passive: The incident had not been reported to her. (*She had not been reported the incident.*)

Other verbs allow two passive versions, and these verbs use either structure 1 or 2 (above) in active sentences. Such verbs are: *bring, give, lend, mail, offer, owe, pay, read, sell, send, show, teach, tell, throw, write,* as in *He gave the book to her = He gave her the book.* The list allows passive versions with either the direct object or the indirect object in the subject position.

active: They brought some food to us = They brought us some food.
passive: Some food (DO) was brought to us (by them).
We (IO) were brought some food (by them).

active: My mother will tell a story to the boys = My mother will tell the boys a story.
passive: A story (DO) will be told to the boys (by my mother).
The boys (IO) will be told a story (by my mother).

active: I have written a letter to Robert = I have written Robert a letter.
passive: A letter (DO) has been written to Robert (by me).
Robert (IO) has been written a letter (by me) (IO subject).

Exercise 1

Change the following active sentences into passive ones. Because of the indirect object, two versions are possible as indicated. Give both:

1. Jonathan wrote a very significant novel last summer.
2. The President will give a medal to the hero. (2)
3. The children have eaten all the apples.
4. The boss will suggest a new plan to the employees.
5. My parents sent me some money in July. (2)
6. He drank a whole bottle of gin.
7. She visits the children every summer.
8. The professor had offered them a better grade. (2)
9. They will describe a new system to the general.
10. His father lent him some money. (2)

THREE TYPES OF SPANISH PASSIVE CONSTRUCTIONS

16.4

Most Spanish grammars describe three types of passive voice sentences. These are (1) the passive with *ser* + PAST PARTICIPLE, the actional form, often called "the true passive," (2) the passive with *estar* + PAST PARTICIPLE, the state of being form, also termed "the apparent passive," and (3) the "passive *se*" whose structure is active in Spanish but rendered as a passive in English. Some Spanish scholars refer the passive *se* as *la pasiva-refleja*. We list examples of these three Spanish passives, identifying each by number:

1. La noticia era conocida por todos.   The news was known by everyone.

2. Está/Estaba prohibido.   It is/was forbidden.

3. Se firmó la paz.   The peace was signed.

Se les atacó en la casa.	They were attacked at home.
Se le dio/dieron a él varias tareas.	He was given various tasks.
	Various tasks were given (to) him.
Se han vendido setenta.	Seventy have been sold.

Although Spanish grammar has three ways of expressing the sense of passivity, a direct correspondence with the English structures does not apply in all instances. The Spanish passive voice occurs much less frequently than in English and is subject to certain restrictions. Spanish often translates the English sense of passivity through active sentences, impersonal locutions, reflexive verb forms, or other non-passive voice means. If a choice between using the active or the passive voice is available, Spanish speakers prefer the active construction since it is more direct and the one most frequently occurring in normal speech. In this regard, the *Academy* gives the following advice:

> Las lenguas francesa e inglesa emplean la pasiva ... en proporciones mucho mayores que la nuestra [española]. Conviene que los traductores tengan en cuenta esta preferencia, para no cometer faltas de estilo y aun incorrecciones gramaticales. Por otra parte, el empleo creciente de la pasiva refleja e impersonal contribuye a limitar la frecuencia de la pasiva con *ser* (Esbozo, §3.12.9).

16.5
THE SPANISH *SER* PASSIVE (The Actional "True" Passive)

The Spanish *ser* passive construction closely parallels the English simple passive formula. English true passive sentences coincide with the Spanish formula, with one significant proviso: An indirect object object from the active sentence cannot become the subject in its corresponding passive structure. (**Nosotros fuimos dados varios regalos*). The basic parts of the Spanish *ser* passive are (1) the "patient" in the position of the subject, (2) the verb phrase, which always includes a form of AUX-*ser* used in any tense and followed by the past participle, inflected for gender and number to agree with the subject and (3) the "agent," omitted or optionally expressed as the object of the preposition *por*.

SUBJECT	VERB PHRASE	AGENT
Mi padre	fue atacado	(por un perro)
Ella	es perdonada	(por su abuela)
Los ladrones	serán acusados	(por la policía)
Nosotras	hemos sido elegidas	(---)

16.6
In *ser* passive sentences, attention is drawn to the recipient of the action (the patient) rather than the doer of the action (the agent). Although an agent might not appear in the sentence, the context generally implies one. The tendency of Spanish speakers to avoid passive constructions, particularly in speech, probably derives from the restrictions mentioned earlier in this section:

- In a *ser* passive sentence, what was an indirect object in the active version of the sentence cannot be used as the subject of the passive version as observed above.

Chapter 16 Passive Constructions

El jefe me dio cincuenta pesos > *Yo fui dado cincuenta pesos por el jefe.

- A *ser* passive sentence cannot have a human subject which, because of the inherent characteristics of the verb, is in any way involved in the action expressed by the verb in the sentence.

    Sus consejos nos traicionaron. > *Fuimos traicionados por sus consejos.

- Active sentences using verbs of perception (eg., *escuchar, ver, oír, sentir,* etc.) rarely occur passivized in Spanish.

    La joven no oyó entrar a su novio. > *El novio no fue oído por la joven.

- Passive *ser* is used freely with inanimate subjects as long as there is an expressed or implied human agent.

    Un alma espiritual frecuenta lugares solitarios. > Algunos lugares solitarios son frecuentados por las almas espirituales.

    La noticia me sorprendió. > Fui sorprendido/a por la noticia.

- All the perfect tenses can occur in *ser* passive sentences.

    El hombre ha sido elegido por sus seguidores en el partido.
    Esa gloriosa obra había sido comenzada en el siglo XV.
    Me pregunto si su obra habrá sido presentada a tiempo.
    Ese trabajo ya habría sido terminado, si me hubieran dejado hacerlo.
    Si a estas alturas su origen no ha sido comprobado por los científicos, no lo será nunca.
    Si la categoría hubiera sido anunciada por los jueces, la joven se habría inscrito.

Exercise 2

Change the following active Spanish sentences into passive ones using *ser* + PAST PARTICIPLE. Some sentences may not be passivized:

1. Sus vecinos la estiman mucho.
2. En todas partes la gente conoce esa noticia.
3. Lo conocían bien en su pueblo.
4. Llamamos a la puerta para avisar de nuestra llegada.
5. Apenas llegó el aviso, se dio la noticia.
6. Unos desconocidos atacan y roban a un anciano.
7. La madre tenía ansias de ver a su hijo.
8. Los oficiales habían firmado el acuerdo antes de marcharse.
9. Ellos tenían nociones sobre este asunto, pero las desconozco.
10. Ya habré terminado mis estudios para antes del verano.

16.7
THE SPANISH PASSIVE WITH *ESTAR* (THE APPARENT PASSIVE)

The passive with *estar* (the "apparent passive") describes the condition, state, location, or posture of a person or thing, and describes the state that results from a completed action. Since English uses only *be* for both state of being and actional (true) passives (whereas Spanish has both *estar* and *ser*), the English speaker must take special care in discerning these differences in Spanish usage. These contrasts within Spanish were covered in Chapter 10.

The basic parts of the Spanish *estar* passive sentence are the same as those for the *ser* passive: the patient (grammatical subject), the verb phrase composed of *estar* plus an inflected past participle used as an adjective and rarely the optional agent. Subjects and agents function as they do in the *ser* passive.

Estar + PAST PARTICIPLE occurs with transitive verbs and is generally found in the simple tenses only—present, imperfect and preterite.

El libro ya está impreso.
La estructura estaba hecha.
Los edificios estuvieron situados aquí; fueron destruidos por el bombardeo.

The *estar* passive appears in the present and the imperfect tenses with punctual verbs such as *acabar, arrancar, lanzar, mandar, ordenar, pagar, prohibir, resolver*, etc.

El dejar piedras en la carretera está/estaba prohibido.

Pronominal reflexive verbs like *adormecerse, arrepentirse, avergonzarse, dormirse, enfadarse, enojarse, entristecerse, sentarse*, etc. expressing the perfection/completion of actions occur with passive *estar* in the present and the imperfect tenses non-pronominally (i.e., without the reflexive pronoun).

Las niñas han estado sentadas desde el comienzo del servicio religioso.
Various sacerdotes están/estaban parados delante del altar.
Los chicos están dormidos desde hace más de cuatro horas.

An agent may accompany an passive *estar* verb phrase when the past participle refers to a durative (non-punctual) action or condition.

El programa está/estaba/estuvo garantizado por el gobierno.

Exercise 3
Change the following sentences into the apparent passive using *estar* + PAST PARTICIPLE:

1. Un jardín de flores rodeaba mi casa en las afueras de la ciudad.
2. Escondieron a sus mujeres cuando llegó el enemigo.
3. Clemente se levantó muy temprano.
4. Tu tío envejeció mucho.
5. Mi hermana administra la tienda de sombreros.
6. El genio se cansó.

7. Se resolvió el problema.
8. Todos se habían dormido cuando llegué.

16.8
AMBIGUITY IN PASSIVES

Possible ambiguities arise between English and Spanish passive sentences using *be* vs. *ser/estar*. The Spanish sentences are less susceptible to confusion than are English ones, since the choice of *ser* over *estar* and *vice versa* in Spanish will dispel ambiguities in most cases. In English there is no ambiguity if a past participle and an attributive adjective derived from the same verb have different forms. When they appear in passive constructions no ambiguity results.

    a. The door was opened. (past participle) Spanish: *ser + abierta* (action)
    b. The door was open. (adjective) Spanish: *estar + abierta* (state)

Sentence (a) strongly implies an agent and stresses the action occurring to the door. The sentence is a true passive. Sentence (b) has no agent, either expressed or implied. Furthermore, no action takes place. The sentence is merely a reflection of the state the door was in, and *open* is an attributive adjective joined to its subject by the copula *was*. However, if the past participle and attributive adjective derived from the same verb are identical, ambiguity may result, particularly if the sentence occurs out of context. Note these examples:

    c. The house was surrounded. (action or state?)
    d. The door was closed. (action or state?)

In example (c), it is impossible to say whether the intended meaning is a passive one, stressing an agent and the action which happened to the house, or whether the emphasis is on the mere condition of the house. Likewise, in sentence (d), either action (the closing of the door) or condition (the state in which the door was found) are possible semantic readings.

Ambiguity as in the preceding English examples cannot occur in Spanish since the actional passive with *ser* describes an action while the apparent passive with *estar* denotes a resultant state or condition. In Spanish, both sentences (c) and (d) would take one or the other structure:

    e. The house was surrounded.   (actional) La casa fue sitiada (por los militares).
                                         (stative) La casa estaba sitiada.

    f. The door was closed.   (actional) La puerta fue cerrada (por el viento).
                                         (stative) La puerta estaba cerrada.

    g. The prices were reduced.   (actional) Los precios fueron reducidos.
                                          (stative) Los precios estaban reducidos.

In addition to the choice between the actional passive *ser* and apparent (stative) passive with *estar*, differences in intended meaning are further clarified when the *por* + AGENT prepositional phrase is added in Spanish. Observe these two contrasting sentences, (h) and (i):

h. La mercancía es pesada (= is weighed) por el comerciante. Here, *pesada* is a past participle.
i. La mercancía es pesada (= is heavy). Now, *pesada* is a predicate adjective.

16.9
THE SPANISH 'PASSIVE WITH *SE*'

The Spanish passive with *se*, the third of its passive structures, occurs with transitive verbs and appears when the performer (agent) of the action's identity is unknown, deemed unimportant or deliberately concealed. In dealing with passive *se*, one must consider whether the recipients of the action are inanimate or animate, but in either case, only third person subjects, both singular and plural, appear in this type of construction due to its impersonal character (See Chapter 13.14). In all cases, however, remember that passive *se* structures are really active-transitive or reflexive constructions, and passive only from the English point-of-view since English translates them all with its passive formulae. They are active structures with passive meaning. *The Real Academia* agrees: *[Son] construcción[es] oracional[es] de significado* **pasivo**, *cuyo verbo, en tercera persona, aparece en* **forma activa** *precedido de se y generalmente sin complemento agente; ej., Esos museos se inauguraron hace cincuenta años.* [English would say, *Those museums were opened fifty years ago*.]

16.10
SPANISH PASSIVE *SE* WITH INANIMATE RECIPIENTS

The information communicated when the passive *se* occurs with inanimate recipients is that something is a direct object (the receiver of the action), but there is no mention of the agent (performer) of that action. Consider the following examples, both of which we discuss from a grammatically analytical point of view.

1. Aquí se alquilan habitaciones.
    ("passive *se*," also termed "the reflexive passive")

2. Aquí se alquila habitaciones.
    (active sentence with an impersonal subject)

In the first sentence, *se* would seem to function as a reflexive pronoun, as the sentence could have the literal translation of **Here rooms rent themselves*. English would translate the sentence with its true passive construction, *Rooms are rented here*, usually expressed as *Rooms for rent*. In the second sentence, *se* acts as an impersonal, indefinite subject or as a passive particle, giving the sentence the literal translation of, *Here one/someone rents rooms*. Again, English would use the true passive rendition of *Rooms are rented here* or more commonly, *Rooms for rent*. Note, however, that in this usage, although *se* acts like a subject pronoun, in the syntax it is distinctly a pronominal/conjunctive/(en)clitic form, inseparable from its verb, and displacing even *no*. A true subject pronoun would show the syntax of *Ella alquila.../Ella no alquila... Se*, even as an indefinite subject, has the syntax of, *Se aquila.../No se aquila....* We made this syntactical observation earlier, in Chapter 13.15.

Native Spanish speakers tend to prefer the first version, *Aquí se alquilan habitaciones*, in which the inanimate recipient and the verb agree, simply because such subject-verb agreement is so characteristic of Spanish. Nevertheless, speakers may disagree concerning which sentence is the most acceptable. The *Academy* recommends the first construction, calling it more traditional, but it does not reject the second.

In the following examples, we show that *se* passive sentences can transform into true passives in Spanish, provided no agent is mentioned. The sentences come from various well-known Spanish grammars, including that of the *Academy*.

SE PASSIVE	*SER* PASSIVE
Se alquilan coches.	Los coches son alquilados.
Se han descubierto sus trampas.	Han sido descubiertas sus trampas.
Se cometieron muchos atropellos.	Muchos atropellos fueron cometidos.
Se suspende la sesión.	La sesión es suspendida.
Se edifican muchas casas aquí.	Muchas casas son edificadas aquí.
La paz se firmó.	La paz fue firmada.
Se venden botellas.	Las botellas son vendidas.
Los pájaros se alborotaron.	Los pájaros fueron alborotados.
Se aceptó el acuerdo.	El acuerdo fue aceptado.
Se han divulgado estas noticias.	Estas noticias han sido divulgadas.

Exercise 4

Change the following Spanish sentences into *se* passives. Notice the original sentences are active, but can be translated impersonally, as passives with *se*: In all cases the recipients are inanimate:

1. Anuncian muchas actividades sociales a través de la televisión.
2. Expresaron su plena satisfacción por la excelencia del vino.
3. Temen otra guerra internacional.
4. Organizaron el Décimo Festival Juvenil.
5. Rechazaron el nuevo proyecto de ley electoral.
6. Vieron en la obra detalles análogos a la poesía de Darío.
7. Observaron las estrellas durante varias horas.
8. Celebraron innumerables fiestas este año.
9. No saben el origen del lenguaje.
10. En esta clase estudian literatura universal.

16.11

SPANISH PASSIVE *SE* WITH ANIMATE RECIPIENTS

When animate recipients are involved, Spanish modifies the structure used for inanimate ones. With inanimate recipients, we can say *Se alquila(n) habitaciones* with the English true passive translation of *Rooms are rented (by someone)/*Rooms rent themselves*, both usually expressed as *Rooms for rent*. But when the recipients are animate, we can, through the use of the personal accusative, say *Se asesinó al dictador*, or *Se asesinaron a los dictadores*. (*Se* in either case is an indefinite subject, *somebody-or-other*.) The constructions are clearly active but translate passively. If the animate recipient occurs first in such sentences, it is pronominally reduplicated with the verb: *Al dictador, se le asesinó./A los dictadores, se les asesinaron.* Worldwide, Spanish is purely *leísta* in this usage.

In our discussion of the Spanish true passive construction (using *ser*), we pointed out that passive *ser* cannot be used with indirect objects. *Ella fue dada un libro* is an ungrammatical translation of *She was given a book*. Spanish has only the passive *se* option for expressing English passives with indirect objects, as can be seen in the following examples. Note that no agent appears in passive *se* sentences with animate recipients as is also the case for inanimate ones.

Se le dio un libro.   She was given a book.
                            A book was given to her.

Se les dio varios libros.   They were given several books.
                            Several books were given to them.

The previous two examples would most commonly be expressed with the "impersonal *ellos*" active construction (*Le dieron un libro/Les dieron varios libros*), both of which English would translate passively: *She was given a book/They were given several books*.

Exercise 5

Translate the following passive constructions, choosing among all three Spanish passive equivalents, and in each case naming the type of passive involved.

1. My parents were mentioned in the letter.
2. The President has been assassinated.
3. They were hanged in the public square.
4. These documents will be studied with care.
5. My friend will be appointed Secretary of State.
6. She is considered (to be) an excellent teacher.
7. The children will be served ice cream at the party.
8. He hasn't been recommended for the position.
9. You will be given a gift at the reception.
10. Nothing had been said to me.
11. Her parents weren't told the whole truth (by her).
12. We weren't invited to your wedding.
13. Several letters have been sent to them.
14. Those men will be taken to jail.
15. No one had been seen in the building.
16. A Mexican meal will be prepared at the reunion.
17. A new governmental program was announced.
18. All the apples have been sold.
19. We will be brought a car early in the morning.
20. Poor children aren't given a good education.

16.12

As previously pointed out, English makes much more frequent use of the passive than does Spanish. Although Spanish has three routes for expressing the sense of passivity, the language

Chapter 16 Passive Constructions

demonstrates a tendency to reject these in favor of the more dynamic, animated structures of the active voice. This frequent lack of direct correspondence between the two languages in this regard should be kept in mind.

The preference for the active voice is illustrated in these examples: *The novel was written by Rómulo Gallegos* can take the Spanish form: *La novela fue escrita por Rómulo Gallegos* (passive). However, a more natural rendition would be, *Rómulo Gallegos escribió la novela* (active), or *La novela la escribió Rómulo Gallegos* (active voice with a change of focus [topicalization]). We include here some very common examples where the two languages are at odds. English expresses the thought passively, while Spanish uses its more direct and natural active voice.

PASSIVE	ACTIVE
I was seated next to the guests. (Ambiguous example in English.)	Me sentaron al lado de los invitados. Estaba sentado/a al lado de los invitados.
We are interested in linguistics.	Nos interesa la lingüística.
That officer was detested by everyone.	Todos detestaban a ese oficial.
We were shown the way.	Nos enseñaron el camino.
He was awarded a consolation prize.	Le otorgaron un premio de consolación.
That role will be played by the understudy.	El suplente desempeñará ese papel.
The children are awakened at seven o'clock.	A los niños los despiertan a las siete.
He was being haunted by his past.	A él lo perseguía su pasado.
We are encouraged to continue with the project.	Nos animan a continuar con el proyecto.
Elementary details are not forgotten the same as more complicated ones.	Uno no se olvida de los detalles básicos igual que de los más complicados.
Indispensable information has been transmitted by the station.	La estación ha transmitido información indispensable.
A control mechanism must be established.	Debe establecerse un mecanismo de control.

Thorough inspection of the above pairs of sentences will provide an additional dimension to the many differences that exist between the Spanish and the English passive systems.

Exercise 6

Translate the following sentences. Many of the English sentences are ambiguous; We have indicated the focus to be used in Spanish.

1. The children were hidden in the old building. (passive *estar*)
2. Mi casa, en Barcelona, estaba rodeada de un jardín de rosas.
3. That type of book is read only by scholars. (passive *ser*)
4. No sabemos quién será elegido presidente en las próximas elecciones.
5. I saw that the windows were closed when I entered the room. (passive *estar*)
6. La puerta derecha debería estar cerrada.
7. My brother has been injured in an accident. (passive *ser*)
8. El edificio estará terminado para fines de mes.
9. An important program will be presented this evening. (passive *ser*)
10. Los cuarenta cuentos de horror fueron escritos por un solo autor.
11. My composition is written. It will be read by my professor. (passive *estar*, passive *ser*)
12. Van a eliminar las curvas de la carretera.
13. We knew they were there because the lights were turned on. (passive *estar*)
14. Esta estructura será elevada a la altura de la otra.
15. This painting will have to be finished by another artist. (passive *ser*)

17

Conditional Sentences and Unreal Comparison

17.1

Both English and Spanish have ways of expressing a hypothesis and a conclusion to it. The clause conveying the hypothesis is often termed the "*if*-clause," and the conclusion, the "result-clause." The word *if* generally introduces the English hypothesis, *si* in Spanish. No specific word introduces the conclusion in either language, although *then* may occur in English. In any conditional structure, the protasis (*if*-clause or hypothesis) may precede the apodosis (*then*-clause or conclusion) or *vice versa* without any change of meaning.

Spanish examples of various types of conditional sentences:

Si ella viene hoy, la veré en mi despacho.
Si ella viniera/viniese quejándose mañana, no la querría/quisiera ver yo.
Si ella fue al casino como dijo, seguramente perdió todo su dinero.
Habría/Hubiera perdido todo si ella hubiera/hubiese ido al casino.

Parallel English examples:

If she comes today, I will see her in my office.
If she came (should come) complaining tomorrow, I wouldn't want to see her.
If she went to the casino as she said, for sure she lost everything.
She would have lost everything if she had gone/had she gone to the casino.

17.2
TYPES OF CONDITIONAL EXPRESSION

Both languages distinguish clearly between neutral conditional sentences and those contrary-to-fact. Neutral conditionals state the hypothesis and its conclusion in such a way as to indicate that both are fully capable of realization. It is completely feasible that the hypothesis put forth and its accompanying conclusion were fulfilled in the past, are being fulfilled in the present, or will be fulfilled at some future time. In both languages only indicative tenses appear in neutral conditional sentences.

Neutral conditional, future:

SPANISH: *si* + (S) + V[PRES INDIC], (S) + V[PRES or FUT INDIC]

Si Eustaquio va al concierto mañana, prometo no decir nada.
Si Eustaquio no llega pronto, no podrá ver el juicio.

ENGLISH: *if* + S + V[PRESENT], S + V[FUTURE]

If Eustace goes to the concert tomorrow, I promise not to say anything.
If Eustace doesn't arrive soon, he won't be able to see the trial.

Neutral conditional, present:

SPANISH: *si* + (S) + V[PRES INDIC], (S) + V[PRES INDIC]

Si Efraín ya está aquí como dices, nadie sabe dónde está.
Si Alicia habla inglés tan bien como dices, seguramente es norteamericana.

ENGLISH: *if* + S + V[PRES], S + V[PRES]

If Ephraim is already here as you say, no one knows where he is.
If Alice speaks English as well as you say, she is surely North American.

Neutral conditional, past:

SPANISH: *si* + (S) + V[PAST INDIC], (S) + V[PAST INDIC]

Si José fue a Argentina como lo anunció, seguramente gastó mucha plata.
Si Josefina hablaba con José, seguramente no le hablaba en inglés.

ENGLISH: *if* + S + V[any PAST TENSE], S + V[any PAST TENSE]

If Joseph went to Argentina as he announced it, he surely spent lots of money.
If Josephine was speaking to Joseph, for sure she wasn't speaking to him in English.

Exercise 1

Translate the following neutral conditional sentences, and determine in each case whether the sentence refers to the past, present, or future.

1. If you gave him the money, he lost it.
2. Si Josefina llega mañana, nadie va a tener tiempo para recogerla.
3. If he has a new car, I want to see it.
4. Si José le dio un regalo a ella, seguramente le gustó mucho.
5. Even if he has a watch, he never knows what time it is.
6. Si escribes sin apretar el lápiz, nadie va a poder leer tu letra.
7. If he didn't go to class, the professor always knew it.
8. Si usted no vio la corona, era porque no estaba en el museo.
9. If you bring your books, we will be able to translate the story.
10. Si lo prefieres, podemos permanecer sentados.

17.3

Contrary-to-fact conditional sentences state the hypothesis and its conclusion in such a way as to imply that the hypothesized event never actually took place in the past nor is it taking place in the present. Since the future has not yet occurred, it cannot be contrary-to-fact, but there is a hypothetical future wherein both the hypothesis and the conclusion express events as highly unlikely of realization at any future time. <u>The Spanish contrary-to-fact present and the hypothetical future use the same verb forms.</u>

Hypothetical future:

SPANISH: *si* + (S) + **V[PAST SUBJ -*ra*/-*se*]**, (S) + **V[COND]**

Si José fuera/fuese a Argentina, gastaría mucha plata.
Si vinieras/vinieses mañana, celebraríamos.

Note: In the conclusion of hypothetical future conditionals, the -*ra* form of the past subjunctive occasionally occurs as a substitute for the conditional. Some speakers consider such sentences to be stylized, however: *Si Bolívar volviera/volviese a vivir entre nosotros, ¿qué pensara de la actual situación política?* It's heard a lot in daily Mexican speech, and is virtually the norm in the perfect tenses (*Lo* **hubiera** *hecho si hubiera podido*) for past counter-factuals. It is not unusual for hypothetical future sentences to be "mixed," i.e., the hypothesis is stated as less likely of realization, while the conclusion is expressed as more likely. Both languages have such future conditionals: *Si llegara tarde tu avión, comeremos allá en el aeropuerto* = *Should your plane arrive late, we'll eat there in the airport.*

ENGLISH: *if* + S + **V[PAST]** , S + **V[COND]**

If John went to Argentina, he would spend a lot.
If you came tomorrow, we would celebrate.

Note: The "past tense" used in this structure is really an old subjunctive inherited from the Germanic (not the Romance) roots of English. In the modern language, it and the modern past tense forms have become identical with one exception, that of the verb *to be,* in which *were* is the correct form for all persons. Increasingly often, English speakers fail to ob-

> serve this distinction, producing such errors as, *If I was you.... Some Spanish varieties say, Yo que tú..., with the meaning of, Si yo fuera tú.... The usage is distinctly colloquial.

Other English structures used to express the hypothetical future are:

if + S + were + INF, S + V[COND]
were + S + INF, S + V[COND]
if + S + should + LV, S + V[COND]
should + S + LV, S + V[COND]

If Joseph were to go to Argentina, he would spend a lot.
Were Joseph to go to Argentina, he would spend a lot.
If Joseph should go to Argentina, he would spend a lot.
Should Joseph go to Argentina, he would spend a lot.

If you were to come tomorrow, we would celebrate.
Were you to come tomorrow, we would celebrate.
If you should come tomorrow, we would celebrate.
Should you come tomorrow, we would celebrate.

Contrary-to-fact present:

SPANISH: *si* + (S) + V[PAST SUBJ *-ra* / *-se*], (S) + V[COND]
(This is the same structure as the one used for the hypothetical future)

Si José tuviera/tuviese tanto dinero, no estaría aquí.
Si Bernardo fuera/fuese francés, no hablaría inglés.
Si vieras/vieses a Juan, no lo conocerías.

> **Note:** Present contrary-to-fact conditionals occasionally take the *-ra* form of the past subjunctive in the conclusion. The usage is again stylistically motivated: *Si ahora mismo hubiera/hubiese un ataque atómico, la población no estuviera preparada.* In the colloquial idiom, the imperfect indicative commonly occurs in the conclusion of present counter factuals: *Si lo supiera, te lo <u>decía</u>*, or when the protasis (*si* clause) is expressed by "*Yo que tú...*": *Yo que tú me lo compraba.* The use of the imperfect tense here instead of the conditional presents the action as more real and less hypothetical.

ENGLISH: *if* + S + V[PAST], S + V[COND]
V[*were, had*] + S, S + V[COND]

If Joseph had/Had Joseph so much money, he wouldn't be here.
If Bernard were/Were Bernard French, he wouldn't speak English.

If you saw John, you wouldn't recognize him.

> **Note:** The last sentence is the only version possible since only the lexical verbs *have* and *be* permit two structures on the basis of subject/verb inversion: *If Joseph had... = Had Joseph...; If Bernard were... = Were Bernard...*

Contrary-to-fact past:

SPANISH: *si* + (S) + V[PLUPERF. SUBJ *-ra /-se*], (S) + V[COND PERF or PLUPERF. SUBJ *-ra* only]

Si José hubiera/hubiese ido a Argentina, habría/hubiera gastado mucho.
Si José hubiera/hubiese estado allí, habría/hubiera visto el accidente.

ENGLISH: *if* + S + V[PLUPERF], S + V[COND PERF]
Had + S + V[PAST PART], S + V[COND PERF]

If Joseph had gone/Had Joseph gone to Argentina, he would have spent a lot.
If Joseph had been/Had Joseph been there, he would have seen the accident.

> **Note:** Modern but inattentive English speakers often simplify past counter-factuals by using *would have*, usually said as "*wudda*," in both clauses, *If you would have studied more, you would have passed the exam*. Spanish accepts this type of "tense leveling" as standard *(Si hubieras estudiado más, hubieras pasado el examen)*. In their written English, students increasingly show confusion between *have* and *of* (both unstressed) in these contexts producing such anomalies as, *"If you would of been here, I would of helped you."* Finally, the Spanish hypothesis in hypothetical future and present and past counter factual sentences can be expressed by *de* (occasionally *con, a* or *al*) + the infinitive, either imperfect *(De tener problemas...= Si tuviera problemas...)* or perfect *(De haber tenido problemas... = Si hubiera tenido problemas...)*. The subject of the hypotheses must be gleaned from the conclusion or from context.

Exercise 2

Translate the following contrary-to-fact (past or present) and hypothetical future conditionals. Determine in each case whether the temporal reference is past, present, or future. Give all possible versions where more than one is acceptable.

1. If I were you, I wouldn't say that.
2. Si acaso vieras a Victoria, no la reconocerías.
3. Had you given him the money, he would have spent it all.
4. Si tuvieses tanto dominio propio como yo, estarías mucho más sereno.
5. Were you to bring a book, I would read you a story.
6. Si tus amigos hubieran venido directamente, no se habrían perdido.
7. If you didn't love your mother, you wouldn't send her flowers.
8. Te enfermarías si bebieras esa clase de vino.
9. There wouldn't be so many taxes should he be elected President.
10. Si un rayo llegase a alcanzarnos, no sobreviviríamos.
11. They would have helped me if they had been my friends.
12. Nadie te hubiera descubierto si hubieras guardado silencio.
13. If you met the President tomorrow, what would you say to him?
14. Si fuese una piedra legítima, ¿cuánto tendría que pagar?
15. We would know what time it is had we a clock.
16. Si yo fuera tú, no pagaría la diferencia.
17. He would have told me his name if I had asked (it of) him.
18. Tendrías que comprar un traje nuevo si quisieras salir conmigo.
19. Would you know him were he to enter the room right now?

20. No hubieras dicho nada si hubieras estado realmente bajo mi influencia.
21. If you left early tomorrow, you would be in León by noon.
22. Si salieses con esa muchacha preciosa, su novio lo sabría al minuto.
23. What would they do were there to be another civil war in El Salvador?
24. ¿Dónde estarías ahora si fueras tan indiferente como tu hermano?

17.4
UNREAL COMPARISON

Spanish makes an unreal comparison with the expression *como si...* which English renders with *as if/as though...*. The idea following these locutions is contrary-to-fact and appears only as a point of comparison. Unreal comparisons may refer either to a time concurrent with the main verb or to a completed/perfected past time. Spanish uses the past subjunctive in either *-ra* or *-se* for the former and its pluperfect subjunctive (*-ra* or *-se*) for the latter. English employs its past tense (except for *be*, becoming *were* in all persons) for unreal comparison concurrent with the main verb and its pluperfect for those viewed as completed.

Unreal comparison, concurrent with the main verb:

SPANISH: **(S) + V[INDIC] +** *como si* **+ (S) + V[PAST SUBJ]**

Ella habla como si conociera/conociese a ese hombre ingenioso.
Él corrió como si fuera/fuese un caballo de carrera.
Ellos llegarán tarde como si no importara/importase la hora de salida.

ENGLISH: **S + V[INDIC] +** *as if (though)* **+ S + V[PAST]**

She speaks as if she knew that witty man.
He ran as though he were a race horse.
They'll arrive late as if the departure time weren't important.

Unreal comparison, prior (and completed) to the main verb:

SPANISH: **(S) + V[INDIC] +** *como si* **+ (S) + V[PLUPERF SUBJ]**

Hablan como si hubieran/hubiesen vivido durante el Imperio Chino.
Parecía tan heroico como si hubiera/hubiese conquistado una nación.
Vendrán hambrientos como si no hubieran/hubiesen comido nada.

ENGLISH: **S + V[INDIC] +** *as if (though)* **+ S + V[PLUPERF]**

They speak as though they had lived during the Chinese Empire.
He appeared as heroic as if he had conquered a nation.
They'll come hungry as if they hadn't eaten anything.

Exercise 3

Translate the following unreal comparisons. In each instance is the unreality/counter-factuality expressed as simultaneous with the main verb or prior to it?

1. Hablas inglés como si lo hubieras estudiado por muchos años.
2. He smokes as if nothing else were important.
3. La niña se comió la fruta como si tuviera mucha hambre.
4. You drink coffee as though you didn't like it very much.
5. Corrieron como si el mismo diablo los persiguiera.
6. He explained everything as if he had studied the lesson already.
7. Norberto hablaba sin expresión, como si estuviera en un trance.
8. The baby is crying as if someone had punished it.
9. El anciano hablaba muy lentamente como si sufriera un intenso dolor.
10. He'll be listening as though he understood every word.

18

Spanish and English Verb + Preposition Constructions

18.1

Both languages often use prepositions after finite verbal forms. Such prepositions operate in one of two ways:

1. As a connector between a conjugated (finite) verbal form and a following dependent but non-conjugated (non-finite) verbal form. As seen in the examples below, the verbal form following prepositions in English is the present participle (-*ing*), while in Spanish, it is the infinitive: *before eating* vs. *antes de comer* (See Chapter 15):

    Vienen **a** comer.
    Soñaron **con** ganar.
    They succeeded **in** entering.

2. As a connector linking a conjugated verbal form with a following noun or pronoun complement.

    Nos acercamos **a** la casa.
    They all laughed **at** him.

18.2

Spanish and English occasionally use these prepositions in a parallel fashion, but these cases are few.

Él insistió **en** salir.　　He insisted **on** leaving. (same preposition)
Él planeó traerlo.　　He planned to bring it. (no preposition used)

Prepositional connector usage more frequently differs from one language to the other as can be seen in the examples which follow.

1. The preposition, if any, appears between a conjugated verbal form and a following dependent but non-conjugated verbal form, as mentioned earlier. Notice the difference between the English and Spanish usage.

    Comenzó **a** llover.　　(Spanish uses a preposition.)
    It began to rain.　　(English uses no preposition since *to rain* is considered the infinitive.)

    She succeeded **in** going.　　(English uses a preposition.)
    Ella pudo ir. / Ella logró ir.　　(Spanish uses no preposition.)

2. The preposition, if any, occurs between a conjugated verbal form and a following noun or pronoun complement.

    Asistieron **al** concierto.　　(Spanish uses a preposition.)
    They attended the concert.　　(English uses none.)

    He looked **for** the wound.　　(English uses preposition.)
    Él buscó la herida.　　(Spanish uses none.)

    Ellos se preocupan **por** las masas.　　(Spanish uses preposition.)
    They worry **about** the masses.　　(English does also, but the prepositions are different.)

18.3

The contrastive analysis of these prepositional usages between English and Spanish often varies according to the particular translation given to lexical items. Note that an obvious contrast exists between the two languages in the following sentences:

Él entró **en/a** la región.　　He entered the region.
Ella se acercó **a** la multitud.　　She approached the multitude.

The contrast occurs because we translate *entrar* as "enter" and *acercarse* as "approach;" that is, they were translated as transitive verbs, and "the region" and "the multitude" are their direct object complements, whereas in Spanish *entrar* and *acercarse* are instransitive. However, in the following examples, no contrasts appear simply because here *entrar* has been rendered as the intransitive "go into" and *acercarse* with the intransitive "go (up) to."

Él entró **en** la región.　　He went **into** the region.
Ella se acercó **a** la multitud.　　She went (**up**) **to** the multitude.

VERB + PREPOSITION CONSTRUCTIONS OF THE TYPE
VERB + PREPOSITION + VERB (See Appendix IV)

18.4
SPANISH USES THE PREPOSITIONS *A, DE ,EN, QUE*; ENGLISH DOES NOT:

The preposition is *A*:

acercarse a*
Él se acercó **a** oponerme resistencia.

to approach
He approached to offer me resistance.

acostumbrarse a
Se acostumbró **a** leer durante el día.

to become accustomed to
He became accustomed to reading during the day.
(NOTE: One could argue that in this example, the *–ing* form is a noun since the English present participle routinely occurs as such, as in, *Reading is often impossible at my house.* You will encounter other such instances.

aprender a
Ella aprendió **a** multiplicar.

to learn
She learned to multiply.

apresurarse a
Me apresuré **a** sonar el timbre.

to hurry
I hurried to ring the bell.

atreverse a
Él no se atreve **a** gastarles una broma pesada.

to dare
He doesn't dare (to) play a practical joke on them.

ayudar a
Ella me ayudó **a** componer poemas.

to help
She helped me (to) compose poems.

bajar a*
Bajaron **a** podar el jardín.

to go/come down
They went/came down to trim the garden.

comenzar a
Pepe comenzó **a** empujarlo.

to begin/to start
Pepe began/started to push him.

correr a*
Corrieron **a** salvarme.

to run
They ran to save me.

empezar a
Empezamos **a** dividir las monedas en partes iguales.

to begin/to start
We began/started to divide the coins in equal parts.

enseñar a

to teach

Ella me enseñó **a** leer.
She taught me to read.

inspirar a
Lo inspiré **a** continuar sus estudios.
to inspire
I inspired him to continue his studies.

invitar a*
Los invité **a** definir su posición en torno a la defensa propia.
to invite
I invited them to define their position on self defense.

ir a*
Fueron **a** rodear el muro.
Van **a** rodear el muro.
to go/to be going
They went to surround the wall.
They are going to surround the wall.

llamar a*
Nos llamaron **a** representar al partido ante el congreso.
to call
They called us to represent the party before the congress.

llegar a*
Llegaron **a** recoger sus papeles.
Llegaron **a** poseer una enorme fortuna.
to arrive/to manage/come
They arrived to collect their papers.
They managed/came to possess an enormous fortune.

pasar a*
Él pasó **a** darme la noticia del siglo.
to pass/come by
He passed/came by to give me the news of the century.

ponerse a
Ella se puso **a** imaginar terribles eventos.
to begin/to start
She began (started) to imagine terrible events.

salir a*
Él salió a unirse **a** la sociedad moderna.
to leave/to go out
He left/went out to join modern society.

subir a*
Ella subió **a** provocar un disgusto.
to go/come up
She went/came up to start a quarrel.

venir a*
Vendrán **a** prestar ayuda a los desposeídos.
to come
They'll come to lend aid to those who suffered ruin.

volver/regresar a*
Regresaron **a** pedir la llave.
Volví **a** llamarte anoche.
to return/to do (something) again
They returned to ask for the key.
I called you again last night.

Note: *These verbs are the so-called "verbs of motion *(ir)* or attraction *(invitar)*." The definition includes verbs which induce one to act purposefully. When a noun complement follows them, they use the connector *a*. In such approach

Chapter 18 Spanish and English Verb + Preposition Constructions 233

> there is no contrast between the two languages: *Corrieron a la tienda = They ran to the store*. However, Spanish requires that *a* also appear before dependent infinitive complements. Compare *Corrieron a ayudarme* with *They ran to help me*. Spanish requires a connector while English uses the *to*-infinitive with no preposition; therefore, the English speaker mistakenly tends to say **Corrieron ayudarme*.

Exercise 1

Translate the following sentences:

1. Volveremos a explicar el procedimiento a seguir.
2. He never became accustomed to eating so late.
3. Subieron a decirnos que nuestro vuelo había llegado.
4. He learned to dance the samba in Rio de Janeiro.
5. Su cuerpo comenzó a temblar de miedo.
6. He won't dare (to) leave his wife there.
7. El genio llegó a ignorar la existencia del placer.
8. They began to study Russian last summer.
9. Van a ofrecer una descripción exacta de la escena dolorosa.
10. My father taught me to make wine.

The preposition is *DE*:

acabar de
Acabo **de** enterarme de la buena noticia.

to have just + PAST. PART.
I have just learned the good news.

acordarse de
Él se acordó **de** reducir el margen de error.

to remember
He remembered to reduce the margin of error.

alegrarse de
Me alegro **de** poder ayudar con el caso.

to be happy
I'm happy to help with the case.

cesar de
Ella cesó **de** fungir como secretaria del Presidente.

to quit/to stop + LV-*ing*
She quit/stopped acting as secretary to the President.

cuidarse de
Se cuidaron **de** no actuar en contra de la voluntad de la naturaleza.

to take care/to be careful
They took care/were careful not to act against the will of nature.

dejar de
Ella dejó **de** satisfacer sus impulsos naturales.

to stop/to quit + LV-*ing*
She quit/stopped satisfying her natural impulses.

disfrutar de
Disfrutan **de** vivir en Hawaii.

to enjoy + LV-*ing*
They enjoy living in Hawaii.

haber de
Has **de** situarlo en la era de los grandes descubrimientos.

to be + INF
You are to place it in the era of great discoveries.

olvidarse de
Juan se olvidó **de** marcarlo en el calendario.

to forget
John forgot to mark it on the calendar.

terminar de
Terminaron **de** recoger una cosecha abundante.

to finish + LV-*ing*
They finished gathering an abundant harvest.

tratar de
Enrique trató **de** echarse la culpa por lo sucedido.

to try/to attempt
Henry tried (attempted) to blame himself for what happened.

The preposition is *EN*:

consentir en
Ella consintió (**en**) tomar la responsabilidad.

to consent
She consented to take the responsibility.

quedar en
Quedaron **en** revolucionar su campaña.

to agree
They agreed to revolutionize their campaign.

tardar en/tardarse en

¿Cuánto tarda uno **en** llegar a El Paso?

Él se tardó mucho **en** cumplir la misión

to take x time+INF/to be late in + LV-*ing*
How much time does it take to get to El Paso?

He was very late in completing the mission.

The connector is *QUE*:
(Note that *que*, which has many functions in Spanish, must be called a "connector" since it rarely operates as a true preposition.)

tener que
Tengo **que** poner más empeño.

to have to
I have to be more persistent.

haber que (3rd pers. sgl. only)
Hay **que** llegar a una conclusión.

one must/it is necessary
One must arrive/It is necessary to arrive at a conclusion.

Exercise 2

Translate the following sentences:

1. One must see it to believe it.
2. Acaban de separarse con dignidad.
3. He had to work last night.
4. Se alegraron de recibir la admiración de los fieles.
5. They agreed to send us the documents.
6. Dejaron de molestarme; por lo tanto soy cordial con ellos.
7. She forgot to bring her books.
8. Trataremos de poner límites a toda acción vulgar.

18.5

ENGLISH USES THE PREPOSITIONS *IN, FROM, ABOUT* BETWEEN THE VERBAL FORMS; SPANISH DOES NOT.

(Note how few instances of this type of contrast there are compared to the large number of cases in which Spanish uses a connector between verbal forms while English does not.)

to succeed in + LV -*ing*
They succeeded **in** raising the building.

lograr/conseguir (=tener éxito)
Lograron/Consiguieron levantar el edificio.

to prevent from + LV -*ing*
I prevented her **from** leaving.

impedir
Impedí que ella saliera.

to think of/about + LV -*ing*
He thought **of** (**about**) giving a party.

pensar
Él pensó dar una fiesta.

(Little contrast with English)

Él pensó en hacer/dar una fiesta.

VERB + PREPOSITION CONSTRUCTIONS OF THE TYPE
VERB + PREPOSITION + NOUN/PRONOUN (See Appendix IV)

18.6

SPANISH USES THE PREPOSITIONS *A, DE, CON, EN*; ENGLISH DOES NOT.

The Preposition is *A*:

acercarse a
Ella se acercó **al** edificio.

to approach
She approached the building.

asistir a

to attend

Asistimos **a** la reunión.
We attended the meeting.

dar a
La construcción da **a** la calle.
to face
The construction faces the street.

entrar a
Entraron a mi clase.
to enter
They entered my class.

jugar a
Juegan (**al**) béisbol.
(NOTE: As a general rule in modern Spanish, the European variety maintains the preposition + article construction, while American Spanish drops it.)
to play
They play baseball.

parecerse a
Te pareces **a** tu padre.
to resemble/to look like
You resemble/look like your father.

unirse a
Roberto se unió **a** la asociación.
to join
Robert joined the association.

The Preposition is *DE*:

acordarse de
Me acordé de tu risa.
to remember/to recall
I remembered/recalled your laugh.

cambiar de
Ella cambió de actitud.
to change
She changed her attitude.

darse cuenta de
No me di cuenta de tu presencia.
to realize/to notice
I didn't realize/notice your presence.

disfrutar de
Disfruté de la leyenda.
to enjoy
I enjoyed the legend.

partir de
Partieron de España.
to leave (a city or a country)
They left Spain.

salir de
Salieron de mi despacho.
to leave (a confined space)
They left my office.

The Preposition is *Con*:

casarse
Él se casó **con** una europea.
to marry/to get married to
He married/got married to a European.

The Preposition is *EN*:

confiar en
Confío **en** tu solución.

to trust
I trust your solution.

entrar en (less common than *entrar a*)
Entré **en** el edificio.

to enter
I entered the building.
(No contrast) I went into the building.

fijarse en
Me fijé **en** su perfil elegante.

to notice/to focus on
I noticed his/her elegant profile.
(No contrast) I focused on his/her elegant profile.

Exercise 3
Translate the following sentences;

1. I noticed his expression of anxiety.
2. Se acercaron al círculo con curiosidad.
3. We entered the class in order to talk to the professor.
4. El año pasado asistí a clase regularmente a pesar de tener tantas preocupaciones.
5. He married a Mexican woman and then they left the country.
6. Me dedico al arte porque disfruto de su variedad.
7. The leftists joined the Communist Party.
8. Se parece a su abuela paterna.
9. Suddenly I remembered the name of his friend.
10. No me di cuenta en absoluto del constante eco que producía el viento.

18.7
ENGLISH USES THE PREPOSITIONS *FOR, TO, AT*; SPANISH DOES NOT USE A PREPOSITION:

to ask for
I asked **for** the address.

pedir
Pedí la dirección.

to listen to
He listened **to** the testimony.
He listened **to** the priest.

escuchar*
Él escuchó el testimonio.
Escuchó al cura.

to look at
She looked **at** her face.
She looked **at** her daughter.

mirar*
Ella miró su rostro.
Miró a su hija.

to look for
They looked **for** a modest home.
They looked **for** the guide.

buscar*
Buscaron un hogar modesto.
Buscaron al guía.

to wait for
We waited **for** the elections.
We waited **for** the children.

esperar*
Esperamos las elecciones.
Esperamos a los niños.

to pay for
I paid **for** the passage/fare.

pagar
Pagué el pasaje.

> **Note:** If Spanish **personal** noun complements follow the verbs marked by *, *a* must precede them. This is the so-called "personal accusative" which belongs to the personal direct object, thus marking it as a person rather than a thing. *Miraron el libro*, but *Miraron a los niños*. For a complete treatment of the personal accusative, See Chapter 22.

Exercise 4
Translate the following sentences:

1. Buscamos el tratado de un filósofo contemporáneo que fue citado.
2. He paid for the car with a personal check.
3. Les pedí consideración, pero me la negaron.
4. They waited for the summer with great anticipation.
5. Escuché la versión del nacimiento sagrado, pero no comprendí nada.
6. He always asks for help with his homework.
7. Tengo que esperar la supuesta partida.
8. She always listens to that ridiculous program.
9. No pude pagar la entrada a la función.
10. We are looking for a good apartment on this street.

18.8
BOTH LANGUAGES USE A PREPOSITION BEFORE A NOUN OR PRONOUN COMPLEMENT, BUT THE PREPOSITIONS ARE DIFFERENT:

contar con
Puedo contar **con** tu trato amable.

to count on
I can count **on** your friendly treatment.

cubrir de
Estaba cubierto **de** una substancia oscura.

to cover with
It was covered **with** a dark substance.

consistir en
La población consiste **en** varios grupos

to consist of
The population consists **of** various

étnicos y religiosos.

depender de
Todo depende **de** la voluntad de Dios.

despedirse de
Me despedí **de** una ilusión perdida.

enamorarse de
Se enamoraron **de** ese paraíso remoto.

interesarse por
Me intereso **por** el progreso continuo de ambos.

pensar en

Pensaron **en** el futuro ecológico del planeta.

preocuparse por
Me preocupo **por** el porvenir de la religión allí.

quejarse de
Ella se quejó **del** volumen de la música tan alto.

soñar con
Ella soñó **con** su novio.

ethnic and religious groups.

to depend on
Everything depends **on** the will of God.

to say goodbye to
I said goodbye **to** a lost fantasy.

to fall in love with
They fell in love **with** that remote paradise.

to be interested in
I'm interested **in** the continuous progress of both (of them).

to think of/about; to ponder/to consider
They thought **of/about** the ecological future of the planet.

to worry/be concerned about
I worry/am concerned **about** the future of religion there.

to complain about
She complained **about** the high volume of the music.

to dream about/of
She dreamed **about/of** her sweetheart.

Exercise 5

Translate the following sentences:

1. I know that we can count on them.
2. Anoche soñé con un ángel de cabello dorado.
3. He covered it with honey and then he ate it.
4. No me gusta que hablen de mí a mis espaldas.
5. In California everything depends on the rains.
6. Ese tonto no se queja de nada.
7. We said goodbye to our friends last week.
8. Me preocupo por una mejor enseñanza para todos.

9. He fell in love with a secretary.
10. El futuro de nuestro movimiento depende del trabajo de todos.

Exercise 6

The following exercise covers all the prepositional contrasts presented in this chapter. After translating each sentence, state the nature of these contrasts. First, determine whether the preposition (if any) occurs between verbs or between a verb and a noun or pronoun complement. Second, do the prepositions occur in both languages, in neither language or in one language but not the other?

1. Where did you learn to speak Spanish?
2. Lograron entrar en el espacio por séptima vez.
3. He approached the bird without making noise.
4. Están mirando el agua cristalina debajo del puente.
5. I know that I can't count on her.
6. Anteayer me invitaron a asistir al doble juego final.
7. You don't have to do anything for that class.
8. Estaban esperando el comienzo del prólogo.
9. Students always complain about examinations.
10. Ella trató de deshacerse de todo pecado, pero no pudo hacerlo.
11. He left Uruguay many years ago.
12. ¿Qué vas a pedir este año?
13. They agreed to come tomorrow at eight o'clock.
14. Hay que pensar en una breve preparación antes de continuar.
15. We didn't realize the danger.
16. Se despidieron de la dictadura recién establecida.
17. The little boy laughed at his puppy.
18. Bajaron a ver a los valientes que acababan de regresar.
19. It hasn't stopped snowing yet.
20. Hemos de asistir a una manifestación popular pasado mañana.
21. They are listening to my new CD's.
22. Adolfo no se atrevió a obligarlos a callar.
23. They came to tell me something sad.
24. No se juega mucho (al) fútbol americano en Sudamérica.
25. I forgot to write you that I had married an artist.

19

Nouns and Articles; Possessive and Partitive Constructions

SPANISH AND ENGLISH NOUNS

19.1
NOUN GENDER

A major difference between Spanish and English nouns is that all Spanish nouns express gender (masculine vs. feminine). English nouns have no gender except, of course, in the case of nouns representing masculine or feminine animate beings—*man/woman, bull/cow, buck/doe, ram/ewe, boy/girl*, etc. When English speakers acquire the meaning of Spanish nouns, they must also learn the gender classification of each one. Following are some useful keys to Spanish noun gender.

19.2

In our presentation of Spanish gender, we owe much to the work of Professor Richard V. Teschner (*Cubre,* 206-221) who organizes the topic around two major headings: 1) Natural Gender (animate beings, particularly humans), and 2) Artificial Gender (inanimate beings). He has, furthermore, made some interesting discoveries, complete with frequency counts, about gender based on word endings. In presenting natural gender we consider masculine and feminine nouns, and others encompassing both genders. Artificial gender is examined in light of semantic groupings and word endings. The chapter concludes with several significant observations.

19.3
NATURAL GENDER (animate beings, especially humans)

Animate nouns ending in –o are usually masculine, and routinely admit a feminine form; (*cocinero/a, gato/a, perro/a, hijo/a, abuelo/a, tío/a*). As regards the professions, some feminine forms are not acceptable to all native speakers, *médico/médica, abogado/abogada*. For animate beings, the language often uses different words to distinguish gender: (*padre/madre, toro/vaca, caballo/yegua, hombre/mujer, yerno/nuera*). Nouns referring to male human beings are of that gender: (*el rey, el cura, el sacerdote, el alcalde*). Such nouns ending in *–ín, -ón* or *–or* add *–a* to specify human females: (*bailarín/a, pastor/a, patrón/a*). Nouns referring to women are feminine (*la reina, la monja*). With titles, especially those of nobility, the feminine form is a different word (*el rey/la reina, el duque/la duquesa, el conde/la condesa*).

A number of animate nouns can be of either gender without a change of form, and in some cases, with no change of article.

Either *el* or *la* may occur before these nouns:

| atleta | bebé | joven | mártir | pareja | testigo |
| agente | intérprete | líder | modelo | siquíatra | |

The article used before the following nouns is fixed, but either gender may apply:

| el ángel | la persona | el personaje | la víctima |

Lastly, with respect to natural gender categories, some endings indicate either of the two genders, each designated by a change of article only. "Nouns of ambivalent gender" is the term used for these:

| -ista | el/la comunista |
| | el /la novelista |

| -ata | el/la burócrata |
| | el/la demócrata |

| -cida | el /la homicida |
| | el/la regicida |

| -ita | el/la menonita |
| | el/la moscovita |

| -ota | el/la patriota |
| | el/la idiota |

| -nte | el/la amante |
| | el/la cliente |

| -(i)ense | el/la canadiense |

	el/la nicaragüense
-al	el/la criminal
	el/la caníbal
-s (in composits)	el/la sacamuelas
	el/la limpiabotas
	el/la chupamedias

Exercise 1

The following are masculine animate nouns. Provide their feminine equivalents, and be able to explain each one:

abogado	gruñón	juez	profesor	testigo
amante	cliente	mártir	lector	trotacalles
amigo	criminal	moscovita	residente	víctima
artista	cuñado	príncipe	matasanos	yerno

19.4
ARTIFICIAL GENDER

Gender based on semantic groupings:

Masculine are:

1. Days of the week : (*el lunes, el miércoles, el sábado*)
2. Months of the year: (*febrero, mayo, setiembre*)
3. Names of languages: (*el árabe, el español, el francés*)
4. Composite forms consisting of a verb + a noun: (*el lavaplatos, el paraguas*)
5. The cardinal numbers: (*el uno, el siete, el once*)
6. Colors, even those not ending in –o: (*el rojo, el azul, el verde, el marrón*)
7. Infinitives used as nouns : (*el querer, el ser, el volar, el caminar*)
8. Post-verbals (nouns derived from verbs): (*el alcance, el cierre*)
9. The names of rivers, lakes, seas, oceans and the cardinal directions: (*El Amazonas, El (Lago) Titicaca, El Caribe, El Pacífico, el norte, el oeste*)
10. Borrowings from other languages: (*el jazz, el campus, el champú, el (e)spray*)
11. Names of trees: However, the fruit they bear are feminine. (*el almendro/la almendra, el naranjo/la naranja, el cerezo/la cereza*)

Feminine are:

The letters of the alphabet: (la "be", la "rr", la "u")

Gender based on noun ending :

Predominantly masculine are:

Nouns ending in *–o*: The vast majority are masculine *(el libro, el caso, el cuarto)*, La mano is feminine, as are shortened forms of longer feminine words *(la foto < la fotografía, la moto < la motocicleta)*

Nouns ending in *–e*: A surprising 90% of these are masculine: *(el aceite, el baile, el coche, el diente, el golpe, el lenguaje, el monte, el nombre, el pie, el timbre, el valle, el vientre)*. The remaining 10% in *–e* are feminine, and a number of these are of such high frequency as to warrant listing here:

la base	la fe	la leche	la noche
la calle	la fiebre	la llave	la nube
la carne	la frase	la masacre	la parte
la catástrofe	la fuente	la mente	la sangre
la clase	la gente	la muerte	la suerte
la corriente	el hambre	la nieve	la torre

1. Nouns ending in *–l*: Virtually all are masculine *(el hotel, el metal, el papel, el sol)* with some very common feminine exceptions: *(la catedral, la cárcel, la piel, la sal, la señal)*.

2. Nouns ending in *–r*: Again, the vast majority are masculine *(el alfiler, el calor, el horror, el lugar)*, with only a few feminine exceptions: *(la flor, la labor)*.

3. Nouns ending in *–ón* are routinely masculine: *(el jabón, el rincón, el algodón, el cajón, el jamón, el cañón)*.

4. Most nouns are masculine if they end in *–n* preceded by one of the following stressed vowels: A, E, I, U: *(el pan, el almacén, el jardín, el atún)*.

5. Nouns ending in *–ión* are rarely masculine, *-ión* being a prototypical feminine ending. The few masculines in *–ión* follow a distinct pattern, in that for them, *-ión* must be preceded by one of the following consonants: B, D, M, P, RR, V, as in the following examples: *(el rabión, el meridión, el camión, el sarampión, el gorrión, el avión)*.

6. Nouns ending in *–az, -oz* and *–uz* are 75% masculine: *(el alcatraz, el altavoz, el avestruz)*. Some frequent feminine nouns also use these endings: *(la cruz, la luz, la paz, la voz)*.

7. Composite nouns made up of a verb + a noun are routinely masculine: *(el abrelatas, el lavaplatos)*.

8. Singular nouns ending in *–s* which are non-composite or do not end in *–sis* or *–tis* are masculine: *(el atlas, el brindis, el compás, el gas, el interés, el mes, el país)*.

Predominantly feminine are:

1. Nouns ending in *–a (la casa, la docena, la vejiga)*, except masculine *el día*. Also masculine are nouns of Greek origin ending in *–ma, -pa, -ta*: *(el tema, el programa, el planeta)*.

2. Nouns ending in *–d*, especially *–dad, -tad, -tud*: (*la verdad, la mitad, la virtud, la pared*) Exceptions are, *el césped* and *el ataúd*)

3. Added to this list of feminines are nouns in *–umbre* and *-ie:* (*la muchedumbre, la legumbre, la serie, la especie*).

4. Nouns ending in *–ión* if the consonant preceding that ending is one of the following: C, G, N, S, T, X: (*la nación, la religión, la opinión, la confesión, la cuestión, la conexión*). The ending *–ión* is normally feminine, although a number of masculines in *–ión* was listed previously.

5. Nouns ending in *–ez* are 85% feminine (*la acidez, la dejadez, la estupidez, la rigidez*), but a few masculine exceptions occur (*el ajedrez, el jerez*).

6. Plural forms in *–s* which admit no singular are all feminine (*las cosquillas, las exequias, las nupcias*).

7. Feminine are nouns ending in *–sis* or *–tis*, derived from Greek, and used primarily in the scientific and medical fields: (*la crisis, la dosis, la tesis, la bronquitis, la apendicitis*). Exception: el oasis

Nouns ending in *–iz* seem equally divided between their gender assignments. Masculine are, *el lápiz* and *el maíz*, but *la nariz* and *la raíz* are feminine.

19.5

Several nouns are of "epicene gender," meaning that they may appear in either gender guise. The classic example is *mar*, usually masculine (*el mar*). In poetry or fixed expressions, it is feminine (*la alta mar, la mar de cosas que hacer*). The nouns *azúcar, puente*, and *sartén* are variable in gender, depending on the regional norms.

19.6

Homophonic nouns are those with identical spelling and pronunciation but different in meaning when of one gender or the other. The following list is fairly complete:

el capital (money)	*la capital* (city)
el cólera (disease)	*la cólera* (anger, fury, rage)
el cometa (comet)	*la cometa* (kite)
el doblez (fold)	*la doblez* (duplicity)
el guía (male guide)	*la guía* (female guide, listing as in *guía de teléfonos*)
el moral (mulberry tree)	*la moral* (morality, ethics)
el orden (listed first to last; peace and tranquility)	*la orden* (command, and item requested, a religious or military organization)
el pendiente (pendent, earing)	*la pendiente* (slope, precipice)
el pez (fish)	*la pez* (pitch from a pine)
el policía (policeman)	*la policía* (police woman, police force)
el radio (radio receiver, element radium, radius)	*la radio* (radio station, broadcast)

19.7
PHONETIC FACTORS AND GENDER

We discuss here feminine nouns beginning with **stressed** *a-* or *ha-*. In the singular, they appear to be masculine because of the article, *el*. This is a historical hangover from Old Spanish where the feminine article, *la*, had two distinct forms (allomorphs): *la*, used before feminine words beginning with a consonant, and *el* with all feminine nouns starting with a vowel. In *El Poema de Mio Cid* we find *el espada* and *el espuela*. In the modern language, *el*, this feminine allomorph of *la* occurs only before feminine nouns with **initial stressed *a-* or *ha-***. Regardless of the historical realities just cited, the usage could be explained to students as, "*El* occurs before feminine nouns beginning with **stressed** *a-* or *ha-* to prevent a word's being lost or misunderstood, *laagua* > *el agua*. Note that any accompanying modifiers take feminine form; *el alma pura, las aguas negras*.

el agua/ las aguas	el alma/las almas	el arma/las armas
el águila/las águilas	el ánima/las ánimas	el habla/las hablas
el ala/las alas	el ansia/las ansias	el hacha/las hachas
el alba/las albas	el área/las áreas	el hambre/las hambres

Note: The noun *arte* is exceptional; masculine in the singular (*el arte moderno*), but feminine in the plural (*las bellas artes*).

Exercise 2
Determine the gender of each of the following inanimate nouns:

1. pared
2. día
3. depresión
4. algodón
5. gorrión
6. disfraz
7. voz
8. timidez
9. cicatriz
10. lombriz
11. dosis
12. atlas
13. metal
14. taller
15. mueble
16. nube
17. paisaje
18. habla
19. ánima
20. nariz
21. lápiz
22. mar
23. sacacorchos
24. barbarie
25. tema
26. género
27. página
28. hache
29. Orinoco (river)
30. este
31. solicitud
32. especie
33. árabe (language)
34. martes
35. costumbre
36. vestirse
37. poeta
38. alma
39. res
40. Pisuerga (river)

Exercise 3
Determine the gender of the following nouns. Which would belong to both genders? Indicate those nouns whose gender cannot be determined from the rules presented.

1. género
2. página
3. x
4. ocho
5. calle
6. caracol
7. avestruz
8. Madre (river)
9. oeste
10. tema
11. virtud
12. comunista
13. serie
14. redacción
15. portugués (language)
16. martes
17. calidad
18. costumbre
19. vestirse
20. actor

Chapter 19 Nouns and Articles; Possessive and Partitive Constructions

NOUN NUMBER IN THE TWO LANGUAGES

Both Spanish and English nouns have the characteristic of number, that is, they are either singular (representing one) or plural (representing two or more). Although the English system of pluralization is more complicated than that of Spanish, the two systems are partially similar, pluralizing with -s or -es in the majority of cases.

19.8
PLURALIZATION OF SPANISH NOUNS

Spanish nouns form their plural according to specific rules:

1. Nouns ending in an unaccented vowel or in an accented -é add: -s *caja/cajas, acto/actos, café/cafés*, . . .

2. Nouns ending in a consonant, in -y, or in any accented vowel (except –é) add -es: *farol/faroles, león/leones, rey/reyes, rubí/rubíes* . . .

3. Nouns ending in -z change the -z to –c- before adding -es: *voz/voces, luz/luces, lápiz/lápices,* . . .

4. If a Spanish singular noun ends in -s and the vowel before the *s* is the stressed vowel of the word, the plural is formed by adding -es: *mes/meses, revés/reveses, inglés/ingleses* . . .

5. However, if the Spanish singular noun ends in -s and the vowel before the -s is unstressed, the singular and the plural forms are identical and only the article indicates whether singular or plural meaning is intended: *el/los lunes, el/los viernes, el/los cumpleaños.*

6. Surnames are pluralized in Spanish by placing the plural form of the article before them. English adds an apostrophe + s ('s) to names and surnames: *Los Rivera/The Riviera's, Los Negrón/The Negron's.* To pluralize a first name (*nombre de pila*) in Spanish, follow rules (1) and (2) above: *las Marías, los Juanes.*

7. In their masculine plural form, many Spanish animate nouns refer either to more than one masculine being or to two or more beings of both sexes: *los reyes 'the kings' or 'the king and queen', los hermanos 'the brothers' or 'the siblings', los padres 'the fathers' or 'the parents.'*

8. Occasionally Spanish presents a plural noun which English translates as singular and *vice versa.*

SPANISH PLURAL:	ENGLISH SINGULAR:
noticias	news
muebles	furniture
helados	ice cream
dulces	candy
consejos	advice

tonterías	nonsense
chismes	gossip
canas	gray hair
vacaciones	vacation

If Spanish uses a singular for the above listed plurals, the meaning is always partitive: *"a piece/a bit of..."*, eg., *un dulce = a piece of candy; un consejo = a bit of advice*. There are a few cases in which a Spanish singular translates as a plural in English: *bosque/woods* (no contrast if translated as *forest*), *pantalón/pants. ropa/clothes*. Of special interest are the words *gente/people*. Both are collective nouns, but *gente* takes a singular verbal form (*La gente sabe...*) while *people* requires a plural (*The people know...*)

Exercise 4

Give the plural form of the following singular nouns and state the rule:

1. columna
2. buey
3. andaluz
4. consejo
5. miércoles
6. cordobés
7. canapé
8. alelí
9. pie
10. pez
11. alemán
12. clase
13. carácter
14. lente

19.9
PLURALIZATION OF ENGLISH NOUNS

In the vast majority of cases, English and Spanish coincide in noun pluralization by adding the suffixes *-s* or *-es* to the singular form. There are some few orthographic adjustments to this process, but by far the most difficult aspect of the English pluralization system for Spanish natives is its oral rendering. Fortunately, however, the phonological rules applied to English plural nouns are identical to those pertaining to the third person singular, present tense form of the English verb already presented in Chapter 2.7. These rules are reviewed as follows:

PHONETIC RULES:

a. A noun ending in a voiceless consonant sound other than the sibilants (See c. below) adds *-s* with the pronunciation of [s]: *pick/picks* [pıks], *bit/bits* [bıts], *rope/ropes* [rops], *fife/fifes* [faɪfs], *bath/baths* [bæθs]. Voiceless consonants that occur in final position in nouns are [**p, t, k, f, θ**].

b. A noun ending in a voiced consonant sound other than the sibilants (Again, see c. below) or in a vowel sound adds *-s*, but with the sound of [z]. As for spelling, nouns ending in *-o* preceded by a consonant usually add *–es* (*torpedo > torpedoes*), and if preceded by another vowel just add *-s* (*radio > radios*). Two common exceptions are *potatoes* and *to-*

matoes. Regardless, both the *-s* and *-es* endings are pronounced as [z]. Since Spanish lacks the [z] sound as a phoneme separate from /s/, the pronunciation in this case requires special attention for the Spanish speaker: *bead/beads* [biidz], *bag/bags* [bægz], *can/cans* [kænz], *name/names* [neɪmz], *tool/tools* [tulz], *car/cars* [karz], *ray/rays* [reɪz], *sea/seas* [siiz], *snow/snows* [snoʊz]. Apart from the sibilants below, the other voiced consonants occurring in final position are **[b, d, g, v, ð, m, n, ŋ, l, r]**.

c. A noun ending in one of the sibilant sounds **[s, z, ʃ, ʧ, ʒ, ʤ]** adds the plural inflection *-s/-es* to the singular form with the pronunciation of [ɪz], an extra syllable: *lass/lasses* [læsɪz], *nose/noses* [nozɪz], *wish/wishes* [wɪʃɪz], *rouge/rouges* [ruʒɪz], *beach/beaches* [biʧɪz], *badge/badges* [bæʤɪz].

d. An English noun ending in *-y* preceded by a vowel adds *-s* to form the plural: *boy/boys, key/keys, day/days*. If, however, the final *-y* is preceded by a consonant, the *y* changes to *i* with *-es* added to form the plural: *spy/spies, fly/flies, century/centuries*. With either orthographic inflection, the pronunciation remains [z].

e. Finally, English has a host of irregularly formed plurals which the Spanish speaker must memorize, since they are especially complicated to classify: *child/children, leaf/leaves, woman/women, mouse/mice, foot/feet, sheep/sheep, goose/geese, tooth/teeth*, etc.

Exercise 5

Give the plural of the following English singular nouns, and state the rule for each pluralization. Provide the phonetic symbol which applies. Identify the plurals that defy convenient classification.

1. singer
2. rack
3. cylinder
4. snap
5. hat
6. church
7. thrush
8. fool
9. toy
10. fly
11. class
12. clash
13. station
14. grudge
15. goose
16. knife
17. breeze
18. man
19. potato
20. thread
21. reply

THE DEFINITE ARTICLES OF SPANISH AND ENGLISH

19.10
The Spanish Definite Article

There are five definite articles in Spanish: *el, la, los, las,* and *lo*. The articles *el, la, los,* and *las* must agree in gender and number with their nouns: *el hombre, la tía, los hombres, las tías*. *Lo* is a neuter definite article which does not show agreement. It appears with both masculine and feminine words, usually adjectives, to produce a nominalization with abstract meaning: *Lo bueno/buena que eres*. (See Chapter 20.12)

The English Definite Article

English has only one written form of the definite article, *the,* with two pronunciations, [ðə] and [ðiį]. Unstressed [ðə] occurs before words beginning with a consonant sound: *the man* [ðə mæn]. Unstressed [ðiį] appears before words beginning with a vowel sound: *the army* [ðiį armiį]. Plural nouns use the same phonetically conditioned forms.

19.11
IDENTICAL USAGE OF THE DEFINITE ARTICLES

Both Spanish and English use the definite article in the same way in many cases, as follow:

1. When the speaker and the listener are aware of both the existence and the identity of the person or thing under discussion:

La ciudad está triste.	The city is sad.
La bandera tricolor es vuestra.	The tricolor flag is yours.

2. With elements of nature:

El cielo es azul.	The sky is blue.
El sol nunca brilla aquí.	The sun never shines here.

3. With animals, plants, or individuals spoken of in the singular as representing their species, sex, race, religion, or nationality:

La zorra es muy astuta.	The fox is very cunning.
La rosa es una flor.	The rose is a flower.
El bautista es protestante.	The Baptist is a protestant.
El argentino no lo haría.	The Argentinian would not do it.
El indígena tiene derechos.	The native has rights.

4. With parts of the body:

El corazón es pequeño.	The heart is small.
El ojo es de menor tamaño.	The eye is smaller in size.

5. With nouns restricted by modifying or defining words:

la flor de papel	the paper flower
la señorita de Cuba	the young lady from Cuba
el número más pequeño	the smallest number

6. With epithets (words used to characterize famous people) and nicknames:

Pedro el Grande	Peter the Great

Chapter 19 Nouns and Articles; Possessive and Partitive Constructions

Bolívar el Libertador   Bolivar the Liberator
Pepe el toro   Pepe the Bull

7. With names of rivers, seas, and oceans:

   El Río Bravo es largo.   The Rio Grande is long.
   La isla se encuentra en el Atlántico.   The island is located in the Atlantic.

8. With the expression of exact dates, provided that English uses the construction *the* + [date] + *of* + [month]:

   Él vino el 20 de abril.   He came (on) the 20th of April.
   Voy el dos de julio.   I'm going (on) the 2nd of July.

> **Note:** Spanish uses the cardinal number but English, the ordinal for dates (*Ellos celebran el Cinco de Mayo* = *They celebrate May fifth*). There is one exception to this practice: Spanish, like English, uses the ordinal number for the first day of the month: *Comienzan el primero de mayo* = *They begin (on) the 1st of May*. Increasingly common, however, is *uno: el 1 de mayo*, said *el uno de mayo*

19.12
DIVERGENT USES OF THE DEFINITE ARTICLES

Spanish uses the definite article while English does not in some instances, or English selects another word in place of the article.

1. With nouns spoken of in a generic sense (Bull, 65), whether concrete or abstract in meaning:

   El griego es difícil.   Greek is difficult.
   No permito los sacrificios.   I don't allow sacrifices.
   El hombre no es divino.   Man is not divine.
   Las drogas causan daño.   Drugs cause harm.
   La ciencia define la naturaleza.   Science defines nature.
   La paz es la tolerancia.   Peace is tolerance.

   Bull also speaks of "unique nouns," entities of common knowledge or experience. These, like the generic nouns, always occur with the definite article in Spanish, but in English, article usage is not so consistent.

   El sol consume hidrógeno.   The sun consumes hydrogen.
   El cielo y el infierno son imaginarios.   Heaven and hell are imaginary.

2. With days of the week and in the expression of exact dates, provided that English uses the construction *on* + [month] + [date]:

   Ella llegó el lunes.   She arrived on Monday.

Chapter 19 Nouns and Articles; Possessive and Partitive Constructions

    La vemos los martes.   We see her on Tuesdays.
    Él vino el diez de mayo.   He came on May 10th.
    Salieron el 24 de agosto.   They left on August 24th.

3. With expressions of the time of day:

    Son las doce en punto.   It's twelve o'clock.
    Eran las cuatro y treinta/media.   It was four-thirty.
    Él nos encontró a las siete.   He met us at seven.

4. With Spanish *en* (English *at*) and Spanish *a* (English *to*) + a commonly frequented or often referred to place or event. Note that Spanish uses the article much more than does English, although in several instances both languages omit it.

    • Spanish uses the definite article; English does not:

        Van al cielo.   They're going to heaven.
        Estoy en la escuela.   I'm in/at school.
        Vas a la cárcel.   You're going to jail.
        Están en la iglesia.   They're in/at church.
        Vas al infierno.   You're going to hell.
        Voy al pueblo.   I'm going to town.
        ¿Vas al mercado?   Are you going to (the) market?

    • Definite article omitted in both languages:

        Están en clase.   They are in class.
        Estoy en casa.   I'm at home.
        Vamos a misa.   Let's go to Mass.

5. Before the name of a country or continent if modified:

    La América Latina   Latin America
    El Asia Central   Central Asia
    La Europa clásica   Classical Europe

6. With classified nouns, i.e., those modified in some way:

    Vivo en la calle Ocho.   I live on Eighth Street.
    Corresponde con la página 25.   It matches page 25.

Surnames bearing titles are also classified nouns, and when they occur in indirect address (i.e., the person involved is referred to rather than directly spoken to) Spanish and English direct article usages differ.

    ¿Dónde está el Sr. Gómez?   Where is Mr. Gomez?
    Es la clase del Dr. Corral.   It's Dr. Corral's class.

7. With nouns used in apposition to a personal pronoun. A noun in apposition is one which identifies a personal pronoun.

Ustedes los rebeldes ...	You rebels ...
Nosotros los técnicos ...	We technicians ...
Vosotros los romanos ...	You Romans ...

8. With parts of the body or articles of clothing. English in these cases uses the possessive adjective rather than the definite article. This lack of correspondence between Spanish and English is one of the most frequent causes of production errors. (See Chapter 13.8)

Me puse el vestido.	I put on my suit (dress).
Él bajó la cabeza.	He bowed his head.
Me quemé el dedo.	I burned my finger.
Ud. se cortó la cara.	You've cut your face.
Ella se quitó los zapatos.	She took off her shoes.

19.13

It is essential to note that English and Spanish have different ways of viewing reality when parts of the body or personal possessions are the topic. When the reference is to bodily parts or articles of clothing found singularly among a group of individuals, Spanish uses the singular form of the noun, meaning that each individual has one item. English employs the plural in these cases since more than one item is involved in the entire group.

| Nos quitamos el sombrero | We took off our hats. |
| (Each person has one hat.) | (There is more than one hat involved.) |

Similarly:
Tenían la boca cerrada.	They had their mouths closed.
Levantaron la mano.	They raised their hands.
Bajaron la cabeza.	They bowed their heads.

But:
| Levantaron las manos. | (Each person raised both his/her hands.) |

| *Bajaron las cabezas. | (The implication is that each person has two heads; therefore, the sentence is ungrammatical) |

Exercise 6

Translate the following sentences:

1. The oak is a very important tree in Portugal.
2. Es obvio que no sabes nada de la cocina francesa.
3. We are going to travel through western France.
4. Me quité los zapatos y me puse las sandalias.

5. He wants to visit us on July 4th.
6. ¿No conoce Ud. a la profesora Serrano?
7. The lungs are very near the heart.
8. No quiero caminar contigo a la cárcel.
9. It's nine o'clock and I have to go home.
10. Los lunes no voy al centro hasta muy tarde.
11. The earth was once considered flat.
12. Leímos la triste historia de Diana la Cazadora.
13. John cut his arm in the accident.
14. No quiero comprar ninguna casa en la calle La Riviera.
15. They live in ignorance and poverty because they lack money.
16. Algunos van al cielo y otros van al infierno.
17. Dr. Brown spoke to Dr. Smith at the meeting.
18. Ustedes los alumnos creen que lo saben todo.
19. They left on Saturday, but they plan to return on Sunday.
20. Abrí los ojos cuando la profesora Roscoe se sentó a mi lado.

THE INDEFINITE ARTICLES OF SPANISH AND ENGLISH

19.14

Spanish has four forms of the indefinite article: *un, una, unos, unas*. There is no neuter indefinite article. Again, the indefinite articles show inflection for gender and number. English has two forms (allomorphs) of its singular indefinite article: *a* and *an*. You use *a* before words beginning with a consonant sound: *a dog, a man, a house, a book, a tiger, a lady*. You use *an* before words with an initial vowel sound: *an apple, an onion, an honor, an eye*. The English plural indefinite article is *some*, and it is often omitted.

SINGULAR	PLURAL
I have a book.	I have (some) books.
She has an answer.	She has (some) answers.
He needs a lesson.	He needs (some) lessons.

The two languages generally use the indefinite article in the same way, although there are some exceptions. With an unmodified singular predicate noun indicating profession or with a singular predicate adjective of nationality, Spanish does not normally use the indefinite article while English does.

Mi padre es capitán.	My father is a captain.
Susana es actriz.	Susan is an actor/actress.
Rafael es mexicano.	Ralph is (a) Mexican.
Ella es alemana.	She's (a) German.

However, when the predicate noun of profession or adjective of nationality is in any way modified, both English and Spanish use the indefinite article.

Mi padre es un capitán de reserva.   My father is a reserve captain.

Chapter 19 Nouns and Articles; Possessive and Partitive Constructions

Susana es una buena actriz.	Susan is a good actor/actress.
Rafael es un mexicano romántico.	Ralph is a romantic Mexican.
Es una alemana curiosa.	She is a curious German.

Finally, if the predicate noun of profession or adjective of nationality assumes plural form, neither language uses the indefinite article, unless--and this applies to Spanish only-- the noun or adjective is modified.

Ellos son dominicanos.	They are Dominican(s).
Mis padres son científicos.	My parents are scientists.
Son médicos.	They are doctors.

But:
Son unos dominicanos ricos.	They are rich Dominicans.

Exercise 7

Translate the following sentences into the other language:

1. Quiero buscar unos documentos de historia en la biblioteca.
2. His father is a businessman.
3. Estos señores son brasileños.
4. Her uncle is a very good doctor.
5. Osvaldo es ingeniero.
6. All your friends are students.
7. ¿Es guatemalteco tu tío?
8. She is (an) Italian.
9. El perro se comió un hueso y unos trozos de carne.
10. Cantinflas was a very famous Mexican comedian.
11. Ellos son unos actores bien conocidos.
12. My parents are French.

EXPRESSIONS OF POSSESSION

The Spanish and English systems used for expressing possession are quite different. Both sets of speakers require considerable practice with the possessive system of the opposing language. The Spanish speaker, however, has more difficulties with the English system than has the English speaker with the Spanish one.

19.15
THE SPANISH SYSTEM

The Spanish system consistently uses the preposition *de* in periphrastic possession expressions.

The formula to show possession is as follows:

POSSESSED THING +	de	+ POSSESSOR
la sonrisa	de	la Virgen
los hijos	de	mis vecinos
el gesto	de	ese héroe
las emociones	de	una madre

When one asks a question concerning who possesses what in Spanish, s/he uses one of the following patterns.

1. *¿De quién(es) es + NOUN [singular]?*
    Example: *¿De quién(es) es esta llave?*

    ¿De quién(es) son + NOUN [plural]?
    Example: *¿De quién(es) son estos dibujos?*

2. *¿A quién(es) + pertenece + NOUN [singular]?*
    Example: *¿A quién(es) pertenece esta llave?*

    ¿A quién(es) + pertenecen + NOUN [plural]?
    Example: *¿A quién(es) pertenecen estos dibujos?*

In the patterns above, the possessor in question is either singular (*¿quién?*) or plural (*¿quiénes?*), both forms accented. English makes no number distinction, and uses either *whose?* or *of whom?*, each with both singular or plural meaning, as seen in 19.17.

19.16
THE ENGLISH SYSTEM

The English system for expressing possession is essentially the reverse of the Spanish one, with some additional features.

- The possessor, expressed in a special form, appears first, followed by the possessed thing.

- No preposition intervenes between the elements of the construction.

- If the possessor (expressed first) is singular, or if it is plural but does not end in *-s*, you then add *-'s* to the word: *John/John's, my niece/my niece's, the men/the men's, the women/the women's.*

- If the possessor (expressed first) is plural and the plural form ends in *-s* as most English plurals do, or is singular and ends in *-s*, then you simply add an apostrophe (') to form the possessive: *the girls/the girls', the boys/the boys', the dogs/the dogs', Agnes/Agnes', Jonas/Jonas'.*

Chapter 19 Nouns and Articles; Possessive and Partitive Constructions 257

The English formula expressing possession is:

POSSESSOR	+	POSSESSED THING
[possessive form]		
Mary's		friend
my brother's		books
Robert's		uncle
his parents'		car
the professors'		salaries
the children's		toys

19.17

An alternate English possessive construction resembles the Spanish formula to a considerable degree. However, the construction occurs more frequently in dialectal speech than in the standard variety.

POSSESSED THING	+	*of*	+	POSSESSOR [possessive form]
the new house		of		my uncle's
that friend		of		Robert's
those boys		of		your sister's
some dogs		of		our neighbors'
this bad feeling		of		mine (possessive pronoun)

When questioning who possesses what in English, you may use one of the four following patterns. The first and third represent the less formal mode of expression, whereas the second and fourth are rather more formal.

1. *whose* + NOUN [sgl./pl.] + *be* + DEMONSTRATIVE PRONOUN

   Whose book is this?
   Whose children are these?

2. *whose* + *be* + DEMONSTRATIVE ADJECTIVE + NOUN [sgl./pl.]

   Whose is this book?
   Whose are these children?

3. *who(m)* + AUX-*do* + DEMONS. ADJ + NOUN [sgl./pl.] + *belong to*

   Who(m) (formal) does this book belong to?
   Who(m) (formal) do these children belong to?

4. *to whom* + AUX-*do* + DEMONS. ADJ + NOUN [sgl./pl.] + *belong*

To whom does this book belong?
To whom do these children belong?

19.18
NOMINALIZATION IN POSSESSIVE STRUCTURES

The nominalization of adjectives in general and its application to possessive and demonstrative adjectives is presented in chapters 20 and 21. It occurs with possessive structures in both languages through the suppression of a word occurring in the first part of the sentence to avoid its repetition in the second sentence segment.

Spanish nominalizes possessive expressions by converting a possessive adjective into a possessive pronoun: *Yo tengo mis problemas, y tú tienes tus problemas* > *Yo tengo mis problemas, y tú tienes los problemas tuyos.* English follows the same pattern: *I have my problems, and you have your problems* > *I have my problems, and you have yours.* However, in possessive nominalizations involving *el/la/los/las* + *de*, where a noun is suppressed between an article and *de* (*el amigo de/la casa de/los productos de/las aventuras de*), English uses its demonstrates (*that/those*) in the translation if a phrase rather than the possessive form of the possessor is chosen:

Tu trabajo y el de tu esposo...
    Your job and your husband's...
    Your job and that of your husband...
Sus preocupaciones y las de sus hijos...
    Her worries and her children's...
    Her worries and those of her children...

Exercise 8
Translate these possessive phrases:

1. my father's brother
2. la bondad de nuestros amigos
3. his brother's son
4. los peligros de mi profesión
5. the children's shoes
6. la cocina de mi madre
7. the girls' dresses
8. las páginas de la declaración
9. the secretary's office
10. las faldas de las chicas
11. Chris' new home
12. las niñas de las mujeres
13. her parents' factory
14. la ópera de Verdi
15. the cat's paws
16. los enemigos de los judíos
17. my articles and the professor's

Chapter 19 Nouns and Articles; Possessive and Partitive Constructions 259

    18. tus clases y las de tus colegas (2 ways)
    19. your solution and that of Einstein
    20. nuestros amigos y los de nuestros padres (2 ways)

Exercise 9

A. Give several Spanish versions of each interrogative possessive pattern (1 and 2) presented in 19.15

B. Give several English versions of each interrogative possessive pattern (1-4) presented in 19.17

19.19

Spanish and English use locutions resembling possessive structures, but these are not possessive. English composes certain lexical items in a manner parallel with its possessive system, but these are other parts of speech.

    I.   An attributive noun precedes a base noun thus forming new word or phrase, for example: *bookstore, dog food, garbage can, alarm clock*.

    II.   The Spanish equivalent may be one word (eg., *alarm clock = despertador*), or a construction using *de*, the first element of English being expressed last in Spanish and the reverse (eg., *housewife = ama de casa, dog food = comida de perros*).

Here are some examples of both types:

- English construction composed of more than one word; one word equivalent in Spanish.

    mailman   cartero
    doorman   portero
    bookstore   librería
    highway   carretera

- English construction composed of more than one word: Spanish uses a construction with *de*, the elements placed in reverse order with respect to English.

    silver chain   cadena de plata
    bathing suit   traje de baño
    silk cape   capa de seda
    dining room table   mesa de comedor

Note: The system is considerably more complex than it would appear at first glance, for example, English one word vs. Spanish two word, *newlyweds* vs. *recién casados*, and English two words vs. Spanish one word, *belly button* vs. *ombligo*.

Exercise 10

Find at least ten examples on your own of English constructions rendered in Spanish by one word and another ten examples of English constructions rendered in Spanish with a construction using *de*.

PARTITIVE CONSTRUCTIONS

19.20
COUNT AND NON-COUNT NOUNS

Both languages have count nouns (nouns that can be counted), eg., *books/libros, houses/casas, friends/amigos, dogs/perros*, and non-count nouns, sometimes called "mass nouns," those that cannot be counted but are described only according to quantity, eg., *water/agua, milk/leche, meat/carne, sugar/azúcar*. Although both languages employ the count/non-count classificatory system, not all nouns are of the same category in each language. One such example is *furniture/muebles*. *Furniture* is a non-count noun in English, whereas *muebles* is a Spanish count noun.

The furniture is new. (non-count)
Two pieces of furniture are broken. (count)
El mobiliario es nuevo. (a non-count Spanish equivalent)
El mueble está roto. (count noun, one item only)
Dos muebles están rotos. (count noun)

19.21
ENGLISH AND SPANISH PARTITIVE SYSTEMS

Count Nouns

With count nouns, English and Spanish use the partitive quantifiers outlined here:

SMALL DEGREE	a few/few	pocos/-as, unos pocos/unas pocas
MEDIUM DEGREE	some	unos/-as algunos/-as, unos cuantos/unas cuantas
LARGE DEGREE	many/lots of/a lot of	muchos/-as

EXAMPLES:
I have a few/few friends.   Tengo/pocos/unos pocos amigos.
I have some friends.   Tengo/unos/algunos/unos cuantos amigos.
I have many/a lot of/lots of friends.   Tengo muchos amigos.

Non-Count Nouns

The partitive system for Spanish and English non-count nouns is as follows:

Chapter 19 Nouns and Articles; Possessive and Partitive Constructions   261

SMALL DEGREE	a little	un poco de
MEDIUM DEGREE	some	algo de/ ø
LARGE DEGREE	a lot of, lots of, much	mucho/a

EXAMPLES:
I carry a little water.   Cargo un poco de agua
I carry some water.   Cargo (algo de) agua
I carry a lot of/lots of/much) water.   Cargo mucha agua.

In the English comparative degree, *less* appears with non-count nouns while *fewer* modifies count nouns: *I drink less water than I should; I have fewer friends than my sister*. In the informal spoken language, however, one hears *less* with both types of nouns: **I have less friends than my sister*.

> **Note:** Some nouns may belong to both categories, count and non-count, for example: *wine/wines* and *vino/vinos*.
>
> **Count:**   **Non-count:**
> There are various wines in the cellar.   I like to drink a little wine with dinner.
> Hay varios vinos en la bodega.   Me gusta beber vino con la cena.

Exercise 11

Translate the following partitive constructions. State in each case whether the italicized item is a count noun or a non-count noun.

1. We don't want to read *many* books.
2. Put *a little* sugar on the fruit.
3. He thinks he can depend on *a few* friends in Brazil.
4. Please buy me *some* cigarettes.
5. She poured *lots of* water into the glass.
6. Why didn't they bring *some* beer?
7. *Few* Europeans live in Paraguay.
8. Do you want *some* orange juice?
9. Please buy me a *little* cheese.
10. Does your car use *much* gasoline?
11. Do they have *a lot of* relatives in Ecuador?
12. We are going to visit *some* friends in Mendoza.

Exercise 12

Translate the following constructions. State in each case whether the italicized item is a count noun or a non-count noun.

1. Tengo *algunos* tíos en Colombia.
2. ¿Tiene *muchos* hijos el profesor de la academia?
3. Algunas mujeres usan *mucho* perfume fino.
4. Esta noche mi esposa va a servir *un poco* de sopa.
5. ¿Dónde podemos comprar trigo?

6. Hay *pocos* católicos en nuestro país.
7. ¿No me dijiste que trajera aceite de oliva?
8. Se le llenó el pecho de *mucha* sangre.
9. ¿Cuándo vas a prestarme *unas* revistas de arte?
10. Tengo *unos cuantos* dólares en el bolsillo.
11. Una buena dieta consiste en *algo de* fruta entre otros alimentos.
12. Durante esta primavera el profesor asignó *mucha* lectura.

20
Descriptive and Limiting Adjectives

20.1

The Spanish adjective always has at least two forms and often four, and in some cases, even five. It is consistently inflected for number (singular vs. plural) and usually for gender (masculine vs. feminine). The English adjective has only one form, unless used in comparisons (See Chapter 25), and is never marked for either gender or number.

20.2
MORPHOLOGICAL CLASSIFICATION OF THE SPANISH ADJECTIVE

Class I

Class I adjectives show a dictionary masculine singular form ending in -o. They always have at least four forms marked for gender and number.

SINGULAR		PLURAL	
MASCULINE	**FEMININE**	**MASCULINE**	**FEMININE**
cómodo	cómoda	cómodos	cómodas
delicioso	deliciosa	deliciosos	deliciosas
sano	sana	sanos	sanas
simpático	simpática	simpáticos	simpáticas

Some adjectives of this class drop their final -o and assume apocopated (shortened) forms **when they precede a masculine singular noun**. These adjectives, then, exhibit five forms—the apocopated form and the other four; most are limiting adjectives expained later.

The following are the main Spanish adjectives of Class I subject to apocopation.

	SINGULAR		PLURAL
MASCULINE	FEMININE	MASCULINE	FEMININE
un(o)	una	unos	unas
algún(o)	alguna	algunos	algunas
ningún(o)	ninguna	ningunos	ningunas
primer(o)	primera	primeros	primeras
tercer(o)	tercera	terceros	terceras
mal(o)	mala	malos	malas
buen(o)	buena	buenos	buenas

20.3
Class II

Class II adjectives have a dictionary masculine singular form ending in a letter other than -o, with the exclusion of the endings mentioned under Class III below. Class II adjectives have two forms and are marked for number but not for gender.

MASCULINE AND FEMININE	
SINGULAR	PLURAL
gris	grises
inteligente	inteligentes
conforme	conformes
genial	geniales
liberal	liberales
feliz	felices
inferior	inferiores

In this class *reciente* has an apocopated form *recién*, like others in Class I.

20.4
Class III

Class III are the adjectives ending in *-án*, *-ón*, *-ín* (except *ruin*), and *-or*, except the comparatives *mejor*, *peor*, *superior*, etc., which belong to Class II. All adjectives of nationality or origin whose masculine singular form ends in other than -o are also included. Class III adjectives always have four forms and are inflected for both gender and number.

	SINGULAR		PLURAL
MASCULINE	FEMININE	MASCULINE	FEMININE
español	española	españoles	españolas
inglés	inglesa	ingleses	inglesas
alemán	alemana	alemanes	alemanas
dulzón	dulzona	dulzones	dulzonas
pequeñín	pequeñina	pequeñines	pequeñinas
labrador	labradora	labradores	labradoras

Exercise 1

Give all possible forms of the following Spanish adjectives and determine their Class, I, II or III.

1. portugués
2. poco
3. holgazán
4. tercero
5. chino
6. remolón
7. superior
8. malo
9. activista
10. infantil
11. permanente
12. profesional
13. chiquitín
14. hablador
15. capaz
16. común
17. santo
18. patán

Exercise 2

Give all possible forms in Spanish for the following English adjectives. Again, determine whether they are Class I, II, or III adjectives in Spanish.

1. poor
2. modern
3. French
4. intelligent
5. first
6. German
7. small
8. racial
9. Spanish
10. useful

20.5

The English adjective precedes the noun it modifies almost without exception.

The **first** man arrived in a **black** car.
The **poor** nations of the **Third** World have many **political** problems.
We live in a **small** house next to the **American** River.

Some exceptions are *court martial, attorney general, heir apparent, notary public,* etc.

Spanish adjectives, however, can precede or follow their noun according to their classification as either limiting or descriptive. Limiting adjectives, often termed "determiners" in English grammars, usually precede nouns while descriptive adjectives generally follow. Many adjectives may assume either position, but always with a change of emphasis or meaning, occasionally substantial.

20.6

SPANISH LIMITING ADJECTIVES

Limiting adjectives relate the noun to its environment *(este edificio)*, describe its order in a succession *(mi segunda clase)*, or state its relative amount or quantity *(dos libros)*. They routinely precede the nouns they modify. Unlike descriptive adjectives, they say virtually nothing about the true nature of the noun itself. In Spanish they include the articles (definite and indefinite), the possessive adjectives (the short, unstressed forms), the demonstrative adjectives, numerical adjectives, adjectives of quantity, indefinites, and so on.

No me gusta **el** gobierno.
Tienen **unos** camaradas venezolanos.
¿Dónde vas a colocar **tu** capa?
Tienen que hablar con **ese** maestro.
Vamos a añadir **dos** ejemplos.
Van a comer **más/menos** frijoles.
Procedió con **toda** tranquilidad.
No podemos revelar **tantos** secretos.
Usa **mucha/poca** corriente eléctrica.
Otro sacerdote murió de viruela.
No vamos a leer **ningún** periódico esta semana.
Llevas la **misma** camiseta que ayer.
Han tirado la **última** edición.
Vivimos en el **cuarto** piso del edificio.
Quiero reunir a los **demás** empleados.

20.7
SPANISH DESCRIPTIVE ADJECTIVES

Descriptive adjectives generally follow their nouns, although several exceptions to this "rule of thumb" will be cited later. These adjectives say something about the nature of their antecedents, that is, they differentiate them from other possible nouns. This function of differentiation may range from classification to contrast.

Classification categories involve color, nationality, social affiliations, technical descriptions, and the like.

Tengo un carro **rojo**
Es un escritor **alemán**.
Fue un presidente **católico**.
Es un suelo **ácido**.

In expressing contrasts, the descriptive adjectives imply the noun belongs to "x category" rather than to a supposed "y category."

Es un príncipe **pobre** (y no **rico**).
Fue un proceso **complicado** (y no **sencillo**).
Es una raza **noble** (y no **inferior**).

Whether they express classification or contrast, true descriptive adjectives follow the noun even when they themselves are modified by adverbs.

Es un país **tan lejano**.
Parece una persona **medio falsa**.
Quiero un vino **bien seco**.

20.8
PREPOSITIONED VS. POSTPOSITIONED SPANISH DESCRIPTIVE ADJECTIVES

In general, the position of Spanish descriptive adjectives depends on the semantic content of the noun/adjective combination. Therefore, although descriptive adjectives generally follow the noun, they may precede it to emphasize the quality being described. Whether the adjective precedes or follows is a function of what we term "relative informativeness," that is, the amount or degree of relevant information provided by the adjective.

In the sentence *Sebastián iba acompañado de su feroz perro*, where the descriptive adjective precedes the noun, relatively little new, significant, or unexpected information is provided about the noun *perro*. What is stressed, is the viciousness of the dog.

In, *Sebastián iba acompañado de su perro feroz*, however, where the descriptive adjective follows, implied is that Sebastián perhaps has more than one dog, some of which are relatively tame. On this occasion, however, he is in the company of a particularly vicious one.

The matter of relative informativeness and descriptive adjective positioning can be further extended. *Bueno, malo, mejor, peor, nuevo, viejo* and *grande* express personal opinions or evaluations. When these precede the noun, an individual's personal estimation or value judgment (*good* vs. *bad*) is emphasized. No contrast of the noun with other nouns of its type is intended.

El guiso adquirió un **buen** gusto.	(Speaker voices pleasure with the taste.)
Tuve una **mala** experiencia.	(Speaker suffered a really bad experience.)
Fue una **verdadera** sorpresa.	(Speaker expresses his true surprise.)
No vuelvo a ese **miserable** salón.	(Speaker really detests the room.)
Ambos sostuvieron una **tremenda** lucha.	(Speaker is impressed by the intensity of the fight.)

When following the noun, the descriptive adjective serves its normal function of differentiation rather than personal estimation such as enhancement or denigration.

Recibí un sueldo **bueno**.	(There are good and bad salaries; this one was good.)
Fue un triunfo **verdadero**.	(Accomplishment was authentic and not a deception.)
Tuvieron una lucha **tremenda**.	(Some spats are insignificant, others relatively more serious; this one was serious!)

20.9
ENGLISH LEXICAL VARIANCE WITH SPANISH PRE- OR POSTPOSED ADJECTIVES

English often uses different lexical items to convey what Spanish accomplishes through mere adjective positioning. The following listing demonstrates this point:

Before the noun (pre-posed):	After the noun (post-posed):
algun(o)	
some (indefinite)	any/none at all (emphtic negative)
algún problema	*No tengo problema alguno.*
some problem	I don't have any problem (at all).

alto

high, *i.e.*, notable	tall
un alto funcionario	*ese funcionario alto*
a high official	that tall official

antiguo

former	old (=aged), ancient
mi antiguo patrón	*mi patrón antiguo*
my former(=old) boss	my old (=aged) boss

cierto

a certain	definite/accurate
Cierto profesor tiene la culpa.	*Siguen buscando una solución cierta.*
A certrain profesor is to blame.	They continue looking for a definite solution.

cualquier(a)

any (selected from a group)	"any" (selected at random)
Cualquier película inglesa sirve.	*Duermo bien en una cama cualquiera.*
Any British film will do.	I can sleep in any bed at all.

dichoso

damned (pejorative)	lucky, fortunate
ese dichoso comerciante	*una persona dichosa*
that damned salesperson	a fortunate person

diferente

various	different
Siempre hay diferentes soluciones.	*Traigo una solución diferente.*
There are always various solutions.	Here I have a different solution.

demonstrative adjectives, eg., este, ese

that (demonstrative adjective)	that (demonstrative, but pejorative)
ese hombre	*el hombre ese*
that man	that guy/creep

gran/grande

great, famous	big, large
Es una gran ciudad.	*Es una ciudad grande.*
It's a great city.	Its a big city.

mismo

the same	himself/herself/itself
El mismo hombre lo hizo.	*Él mismo nos lo dijo*
The same man did it.	He himself told it to us.

nuevo

different	brand new
Se puso una nueva camisa.	*Se puso una camisa nueva.*
He put on a different shirt.	He put on a new shirt.

pobre

unfortunate
una pobre mujer
an unfortunate woman

poor (financially)
una mujer pobre
a poor woman

propio

one's own
mi propio motivo
my own motive

appropriate, suitable
un motivo propio para impresionarnos
a motive suitable for impressing us

puro

sheer, nothing but
nada más que puras mentiras
nothing but sheer lies

pure (not contaminated)
No bebe más que agua pura.
She doesn't drink anything but pure water.

semejante

such a
Jamás he visto semejante cosa.
I've never seen such a thing.

similar
A ella le pasó una cosa semejante.
Something similar happened to her.

simple

just a . . . /mere
Fue una simple camarera.
She was just a maid.

simple-minded
Lo hizo una camarera simple.
A simple-minded maid did it.

triste

without status/lowly
Ese triste peón no gana nada.
That lowly worker doesn't earn anything.

sad, melancolic
una persona triste
a sad (depressed) person

único

the only/sole
Tiene la única solución.
She has the only solution.

unique/one-of-a-kind
Nos sugirió una solución única.
She suggested a unique solution to us.

varios

several
Llegó con varios amigos
He arrived with several friends.

miscellaneous
Vende cosas varias.
He sells miscellaneous items.

viejo

of long standing
Piensa visitar a su viejo amigo.
He plans to visit his longtime friend.

aged, old, elderly
Ese hombre viejo sigue trabajando.
That elderly man continues working.

20.10
THE PROBLEMATIC ADJECTIVE *GRANDE*

When following a noun, *grande* and its plural *grandes* carry the descriptive meaning of *large/big*, stressing physical size.

| Es una estancia **grande**. | It is a large estate. |
| Son una niñas **grandes**. | They are big girls. |

When preceding a singular noun of either gender, *grande* assumes the apocopated form *gran* and must then be translated as *great*, *grand*, or *famous*.

| Pasamos un **gran** rato. | We had a great/grand/fabulous time. |
| Fue una **gran** reina. | She was a famous/great queen. |

Grandes expresses the English idea of *famous/great* when it occurs before a plural noun.

Fernando e Isabel fueron unos **grandes** reyes.
Ferdinand and Isabel were great monarchs.

La producción en el teatro prescinde de **grandes** actores.
The theater production does without famous actors.

Exercise 3

Translate the following sentences placing limiting adjectives before the noun and descriptive adjectives after.

1. I am reading the same book.
2. They arrived in a large airplane.
3. He needs another glass.
4. You missed an important meeting.
5. She came to my house three times.
6. I want a cup of hot tea.
7. They sell fortified rice in that store.
8. There was a general strike in the second factory.
9. Some friends live on the fifth floor.
10. I bought the first book with my Mexican pesos.
11. The same man solved three difficult problems.
12. This complicated machine didn't cost much money.

Exercise 4

Write original Spanish sentences in which the following adjectives occur before nouns.

1. alto   4. estúpido   7. malo   10. pequeño
2. bendito   5. gran   8. mejor   11. tremendo
3. bueno   6. loco   9. peor   12. verdadero

Exercise 5

Translate the following pairs of sentences. Use the same adjective in your translation, Your placement of the adjective with respect to its noun will produce the intended meaning.

1. He is an old employee. (aged)
   He is an old employee. (long-time employee)

2. He arrived in a different car.
   He arrived in a new car.

3. It is a poor country. (It has many wars and other difficulties.)
   It is a poor country. (economically)

4. I am looking for a certain answer.
   I am looking for an accurate answer.

5. It contains pure milk.
   He opened it with pure (sheer) force.

6. Among my own clothes, I have clothes suitable for work.

7. She has big hands.
   She is a great teacher.

20.11
NOMINALIZATION OF SPANISH AND ENGLISH ADJECTIVES

Nominalization is the grammatical process by which adjectives are converted into nouns. Spanish has a rather simple system: It simply omits the noun in a **article + noun + adjective** construction, leaving both the article and the adjective. Nominalizations must occur in a clear context to be meaningful.

Ya no me atraen las mismas causas.	Por eso, me atrevo a apoyar una ~~causa~~ diferente.
Necesito cursos en la mañana;	No me convienen los ~~cursos~~ nocturnos porque trabajo de noche.
Nos hacen faltan más recursos,	así que vamos a necesitar unos ~~recursos~~ privados.

Hemos obtenido tantos logros,   y tenemos que conservar los ~~logros~~ más sobresalientes.

The English system for adjectival nominalization follows the Spanish one only in a few cases with singular nouns.

A blonde ~~lady~~ just arrived.
I must speak to the brunette ~~girl~~.

If English follows the Spanish system of merely omitting a noun and leaving an **article + adjective** combination, the resulting nominalization normally refers to plural entities only, usually human.

I refuse to have any more to do with the poor ~~people~~.
He feels we should tax the rich ~~people~~.
What will be done with the sick ~~people~~ and the aged ~~people~~?
There are no more institutions for the insane ~~people~~.

English most often nominalizes adjectives by omitting the noun, replacing it with the indefinite pronoun *one* if the noun is singular, or *ones* if it is plural, and retaining any article or other noun marker. Compare the Spanish examples below with the usual English method of nominalization.

los ~~hombres~~ ricos	the rich ~~men~~ ones
la ~~mujer~~ mayor	the older ~~lady~~ one
esa ~~chica~~ de los ojos verdes	that ~~girl~~ one with the green eyes
Este ~~libro~~ está roto.	This ~~book~~ one is torn.
unos ~~libros~~ más grandes	some larger ~~books~~ ones
diez ~~mujeres~~ casadas	ten married ~~women~~ ones
otro ~~perro~~ mejor	another better ~~dog~~ one
una ~~casa~~ más pequeña	a smaller ~~house~~ one
la ~~muchacha~~ que viste ayer	the ~~girl~~ one you saw yesterday

Exercise 6

Rewrite the following English and Spanish sentences. The italicized phrases should be nominalized.

1. If I can't buy a new car, then I'll buy *a used car*.
2. La línea verde está cerca de *la línea amarilla*.
3. I don't have any *good pencils* left.
4. Voy a comprar unas frutas dulces, porque no me gustan *las frutas agrias*.
5. The book on the table is *a very valuable book*.
6. Los conocidos nuevos son más interesantes que *los conocidos viejos*.
7. Poor people are often forced to beg for money from *the rich people*.
8. Busco un clima más templado porque *el clima* de aquí es muy fresco.

20.12

Spanish has a system using the neuter article *lo* with adjectives, adverbs, and even prepositions to produce nominalizations with abstract meanings. English must rely upon a variety of constructions to convey such ideas. The most commonly used English equivalents of Spanish abstract nominalizations with *lo* are listed here.

a. **how + ADJ/ADV**
   No sabes lo claro que es el cielo.   You don't know how clear the sky is.
   Veo lo rápido que él conduce.   I see how fast he drives.

b. **the + ADJ + aspect/thing/part**
   Eso es lo bonito de mi vida.   That's the pretty aspect of my life.
   Es lo más fácil de mi asignatura.   It's the easiest part of my assignment.

c. **the (that) business (stuff) about**
   Lo de Josué no me importa.   I don't care about that stuff about Joshua.
   Lo de tu marido me preocupa.   The business about your husband worries me.

d. **the + NOUN[-ness] + of**
   Me gustó lo conciso de tu ensayo.   I liked the conciseness of your essay.
   Vas a comprender lo inútil de este método.   You will understand the uselessness of this method.

e. **what** (non-interrogative, followed by a clause)
   Él me dijo lo que necesitaba.   He told me what he needed.
   Él no te puede decir lo que dijo ella.   He can't tell you what she said.

Exercise 7

Translate the following sentences involving abstract ideas.

1. I haven't words to tell you how funny that movie is.
2. Lo interesante es que ya habían recibido la comunicación.
3. The bad part is that I have to get up so early.
4. Algún día te voy a contar lo mucho que he sufrido en esta vida.
5. You can't imagine how badly he reads.
6. Haz lo que quieras con lo que tienes.
7. That business about Susan is not as serious as that stuff about her mother.
8. No me gusta ese novelista por lo revolucionario que es su estilo.
9. I scolded him for the ridiculousness of his actions.
10. Lo de tu padre es triste, pero peor es lo que tú hiciste.
11. What I do with my time is my own business.
12. Nadie se ha enterado de lo malo que son.

21

Possessive and Demonstrative Adjectives and Pronouns

21.1
POSSESSIVE ADJECTIVES

Whereas English has only one set of possessive adjectives, Spanish has two. These are the unstressed set, which precede nouns, and the stressed possessives, which follow them. The possessive adjectives of the stressed set can be nominalized, that is, converted into pronouns (*mi casa* > *la casa mía*).

	SINGULAR			**PLURAL**	
	UNSTRESSED	**STRESSED**		**UNSTRESSED**	**STRESSED**
my	mi, mis	mío, mía míos, mías	**our**	nuestro, -a nuestros, -as	nuestro, -a nuestros, -as
your	[FAMILIAR] tu, tus	[FAMILIAR] tuyo, tuya tuyos, tuyas	**your**	[FAMILIAR] vuestro, -a vuestros, -as	[FAMILIAR] vuestro, -a vuestros, -as
your	[FORMAL] su, sus	[FORMAL] suyo, suya suyos, suyas de usted	**your**	[FORMAL] su, sus	[FORMAL] suyo, suya suyos, -as de ustedes

his/her	su, sus	suyo, suya suyos, suyas	**their**	su, sus	suyo, suya suyos, suyas de ellos, de ellas
his	su, sus	de él			
her	su, sus	de ella			
its	su, sus	de él, de ella, de ello			

21.2
PEDAGOGICAL IMPLICATIONS

The Spanish unstressed possessive adjective always precedes the noun and is consistently inflected for number (singular vs. plural), providing two forms. In the first and second persons plural, it is shows gender inflection also, producing four forms. The Spanish stressed possessive adjective always follows its noun and is inflected for both gender and number, giving four forms. It is routinely used with the fully inflected article, either definite or indefinite. As we have mentioned in other chapters of the book, a Spanish speaker's mode of expression frequently reflects a different way of viewing reality than that of the English native. The Spanish possessive adjective, whether stressed or unstressed, agrees with the noun possessed rather than with the possessor.

>   mi(s) casa(s)   la(s) casa(s) mía(s)
>   su(s) libro(s)   lo(s) libros suyo(s)
>   nuestra(s) casa(s) la(s) casa(s) nuestra(s)

Just the opposite is the case with English possessives since they agree with the possessor, whose gender and number are reflected only in the third person possessive adjectives.

>   his/her/their house(s)
>   his/her/their book(s)

The complete lack of correspondence in this area contributes greatly to the confusion and uncertainty experienced by both Spanish and English speakers when they carry their linguistic intuitions into the respective target languages. The unstressed Spanish possessive adjective *su(s)* is problematic for the English speaker since, as can be seem from the preceding chart and in the following sentence examples, it has at least six possible English translations.

a) Martha no encuentra su auto en el estacionamiento (her car).
b) Pedro no encuentra su auto en el estacionamiento (his car).
c) Señor(a), ¿no puede encontrar su auto en el estacionamiento? (your car, formal).
d) Los Gómez no encuentran su auto en el estacionamiento (their car).
e) Chicos, ¿no pueden encontrar su auto en el estacionamiento? (your car, plural).
f) En la neblina, el barco perdió su destino (its destination).

Had the possessed noun in the previous examples been *llaves*, the possessive adjective would have been *sus*. By the same token, the Spanish speaker will confuse *su casa (de él)*, which means *his house* (often rendered mistakenly as *her house* [because of the feminine gender of *casa*], with *su casa (de ella)*, which means *her house*. Likewise, *su libro (de ella)* is frequently translated as *his* book since *book* is a masculine noun. This confusion is due to the differing focus on agreement in the two languages. Again, the Spanish speaker aligns the possessive adjective's gender and number agreement with that of the object possessed, whereas the English speaker relates gender and number to that of the possessor.

In modern Spanish usage, the stressed possessive adjectives *suyo, suya, suyos,* and *suyas* generally refer to the addressee (the person being spoken to), that is *you* (singular) or *you* (plural). *La casa suya* usually means *your* (singular or plural) *house. Suyo* and *suya* can, however, refer to third person possessors, depending upon context. Should ambiguity result, an alternate prepositional construction is always available. Note the following examples:

(*la casa suya = his house*), more often expressed as *la casa de él*
(*la casa suya = her house* > *la casa de ella*)
(*la casa suya = their house* > *la casa de ellos, de ellas*)
(*la casa suya = your house* > *la casa de usted,* formal)
(*la casa suya = your house* > *la casa de ustedes*)

The unstressed possessive adjective of Spanish must precede the noun, and no article appears in the construction: *mi comida, tu lado, sus dientes*. However, the stressed possessive adjective follows the noun, and the noun takes an article or some other type of determiner or noun marker: *la comida mía, este problema tuyo, diez dientes suyos*.

Exercise 1
Give both unstressed and stressed versions:

1. her cousin (masc.)
2. my adventure
3. our aunt
4. your (familiar s.) cigarettes
5. their brothers
6. your (formal s.) dog
7. his grandmother
8. your (formal pl.) uncle
9. its paws
10. your (familiar pl.) ballpoint pen

21.3
POSSESSIVE PRONOUNS

The English possessive pronoun is generally a different form from the possessive adjective, as can be seen by comparing this chart with the chart in 21.1. The Spanish possessive pronoun is merely a nominalized form of the stressed possessive adjective. The noun of the stressed possessive adjective construction is suppressed, but the article retained, thereby inducing a nominalization.

	SINGULAR		**PLURAL**
mine	el mío, la mía	**ours**	el nuestro, la nuestra

	los míos, las mías		los nuestros, las nuestras
	[FAMILIAR]		[FAMILIAR]
yours	el tuyo, la tuya	**yours**	el vuestro, la vuestra
	los tuyos, las tuyas		los vuestros, las vuestras
	[FORMAL]		[FORMAL]
	el suyo, la suya		el suyo, la suya
	los suyos, las suyas		los suyos, las suyas
	el/la/los/las de usted		el/la/los/las de ustedes
his	el suyo, la suya	**theirs**	el suyo, la suya
	los suyos, las suyas		los suyos, las suyas
	el de él, la de él		el de ellos, el de ellas
	los de él, las de él		la de ellos, la de ellas
			los de ellos, los de ellas
hers	el suyo, la suya		las de ellos, las de ellas
	los suyos, las suyas		
	el de ella, la de ella		
	los de ella, las de ella		

Note: When a possessive pronoun follows a form of *ser*, the article may or may not occur to this effect: With no article, only possession is expressed: *El problema es tuyo.* With the article, contrast is implied: *Este es el mío; ese, el tuyo.*

Exercise 2

Translate these short possessive pronoun phrases. Example: *It's ours (the car)* = *Es nuestro; Vi la de ellos (casa)* = *I saw theirs.*

1. It's mine. (= house)
2. Vi el de él. (= libro)
3. I met yours. (= friends)
4. Hirieron a los suyos. (= enemigos de Ud.)
5. We enjoyed ours. (= party)
6. Detén la tuya. (= aventura)
7. They smoked theirs. (= cigars)
8. Defendió a las de ellas. (= amigas de ellas)
9. He has finished his. (= work)
10. Cultivamos las nuestras. (= flores)

Exercise 3

Rewrite the following sentences by replacing the second possessive adjective constructions with possessive pronoun nominalizations.

1. Mi secretaria está hablando con tu secretaria.
2. Their cousins want to meet our cousins.

3. Su carro está junto a tu carro.
4. Our money was all spent along with his money.
5. Su copia (de ella) llegó junto con nuestra copia.
6. Your nephew is fighting with my nephew.
7. Nuestros ciudadanos son mejores que sus ciudadanos (de ellos).
8. Their parents don't know your parents.
9. Su papá (de Uds.) quiere ver al papá de ella.
10. His books seem to be locked up with my books.

21.4
DEMONSTRATIVE ADJECTIVES

Demonstrative adjectives precede their nouns in both English and Spanish. They are used to indicate relative proximity of persons or things from the speaker, either in spatial relation or in time.

	SINGULAR			**PLURAL**	
this	este	esta	**these**	estos	estas
that	ese	esa	**those**	esos	esas
	aquel	aquella		aquellos	aquellas

The English demonstrative adjectives distinguish formally only between a singular and a plural. Spanish demonstrative adjectives are marked for both gender and number as depicted above.

Spanish also distinguishes between *that* (*ese, esa*) and *those* (*esos, esas*), which are relatively nearer to the speaker in either space or time, and *that* (*aquel, aquella*) and *those* (*aquellos, aquellas*), designating a relatively farther distance from the speaker, again, either spatially or temporally. No such differentiation occurs in modern English unless you use extra words in association with the demonstrative. For example, *ese barco* would be translated as *that boat*, but *aquel barco* would best be rendered as *that boat over there* or as *that boat (over) yonder*. *Yonder* is a more dialectal and usually deemed archaic.

Exercise 4
Translate the following sentences:

1. I don't want to buy those bananas. (near)
2. El director no va a utilizar a aquellos personajes en la comedia.
3. My parents say that they are going to buy that house. (far)
4. No me dejaron cruzar ese parque; por eso subo por este camino.
5. They gave me five dollars for this old watch.
6. En aquel gobierno estos diputados formaron una junta independiente.
7. During that (near) time, we swam in this river every day.
8. Este fraile quiere hablar con aquella señora.

9. These books are old, but those books (near) are very new.
10. Si quieres comprar esta empresa, debes comunicarte con ese señor.

21.5
DEMONSTRATIVE PRONOUNS

As we have seen, both languages have possessive adjectives and pronouns; likewise both use demonstrative adjectives and pronouns. The demonstrative pronouns in the two languages are merely nominalized versions of the demonstrative adjectives. They are pronouns since they substitute for persons or things rather than modify them.

	SINGULAR		PLURAL		NEUTER	
this one	este	esta	**these**	estos estas	**this**	esto
that one	ese	esa	**those**	esos esas	**that**	eso
	aquel	aquella		aquellos, aquellas		aquello

Nominalization takes place in Spanish by omitting the noun of the demonstrative adjective construction. Until recently a graphic accent appeared on the resulting demonstrative pronoun. This orthographic requirement no longer applies but can be resurrected when there is any possibility of ambiguity:

Me dice que **esta** mañana va a ir a la estación. (He is telling me (that) he's is going to go to the station this morning.)

Me dice que **ésta** mañana va a ir a la estación. (He is telling me that this one (a female) is going to go to the station tomorrow.)

In English the singular nominalization takes the form of omitting the noun and replacing it with the indefinite pronoun *one*. In the plural, the noun is simply omitted, and no other word is required, although *ones* is sometimes used.

"Tell me about these notebooks."
"Well, this one is the teacher's, but those (ones) can be used again."

As seen in the graphic, both languages have neuter demonstrative pronouns. These refer to items whose gender cannot be determined or to entire ideas or abstractions. In English the neuter demonstrative pronouns are simply the singular demonstrative pronoun without the pronoun *one*.

I don't understand this. (= No entiendo esto.)
They refused to do that. (=Se negaron a hacer eso.)

The Spanish neuter forms always end in –o. Neither language has a plural form.

Chapter 21 Possessive and Demonstrative Adjective and Pronouns

Exercise 5

Rewrite the following English and Spanish sentences using a demonstrative pronoun where appropriate. For some of the sentences no rewrite is possible.

1. I don't like these grapes; let's buy those grapes.
2. Este alcalde es muy buen amigo de ese otro alcalde.
3. I don't know anything about this.
4. Este capítulo del libro llegó ayer, pero aquel capítulo llegó anteayer.
5. Are you going to speak to your boss about that?
6. Aquellos ministros convencen al pueblo, pero estos ministros, no.
7. Before buying this apartment, you should see those apartments.
8. Aquello constituye un grave problema.
9. He brought me those letters, but I can answer only this letter today.
10. Insistió en que aceptáramos estos artículos, pero no esos otros.

22

Adverbs and Prepositions

Before beginning this chapter, please see the Glossary for definitions and examples of these two parts of speech.

22.1

Spanish and English adverbs and related prepositional constructions are frequently difficult for both English and Spanish speakers. In the following contrastive listings, note that the Spanish adverb often converts into a prepositional construction by using the preposition *de*. In English, however, the adverb and the preposition are often identical. There are, however, many exceptions in both languages.

SPANISH		ENGLISH	
ADVERB	**PREPOSITION**	**ADVERB**	**PREPOSITION**
(-------)	ante	before (space)	before
(a)delante	delante de	in front	in front of
(a)dentro	(a)dentro de	inside within	inside (of) within
(a)fuera	(a)fuera de	outside	outside (of)
abajo	debajo de, bajo	below, beneath downstairs	below, beneath under(neath)
además	además de	besides	besides

antes	antes de	before (time)	before
arriba	arriba de	above, upstairs	above
atrás	atrás de	behind	behind
cerca	cerca de	near, nearby	near
después	después de	afterwards	after
detrás	detrás de (moved)	in back	in back of
encima	encima de	on top above	on top of above
lejos	lejos de	far (away)	far from

22.2

Note that there are few troublesome contrasts in the following English-Spanish adverbial pairs.

Él nunca vino aquí antes.	He never came here before.
Mis tíos viven cerca.	My aunt and uncle live near/nearby.
Después escribieron la crónica.	Afterwards they wrote the chronicle.
La frontera no está lejos.	The border isn't far (away).
El recién nacido está arriba.	The newborn is upstairs.
Nadie está (a)dentro.	No one is inside.
Se oyó un grito afuera.	A scream was heard outside.
Mi cuarto está abajo.	My room is below/downstairs.

22.3

However, in the following pairs involving prepositional constructions, contrastive differences appear in virtually every case.

Él llegó antes **de** la revolución.	He arrived before the revolution.
Vivo cerca **de** la plaza pública.	I live near the public square.
Hablé después **del** representante.	I spoke after the representative.
La caja está arriba **de** esa otra.	The box is above that other one.
Ella está dentro **de** la casa.	She's inside the house.
Viven aislados fuera **de** la ciudad.	They live isolated outside the city.
El cuadro está detrás **de** la pared verde.	The picture is behind the green wall.

Exercise 1

Translate the following sentences into the other language. State in each case whether you are dealing with an adverb or with a prepositional construction. Also note whether a significant English-Spanish contrast exists and what the nature of it is.

1. Besides apples, he wants to buy oranges.
2. El interesado está nervioso porque no quiere estar afuera.
3. Before the opera we went to a small café.
4. Rubén se quedó atrás, pero Alejandra se fue (a)delante/por delante.
5. I think he was working near that machine.
6. No creíamos que nadie estuviera adentro.
7. After the dance she went home with a friend.
8. Mis amigos están abajo con mis abuelos.
9. I couldn't see him because he was behind the car.
10. ¿Se coloca la materia arriba o debajo de la superficie?

22.4
ADVERB FORMATION IN ENGLISH AND SPANISH

Adverbs usually derive from adjectives or from nouns in both languages.

The English adverb is formed by adding the suffix *-ly* to an adjective.

ADJECTIVE	ADVERB
pleasant	pleasantly
great	greatly
rapid	rapidly
rich	richly

The Spanish adverb is formed in one of two ways:

- By placing the preposition *con* before the noun.

NOUN	ADVERB
mérito	con mérito (meritoriously)
acierto	con acierto (successfully, skillfully)
tristeza	con tristeza (sadly)
gratitud	con gratitud (greatfully)

- By adding the suffix *-mente* to a Class II adjective or to the feminine form of a Class I adjective (See Chapter 20). If the adjective bears a graphic accent, it is retained in the derived adverb.

ADJECTIVE	ADVERB
peligroso (I)	peligrosamente (dangerously)
fácil (II)	fácilmente (easily)
rápido (I)	rápidamente (rapidly)
especial (II)	especialmente ([e]specially)

22.5

In both languages some adjectives assume adverbial force without any change of form. English says:

Don't go *fast;* go *slow!*
He spoke *loud* and *clear*.
She came back *quick*.

Spanish examples include:

No puedo verlo muy *claro*.
Mi carro viejo va muy *lento*.
Hablaron *largo* y *tendido*.
¡Qué *rápido* corres!

Exercise 2

Translate the following adverbial expressions.

1. con grandeza
2. (e)specially
3. probablemente
4. happily
5. con simpatía
6. easily
7. fríamente
8. sadly
9. con gracia
10. beautifully
11. solamente
12. clearly
13. con pasión
14. fast
15. descuidadamente

VARIOUS PREPOSITIONS AND THEIR USES

22.6

The English prepositions *in, on, at,* and *to* versus Spanish *en* are put in perspective here. English employs four locative prepositions, *in, on, at,* and *to* while Spanish generally uses only one, *en*. Thus, Spanish speakers learning English have considerable difficulty discerning which of the four English locative prepositions to use in any given case. The following guides should prove helpful.

22.7

In (= *en*) is used with objects or people found within the confines of some container or physical location, or with months and years, as does Spanish

The feather is in the box.	La pluma está en la caja.
The reader is in the library.	El lector está en la biblioteca.
The salt is in the container.	La sal está en el envase.
I work in an assembly plant.	Trabajo en una maquiladora.
He came in July.	Él vino en julio.
We arrived in 1999.	Llegamos en 1999.
They live in the village.	Ellos viven en la aldea.

22.8

On (= *en*) indicates that an object or person touches the surface of something while not being located within its confines. It is also used for dates and days of the week, whereas Spanish employs the definite articles *el* and *los*: on Monday(s) = *el/los lunes*

I saw her on Thursday.	La vi el jueves.
I found it on the corner.	Lo encontré en la esquina.
He came on May 3rd/the 3rd of May	Él llegó el 3 de mayo.
The picture is on the wall.	El cuadro está en la pared.
I live on this street.	Vivo en esta calle.
A ring is on her finger.	Ella tiene un anillo en su dedo.
There is nothing on the table.	No hay nada en la mesa.
There is no class on Mondays.	No hay clase los lunes.

English *on* accompanies most modes of conveyance (i.e., vehicles one climbs onto/into), although the person or thing traveling is actually within the confines of the conveyance.

They weren't on that plane.	Ellos no estaban en ese avión.
He arrived on a bus.	Él llegó en un autobús.
Let's celebrate on the ship.	Vamos a celebrar en el barco.
She died on a train.	Ella se murió en un tren.
He was on his bike.	Él estaba en su bicicleta.
There is iron on that truck.	Hay hierro en ese camión.

But, when small, four-wheeled motor vehicles are the mode of conveyance, English uses *in*, which seems logical to the Spanish speaker.

He was in a taxi.	Él estaba en un taxi.
I was born in an ambulance.	Nací en una ambulancia.
She went in a car.	Ella se fue en un auto.

22.9

At (= *en*) expresses the location where an activity takes place, but it does not specify that either people or things are actually within the confines of that place. It is also used like Spanish *a* to mark the time an event takes place. It is doubtlessly the most difficult locative preposition for the Spanish speaker when location in space rather than in time is designated.

Location in space:

I saw her at the market.	La vi en el mercado.
He's at the airport.	Él está en el aeropuerto.
Meet me at the station.	Búscame en la estación.
The party was at my house.	La fiesta fue en mi casa.
I bought it at the store.	Lo compré en la tienda.
He was at the doctor's office.	Él estaba en el consultorio del médico.
I work at the university.	Trabajo en la universidad.

Location in time:

She arrived at one.	Ella llegó a la una.
I left at two.	Salí a las dos.
We have and appointment at noon.	Tenemos una cita al mediodía.

22.10

To (= *en*) is frequently used as a locative preposition in English. This use reveals a semantic confusion with *to*, the English preposition expressing motion toward some destination. Since English says, *I have gone to Mexico several times*, expressing movement toward a goal, *to* has developed a locative meaning: *I have been to (=in) Mexico several times*. The usage is standard but limited to the verb *to be* in the present perfect or the pluperfect tenses.

I have never been to Spain.	Nunca he estado en España.
He had been to Denmark.	Él había estado en Dinamarca.
I've been to your house repeatedly.	He estado en tu casa varias veces.
Who's been to my house?	¿Quién ha estado en mi casa?
You haven't been to the port yet.	Ud. no ha estado en el puerto todavía.

Exercise 3

Translate the following Spanish sentences using *in, on, at,* or *to* for Spanish locative *en*. More than one choice may be possible in some cases. State the reason(s) for your prepositional selection.

1. ¿Has estado alguna vez en la Costa Azul?
2. El río Tajo se halla en la Península Ibérica.
3. Tus llaves están en mi bolsillo.
4. Creo que te conocí en otra actividad parecida.
5. ¿Qué tiene Daniel en la mano izquierda?
6. Estábamos en el cine cuando pasó algo misterioso.
7. El perro se sentó en el rincón.
8. No se veía una sola nube en el cielo infinito.
9. Mis amigos nunca han estado en San Juan.
10. El señor que está en el avión es el profesor Santana.
11. Me senté en la silla que estaba en el balcón.

12. La Segunda Guerra Mundial comenzó en 1939 y terminó en 1945.
13. Mi padre enseña inglés en la Universidad de Salamanca.
14. ¿Has estado alguna vez en el pueblo donde nací?
15. El Presidente estaba en un coche cuando fue asesinado.
16. Sandra estaba en el autobús cuando le habló el anciano.
17. Hay muchas páginas en esta unidad.
18. Paquito, ¿qué tienes en la boca?
19. Mi auto no está ni en el garaje ni en la calle sino en la estación de trenes.
20. Querían venir en octubre, pero llegaron el 2 de noviembre.

22.11

The English prepositions *in*, *at*, and *on* appear in a host of idiomatic expressions. The following list, by no means complete, gives some idea of their frequency.

in		**at**	**on**
in addition	in progress	at all	on account of
in a hurry	in the afternoon	at any rate	on fire
in all	in the beginning	at best/worst	on my way to
in a way	in the end	at first	on purpose
in a while	in the evening	at last	on second thought
in detail	in the event of	at least	on several occasions
in distress	in the future	at night	on that block
in every way	in the meantime	at once	on that show
in fact	in the middle	at present	on the contrary
in favor of	in the morning	at the beginning of	on the left/right
in front/back	in the news	at the end of	on the other hand
in general	in the presence of	at the moment	on the phone
in many/most ways	in the sky	at the side of	on the whole
in mind	in this/that case	at this/that time	on time
in no time	in tears		on social media
in order to	in time for		
	in touch		
	in town		
	in trouble		

Exercise 4

See the English idiomatic prepositional expressions above and find a Spanish equivalent for each. Use each in an English sentence and translate.

22.12

Spanish uses *de* and *por* while English uses *in* with time divisions of the day. When a specific time of a specific division of the day is mentioned, Spanish *de* translates English *in*.

Ella llegó a las ocho de la mañana.	She arrived at eight in the morning.
No salimos hasta las tres de la tarde.	We didn't leave until three in the afternoon.

Spanish *por* is used for English *in* when only the division of the day is mentioned, but no specific hour. *En*, however, appears with ever increasing frequency here.

Andrés no trabaja por (en) la mañana.	Andrew doesn't work in the morning.
Tengo clases por (en) la tarde.	I have classes in the afternoon.
¿Qué haces por (en) las noches?	What do you do in the evenings?
But,	What do you do *at* night?

Exercise 5

Translate the following sentences using *de* and *por/en* to translate English *in*.

1. My friends have to work in the afternoon.
2. Julio arrived at nine o'clock in the morning.
3. Do you do anything in the evenings?
4. What could she be doing at five o'clock in the morning?
5. I have classes in the evenings, but I don't in the afternoons.

22.13

Spanish uses *con* and *de* for English *with*. In Spanish, *con* (= *with*) occurs to convey the idea of the person or object's being in the company of or associated with another person, object, or abstract entity.

Leonardo llegó con su amigo.	Leonard arrived with his friend.
Siempre tomo café con leche.	I always take my coffee with milk.
Sustituimos lo viejo con lo nuevo.	We replaced the old with the new.

Spanish *de* (= *with/in*) appears for identification, that is, the person or thing is identified by the phrase following *de*. It also indicates the state of people or things.

¿Conoces a la de los ojos claros?	Do you know the one with the blue eyes?
La de la falda me gusta más.	I like the one with/in the skirt more.
Él llegó cubierto de polvo.	He arrived covered with/in dust.
Ella tiene la cara cubierta de sangre.	Her face is covered with/in blood.

Exercise 6

Translate the following sentences, determining whether to use *con* or *de* to translate English *with* or *in*.

1. The girl in the blue dress is my sister.
2. His shirt was all covered with grease.
3. The man arrived with a large dog.
4. The man with the dog is a friend of mine.
5. Those boys with the long hair smoke marijuana.
6. He came with the beer and spoke to the man in the hat.
7. His face was covered with bandages.
8. My students arrived with their books.
9. It's covered now with a sheet.
10. The car with the new tires is mine.

22.14

English generally uses a phrase to indicate possession or identification, whereas Spanish more normally employs a clause. Spanish may also follow the English model, but with an identification phrase introduced by *de*.

| the young man with the short legs | el joven que tiene las piernas cortas |
| | el joven de las piernas cortas |

| the man with the defect in his shoulder | el hombre que tiene el defecto en el hombro |
| | el hombre del defecto en el hombro |

| the people with prestige | la gente que tiene prestigio |
| | la gente de prestigio |

English also generally uses a phrase to indicate location, but Spanish prefers a clause.

the women in the store	las mujeres que están en la tienda
the boys in the field	los chicos que están en el campo
the girl in the car	la chamaca que está en el carro

Exercise 7

Translate the following sentences into Spanish using a clause to express possession, identification, or location where English uses a phrase.

1. I want to meet the girl with the new car.
2. The people in the library don't speak Spanish.

3. The book on the table is about Chilean wines.
4. We don't like the house with the blue door.
5. That dog in your house really barks a lot.
6. The stores in the country towns are small.
7. We met a woman with a sick husband.
8. The houses on my street are very expensive.
9. Look! The girl at the window is crying.
10. The boys with the coin collection live in that building.

22.15

Finally, English generally uses only one preposition before a compound prepositional complement (a complement composed of more than one element), but Spanish repeats the preposition before each element.

They have a formidable impression of you and me.
Tienen una impresión formidable de ti y de mí.

They promoted him for being honest and humble.
Lo ascendieron por honrado y por humilde.

I want to live with love and respect.
Quiero vivir con amor y con respeto.

> **Note:** Compound prepositional objects, especially when pronouns, regularly confound even educated native English speakers. A hypercorrective explanation could be advanced. Children, to the dismay of their parents, are corrected for saying, *Me and him are going to the movies, where object(ive) pronouns substitute for the subject pronouns, and in the wrong order. The correct versión is, He and I are going to the movies. Speakers so corrected then subsconciously develop an aversión to the object(ive) pronouns even in structures where they belong (i.e., as prepositional, direct and indirect objects), particularly when compound. They come up with such utterances as, *He doesn't know my father and she; *He had a very bad impression of my wife and I. Repeating the preposition before each compound object causes the error to "self-correct" (...of my wife and of me).

Exercise 8

Translate the following sentences, and use the preposition before each element of the compound complement.

1. They gave flowers to my mother and aunt.
2. I know all the business about your brother and nephew.
3. They came by for my father and mother.
4. My father works with Dr. Blanc and Dr. Porrata.
5. You can't leave without your hat and coat.

THE SPANISH PERSONAL ACCUSATIVE

22.16

In Spanish whenever a noun or an interrogative (¿quién-es?) or relative (el/la/los/las que/cual-es) pronoun referring to a person or to a named animal occurs as the direct object, it must be preceded by *a*, the so-called "personal *a*" or "personal accusative." The rule does not apply to the conjunctive (clitic/"with-verb") pronouns. English has no system for marking personal direct objects, so mastery of this feature of Spanish grammar presents a persistent learning problem for English natives.

Examples of the Spanish personal accusative:

No veo a Raquel.
Gabriel no conoce a la señora Dennis.
Mi padre cree que vio a alguien en el patio.
Geraldo nunca visita a nadie.
Acusaron a Milagros de matar a alguien.
¿A quién quiere usted ver, por favor?
Paseo a mi perro Beto todos los días.
No sé a quiénes te refieres.
Queremos conocer a los que hablan español.

22.17

The verb *tener* vacillates in taking the particle as seen in these two examples.

Tengo muchos hijos.	Tengo una sobrina en México.
vs.	
Ya no tengo a nadie.	Tengo a mi sobrina conmigo.

Tener may emphasize either existence or possession. When Spanish speakers say *Tengo una sobrina en México*, they are calling attention to the mere existence of such a person so related to them. *Tener* then does not take the personal accusative. But in *Tengo a mi sobrina conmigo*, the existence of the niece has already been established. What is actually expressed is possession/accompanyment, and in such cases *tener* is followed by the personal accusative.

The verb *querer* can also be problematic. When it means *to love*, the personal accusative is required:

Quiero a mi novia con todo mi corazón.

However, when it means *to want*, one finds more variation:

Quiero un médico (Non–specific or 'any' doctor)

But:

¡Quiero a mi mamá! (Said by a child crying out for his mother)

Almodóvar quiere a Sara Montiel para su próxima película. (Whitley 2002:224-5)

The personal accusative personifies inanimate direct objects:

El científico vio a la Muerte.

Occasionally it grammatically identifies the direct object, be it animate or not:

Y siguió a la angustia la fatiga. (A Machado)
Los perros persiguen a los gatos.
Persiguen a los gatos los perros.
El bullicio siguió al silencio.
Alcanzó al vapor el yate.
(Whitley 2002:224)

This last function is clearly due to the greater syntactic flexibility of Spanish, which, in addition to the preferred SVO (Subject-Verb-Object) order, also allows for VSO or VOS.

Finally, the personal accusative can be omitted with human direct objects if they are presented as non-specific, as seen above in the sentence *Quiero un médico*:

Buscan secretarias bilingües. (Any bilingual secretaries)
vs.
Busco a mi secretaria. (A specific person)

Furthermore, the personal *a* before a human direct object can be suppressed in order that this direct object be distinguished from a human indirect object, as in, *La mamá le dio (a) el niño* [DO] *a la niñera* [IO]. The problema of determining "who is giving whom to whom" is thus resolved. Yet there remain cases like, *Te quisiera presentar a mi amigo, Miguel*, where *te* and *a mi amigo* could both function either as direct or indirect objects, and ambiguity concerning "whom to whom" seems insoluble.

22.18

Sometimes in Spanish the personal direct object noun preceded by the personal accusative occurs as a unit before the verb. In these cases, the direct object is then repeated (reduplicated) pronominally before the verb. (See Chapter 11.13.) The structure is used for emphasis, or for contrast as in the first example below:

A Elena no la conozco, (pero a su novio, sí).
A tus padres no los he visto por aquí.
Al Presidente de la República lo mataron.
A los habitantes desamparados no los puede ayudar el gobierno.

The direct object noun may convert into a pronoun, and again reduplicates pronominally.

A él (= Al Director) lo vi ayer.

Exercise 9

Translate the following English sentences, providing the personal accusative where appropriate.

1. We don't want to see your friends now.
2. I think John killed someone last night.
3. They want to have at least three children.
4. I know Dr. Johnson, but I don't know his wife.
5. We didn't see anyone on the street.
6. Who(m) are you going to bring to my party?
7. All my students have to bring books to class.
8. I see some of them (people), but I don't see their cars.
9. Who was with you when you met the ambassador?
10. Did someone say something to Dr. Smith?
11. They want to know who(m) we saw in class.
12. My friends don't know anyone in Mexico.
13. We plan to meet a lot of people during our trip.
14. Who(m) did they take to the airport?
15. John brought his little dog to class yesterday.

Exercise 10

Write in the personal *a* where necessary:

1. Miro _____ las noticias todos los días.
2. Visitaremos _____ ese museo mañana.
3. ¿Llamaste _____ tu novia?
4. No reconocimos _____ tus hermanos.
5. ¿_____ quién visitaste hoy?
6. ¿_____ qué viste hoy?
7. Estoy buscando _____ mis libros.
8. Estoy buscando _____ mi esposa.
9. Estoy buscando _____ una esposa.
10. No entiendo _____ nada.
11. No entiendo _____ nadie.
12. Tiene _____ hermanos.
13. Tiene _____ su hijo en una escuela privada.
14. Quiero _____ un mecánico que no cobre mucho.
15. Quiero _____ mi novia con todo mi corazón.
16. _____ ella la vimos, pero _____ él, no.

POR VERSUS PARA

22.19

English uses a variety of prepositions to translate the two Spanish prepositions *por* and *para*. English *for* is especially difficult since both *por* and *para* are possibilities. Gili Gaya classifies *por* as a causal preposition and *para* as a preposition denoting aim, purpose, or result. He observes that, "*En nuestros días se ha consumado casi totalmente la distinción entre el sentido final de para y el causal de por*" (Gili Gaya, *Curso superior*, §193).

When reading the following section, keep in mind that the Spanish speaker often uses these two prepositions more on the basis of his/her feelings for them than on the basis of any dictates of grammar: *...mi amor por/para mi patria*. The following discussion should prove helpful to both the English and Spanish speaker.

22.20
USES OF *POR*

Here are the most frequent usages of the preposition *por* together with plausible equivalent translations in English. At the end of the section is a list of common idiomatic expressions with *por* along with an explanation of its usage when followed by an infinitive (See items 13 and 14, below).

Por **is used:**

1. To express the agent in the true passive constructions—English uses *by*. (See Chapter 16)

    Ese edificio fue construido por un arquitecto muy conocido.
    That building was built by a well-known architect.

    Don Quijote fue escrito por don Miguel de Cervantes Saavedra.
    Don Quixote was written by Miguel de Cervantes Saavedra.

    La sexta versión fue bien recibida por todos.
    The sixth version was well received by all.

2. To express the manner or means by which something is accomplished— English uses *by, through*.

    Lo logró por gastar todos sus ahorros.
    He accomplished it by spending all his savings.

    Conseguí el trabajo por un amigo.
    I got the job through a friend.

3. To express a motive or reason why—English uses *because of, out of, due to, on account of*.

    Ella no fue a la manifestación principalmente por miedo.
    She didn't go to the demonstration principally because of (out of) fear.

No pudimos salir por la lluvia.
We were unable to leave due to the rain.

4. To express the act of going for something or someone. The verbs most commonly used here are verbs of motion: *ir, venir, mandar, enviar, volver, regresar,* and *pasar.* English uses *for.*

    Fuimos por lana y volvimos trasquilados.
    We went for wool and came back shorn.

    No pude pasar por ti anoche.
    I was unable to come by for you last night.

5. To express an opinion of someone or something—English uses *as.*

    Indudablemente lo tienen a él por loco.
    Undoubtedly they consider him (as) crazy.

    Absolutamente todos lo rechazaron por ladrón.
    Absolutely everyone rejected him as (because he was) a thief.

6. To express duration of time or distance—English uses *for.*

    Se suscribió por un año a la revista *Buen Hogar.*
    She subscribed for one year to *Good Housekeeping* magazine.

    Viajamos por más de cien kilómetros.
    We traveled for more than one hundred kilometers.

7. To express movement *along, through,* or *by,* or to express imprecise time:

    Paseamos por la Gran Vía.
    We strolled along the Gran Vía.

    El tren pasó por el túnel.
    The train passed through the tunnel.

    Entraron por esa ventana.
    The entered through/by that window.

    No hago nada por (en) las mañanas.
    I don't do anything in the mornings.

8. To express the exchange of one item for another—English uses *for.*

    A él le di mucho dinero por el carro.

I gave him a lot of money for the car.

Ni me dieron las gracias por el favor que les hice.
They didn't even thank me for the favor I did them.

9. To express occurrences in a sequence—English uses *by, for*.

   Iban preguntando casa por casa.
   They went around asking house by house.

   Aquí tienes lo que dijo ella, palabra por palabra.
   Here's what she said, word for word.

10. To express whatever unit of measure is being used—English uses *per, a*.

    Los compré a tres dólares por docena.
    I bought them at three dollars a/per dozen.

    El avión 747 puede volar a 550 millas por hora.
    The Boeing 747 can fly at 550 miles an hour.

    Él gana más de sesenta mil dólares por/al año.
    He earns more than sixty thousand dollars a year.

11. To express the term *times* in math problems involving multiplication.

    Dos por dos son cuatro.
    Two times two is four.

    ¿Cuántos son cinco por cuatro?
    How much are five times four?

12. To express on behalf of someone or in place of someone (proxy)—English uses *for*.

    Naturalmente todo lo hacemos por nuestra patria.
    Naturally we do it all for our country.

    Él habló por su padre, que tuvo que asistir a otra reunión.
    He spoke for (in place of) his father, who had to attend another meeting.

13. *Por* + INF expresses something remaining to be done.

    Todavía nos quedan detalles pendientes por hacer.
    We still have some details left to do.

    No nos dejaron muchos ensayos por corregir.
    They didn't leave us many essays to correct.

14. *Por* is used in a variety of Spanish idiomatic expressions. We list some of the most common ones here.

por ahora	for now/for the present
por cierto	certainly/for sure
por Dios	for heaven's sake
por eso	for that reason/therefore
por favor	please
por fin	at last/finally
por lo general	in general
por lo menos	at least
por lo visto	apparently
por más/menos que	however more/less
por otra parte	elsewhere/on the other hand
por supuesto	of course
por una parte	on the one hand

22.21
USES OF *PARA*

The most common usages of the preposition *para* along with their English equivalents follow. A careful study of this and the preceding section should benefit the English speaker in choosing between *por* and *para* to express *for*.

Para is used:

1. To express the person or thing for which something is intended—English uses *for*.

   Aquí tengo una carta para ti.
   Here is a letter for you.

   No pienso traer nada para ella.
   I don't plan to bring anything for her.

2. To express an unexpected comparison—English uses *for*.

   Para ser extranjero Usted habla español muy bien.
   You speak Spanish very well for (being) a foreigner.

   Para ser mayo hace mucho frío.
   It's very cold for May.

3. *Para* is used to express English *only to* or *not/never to*.

Salió el sol para esconderse luego detrás de las nubes.
The sun came out only to be hidden later behind the clouds.

Ella se fue a Brasil para no volver.
She went off to Brazil never to return.

4. To express a time deadline—English uses *by*.

   Tenemos que terminar de imprimir el libro para mañana.
   We have to finish printing the book by tomorrow.

   A él le dije que me lo trajera para el miércoles.
   I told him to bring it to me by Wednesday.

5. To express the purpose of or reason for an action (*para* + INF = *to/in order to*), or to express an actual destination (*para* + GOAL = *for*).

   Harás lo que sea necesario para lograr tus fines.
   You will do whatever is necessary (in order) to achieve your goals.

   Saldremos para el Perú mañana.
   We shall leave for Peru tomorrow.

6. *Estar para* + INF expresses the concept of being about to or being on the verge of doing something. *Estar a punto de* is perhaps more common in the colloquial language. Some educated native speakers will argue that *estar por* + INF is possible, even preferable in this context.

   Estamos para/por salir.
   We are about to leave.

   Yo no quería decir más porque ella estaba para/por llorar.
   I didn't want to say any more because she was on the verge of crying.

Exercise 11

Translate the following English sentences. Be able to state by number the reason for your choice of *por* or *para*.

1. You speak English very well for being a foreigner.
2. I went along the street, but they went through the park.
3. What are you going to do in the evenings?
4. We have to spend a lot of money (in order) to travel.
5. Is this package for you or for me?
6. How much did they give you for the horse?
7. She read this difficult book page by page.

Chapter 22 Adverbs and Prepositions

8. Because of the lack of water, we almost died of thirst.
9. They attacked him as (being) a rebel.
10. I returned for the car, but nobody was there.
11. That picture was painted by El Greco.
12. We are about to leave. We have to be there by seven o'clock.
13. He entered a monastery never to leave again.
14. They were here for two hours, and they brought candy for the kids.
15. Mrs. Martínez sacrifices herself for her son.
16. I don't want to speak for (on behalf of) my brother.
17. May I exchange this dictionary for another one?
18. Berta was in a hurry because her shopping remained to be done.
19. How much do you earn an/per hour?
20. I found out through my sister that you had been ill.
21. For a professor of languages, you seem to know a lot about physics.
22. At last they arrived. They had bought flowers for my sister.
23. Apparently we will finish it by tomorrow.
24. We came by for Mary, but she couldn't come with us on account having to work.
25. In order to arrive on time, we had to run through the library.

23
Interrogatives, Admiratives, Ellipsis and Verification Tags

INTERROGATIVES

23.1
SPANISH INTEGRATED VS. ENGLISH SEPARABLE INTERROGATIVES

The two languages have interrogative words and expressions, those used in content questions. This chapter focuses on the varieties of the interrogative words and expressions themselves, paying close attention to syntax.

Spanish consistently integrates (keeps together) the elements of its interrogatives if they consist of more than one word. English, however, allows the elements of the interrogative unit to separate, the first element occurring at the beginning of the question and the remaining one placed last. Examine the following contrasting examples of Spanish integrated vs. English separable interrogative constructions.

¿*De dónde* es usted?	*Where* are you *from*?
¿*Para qué* lo quieres?	*What* do you want it *for*?
¿*De qué* están hablando?	*What* are they talking *about*?
¿*Con qué* lo abrió él?	*What* did he open it *with*?
¿*Debajo de qué* lo viste?	*What* did you see it *under*?
¿*Para quién* es esto?	*Who(m)* is this *for*?
¿*A quién* le doy la caja?	*Who(m)* do I give the box *to*?
¿*De quién* recibió ella eso?	*Who(m)* did she get that *from*?
¿*Para cuándo* lo pedimos?	*When* did we order it *for*?

304   *Chapter 23 Interrogatives, Admiratives, Ellipsis and Verification Tags*

Modern English usage recommends that when interrogative *who* is preceded by a preposition, it must assume the object(ive) form *whom*: *From whom did you receive the letter?* However, if this prepositional construction is in separable form, *who* is acceptable: *Who did you receive the letter from?* Although prescriptive grammar recommends *whom* over *who* in the last example, few are the speakers who follow this dictate. *Whom* is the object(ive) form of *who*, used in the formal language as the direct object (*Who[m] do you know there?*), indirect object (*Who[m] did you write [to]?*) and prepositional object (*With whom* [obligatory] *do you plan to live?*).

Exercise 1

Translate the following Spanish interrogative sentences. Provide both integrated and separable interrogative constructions.

1. ¿Para cuándo los necesitas?
2. ¿De dónde son esos aborígenes?
3. ¿De qué período hablas?
4. ¿A qué vas al extranjero constantemente?
5. ¿Para quién horneaste ese pastel?
6. ¿Encima de qué casa está el animal?
7. ¿Con quiénes vas al teatro?
8. ¿En qué alternativa estás pensando?
9. ¿Por quién fue escrita la carta?
10. ¿Acerca de qué hablaron anoche?

Exercise 2

Translate the following English interrogative sentences. In all cases, the interrogative will be integrated:

1. Who(m) did you do it for?
2. What do we want that for?
3. Who(m) does she wish to speak with?
4. What are you drinking that for?
5. Where is your professor from?
6. What are they writing about?
7. Who(m) am I going to leave with?
8. When do you want it for?
9. What did they find it under?
10. About whom is he going to speak?
11. With whom is she speaking?
12. Where are you coming from?

23.2

Spanish and English simple interrogative words correspond well, except in the few cases illustrated here. The interrogative for unidentified persons in Spanish is *¿quién?*; it has a plural, *¿quiénes?*. Either word functions as the subject in a question. Since English does not designate number in its interrogatives, both *¿quién?* and *¿quiénes?* are translated by *who?* if in subject position. English may distinguish between singular and plural by adding the word *all* for the plural.

| ¿Quién quiere ir? | Who wants to go? |
| ¿Quiénes quieren ir? | Who (all) want to go? |

When *¿quién?* and *¿quiénes?* function as either direct or indirect objects, they are preceded by *a*. In the case of direct objects, *a* is the personal accusative and belongs to the personal direct object interrogative. However, the *a* preceding an indirect object is a true preposition and is translated with *to*, as seen below.

DIRECT OBJECT

| ¿A quién viste? | Who(m) did you see? |
| ¿A quiénes visitarán? | Who(m) (all) will they visit? |

INDIRECT OBJECT

¿A quiénes (les) escribieron?	To whom (all) did they write?
	Who(m) (all) did they write to?
¿A quién (le) diste el dinero?	To whom did you give the money?
	Who(m) did you give the money to?

Once more, standard "correct" English prefers *whom* in the translation, although *who* is acceptable and increasingly more frequent than *whom*. Again, *whom* is obligatory only after a preposition.

23.3

The English interrogative for unidentified things is *what*. It has three Spanish equivalents: *¿qué?, ¿cuál?* and *¿cuáles?* In sentences involving the verb *ser*, the Spanish speaker employs either *¿qué?* or *¿cuál/cuales?* You use *¿cuál(es)?* when the subject of the question follows a form of *ser*, except when a mere definition is asked for.

¿Cuál es la fecha de hoy?	What is the date today?
¿Cuál es tu número de teléfono?	What is your telephone number?
¿Cuáles son los meses del otoño?	What are the months of autumn?

But,

| ¿Qué es una *visión*? | What is a *vision*? |
| ¿Qué es una *hipótesis*? | What is a *hypothesis*? |

Note: In the last two examples, a mere definition is sought. The word *cosa* could be placed after interrogative *¿qué?* in each case: *¿Qué cosa es una hipótesis?*

Interrogative *¿qué?* occurs when the subject of the question directly follows it and both precede a form of *ser*. In Latin American usage, *¿cuál?* frequently substitutes.

¿Qué fecha sería mejor?	What date would be better?
¿Qué número es mayor?	What number is larger?
¿Qué meses te gustan más?	What months do you like best?
¿Qué (cosa) es una hipótesis?	What is a hypothesis?

23.4

The English interrogatives *which (one)/which (ones)* are usually rendered by *¿cuál/cuáles?*. These interrogatives may refer to either personal or non-personal objects. In references of this type, the listener is asked to select one or more elements from a supposed grouping or actual listing of items.

| ¿Cuál de las afirmaciones prefieres? | Which (one) of the affirmations do you prefer? |
| ¿Cuáles escogiste? | Which (ones) did you choose? |

Exercise 3

Translate the following English interrogative sentences using *¿quién?*, *¿quiénes?*, *¿cuál?*, *¿cuáles?*, and *¿qué?*.

1. What are the most important cities in the United States?
2. Who(m) did you sell it to?
3. What book did you find at the bookstore?
4. Which (ones) of your students know Portuguese?
5. What was their flight number?
6. What museum do they want to visit?
7. Who (all) are in the library?
8. What is a *kangaroo*?
9. Which (one) are you going to buy?
10. What will be the result of our actions?
11. Who(m) did he help?
12. What was her problem?

ADMIRATIVE EXPRESSIONS

23.5

Both languages have formulas expressing admiration, surprise or contempt.

What a sensation!	¡Qué sensación!
How horrible!	¡Qué horror!
How fast you run!	¡Qué rápido corres!

The Spanish formulas for admirative expressions used with nouns are more consistent and simpler than those of English. The term "count nouns" refer to items that can be counted, for example, *dogs/perros*, *friends/amigos*, *problems/problemas*. "Non-count (or 'mass') nouns" cannot be counted, and are measurable only by their quantity; *water/agua*, *smoke/humo*, *milk/leche* (See Chapter 19).

Chapter 23 Interrogatives, Admiratives, Ellipsis and Verification Tags

An admirative expression of a singular count noun is as follows:

ENGLISH: **what** + INDEF. ART. + (ADJ) + NOUN

    What a man!
    What a large proportion!
    What a novel!
    What a difficult course!

SPANISH: **qué** + NOUN + (*tan/más* + ADJ)

    ¡Qué hombre!
    ¡Qué proporción más (tan) grande!
    ¡Qué novela!
    ¡Qué curso tan (más) difícil!

An admirative expression of a non-count noun or of a plural noun employs the following formulas:

ENGLISH: **what** + (ADJ) + NOUN

    What men!
    What strong women!
    What books!
    What good coffee!

SPANISH: **qué** + NOUN + (*tan/más* + ADJ)

    ¡Qué hombres!
    ¡Qué mujeres más (tan) fuertes!
    ¡Qué libros!
    ¡Qué café más (tan) bueno!

The admirative expression of an English adjective, adverb or verb has this formula:

how + ADJ	How beautiful!
how + ADV	How quickly they answered!
how + S + V	How you talk!

In Spanish admirative expressions with adjectives and adverbs use a different formula from the one involving verbs:

qué/cuán + ADJ/ADV   ¡Qué falso! ¡Cuán temprano!
(*Qué* is far more frequent than *cuán* in this setting)

cómo + V + (S)   ¡Cómo hablas (tú)!
                          ¡Cómo corre (Juan)!

Exercise 4

Translate the following admirative expressions into the other language. Determine whether you are dealing with count nouns, non-count nouns, or with adjectives, adverbs or verbs.

1. ¡Qué rápido corre tu carro!
2. What a tall boy John is!
3. ¡Qué bien sabes tus lecciones!
4. What good wine!
5. ¡Cómo me preocupa esa señora!
6. How slowly you work!
7. ¡Qué sutil es ese sabor!
8. What bad beer they served us!
9. ¡Qué dura e intolerable es esta vida!
10. How well you teach Spanish!

23.6

Two additional forms of admirative expression require attention. One occurs in English, the other in Spanish. The interlingual contrasts are significant.

Colloquial English sometimes uses an affirmative *Yes/No* question structure (but always with descending intonation) to express admiration. An interjection is usually present, for example, *Man!, Wow!, Boy!, Gosh!*, etc. Of course, Spanish speakers may be confused by the English *Yes/No* question structure's being used in this way, so they should be "on the look-out" for such utterances.

Man! Does he speak Spanish well!	¡Qué bien habla español!
Wow! Is this food (ever) delicious!	¡Qué deliciosa está esta comida!
Boy! Does he say romantic things!	¡Qué cosas tan (más) románticas dice!
Gosh! Did she get annoyed!	¡Qué molesta se puso!

Spanish uses *lo* + ADJ/ADV + *que* for English *how* when the English word introduces an assertive subordinate clause following the main clause. The locution *qué* + ADJ/ADV (with subordinating *que* suppressed) also occurs: *No sabes lo importante que es = No sabes qué importante es.*

You don't know how hard we worked.	No sabes lo duro que trabajamos.
If you knew how mean he is, ...	Si supieras lo malo que es, ...
I want you to tell me how far it is.	Quiero que me digas lo lejos que está.
I hope you know how difficult it is.	Espero que sepas lo difícil que es.

Exercise 5

Translate the following admirative sentences into the other language, drawing from all the structures presented in this section.

1. You don't know how fast I can run!

2. ¡Qué rápido corría ese tren!
3. Don't they see how bad he is!
4. ¡Qué furiosa se puso la profesora!
5. She won't tell you how ridiculous it is!
6. ¡Qué bonita va a ser la casa de ellos!
7. I don't want to know how handsome he is!
8. ¡Qué chica más bonita la que vimos en la playa!
9. He doesn't know how sick they are!
10. ¡Qué contento está mi hermano!

ELLIPTICAL VERBAL USAGES

23.7

Spanish usually answers simple affirmative or negative *Yes/No* questions with a simple *sí* or *no*.

¿Vives en San Francisco?   Sí.
¿Vas a venir mañana?   No.

English may follow the Spanish model, but also has the option of employing its auxiliary verbal system in the answer. In addition to a simple *yes* or *no* response, there may follow a substitute pronoun for the subject of the statement combined with a corresponding auxiliary serving as an anaphoric elliptical echo of the original statement.

YES/NO QUESTION	AFFIM. RESPONSE	NEG. RESPONSE
Is your father working?	Yes, he is.	No, he isn't.
Does she live here?	Yes, she does.	No, she doesn't.
Did your friends go?	Yes, they did.	No, they didn't.
Will they come home?	Yes, they will.	No, they won't.
Would your brother like her?	Yes, he would.	No, he wouldn't.
Has she studied French?	Yes, she has.	No, she hasn't.
Had they come early?	Yes, they had.	No, they hadn't.
Do you have a book?	Yes, I do.	No, I don't.
Have you a book? (British)	Yes, I have.	No, I haven't
Should the boy be here?	Yes, he should.	No, he shouldn't.
Can your friends come?	Yes, they can.	No, they can't.

The structure for the affirmative response is:

Yes, S[PRONOUN] + AUX[*be, do, have*, or **MODAL**]

The structure for the negative response is:

No, S[PRONOUN] + AUX[*be, do, have*, or **MODAL**]** + *not*

Note: The double asterisk (**) denotes a generally mandatory contraction of *not* with all auxiliaries. However, by avoiding the contraction the speaker can intensify the negative response: *No, I'm not > No, I am not*.

Exercise 6

Give both affirmative and negative English elliptical responses for the following *Yes/No* questions.

1. Are you rich?
2. Were your parents here yesterday?
3. Is he working at the plant this month?
4. Were you in school last semester?
5. Did the students try to do the work?
6. Have you a car in the city? (British)
7. Do they have many friends in Honduras?
8. Have your friends left yet?
9. Has your brother written to your family?
10. Had they ever been there before?
11. Will the professor help me?
12. Would they like to see the old part of the city?
13. Can you show me the exercises?
14. Should we wait for them?
15. Am I really sick?

23.8

In compound sentences, English often uses an elliptical verbal construction in the second clause to avoid repeating the verb in the first one. As in the case of elliptical responses to the affirmative or negative *Yes/No* questions, only the auxiliary remains in the second clause. Observe the following examples:

First and second clauses are negative:
   He doesn't like his car, and I don't either. (and neither do I / nor do I)
   I don't reside in Miami, and she doesn't either. (and neither does she / nor does she)

First clause is negative; second is not:
   They can't go, but I can.
   They haven't been to Spain yet, but I have.
   I hadn't met her before, but they had.

First and second clauses are affirmative statements:
   He likes his car, and so do I. (and I do too/also/as well)
   I reside in Chicago, and so does he. (and he does too/also/as well)
   He would've helped you, and so would've I. (and I would've too/also/as well)

First clause is affirmative; second is not:
   He'll be here tomorrow, but I won't.
   He would've helped you, but she wouldn't have.

Chapter 23 Interrogatives, Admiratives, Ellipsis and Verification Tags

Regarding the examples just presented, if *and* introduces the second clause, two different patterns can be used, both affirmative and negative:

Pattern 1:

Affirmative:	Negative
...and + S + V[always aux] + too/also/as well	...and + S + V[always aux]** + not + either
...and we can too/also/as well.	...and we can't either.
...and they did too/also/as well	...and they didn't either.
...and you should too/also/as well.	...and you shouldn't either.

Pattern 2:

Affirmative:	Negative
...and + so + V[always aux] + S	...and + neither + V[always aux] + S
...and so can we.	...and neither can we
....and so did they.	...and neither did they
...and so should you.	...and neither should you.

The negative structures for both patterns above have a third version. If the word *and* is replaced by *nor*, the structure is **nor + aux + s.**

> He won't go, nor will I.
> You don't know it, nor do they.

All three possible negative structures are used below:

We shouldn't do that,	and our students shouldn't either.
	and neither should our students.
	nor should our students.

Spanish expresses this type of construction with a simple subject plus *sí* or *no*, or with a similar non-verbal construction (*y a mí también*), as in these examples.

First and second clauses are negative statements:
    A él no le gusta su carro, ni a mí tampoco.
    Yo no resido en Miami, ni ella tampoco.

First clause is negative; second is not:
    Ellos no pueden ir, pero yo sí.
    No han estado en España aún, pero yo sí.
    Yo no la había conocido antes, pero ellos sí

First and second clauses are affirmative statements:
    A él le gusta su carro y a mí también.
    Yo resido en Chicago y él también.
    Él te hubiera ayudado y yo también.

First clause is affirmative; second is not:
El estará aquí mañana, pero yo, no.
Él te hubiera ayudado, pero ella, no.

Exercise 7

Translate the following Spanish sentences using a verbal ellipsis in the second clause. For sentences marked with "(2)" give both possible versions of the second clause. Sentences designated "(3)" (all negative) have three second-clause versions: Give them all.

1. Rey está en casa, pero Julia no.
2. Estábamos traduciendo del latín y ellos también. (2)
3. Yolanda no es egoísta, ni su hermana tampoco. (3)
4. El príncipe no fue asesinado, pero el conde sí.
5. Ella no piensa en ti, pero yo sí.
6. Yo tengo muchas preocupaciones, pero mi padre no.
7. Mi madre siempre mantiene el mismo peso, pero mi tía no.
8. Ellos no hablaban de sus virtudes, ni nosotros tampoco. (3)
9. Ella no padecía de nada, pero él sí.
10. Yo he visto a Roberto, pero a Jaime, no.
11. Casi nadie había hecho la tarea, pero Paulina sí.
12. Ellos no tenían deseos de bailar, pero yo sí.
13. Ella no tiene voto, pero mi hermana sí.
14. Ellas no aparecen en la lista publicada, pero yo sí.
15. Pablo no resolverá ni siquiera la mitad del misterio, ni ella tampoco. (3)
16. Yo no pude abrir la puerta, pero ellos sí.
17. Este libro habla de la evolución, pero ese otro no.
18. Ellos no pudieron viajar al Mediterráneo, pero tú sí.
19. Mis padres no vivían en la nueva urbanización, ni yo tampoco. (3)
20. Nadie más te ha visto esa mirada, pero yo sí.

23.9

Finally, English may make an ellipsis of its infinitive in the second clause of a compound sentence. This is done by removing the lexical verb and leaving behind only the particle *to* of the infinitive phrase. Such an ellipsis again avoids a redundant verb. Spanish must repeat the infinitive or bring it to mind with the substitute *hacer*.

ENGLISH EXAMPLES:
We haven't read it yet, but we plan to tomorrow.
He wants to write a book, and he hopes to soon.
She didn't leave a message, but she's going to tonight.
I haven't met them, but I expect to at the party

SPANISH EXAMPLES:
Aún no lo hemos leído, pero pensamos hacerlo mañana.

Él quiere escribir un libro y espera hacerlo pronto.
Ella no dejó ningún recado, pero va a dejar uno esta noche.
No los he conocido, pero espero conocerlos en la fiesta.

Exercise 8

Translate the following sentences. Make an elliptical construction for the infinitive occurring in the second segment of the compound sentence.

1. No han traído los noventa libros, pero piensan traerlos esta noche.
2. Quiero decírtelo y voy a hacerlo cuando te vea.
3. No hemos hablado con el profesor, pero tenemos que hacerlo mañana.
4. No puedo hablarte ahora, pero necesito hacerlo más tarde.
5. Debo escribir una composición y voy a hacer eso esta tarde.
6. No le hemos contado la historia, pero esperamos contársela dentro de poco.

VERIFICATION TAGS

23.10

SPANISH TAGS

In any language, a speaker may make a statement (affirmative or negative) and then follow it with a request for confirmation. This is done by appending a so-called "verification tag" to the statement. The Spanish system for verification tags, called *preguntas retóricas*, is relatively simple. The English system is considerably more complex.

In Spanish, if the tagged statement is affirmative, either of the tags ¿no? or ¿verdad? may be used. ¿No es así? also occurs, especially in informal speech.

Zoraida viene esta noche,	¿verdad?/¿no?
Esa técnica es confusa,	¿verdad?/¿no?
Vicente va a Santo Domingo a vivir,	¿verdad?/¿no?
Ella llegó a las siete,	¿verdad?/¿no?

If the Spanish tagged statement is negative, only ¿verdad? appears.

Zoraida no viene esta noche,	¿verdad?
Esa técnica no es confusa,	¿verdad?
Vicente no va a Santo Domingo a vivir,	¿verdad?
Ella no llegó a las siete,	¿verdad?

Exercise 9

Determine which tags, ¿verdad?, ¿no?, or both, could be used with the following Spanish affirmative and negative statements.

1. Los críticos de drama no vienen esta noche,
2. Su colección contiene muchas figuras de cristal,

3. Juanillo no fue a Uruguay,
4. Tus amigos siempre llegan con alegría,
5. Ellos no van a estar en la fiesta el sábado,
6. Los Estados Unidos de América es un país muy rico,
7. Venezuela se encuentra al lado de Colombia,
8. Mis padres no conocen a tus padres,
9. La ciudad más grande del mundo es Tokio,
10. No fumas a diario,

23.11
ENGLISH TAGS

English restates an affirmative statement as a negative question and the reverse. The tense remains the same, but the verb phrase of the original statement is reduced to its first auxiliary or to *do* if no other auxiliary is present. When the main verb of a sentence is any form of *be* or *have*, these are repeated in the tag. The subject of the tagged statement is mandatorily restated as a pronoun in the tag itself, just as in the case of the elliptical responses to English *Yes/No* questions. As was explained in Chapter 5, mandatory contractions occur in most negative responses. Colloquial English ever more frequently takes the easy way out, tagging both affirmative and negative statements with *right*?: *You will/won't be here tomorrow, right?*

AFFIRMATIVE STATEMENT	NEGATIVE TAG AUX** + *not* + S[PRONOUN] **Mandatory contraction with *not*. Note: British English often uses, AUX + S[PRONOUN] + *not*
He is here,	isn't he? / is he not?
Your parents live here,	don't they? / do they not?
Susan will arrive on time,	won't she? / will she not?
Your son has been working,	hasn't he? / has he not?
You had been sick,	hadn't you? / had you not?
The cause would be lost,	wouldn't it? / would it not?
We met your father,	didn't we? / did we not?
John should visit her,	shouldn't he? / should he not?
Your parents have a car,	don't they? / do they not? haven't they? / have they not?

Note: In spoken American English; If the subject is *I* and the verb is *be* in the present tense, the negative tag is as follows: *I'm pretty, aren't I?*; *I'm in a warehouse, aren't I* ? Careful speakers will select the alternate, more correct negative tag, *Am I not?*

Chapter 23 Interrogatives, Admiratives, Ellipsis and Verification Tags

NEGATIVE STATEMENT	AFFIRMATIVE TAG AUX + S[PRONOUN]
They aren't here,	are they?
She doesn't live here now,	does she?
Janice won't arrive on time,	will she?
My son hasn't been working,	has he?
Harry hadn't been sick,	had he?
The cause wouldn't be lost,	would it?
They didn't see your cousin,	did they?
Our friends can't come home,	can they?
Her father doesn't have a car,	does he?

Exercise 10

Write the English verification tags for the following affirmative and negative statements, then translate each with their tags into Spanish.

1. You have a house in the country,
2. You didn't bring a car to school today,
3. You see my friends on the corner,
4. She is an American student,
5. They aren't working in Europe this summer,
6. They are your cousins from Argentina,
7. Your uncle wasn't living in Guatemala,
8. The children had been sick with the measles,
9. Your little girl hasn't seen a circus,
10. His family will be here for the whole month,
11. Your brother wouldn't do a thing like that,
12. They know Spanish very well,
13. Your sister can write English,
14. She couldn't open the window,
15. The professor lives near the university,
16. The school is on this block,
17. Those boys had given her a ride home,
18. All the students know the material,
19. Your nephew has to pay a fine,
20. Your party is going to be a huge success,

24

Spanish and English Contractions

24.1

Spanish has only two contractions; these are the prepositions *a* and *de* contracted with the definite article *el* to form *al* and *del* respectively.

a + el > al
>Descansemos al aire libre.
>El hombre trató de lograrlo al instante.
>Se asomaron al borde de la fuente.

de + el > del
>Los individuos huyeron del bosque.
>Admiramos la colección del museo.
>Lo descubrí al extremo de la orilla del mar.

> **Note:** The two contractions do not occur if *el* is part of a place name or title: *Los estudiantes salieron de El Ganso Negro y fueron a El Gusano Muerto a seguir bebiendo.*

24.2

Unlike Spanish, English has various types of contractions. They may occur at any level of speech but are most common in the spoken language. English contractions can be very difficult for Spanish speakers in both the passive and productive skills. English contractions are always optional, with the one exception of that occurring between the AUX and *not* in the negative Yes/No question structure: *Haven't we been here before?* (See Chapter 5.10) Only one contraction per simple sentence occurs in standard English. In the following sentence, the underlined segments show where a contraction is theoretically possible: *She is not going*. But the sentence can be rendered in contracted form in only one or the other of the two possible ways.

She's not going, or
She isn't going.

CLASSIFICATION OF ENGLISH CONTRACTIONS

24.3

There are three major classifications for English contractions:

Class 1. Contractions occurring between a subject pronoun and the verbs *be* (forms *am, is,* and *are* only, used as an AUX and non-AUX); *have/has/had* (AUX and non-AUX); and modals *will/would*.

I'm in school now. (am)
She's working in an atomic plant. (is)
You've bought a new car. (have)
They'd been living there for years. (had)
He'll be here in a few minutes. (will)
We'd rather be in Texas. (would)

Class 2. Contractions occurring between a subject noun or interrogative word and the verbs *be* (forms *is, are* used as an AUX or non-AUX); *have/has/had* (AUX and non-AUX); and the modals *will/would*. This type of contraction is less frequent in English.

Mary's in school today. (is)
Both John and David're working in the State Department. (are)
Who's been working here lately? (has)
Where'll you be this time next year? (will)
What's your name, little boy? (is)
Billy'd go to Spain if he could. (would)

Class 3. Contractions occurring between the following verb forms: *be* (forms *is, are, was, were* used as an AUX or non-AUX), *have/has/had* (AUX or non-AUX), *do/does/did* (AUX), most of the modal auxiliaries and the negative particle, *not*.

They aren't here now. (are not)
She isn't working here these days. (is not)
We weren't studying much last year. (were not)
I wasn't trying to open your door. (was not)
He hasn't any friends in Florida. (Brit.) (has not)
They haven't gone yet. (have not)
We hadn't seen him for several weeks. (had not)
I don't know your name. (do not)
They didn't know any of the answers. (did not)
She doesn't want to see them now. (does not)

Jane wouldn't say a thing like that. (would not)
We won't be there when you arrive. (will not)
Why can't you help me? (cannot)
They couldn't find their friends. (could not)
We shouldn't have bought so much bread. (should not)

24.4
CONFUSING CONTRACTIONS IN ENGLISH

Here are some particularly confusing English contractions.

a. A contraction like *Mary's* may have the following meanings:
Mary is... *Mary's here and needs to see you.*
Mary has... *Mary's done all her work.*
The possessive form: *Mary's brother is Tom.*

b. *its* vs *it's*
Its is a possessive adjective. *I don't like its color.*
It's is the contracted form of *it is* or *it has*. *It's an old chair; it's been broken for a long time.*

c. *there's* vs *theirs*
There is... *There's a book on the table.*
There has... *There's been a terrible accident.*
Theirs is a possessive pronoun: *The house is theirs after the first of the month.*

d. *they're* vs *there* and *their*
They're is the contraction of *they are*: *They're ready to go.*
There is an adverb of location: *The students are over there.*
Their is a possessive adjective: *They love their children.*

e. *I'd* and similar contractions: *she'd, he'd, you'd, we'd, they'd* etc.
I would... *I'd be a liar if I told you that.*
I had... *I'd told him several times before not to do that.*

Exercise 1
Rewrite the following English sentences, making all possible contractions. Some sentences may have at least two versions. Analyze the elements comprising each contraction and classify them under the appropriate class outlined in 24.3.

1. We are not at home now.
2. They have not been traveling much.
3. You would not say a thing like that.
4. Marianne did not come home last night.
5. Your father has not been feeling well.
6. Frederick is trying to do much better work.

7. Who is not studying chemistry this year?
8. They will unlock the door soon.
9. I will not be at home when you arrive.
10. He would bring it if his father let him.
11. She had bought that in Peru.
12. Your brother did not see us.
13. Our sister has not arrived yet.
14. What is he going to say to us?
15. Where will I be able to find you?
16. You should not go out with her.
17. He could not open it with her key.
18. You would have a good time in Yucatan.
19. Your mother is here now.
20. That is not who(m) I wish to see right now.

25

Degrees of Comparison

25.1

Both languages distinguish between three degrees of comparison with adjectives and adverbs: (1) the positive degree (also called "the absolute degree"), (2) the comparative degree and (3) the superlative degree. These three degrees in English are distinguished morphologically.

	ADJECTIVE		ADVERB	
POSITIVE:	frank	franco	fast	rápido
COMPARATIVE:	franker	más franco	faster	más rápido
SUPERLATIVE:	frankest	el más franco	fastest	el más rápido

25.2
DEGREES OF GRADATION

The **positive degree** in either language is the simple dictionary form of the adjective or the adverb. The **Spanish comparative degree** of an adjective or adverb is regularly formed by placing the words *más* or *menos* before the positive form (*más/menos escaso, más/menos lógico, más/menos profundo*).

Several comparative forms, however, are irregular:

POSITIVE	COMPARATIVE
mucho	más
poco	menos
bueno	mejor
malo	peor

grande	mayor/más grande
viejo	mayor/más viejo
pequeño	menor/más pequeño
joven	menor/más joven

> **Note:** *Mayor* appears more than *más viejo* when age is the reference. *Más grande* is preferred to *mayor* when physical size is stressed. Similarly, *menor* generally refers to age, while *más pequeño/chico* is more common when referring to physical size.

The **English comparative degree** of an adjective or adverb is formed synthetically by adding the suffix *-er* to a word of one syllable, for example, *faster, richer, harder, softer, brighter, bigger, nicer*. Two syllable words ending in the sounds [i], [o], and some ending in the sound [l] also add *-er*: *funnier, sillier, yellower, mellower, littler, simpler*. Other two syllable words generally make the comparative by placing the words *more* or *less* before the positive form: *more handsome, less bookish, more standard*. English adjectives or adverbs of more than two syllables invariably produce the comparative with *more/less* before the positive form: *more intelligent, less rigorously, more influential, less generously*.

Like Spanish, English has several irregularly formed comparatives:

POSITIVE	COMPARATIVE
good (well)	better
bad (badly)	worse
much	more
little (with non-count nouns)	less (with non-count nouns)
far	farther/further
many (with count nouns)	fewer (with count nouns)

25.3

The **Spanish superlative degree** of comparison places a fully inflected definite article before an adjective or adverb in the comparative degree. This unit then generally follows the modified noun. Some examples are, *el jefe más poderoso, la chica más bella, los animales más vivos, las preguntas más vitales, los mejores, el más cerca*. Note that the last two are nominalizations and that the others could be nominalized as well: *la chica más bella > la más bella*.

The **English superlative degree** of comparison in is formed by placing the article before the superlative form of the adjective or adverb. English generates such superlatives as follows:

- The suffix *-est* is added to a positive form of one syllable, or to a two syllable positive form ending in the sounds [i], [o], and in many cases [l]. The definite article must accompany the superlative form: *the largest, the strongest, the fastest, the ugliest, the yellowest, the simplest*. To form the opposite type of superlative, the definite article + *least* is placed before the positive degree adjective: *the least strong, the least likely*.

- The superlative form of other two syllable words or of words of three or more syllables places the definite article + *most/least* before the positive form: *the most evident, the least intelligent, the most influential, the least efficient*.

- The English adjectives and adverbs which have irregular comparative forms also have irregular superlatives.

COMPARATIVE	SUPERLATIVE
better	the best
worse	the worst
more	the most
less	the least
farther/further	the farthest/furthest

25.4

Spanish has a so-called "absolute superlative" formed by adding the inflected suffix *-ísimo* to a positive degree adjective or adverb. English translates this form with *very, exceedingly, extremely, highly* or *really* + positive adjective/adverb. Some examples of this Spanish superlative are, *ancho > anchísimo, generoso > generosísimo, hondo > hondísimo, ilustre > ilustrísimo*. Respective translations of these Spanish forms are, *exceedingly wide, extremely generous, highly illustrious* and *really deep*. Absolute superlatives never occur in sentences where one item or person is compared with another.

Exercise 1

Give both the comparative and superlative degrees of the following English and Spanish positive degree adjectives and adverbs.

1. inteligente
2. agudo
3. enfermo
4. lento
5. bueno
6. alto
7. débil
8. valiente
9. joven
10. viejo.

1. wonderful
2. callow
3. expensive
4. filthy
5. careful
6. loud
7. bad
8. simple
9. sunny
10. slick

25.5

THE COMPARISON OF INEQUALITY

In the comparison of inequality, one item or person is compared unequally with a second item or person. The two languages use virtually identical systems.

He is richer than I (am).	Él es más rico que yo.
They are more intelligent than we (are).	Son más inteligentes que nosotros.
I am happier than she (is).	Soy más feliz que ella.
This is worse than that.	Esto es peor que eso.

The *de/que* choice for the linking preposition can be troublesome:

De (not *que*) is used in affirmative comparisons involving numbers, amounts or quantities:

Le di más de cien quetzales.
Comieron más de la mitad.
Estudia más de lo normal.

In negative comparisons involving numbers, amounts or quantities, either *de* or *que* may be used, but there is always a difference in meaning:

No más que + numerical...   = just/only X amount...
No le di más que diez quetzales.   I gave him just/only ten quetzales.
                                      (i.e., that is all I gave him.)

No más de + numerical...   = not more than...
No le di más de diez quetzales.   I gave him no more than ten quetzals.
                                      (i.e., I gave him 10 quetzals or less.)

When the element following *than/que* is a clause, the two language systems are at considerable variance. In the English system the connective is always *than*.

He is richer than you think.
He has more friends than we know about.
She has more money than she can spend.
They are better than we thought.

A number of connectives appear in the Spanish system when the second element is a clause. If an adjective or an adverb is found in the first element, *de lo que* is the connective used to introduce the following clause.

Es más rico de lo que tú crees.
Ella sabe más de lo que demuestra.
Ese carro corre más rápido de lo que puedes imaginar.

If a noun occurs in the first element, *del, de la, de los, de las* + *que* are the connectives used with the following clause, each recalling the gender and number of the noun appearing in the first clause:

Ellos tienen más dinero del que pueden gastar.
Siento más pena de la que puedo expresar.
Trajeron más libros de los que pueden leer.
Compré más papas de las que necesitamos.

Exercise 2

Translate the following comparisons of inequality into the other language. Take particular care with the connectives used between the first and the second elements of the comparison, especially if the second element is clausal.

1. He has more classes than I (have).
2. La figura tiene más ángulos de los que debe tener.
3. We need less gasoline than they do.
4. Amelia es más alta que su hermana.
5. Texas is poorer than you believe.
6. ¿Es tu padre mayor que tu madre?
7. He brought more food than they could eat.
8. Tengo más práctica que usted.
9. They spent more money than we could believe.
10. Ella es más amable que el resto del grupo.
11. She is more intelligent than she knows.
12. Fumo más cigarrillos de los que debo fumar.
13. We need more sugar than we can buy.
14. Hablan español mejor que nosotros.
15. He spoke worse than anyone would have imagined.
16. Ella ganó más plata de la que pudo gastar.
17. There is more smoke in the room than ever.
18. Había más ruido en el edificio del que esperábamos.
19. Do you write English better or worse than you sister?
20. Tomás piensa traer a más visitas de las que podemos atender.
21. She has no more than twenty dollars.
22. No tuvimos que pagar más de mil pesos.

25.6
THE SUPERLATIVE DEGREE OF COMPARISON

The **English and Spanish superlative degree** structures are shown below.

He is the fastest boy in the group.
She is the least naive girl in the class.
That is the poorest family in the neighborhood.
He is the best student in the class.

Es el muchacho más rápido del grupo.
Es la muchacha menos ingenua de la clase.
Esa es la familia más pobre del barrio.
Es el mejor estudiante de la clase.

In a superlative degree construction in either language, the main noun may be suppressed if it is clearly understood from context. This is the standard process of nominalization presented in Chapter 20.11. The article must remain to imply the noun. English may optionally substitute *one(s)* for the suppressed noun.

Es el ~~muchacho~~ más rápido del grupo.
He is the fastest (one) in the group.

Es la ~~familia~~ más pobre del barrio.
It's the poorest (one) in the neighborhood.

When stated in the superlative degree, an adjective precedes the noun in English: *the fastest boy, the most pleasant gentleman*. In the Spanish superlative the adjective construction normally follows the noun: *el muchacho más rápido, el caballero más agradable*. The connectives *in* or *on* of English are routinely rendered as *de* in Spanish.

the tallest man *in* the world	el hombre más alto *del* mundo
the cleanest house *on* the block	la casa más limpia *de* la cuadra

Finally, English has a special way of expressing the superlative when only two beings are compared. It uses the definite article *the* + the comparative degree of the adjective. Examples follow:

I own two large dogs, Frida and Diego; Frida is the more intelligent (of the two).
My father has two aunts who live alone. Aunt Sadie is the elder (of the two).
   (*Elder* is an archaic form of *older* and appears as an adjective only in this type of superlative expression.)
The Lions and the Bears are two football teams. The Bears are the better team.

Exercise 3

Translate the following superlative degree comparisons in into the other language, making nominalized structures where indicated by the items enclosed in parentheses.

1. Usted es el (hombre) más considerado del grupo.
2. Who is the tallest student in your class?
3. Esther es la más sentimental de todas.
4. Are they the most intelligent (men) in the United States?
5. ¿Eres la persona más animada de tu familia?
6. Which is the largest country in South America?
7. Ese lugar tiene el paisaje más maravilloso del estado.
8. Which is the best (wine) in the world?
9. Esa es la peor (tienda) del pueblo.
10. Pepe is the strongest player on the team.
11. Es la chica más extraordinaria de la escuela.
12. They are the poorest (people) in our neighborhood.
13. ¿Quién sabe cuál era la civilización más antigua del mundo?
14. This has to be the ugliest (city) in the country!
15. Vivo con la (mujer) más divina del mundo.

25.7

In superlatives involving modified adverbs, English uses the structure *as* + positive adverb + *as* + modification.

Come as soon as possible.

He spoke as loud as he could.

Spanish modified adverbial superlatives use the structure *lo* + *más* + positive adverb + modification. More colloquial, but completely standard, is *tan* + positive adverb + *como* + modification.

Ven lo más pronto posible.
Ven tan pronto como posible.

Ella habló lo más alto que pudo.
Ella habló tan alto como pudo.

Exercise 4

Translate the following superlatives involving modified adverbs into the other language, using the structures presented above.

1. Raúl salió lo más pronto posible.
2. He ran as fast as he could.
3. Lo puse tan alto como pude.
4. They did it as slowly as possible.
5. La joven habló lo más expresivamente que podía.

25.8
THE COMPARISON OF EQUALITY

The English comparison of equality with nouns follows:

as + much + non-count noun + as

He has as much money as I (have/do).
She drinks as much milk as they (do).

as + many + count noun + as

They know as many sayings as we (do).
He has as many friends as you (do).

The Spanish system for comparison of equality with nouns is:

tanto/-a* + non-count noun + *como

Usted tiene tanto dinero como yo.
Bebo tanta leche como ellos.

tantos/-as* + count noun + *como

Saben tantos dichos como nosotros.
Alicia tiene tantas amistades como tú.

When no noun occurs in these comparisons, and only the extent of the verb appears adverbially as equal between two entities, English uses *as much as* while Spanish employs *tanto como*.

They don't read or write as much as my students.
No leen ni escriben tanto como mis estudiantes.

English structures with adjectives and adverbs in equality comparison are as follows:

as + adjective/adverb + as

He is as poetic as she (is).
He eats as rapidly as a machine.

Spanish uses:

tan + adjective/adverb + como

Es tan poético como ella.
Él come tan rápido/rápidamente como una máquina.

Exercise 5

Translate the following comparisons of equality into the other language. Keep in mind whether you are dealing with nouns or with adjectives and adverbs.

1. I want to earn as much money as you.
2. Alberto tiene unas referencias tan buenas como cualquiera.
3. They don't know as much as I (do).
4. Ese escrito tiene un sentido tan profundo como aquel.
5. Our street doesn't have as many trees as yours (has/does).
6. Noé no fuma tanto como yo.
7. Do they sell as much fruit here as they do in the market place?
8. El desarrollo bajo su reino fue tan extenso como bajo el anterior.
9. Most Latin Americans don't speak Spanish as fast as the Spaniards (do).
10. La vía estrecha no se inclina tanto como la ancha.
11. Do you study as much as your brother (does)?
12. El gobierno militar va a gastar tanto dinero como el civil.
13. I hope to receive as many presents as my sister.
14. No puede ser tan flexible como los otros administradores.
15. Do you know as much as she (does)?
16. Ella demuestra tanto cariño como su hermana.
17. My grandmother isn't as nice as my mother.
18. Arizona no tiene tanta población como California.

25.9
CORRELATIVE CONSTRUCTIONS

The English structure for correlative constructions is *the more/less. . . the more/less. . .*

The more I study, the less I learn.
The less I work, the more I earn.

The Spanish structure for correlative constructions is *cuanto más/menos ... (tanto) más/menos ...* or *mientras más/menos ... (tanto) más/menos ...*

Cuanto más estudio, (tanto) menos aprendo.
Mientras más estudio, (tanto) menos aprendo.

Cuanto menos trabajo, (tanto) más gano.
Mientras menos trabajo, (tanto) más gano.

Such constructions often require the subjunctive in the dependent clause because of a reference to future time: *Cuanto/mientras más estudie, (tanto) más aprenderé.*

Exercise 6
Translate the following correlative constructions into the other language. Give all possible versions.

1. The more I eat, the fatter I get.
2. Cuanto más aprendo, (tanto) menos sé.
3. The more he drank, the sicker he became.
4. Mientras menos leo, (tanto) menos me confundo.
5. The more time I spend with you, the more I like you.
6. Cuanto más fumo, (tanto) más me preocupo por mí mismo.
7. The less you spend, the more you will have.
8. Mientras más gano, (tanto) más gasto.
9. The less I see her, the happier I am.
10. Cuanto menos te llamo, (tanto) menos sé de ti.

26

Relative Words Used Between Clauses

26.1
COMPOUND VS. COMPLEX SENTENCES:

A compound sentence is composed of two clauses, each of which could stand alone as an independent, meaningful utterance. The connectors used between the clauses in these sentences are coordinating conjunctions such as, *and/y, but/pero, since/ya que, because/porque,* etc,

I said goodbye to her, **and** I will never see her again.
Me despedí de ella **y** nunca volveré a verla.

She left for work, **but** she never arrived at the office.
Salió para el trabajo, **pero** nunca llegó a la oficina.

Since we had such a good time, we decided to return to Hawaii.
Ya que nos divertimos tanto, decidimos volver a Hawaii.

My parents sold the business **because** my father wanted to retire.
Mis padres vendieron el negocio **porque** mi padre quería jubilarse.

In compound sentences, both clauses have an expressed subject which may be identical or different between the two elements. If no subject is expressed in the second clause, then it is assumed that subject of the first clause governs the verb of both elements, resulting in a compound predicate, but not necessarily a compound sentence. Note that *sino que* replaces *pero* when the first clause is negated and the second asserted in its place. *Sino* alone subsistutes for *pero* similarly, but only when no clause is involved: *No me trajeron flores, sino caramelos.*

His girlfriend left early **but** arrived late for work.
Su novia salió temprano **pero** llegó tarde al trabajo.
(The *girlfriend* [*novia*] did both actions in the compound [two-part] predicate, *left/salió* and *arrived/llegó*.)

Not only did my niece go with us to the country **but** she prepared/made/fixed us a paella.
Mi sobrina no solo nos acompañó al campo **sino que** nos preparó una paella.

26.2

A complex sentence is also composed of two clauses, but one is subordinated to or dependent on the other, that is, it does not convey a coherent thought or make much sense without the main clause to which it is attached. Since complex sentences are the primary topic of this chapter, we focus on the variety of words and their grammatical function that subordinate dependent clauses to their main clauses. The subordinate (dependent) clauses may be noun, adverbial or adjectival, all three of which were discussed in Chapter 7. Adjective clause subordination has by far the most variety of subordinators/connectors.

Subordinate/Dependent noun clause: The connector is a subordinating conjunction:

We know (**that**) they live in the suburbs.
Sabemos **que** viven in las afueras de la ciudad.

His teachers insist (**that**) he come prepared for class.
Sus maestros insisten en **que** venga preparado para sus clases.

Subordinate/Dependent adverbial clause: The connector is a subordinating adverbial conjunction, expressing manner, time, etc.

Scholars haven't determined **when** he wrote the play
Los eruditos no han determinado **cuándo** escribió la comedia.

They won't do it until they have the time
No van a hacerlo **hasta que** se dispongan del tiempo.

Subordinate/Dependent adjective clause: The connector is generally a relative pronoun which refers to an antecedent (in italics) in the main clause:

The *garage* **under which** the raccoon lives is very old.
El *garage* **debajo del que/cual** vive el mapache es muy viejo.

The police arrested the *men* **who** robbed the bank.
La policía llevó presos a los *hombres* **que** asaltaron al banco.

26.3
NOUN CLAUSE SUBORDINATION:

The subordinating conjunction *que* routinely introduces Spanish dependent noun clauses. The English equivalent is *that*, and its frequent omission troubles the Spanish speaker since *que* is almost never left out. Compare the English sentences on the left, which use the conjunction *that*, with those on the right, where *that* is suppressed. Note, however, that both sets of sentences make sense and express exactly the same ideas.

CONJUNCTION *THAT* EXPRESSED	CONJUNCTION *THAT* SUPPRESSED
I know that you see me.	I know you see me.
He thinks that we live here.	He thinks we live here.
They believe that I know you.	They believe I know you.
She said that she could do it.	She said she could do it.
Please remember that I need it.	Please remember I need it.

The conjunction *that* is so frequently omitted in English that the following statement might be totally incomprehensible to the Spanish speaker at first glance. (A diagonal appears where *that* has been suppressed.): *I know / you believe / you understand what you think / I said, but I'm not sure / you realize / what you heard is not what I meant.*

Exercise 1

Translate the English sentence examples given above under "CONJUNCION *THAT* SUPPRESSED" into Spanish. Note that in each case the Spanish coordinating conjunction *que* must be supplied.

26.4
ADVERBIAL CLAUSE SUBORDINATION

The subordinating words for dependent adverb clauses are themselves adverbs, which, since they function as conjunctions, may rightly be termed "subordinating adverbial conjunctions." They express the usual adverbial concepts of manner (*como/según*), time (*cuando, hasta que*), etc. Some examples of subordinate adverbial clauses follow:

I'll always be here **when** you need me.
Siempre estaré aquí **cuando** me necesites.

They prepared their homework **as** the teacher explained it to them.
Prepararon su tarea **como** el maestro se la explicó.

We always wait on the corner **until** the bus arrives.
Siempre esperamos en la esquina **hasta que** llega el autobús.

Exercise 2

Write original Spanish sentences in which the following subordinating adverbial conjunctions connect main clauses to subordinate adverbial clauses. Translate each sentence into English.

1. según
2. para que
3. siempre y cuando
4. en cuanto

5. sin que
6. a menos que
7. cuando
8. hasta que
9. después que
10. antes (de) que

26.5
ADJECTIVE CLAUSE SUBORDINATION

The subordinators for dependent adjective clauses are varied and rather complex since in all cases they have an antecedent (modified word) in the main clause. The nature of the antecedent (gender, number, grammatical category, etc.) all come into play when one selects the correct subordinator. In general, the subordinators for dependent adjective clauses are called relative pronouns.

Notice that although routinely classified as an adverb, *donde* as a subordinator is a relative pronoun, as shown in the following comparative examples:

Lo puse **donde** me dijiste = Lo puse en *el lugar* **que** me dijiste.
Lo voy a poner **donde** me digas. = Lo voy a poner en *el lugar* **que** me digas.

Subordinate adjective clauses are of two types: restrictive and non-restrictive. A restrictive adjective clause provides essential or clarifying information about its noun antecedent, as in the following examples, where the antecedent is italicized and the relative pronoun is in bold print:

My *brother* **who/that** lives in Washington is a lawyer.
Mi *hermano* **que** vive en Washington es abogado.
(The speaker may have other brothers; this one is identified by his living in Washington and being a lawyer.)

The *car* **which/that** hit the child was driven by a madman.
El *carro* **que** arrolló al niño era conducido por un energúmeno.
(There may have been many cars around; here a particular car is being cited.)

Non-restrictive adjectives clauses present only parenthetical information about their antecedents; nothing expressed is essential to identifying or distinguishing the antecedent from other possible ones. In speech such clauses have a slight pause before and after, while in writing they are set off by commas.

My *little brother*, **who** is only three, is the joy of my family.
Mi *hermanito*, **que/(quien/el que/el cual)** tiene solo tres añitos, es la alegría de mi familia.

Her *bedroom*, **which** faces the pool, is really where she lives.
Su *recámara*, **que/(la que/la cual)** da a la alberca, es en realidad donde vive.

Observe with regard to the previous Spanish examples that non-restrictive adjective clauses have various possible relative pronoun subordinators, while restrictive ones have fewer.

The following discussion shows the possible grammatical relationships subordinate restrictive adjective clauses have to their antecedents. The antecedents require classification as either animate or inanimate in main clauses. The subordinate adjective clauses relate to these as subjects or objects (DO, IO, or prepositional). In the examples, independent sentences will be re-cast into one composed of a main clause with an antecedent + a relative pronoun construction + the subordinate adjective clause referring to its antecedent in the main clause. Only Spanish examples are presented, since when the English relative pronoun system is explained, it will follow similar patterns:

1. **Antecedent is animate;** relative pronouns re-cast it as a subject:
   *El hombre es carpintero. El hombre vino a mi casa. > El hombre **que** vino a mi casa es carpintero.*

2. **Antecedent is inanimate;** relative pronouns re-cast it as a subject:
   *El árbol es enorme. El árbol está en el parque. > El árbol **que** está en el parque es enorme.*

3. **Antecedent is animate;** relative pronouns re-cast it as a direct object:
   *El hombre es carpintero. Yo conozco al hombre. > El hombre **que/a quien** conozco es carpintero.*

4. **Antecedent is inanimate;** relative pronouns re-cast it as a direct object:
   *El árbol es enorme. Yo vi el árbol en el parque. > El arbol **que** vi en el parque es enorme.*

5. **Antecedent is animate;** relative pronouns re-cast it as an indirect object:
   *La persona es Jorge. A Jorge (yo) le encargué el negocio. > La persona **a quien/(a la que /a la cual)** (yo) le encargué el negocio es Jorge.*

6. **Antecedent is inanimate;** reative pronoun re-casts it as an indirect object: *El café está delicioso. Yo le puse crema al café. > El café **al que/al cual** le puse crema está delicioso.*

7. **Antecedent is animate;** relative pronouns re-cast it as a prepositional object:
   *La persona es el Presidente. Yo hablaba con la persona. > La persona **con quien/(con la que/con la cual)** hablaba es el Presidente.*

8. **Antecedent is inanimate:** relative pronouns re-cast it as a prepositional object:
   *El libro está en la mesa. Yo te hablé del libro. > El libro **de que/(del que/del cual)** te hablé está en la mesa.*

SPANISH AND ENGLISH RELATIVE PRONOUNS

26.6

The following is a contrastive listing of the Spanish and English relative pronouns introducing relative adjective clauses. These always refer to an antecedent in the main clause. Note that the Spanish words are in many cases identical to the Spanish interrogative words, but as relative pronouns they are unstressed and never bear an orthographic accent.

RELATIVE PRONOUNS

que	which, that, who, whom
(a) quien, (a) quienes	who, whom
(al) el cual, (a) la cual, (a) los cuales, (a) las cuales	which, that, who, whom
(al) el que, (a) la que, (a) los que, (a) las que	the one who/which/that, the ones who/which/that

> **Note:** The variants using the preposition *a* in the previous two listings involve either personal direct object antecedents (...*el hombre al que vi en mi cuarto*) or indirect object antecedents (...*el hombre al que/a quien le voy a vender mi carro*).

lo que, lo cual	what, which
cuyo, cuya, cuyos, cuyas	whose
donde	where

26.7

Que is the most commonly used relative pronoun of all in Spanish. It can have as its antecedent both people and things of either gender or number.

Ella es la persona **que** vi.	She is the person (**who[m]/that**) I saw.
Son los libros **que** compré.	They are the books (**that**) I bought.
Son las señoras **que** llegaron.	They are the ladies **who/that** arrived.

26.8

The relative pronouns **quien** and **quienes** refer only to people. They generally appear in lieu of **que** when preceded by a preposition.

¿Es ella la persona **a quien** (indirect object) le escribiste?	Is she the person **to who(m)/that** you wrote/**who(m)/that** you wrote **to**?
Julio es el hombre **a quien** (direct object) viste en la calle	Julio is the man **who(m)/that** you saw in the street.
Ellos son los jóvenes **con quienes** hablé.	They are the young men **with whom** I spoke/**who(m)/that** I spoke **with**.

26.9

El/(al) cual, la/(a la) cual, los/(a los) cuales, las/(a las) cuales are frequently used after compound prepositions (prepositions composed of more than one element, e.g., *encima de*), or the prepositions *por, según* and *sin*. They are far more characteristic of the formal, written language than they are of everyday speech.

Tiene cuatro hijos, dos **de los cuales** ya están casados. (partitive)
She has four children, two **of who(m)/which** are already married.

La razón **por la cual** lo hice...
The reason (**that**) I did it...

Su buen humor, **sin el cual** no es el mismo...
His high spirits, **without which** he's not the same...

El árbol **debajo del cual** lo encontré...
The tree **beneath/under which** I found it...

Existe una segunda versión **según la cual** el héroe muere en un duelo.
There exists a second version **according to which** the hero dies in a duel.

26.10

El/(al) que, la/(a la) que, los/ (a los) que, las/ (a las) que are used when the articles *el, la, los,* and *las* are the only antecedents expressed. They indicate a nominalization, that is, the suppression of a noun between the article and the relative word *que*. For these expressions introduced by *de* in comparative structures, see Chapter 25.5

La que (= la chica que) lo dijo...	**The one who/that** said it...
El que (= el hombre que) lo trajo...	**The one who/that** brought it...
No vi **los que** (= los libros que) mandaste.	I didn't see **the ones (that)** you sent.
¿No ves **las que** (= las revistas que) leí?	Don't you see **the ones (that)** I read?
No conozco **al que** (= al estudiante que) mencionaste.	I don't know **the one (that)** you mentioned.

26.11

Either *lo que* or *lo cual* occur as subordinators in reference to a previously mentioned idea or to a genderless abstraction. English uses *which* in the translation. (*Lo que* equivalent to the English relative *what* appears in Chapter 7.20; For *de lo que*, see Chapter 25.5) *Lo cual* is merely an emphatic variation upon *lo que*.

César no vino, **lo que** (lo cual) me preocupa.
Cesar didn't come, **which** worries me.

Pusieron las letras en relieve, **lo que** (lo cual) se ve mejor.
They made the letters stand out, **which** looks better.

Llovió toda la semana, **lo que** (lo cual) es raro.
It rained all week long, **which** is unusual.

26.12

Donde in its relative function:

Me encantan los lugares **donde** hay mucho bullicio.
I like places **where** there is a lot of activity.

Volvamos a la playa **donde** perdiste las llaves.
Lets go back to the beach **where** you lost the keys.

26.13

Cuyo, cuya, cuyos, cuyas have as their English equivalent ***whose***, a relative possessive pronoun. The Spanish words agree in gender and number with the possessed thing rather than with the possessor, as do the Spanish possessive adjectives. This relative pronoun is virtually extinct in the spoken language, but continues to appear in the formal, written idiom.

Cristina, **cuyos** padres (los padres **de quien/de la cual**) viven muy cerca...
Christine, **whose** parents live very close by...

El pájaro, **cuyo** cuello (el cuello **del que/del cual**) está roto...
The bird, **whose** neck is broken...

Los aztecas, **cuya** cultura (la cultura **de quienes/de los cuales**) era única...
The Aztecs, **whose** culture was unique...

Los niños, **cuyas** manos (las manos **de quienes/de los cuales**) están muy sucias...
The children, **whose** hands are very dirty...

Exercise 3

Translate the following English sentences or sentence fragments into Spanish, using relative pronoun constructions.

1. My friend, whose books are on the table...
2. He didn't say anything, which surprised me a lot.
3. The one you know is a Venezuelan girl.
4. My grandparents, whose house is in Morelia...
5. That is the man with whom she lives.
6. I didn't understand what he was saying.
7. The building behind which I work...
8. There is someone that I write to in Honduras...
9. The Sánchez family, whose house is on the corner...
10. He doesn't want to know what you think about it.
11. They earned a lot of money, which makes me angry.
12. Do you know the ones (boys) who have the new car?
13. The house in front of which he fell down...
14. The girls to whom you gave the money spent it all.
15. The students who came late didn't hear what he said.
16. The ones who saw us also saw the professor who is from Nicaragua.
17. I know what I want, but I don't want what I see.
18. Is that the student for whom you wrote the recommendation?

19. He had a menacing look which frightened her.
20. The man who said that is the one who left early.
21. This is the place where the children saw the Virgin.

26.14

The English relative pronoun system is somewhat different from the Spanish one, and its grammatical analysis entails posing several questions.

- Is the relative's antecedent animate or inanimate?
- Does the relative function as a subject or as an object (direct, indirect, or prepositional) **in its own clause**?
- Can the relative pronoun be omitted?
- If the relative can be suppressed, does this cause another possible syntactic arrangement of the relative pronoun construction?
- How many ways are there of expressing the same idea when English relative pronouns are involved?

In the following examples of relative pronoun clausal constructions, note that **(Ø)** indicates the suppression of a relative pronoun which would normally be found introducing the clause. **This happens only when the relative is the object (direct or indirect) of its own clause or the object of a preposition:** *The man (that) we met.../The man (that) you wrote to/The man (that) you talked about...* When the relative is the subject of its own clause, however, the relative pronoun is required: *The woman that/who prepared the meal...* Remember that in Spanish the relative pronoun must always be expressed. To review relative pronoun usages in both languages, we provide a Spanish version of each English sentence. All of the relative clause usages are restrictive.

1. The relative's antecedent is inanimate; the relative is the subject of its own clause:

    This is the letter **that/which** came in the mail.
    *Esta es la carta **que** llegó con el correo.*

    Here is the book **that/which** tells the whole story.
    *Aquí tienes el libro **que** cuenta la historia total.*

    There is the truck **that/which** killed the little boy.
    *Allí está el camión **que** mató al niño.*

2. The relative's antecedent is inanimate; the relative is the direct object of its own clause:

    This is the letter **that/which/(Ø)** you wanted to read.
    *Esta es la carta **que** querías leer.*

    Here is the book **that/which/(Ø)** the professor wrote.
    *Aquí tienes el libro **que** escribió el professor.*

There is the truck **that/which/(Ø)** I saw go by last night.
*Allí está el camión **que** vi pasar anoche.*

3. The relative's antecedent is animate; the relative is the subject of its own clause:

   He is the man **who/that** was on the bus.
   *Es el hombre **que** estaba en el autobús.*

   They are the boys **who/that** won the race.
   *Son los chicos **que** ganaron la carrera.*

   You are the woman **who/that** screamed at me.
   *Usted es la mujer **que** me gritó.*

4. The relative's antecedent is animate; the relative is the object of its own clause:

   He is the man **who(m)/that/(Ø)** I saw.
   *Es el señor **que/a quien** vi.*

   They are the boys **who(m)/that/(Ø)** I met in Zacatecas.
   *Son los chicos **que/a quienes** conocí en Zacatecas.*

   You are the woman **who(m)/that/(Ø)** they attacked.
   *Usted es la mujer **que/a quien** atacaron.*

5. The relative's antecedent is animate; the relative is the indirect object of its own clause:

   This is the senator **to whom** we wrote the letter.
   This is the senator **(that/who)** we wrote the letter **to**.
   *Este es el senador **a quien** escribimos la carta.*

   Those are the children **for whom** you made the swings.
   Those are the children **(that/who)** you made the swings **for**.
   *Esos son los niños **para quienes** hiciste el colúmpio.*

6. The relative's antecedent is inanimate; the relative is the object of a preposition.

   This is the table **under which** I found it.
   This is the table **which/that/(Ø)** I found it **under**.
   *Esta es la mesa **debajo de la cual** lo encontré.*

   This is the place **about which** I spoke.
   This is the place **which/that/(Ø)** I spoke **about**.
   *Este es el lugar **del que/del cual** te hablé.*

   Here are the dishes **for which** she came.

Here are the dishes **which/that/(Ø)** she came **for**.
*Aquí están los platos **por los cuales/que** vino ella.*

7. The relative's antecedent is animate; the relative is the object of a preposition.

This is the man **about whom** I spoke.
This is the man **who(m)/that/(Ø)** I spoke **about**.
*Este es el señor **de quien/del cual** te hablé.*

These are the boys **for whom** he did it.
These are the boys **who(m)/that/(Ø)** he did it **for**.
*Estos son los jóvenes **para quienes/para los cuales** lo hizo.*

Do you want to see the girl **with whom** he works?
Do you want to see the girl **who(m)/that/(Ø)** he works **with**?
*Quieres ver a la chica **con quien/con la que** trabaja.*

The English relatives *the one(s) who, the one(s) that, the one(s) which,* and *(Ø)* have as their Spanish equivalents *el (al) que, la (a la) que, los (a los) que, las (a las) que* and represent mere nominalizations. They can be used with all the structures and their variations presented above in (1)–(7).

Note: In the English examples under (4, 5, and 7 above), *who(m)* appears. As it functions as a direct or indirect object in its own clause, the English objective case form *whom* is preferred, certainly in formal writing. *Who* is the usual form in everyday speech. Observe, however, that *whom* is the only form allowable if it is the object of a preposition.
Also, when prepositions occur in English relative constructions, either as markers of indirect objects or as indicators of prepositional objects, English often allows positioning the preposition after the relative word (*the lady to whom I wrote* > *the lady [who(m)] I wrote to; the man with whom she arrived* > *the man [who(m)/that] she arrived with*). This doesn't occur in Spanish relative word usage. A related syntactical matter is taken up in the first part of Chapter 23.

Exercise 4

Where possible rewrite the following English sentences, giving all English versions of the original sentences. Be able to classify each sentence under the headings above in (1) through (7) in order to show your knowledge of the type of relative sentence you are dealing with.

1. I want to see the person who/that owns that car.
2. Do you want to buy the book my father wrote?
3. We went to the bank which/that opened yesterday.
4. Please say something nice to that Chilean girl we met yesterday.
5. Are you going to read the letter my mother spoke about?
6. I don't know the woman who he gave the money to.
7. Where is the building under which they discovered it?
8. I'm trying to find the gold watch (which/that) I lost at your party.
9. Do you see the children that are on that bus?
10. Do you know the students about whom the professor spoke?

Exercise 5

Translate the English sentences in Exercise 4 into Spanish. Note that Spanish does not allow the great variety of versions that English permits, nor does it allow any suppression of the relative words.

27
Affirmative Words and their Negative Counterparts

27.1

Chapter 5 shows that the negation systems of English and Spanish function differently on a syntactic level. In this chapter, and after the following chart, we first present the syntactical differences between affirmation and negation in the two languages and then deal with the affirmative and negative words themselves. We chose to term these generically as "words" because most fall under various grammatical categories including limiting adjectives and their nominalization, indefinite pronouns and adverbs.

GENERAL PATTERNS FOR AFFIRMATIVE AND NEGATIVE WORD USAGE IN SPANISH AND ENGLISH

27.2

> **Note:** In the English negative examples, sentences using affirmative words have been tagged with the symbol #. Such sentences will be explained presently under "Rules for Negation in English."

AFFIRMATIVE	NEGATIVE
1. Referring to people (indefinite pronouns)	
Alguien está aquí.	**Nadie** está aquí. No está aquí **nadie**
Someone/Somebody is here.	**No one/Nobody** is here. There is **no one/nobody** here. #There is**n't** **anyone/anybody** here.

2. Referring to things (indefinite pronouns)

Hay **algo** sobre la mesa.	**No** hay **nada** sobre la mesa.
Something is on the table.	**Nothing** is on the table. There is **nothing** on the table. #There is**n't anything** on the table.

3. As temporal adverbs

Siempre voy a España.	**Nunca/Jamás** voy a España. **No** voy a España **nunca/jamás**.
I **always** go to Spain.	I **never** go to Spain. #I do**n't ever** go to Spain.
Algún día iré a España.	**Nunca/Jamás** iré a España. **No** iré a España **nunca/jamás**.
Someday I'll go/I'm going to Spain.	I'll **never** go/I'm **never** going to Spain. #I wo**n't ever** go to Spain. #I'm **not ever** going to Spain.

4. Expressing selection from a supposed group of people or things

Ha de haber **algún** problema.	**No** ha de haber **ningún** problema. **No** ha de haber problema **alguno**.
There must be **some** problem.	There is probably **no** problem #There probably is**n't any** problem.

5. Expressing inclusion/exclusion

Nosotras **también** vamos.	Nosotras **tampoco** vamos. **No** vamos nosotras **tampoco**.
We are going **too/also/as well**.	**Neither** are we going. #We're **not** going **either**.

6. Expressing alternates

Va a ir uno de los dos, Héctor **o** Marta.	**Ni** Héctor **ni** Marta van. **No** van **ni** Héctor **ni** Marta.

| **Either** Hector **or** Martha is going. | **Neither** Hector **nor** Martha is going. (There is no version here using an affirmative word with a negative bias.) |

27.3
RULES FOR NEGATION IN SPANISH:

Rule 1: If a negative word (other than *no*) precedes the verb, no other negative word is required in the sentence, although some may occur since double negatives are a valid part of Spanish syntax. When the negative word precedes the verb, the verb becomes fully negated.

Nadie vio la sombra.
Nada se puede presumir en este caso.
Nunca/Jamás iré por esos horizontes.
Yo **tampoco** estoy dispuesto a hablar.
Ni Héctor **ni** Marta estarán expuestos al peligro.

Rule 2: If negative words other than *no* follow the verb, then the word *no* must precede it; this results in the use of at least two negative forms in this type of sentence. Note that the following sentences have the same meaning as those listed under rule (1) above.

No vio **nadie** la sombra.
No se puede presumir **nada** en este caso.
No iré por esos horizontes **nunca/jamás**.
Yo **no** estoy dispuesto a hablar **tampoco**.
No estarán expuestos al peligro **ni** Héctor **ni** Marta.

In the first set of sentences above, only one negative element is present. In the second set, at least two negative elements occur. English allows the first type of construction, but never the second. An English speaker's approach to a sentence with two negatives would logically be to assume that a second negative cancels the first; hence the statement reverts to a positive assertion. Logic and accepted usage are often in conflict in languages. ***Nadie nunca* dijo *nada* a *ninguno* de ellos*** is a completely grammatical Spanish utterance.

Exercise 1
Give two negative versions of the following Spanish affirmative sentences: (1) a negative word other than *no* precedes the verb, and (2) *no* precedes the verb, and a negative word other than *no* follows it.

1. Alguien estaba en mi cuarto cuando entré.
2. Algún día iremos a vivir a Puerto Rico.
3. Algo llegó hoy para ti en la correspondencia.
4. Alguien quiere verte a las ocho mañana.
5. Yo también tengo amigos en Acapulco.
6. Van a venir a verlo mi hermano o mi hermana.

7. Siempre pienso en ser una persona ejemplar.
8. Alguien quiere hablarte ahora.
9. Un bicho pasó por debajo de la puerta.
10. Anoche dejaron algo sobre la mesa.
11. También voy a ver a mi novia.
12. Vi en la sala al perro o al gato.

27.4
RULES FOR NEGATION IN ENGLISH

Rule 1: An English affirmative sentence may be made negative by using a negative word or phrase somewhere in the sentence, usually before the verb.

He **always** goes to Spain.
He **never** goes to Spain.

Someone/Somebody wants to see you.
No one/Nobody wants to see you.

Rule 2: English has an alternate way of making affirmative sentences negative. If the verb is already negated, that is, if the word *not* or the contracted form *-n't* occurs in the sentence, an affirmative words must be used. (Sentences of this type are marked with # in the chart.) Unlike Spanish, English does not allow more than one negative element per negative sentence. In some forms of vernacular English, double negatives are found; however, the usage is ungrammatical and inveighed against by teachers and parents alike.

STANDARD	VERNACULAR NEGATIVE
He always goes to Spain.	
He does**n't ever** go to Spain.	*He don't never go to Spain.
Something is under the table.	
There is**n't anything** under the table.	*There ain't nothing under the table.
I want to see someone about it.	
I do**n't** want to see **anyone** about it.	*I don't want to see nobody about it.

Exercise 2

Rewrite the following English sentences by negating the verb and using an affirmative word with the negated verb.

1. Did no one see the man?
2. Nothing was in the mailbox.

3. They never speak Portuguese to me.
4. Has no one heard the news?
5. We never have good parties at school.
6. No children were at the movie.
7. Neither are we going to the meeting.
8. Is neither he nor she going?

Exercise 3

Translate the following Spanish negative sentences into English, giving two versions for each: (1) with a negative word accompanying the verb, and (2) with a negated verb accompanied by an affirmative word with negative bias.

1. Nadie hace el trabajo en esta casa.
2. Nada sucede en la asociación.
3. Mis padres nunca les ponen atención a los lujos.
4. Ningún estudiante tiene rasgos de enfermedad mental.
5. Yo no tengo tan amplia imaginación tampoco.
6. Jamás conduces por esa ruta.
7. No te conceden nada.
8. No voy a referirme a nadie.
9. No queremos verla nunca.
10. No creo en la justicia tampoco.
11. No quieren luchar con nadie.
12. Esa oración no tiene ningún sujeto.

27.5
OBSERVATIONS CONCERNING THE AFFIRMATIVE AND NEGATIVE WORDS.

The numbering of the following paragraphs corresponds to that used in the chart under 27.2.

1. The English and Spanish affirmative and negative words referring to people are grammatically indefinite pronouns. *Someone/Somebody* and *no one/nobody* occur with equal frequency with no difference in meaning or level of formality. As for Spanish *alguien/nadie*, when occurring as direct objects, they must use the personal accusative, since the reference is human: *¿Conoces **a** alguien aquí? No, no conozco **a** nadie.*

2. *Algo/Nada* along with *something/nothing* are also indefinite pronouns. *Algo* has an additional function; that of an adverb, as in, *Es **algo** exigente = He's **somewhat** demanding.*

3. *Siempre/Nunca=Jamás* and *always/never* are temporal adverbs. Spanish has a number of these composed of two words: *alguna(s) vez(ces) = sometime(s); una, dos vez(ces) = once, twice; algún día = someday; a/algunas veces = sometimes.* Their negative equivalents remain *nunca=jamás* and *never*.

4. *Alguno/Ninguno* are especially difficult. They are always apocopated when occurring as limiting adjectives before masculine, singular nouns (*algún día, nungún problema*), and when postposed as adjectives in negative sentences, *alguno/-a* assume negative force: *No tengo problema alguno.* They rarely occur in the plural as adjectives or nominalizations thereof in negative sentences: *¿Te preocupan algunas cuestiones financieras? No, no me preocupa ninguna.*

As indefinite pronouns, *alguno/ninguno* stand alone and may be inflected for number and gender: *Algunos (de ellos) querían hablar, pero el jefe no permitió que ninguno (nadie) lo hiciera.* Finally, if these indefinite pronouns refer to persons and occur as direct objects, the personal accusative must precede them: *¿Conoces **a** alguno (de ellos)? No, no conozco **a** ninguno.* This is also the case if these words function as limiting adjectives or as nominalizations: *Van a entrevistar **a** algunos estudiantes/**a** algunos.* The words also occur as indirect objects, with the accompanying indirect object marker *a*, translated as *to* in English: *No pienso enviar saludos a ninguno (de ellos).*

Some sustained questioning of native Spanish speakers, both language specialists and laymen, by one of our authors has led him to the following unconfirmed conclusion: Modern informal, spoken usage tends to prefer *alguien/nadie* and *algo/nada* over such locutions as *algún/ningún señor* and *alguna/ninguna cosa*: *Ningún señor quería hacerlo > Nadie quería hacerlo; No encontraron ninguna cosa > No encontraron nada.* Furthermore, natives seem to feel that *alguno/ninguno* are appropriate as adjectives or nominalizations only in sentences involving conjecture or speculation, for example, *Habrá algún problema con la computadora; No ha de haber ninguna solución/solución alguna.*

Alguno/Ninguno still occur in the more formal spoken and written language, and when they do, there is the implication that a selection is being made from a known or supposed group of people or things. The following examples are illustrative:

--¡Que alguno de ellos (alguien) venga a ayudarme!
"Have one of them come help me."
--Pero ninguno (nadie) está disponible.
"But, no one is available."

--Quisiera conocer a alguna (una) de tus dos hermanas.
"I'd like to meet one of your two sisters."
--Pues, no te va a gustar ninguna.
"Well, you wouldn't like either one."

--¿Has encontrado a algún chico (alguien) que te interese?
"Have you met any boy (someone/anyone) that interests you?"
--No, no he econtrado a ninguno (nadie).
"No, I haven't met any/anyone."

--¿No han llegado ningunas noticias del frente?
"Hasn't any news arrived from the front lines?"
--No, no ha llegado ninguna.
"No, none has arrived."

Alguno/Ninguno occur in some locative adverbial locutions, to wit,

| PREP + alguna parte | ninguna parte |
| algún lugar/sitio/lado | nungún lugar/sitio/lado |

| somewhere | nowhere/not anywhere |

Both are found in a few adverbial locutions of manner:

| de algún modo | de ningún modo |
| de alguna manera | de ninguna manera |

| somehow/(in) some way | in no way/by no means/not at all/not in any way |

Appendix I
List of Principle Irregular English Verbs

PRESENT	PAST	PAST PARTICIPLE
A		
abide	abode/abided	abode/abided
arise	arose	arisen
awake	awoke	awaken
B		
be (am, is, are)	was/were	been
bear	bore	borne (carry)
bear	bore	born (birth)
beat	beat	beaten
become	became	become
begin	began	begun
bend	bent	bent
bet	bet/betted	bet/betted
bid	bid	bid
overbid	overbid	overbid
bind	bound	bound
bite	bit	bitten
bleed	bled	bled
blow	blew	blown
break	broke	broken
breed	bred	bred
crossbreed	crossbred	crossbred
inbreed	inbred	inbred
interbreed	interbred	interbred
bring	brought	brought
build	built	built
overbuild	overbuilt	overbuilt
prebuild	prebuilt	prebuilt
rebuild	rebuilt	rebuilt
burst	burst	burst
buy	bought	bought
C		
cast	cast	cast
broadcast	broadcast	broadcast
forecast	forecast	forecast
catch	caught	caught
choose	chose	chosen

cling	clung	clung
come	came	come
overcome	overcame	overcome
cost	cost	cost
creep	crept	crept
cut	cut	cut
undercut	undercut	undercut

D

deal	dealt	dealt
dig	dug	dug
dive	dove/dived	dived
do	did	done
outdo	outdid	outdone
overdo	overdid	overdone
draw	drew	drawn
overdraw	overdrew	overdrawn
redraw	redrew	redrawn
withdraw	withdrew	withdrawn
dream	dreamed/dreamt	dreamed/dreamt
daydream	daydreamed/daydreamt	daydreamed/daydreamt
drink	drank	drunk
outdrink	outdrank	outdrunk
drive	drove	driven
dwell	dwelt	dwelt

E

eat	ate	eaten
overeat	overate	overeaten

F

fall	fell	fallen
feed	fed	fed
overfeed	overfed	overfed
underfeed	underfed	underfed
feel	felt	felt
fight	fought	fought
find	found	found
fit	fit	fit
flee	fled	fled
fling	flung	flung
fly	flew	flown
forbid	forbade	forbidden
forsake	forsook	forsaken
freeze	froze	frozen

G

get	got	got/gotten
forget	forgot	forgot/forgotten
give	gave	given
forgive	forgave	forgiven
go	went	gone
forego	forewent	foregone
undergo	underwent	undergone
grind	ground	ground
grow	grew	grown
outgrow	outgrew	outgrown
regrow	regrew	regrown

H

hang	hung	hung
hang (regular)	hanged (law)	hanged (law)
have	had	had
hear	heard	heard
overhear	overheard	overheard
hide	hid	hidden
hit	hit	hit
hold	held	held
uphold	upheld	upheld
withhold	withheld	withheld
hurt	hurt	hurt

K

keep	kept	kept
kneel	knelt/kneeled	knelt/kneeled
knit	knit	knit
know	knew	known

L

lay	laid	laid
inlay	inlaid	inlaid
mislay	mislaid	mislaid
waylay	waylaid	waylaid
lead	led	led
mislead	misled	misled
leap	leapt	leapt
leave	left	left
lend	lent	lent
let	let	let
lie (down)	lay	lain
underlie	underlay	underlain
light	lit	lit
lose	lost	lost

M

make	made	made
premake	premade	premade
remake	remade	remade
mean	meant	meant
meet	met	met
mow	mowed	mowed/mown

P

pay	paid	paid
prepay	prepaid	prepaid
repay	repaid	repaid
prove	proved	proven/proved
put	put	put

Q

quit	quit	quit

R

read [rijd]	read [rɛd]	read [rɛd]
misread	misread	misread
proofread	proofread	proofread
reread	reread	reread
rid	rid	rid
ride	rode	ridden
override	overrode	overridden
ring	rang	rung
rise	rose	risen
run	ran	run
outrun	outran	outrun
overrun	overran	overrun

S

saw	sawed	sawn/sawed
say [sej]	said [sɛd]	said [sɛd]
see	saw	seen
foresee	foresaw	foreseen
oversee	oversaw	overseen
seek	sought	sought
sell	sold	sold
outsell	outsold	outsold
send	sent	sent
set	set	set
preset	preset	preset
reset	reset	reset
upset	upset	upset
sew	sewed	sewn/sewed
shake	shook	shaken
shear	sheared	shorn
shed	shed	shed

Appendix I

shine	shone	shone
outshine	outshone	outshone
shoot	shot	shot
overshoot	overshot	overshot
show	showed	shown
shrink	shrank	shrunk
shut	shut	shut
sing	sang	sung
sink	sank	sunk
sit	sat	sat
slay	slew	slain
sleep	slept	slept
oversleep	overslept	overslept
slide	slid	slid
backslide	backslid	backslid
sling	slung	slung
slink	slunk	slunk
slit	slit	slit
sow	sowed	sown
speak	spoke	spoken
misspeak	misspoke	misspoken
speed	sped	sped
spend	spent	spent
misspend	misspent	misspent
outspend	outspent	outspent
overspend	overspent	overspent
underspend	underspent	underspent
spin	spun	spun
spit	spit/spat	spit/spat
split	split	split
spread	spread	spread
spring	sprang	sprung
stand	stood	stood
misunderstand	misunderstood	misunderstood
understand	understood	understood
withstand	withstood	withstood
steal	stole	stolen
stick	stuck	stuck
sting	stung	stung
stink	stank	stunk
stride	strode	stridden
strike	struck	struck/stricken
string	strung	strung
strive	strove	striven
swear	swore	sworn
sweep	swept	swept

swell	swelled	swollen/swelled
swim	swam	swum
swing	swang	swung

T

take	took	taken
mistake	mistook	mistaken
overtake	overtook	overtaken
partake	partook	partaken
retake	retook	retaken
undertake	undertook	undertaken
teach	taught	taught
tear	tore	torn
tell	told	told
foretell	foretold	foretold
retell	retold	retold
think	thought	thought
rethink	rethought	rethought
throw	threw	thrown
overthrow	overthrew	overthrown
thrust	thrust	thrust
tread	trod	trodden

W

wake	woke	woken
wear	wore	worn
weave	wove	woven
interweave	interwove	interwoven
weep	wept	wept
wet	wet	wet
win	won	won
wind	wound	wound
overwind	overwound	overwound
rewind	rewound	rewound
unwind	unwound	unwound
wring	wrung	wrung
write	wrote	written
rewrite	rewrote	rewritten
underwrite	underwrote	underwritten

Appendix II

Verb Tense Terminology

NON-FINITE FORMS

THIS EDITION	ALSO CALLED	LA REAL ACADEMIA	OTHER SPANISH GRAMMARIANS
infinitive *amar* to love		infinitivo	
gerund *amando* loving	present participle; imperfect participle; gerund; *-ing* form	gerundio	gerundio de presente; participio de presente
past participle *amado* loved	perfective participle perfect participle	participio	participio pasivo; participio pretérito

IMPERATIVE MOOD

THIS EDITION	ALSO CALLED	LA REAL ACADEMIA	OTHER SPANISH GRAMMARIANS
imperative *ama (tú)* love	commands	imperativo presente	imperativo

INDICATIVE MOOD

THIS EDITION	ALSO CALLED	LA REAL ACADEMIA	OTHER SPANISH GRAMMARIANS
present *amo* I love	simple present	presente	presente imperfecto
imperfect *(yo) amaba* I loved		pretérito imperfect	copretérito; imperfecto

preterite *amé* *I loved*	simple past; past preterite	pretérito indefinido	pretérito; pretérito perfecto absoluto
future *amaré* *I will love*		futuro imperfecto	futuro; futuro simple; futuro absoluto; postpresente
conditional *(yo) amaría* *I would love*		potencial	condicional simple; prospretérito; futuro hipotético

SUBJUNCTIVE MOOD

There are only two simple tenses in the subjunctive mood, the present subjunctive *(ame)* and the past subjunctive *(amara/-se)*. Most authorities refer to the past subjunctive as the **imperfect subjunctive** *(imperfecto de subjuntivo)*. The authors prefer the term "past subjuctive" because the forms may denote both perfective and imperfective aspects.

PERFECT TENSES

THIS EDITION	ALSO CALLED	LA REAL ACADEMIA	OTHER SPANISH GRAMMARIANS
present perfect *he amado* *I have loved*	presente anterior; past indefinite	pretérito perfecto	antepresente; pretérito perfecto actual; perfecto
pluperfect *(yo) había amado* *I had loved*	past perfect; imperfecto anterior	pretérito plus- cuamperfecto	antecopretérito; pluscuamperfecto; antepretérito
preterite perfect *hube amado* *I had loved*	pretérito anterior	pretérito anterior	antepretérito
future perfect *habré amado* *I will have loved*	future anterior	futuro perfecto	futuro compuesto; antefuturo
conditional perfect *(yo) habría amado* *I would have loved*	conditional anterior	potencial com- puesto	condicional compuesto; ante-pospretérito; antefuturo hipotético

Appendix III
List of Principle Irregular Spanish Verbs

Only the tenses in which irregularities of some type occur are listed. Irregular forms are shown in bold, regular ones are in standard type. Note the following restrictions:

1. As most of them are not truly irregular, orthographically-changing verbs (*llegar > llegue; rezar > rece*, etc.) are not listed. **(See Chapter 3.7)**
2. In the imperative, only the affirmative *tú* irregular forms are listed, since all the regular forms are the third person singular, present indicative. All *vosotros* affirmative forms are regular, and the other imperative forms, both affirmative and negative, are derived from the present subjunctive, which itself has both regular and irregular forms.
3. Some verbs are listed as models for others, as noted.
4. With respect to the radically (or stem-changing verbs), model verbs appear for the three classes under which these are grouped. **(See Chapter 4.2-6)**

Adquirir
(One of very few verbs in which *i > ie*. It operates like *sentir*, a Class II radically-changing verb, but only the stressed forms [form where the stress falls on the root] are affected.)

INDICATIVE
Present **adquiero, adquieres, adquiere**; adquirimos, adquirís, **adquieren**

SUBJUNCTIVE
Present **adquiera, adquieras, adquiera**; adquiramos, adquiráis, **adquieran**

Andar

INDICATIVE
Preterite **anduve, anduviste, anduvo; anduvimos, anduvisteis, anduvieron**

SUBJUNCTIVE
Past **anduviera/se, anduvieras, anduviera; anduviéramos, anduvierais, anduvieran**

Caber

INDICATIVE
Present **quepo**, cabes, cabe; cabemos, cabéis, caben
Preterite **cupe, cupiste, cupo; cupimos, cupisteis, cupieron**
Future **cabré, cabrás, cabrá; cabremos, cabréis, cabrán**
Conditional **cabría, cabrías, cabría; cabríamos, cabríais, cabrían**

SUBJUNCTIVE
Present **quepa, quepas, quepa; quepamos, quepáis, quepan**
Past **cupiera/se, cupieras, cupiera; cupiéramos, cupierais, cupieran**

Caer

INDICATIVE
    Present **caigo**, caes, cae; caemos, caéis, caen
    Preterite caí, caíste, **cayó**; caímos, caísteis, **cayeron**

SUBJUNCTIVE
    Present **caiga, caigas, caiga; caigamos, caigáis, caigan**
    Past **cayera/se, cayeras, cayera; cayéramos, cayerais, cayeran**

PARTICIPLES
    Present (-*ndo*) **cayendo**

Conducir
(Model for all verbs ending in –*ducir; traducir, deducir, producir,* etc.)

INDICATIVE
    Present **conduzco**, conduces, conduce; conducimos, conducís, conducen
    Preterite **conduje, condujiste, condujo; condujimos, condujisteis, condujeron**

SUBJUNCTIVE
    Present **conduzca, conduzcas, conduzca; conduzcamos, conduzcáis, conduzcan**
    Past **condujera/se, condujeras, condujera; condujéramos, condujerais, condujeran**

Conocer
(Model for all verbs ending in a <u>vowel</u> + -*cer* [*parecer*] or –*cir* [*lucir*], except *decir* and *hacer*)

INDICATIVE
    Present **conozco**, conoces, conoce; conocemos, conocéis, conocen

SUBJUNCTIVE
    Present **conozca, conozcas, conozca; conozcamos, conozcais, conozcan**

Construir
(Model verb for all ending in –*uir*)

INDICATIVE
    Present **construyo, construyes, construye**; construimos, construís, **construyen**
    Preterite construí, construiste, **construyó**; construimos, construisteis, **construyeron**

SUBJUNCTIVE
    Present **construya, construyas, construya; construyamos, construyáis, construyan**
    Past **construyera/se, construyeras, construyera; construyéramos, construyerais, construyeran**

PARTICIPLES
    Present (-*ndo*) **construyendo**

Contar
(A model Class I, first conjugation radically changing verb in which *o > ue*)

INDICATIVE
    Present **cuento, cuentas, cuenta**; contamos, contáis, **cuentan**

SUBJUNCTIVE
    Present **cuente, cuentes, cuente**; contemos, contéis, **cuenten**

Dar

INDICATIVE
    Present **doy**, das, da; damos, dais, dan
    Preterite **di, diste, dio; dimos, disteis, dieron**

SUBJUNCTIVE
    Present **dé, des, dé; demos, deis, den**
    Past **diera/se, dieras, diera; diéramos, dierais, dieran**

Decir
(Model for all derivatives; *bendecir, maldecir, contradecir*)

INDICATIVE
    Present **digo, dices, dice**; decimos, decís, **dicen**
    Preterite **dije, dijiste, dijo; dijimos, dijisteis, dijeron**
    Future **diré, dirás, dirá; diremos, diréis, dirán**
    Conditional **diría, dirías, diría; diríamos, diríais, dirían**

SUBJUNCTIVE
    Present **diga, digas, diga; digamos, digáis, digan**
    Past **dijera/se, dijeras, dijera; dijéramos, dijerais, dijeran**

Tú **IMPERATIVE** **di**

PARTICIPLES
    Present (*-ndo*) **diciendo**
    Past **dicho**

Dormir
(Model Class II, third conjugation, radically changing verb: *o > ue/u*)

INDICATIVE
    Present **duermo, duermes, duerme**; dormimos, dormís, **duermen**
    Preterite dormí, dormiste, **durmió**; dormimos, dormisteis, **durmieron**

SUBJUNCTIVE
    Present **duerma, duermas, duerma; durmamos, durmáis, duerman**

    Past **durmiera/se, durmieras, durmiera; durmiéramos, durmierais, durmieran**

PARTICIPLES
 Present (*-ndo*) **durmiendo**

Errar
(Class I, first conjugation radically changing verb in which initial *e* > *ie*, spelled "ye-")

INDICATIVE
   Present **yerro, yerras, yerra**; erramos, erráis, **yerran**

SUBJUNCTIVE
   Present **yerre, yerres, yerre**; erremos, erréis, **yerren**

Estar

INDICATIVE
   Present **estoy, estás, está**; estamos, estáis, **están**
   Preterite **estuve, estuviste, estuvo; estuvimos, estuvisteis, estuvieron**

SUBJUNCTIVE
   Present **esté, estés, esté**; estemos, estéis, **estén**
   Past **estuviera/se, estuvieras, estuviera; estuviéramos, estuvierais, estuvieran**

Haber

INDICATIVE
   Present **he, has, ha; hemos,** habéis, **han**
   Preterite **hube, hubiste, hubo; hubimos, hubisteis, hubieron**
   Future **habré, habrás, habrá; habremos, habréis, habrán**
   Conditional **habría, habrías, habría; habríamos, habríais, habrían**

SUBJUNCTIVE
   Present **haya, hayas, haya; hayamos, hayáis, hayan**
   Past **hubiera/se, hubieras, hubiera; hubiéramos, hubierais, hubieran**

Hacer

INDICATIVE
   Present **hago**, haces, hace; hacemos, hacéis, hacen
   Preterite **hice, hiciste, hizo; hicimos, hicisteis, hicieron**
   Future **haré, harás, hará; haremos, haréis, harán**
   Conditional **haría, harías, haría; haríamos, haríais, harían**

SUBJUNCTIVE
   Present **haga, hagas, haga; hagamos, hagáis, hagan**
   Past **hiciera/se, hicieras, hiciera; hiciéramos, hicierais, hicieran**

Tú **IMPERATIVE** **haz**

PARTICIPLES
    Past **hecho**

Ir

INDICATIVE
    Present **voy, vas, va; vamos, vais, van**
    Preterite **fui, fuiste, fue; fuimos, fuisteis, fueron**
    Imperfect **iba, ibas, iba; íbamos, ibais, iban**

SUBJUNCTIVE
    Present **vaya, vayas, vaya; vayamos, vayáis, vayan**
    Past **fuera/se, fueras, fuera; fuéramos, fuerais, fueran**

***Tú* IMPERATIVE**   **ve**

PARTICIPLES
    Present *yendo*

Jugar
(One of a few Class I, first conjugation radically changing verbs in which *u > ue*)

INDICATIVE
    Present **juego, juegas, juega**; jugamos, jugáis, **juegan**

SUBJUNCTIVE
    Present **juegue, juegues, juegue**; juguemos, juguéis, **jueguen**

Leer
(The verb *creer* and a few other second conjugation verbs whose root ends in a vowel follow this pattern)

INDICATIVE
    Preterite leí, leíste, **leyó;** leímos, leísteis, **leyeron**

SUBJUNCTIVE
    Past **leyera/se, leyeras, leyera; leyéramos, leyerais, leyeran**

PARTICIPLES
    Present (*-ndo*) **leyendo**

Oír

INDICATIVE
    Present **oigo, oyes, oye**; oímos, oís, **oyen**
    Preterite oí, oíste, **oyó**; oímos, oísteis, **oyeron**

SUBJUNCTIVE
    Present **oiga, oigas, oiga; oigamos, oigáis, oigan**

Past **oyera/se, oyeras, oyera; oyéramos, oyerais, oyeran**

PARTICIPLES
Present (-*ndo*) **oyendo**

Oler
(One of a few radically changing verbs in which the initial *o* > *ue*, spelled "hue-")

INDICATIVE
Present **huelo, hueles, huele**; olemos, oléis, **huelen**

SUBJUNCTIVE
Present **huela, huelas, huela**; olamos, oláis, **huelan**

Pedir
(A model Class III, third conjugation radically changing verb in which *e* > *i/i*)

INDICATIVE
Present **pido, pides, pide**; pedimos, pedís, **piden**
Preterite pedí, pediste, **pidió**; pedimos, pedisteis, **pidieron**

SUBJUNCTIVE
Present **pida, pidas, pida; pidamos, pidáis, pidan**
Past **pidiera/se, pidieras, pidiera; pidiéramos, pidierais, pidieran**

PARTICIPLES
Present (-*ndo*) **pidiendo**

Pensar
(A model Class I, first conjugation radically changing verb in which *e* > *ie*)

INDICATIVE
Present **pienso, piensas, piensa**; pensamos, pensáis, **piensan**

SUBJUNCTIVE
Present **piense, pienses, piense**; pensemos, penséis, **piensen**

Perder
(A model Class I, second conjugation radically changing verb in which *e* > *ie*)

INDICATIVE
Present **pierdo, pierdes, pierde**; perdemos, perdéis, **pierden**

SUBJUNCTIVE
Present **pierda, pierdas, pierda**; perdamos, perdáis, **pierdan**

Poder

INDICATIVE
- Present   **puedo, puedes, puede**; podemos, podéis, **pueden**
- Preterite   **pude, pudiste, pudo; pudimos, pudisteis, pudieron**
- Future   **podré, podrás, podrá; podremos, podréis, podrán**
- Conditional   **podría, podrías, podría; podríamos, podríais, podrían**

SUBJUNCTIVE
- Present   **pueda, puedas, pueda; podamos, podáis, puedan**
- Past   **pudiera/se, pudieras, pudiera; pudiéramos, pudierais, pudieran**

PARTICIPLES
- Present (-*ndo*)   **pudiendo**

Poner
(Model for all derivatives; *postponer, imponer, exponer*, etc.)

INDICATIVE
- Present   **pongo**, pones, pone; ponemos, ponéis, ponen
- Preterite   **puse, pusiste, puso; pusimos, pusisteis, pusieron**
- Future   **pondré, pondrás, pondrá; pondremos, pondréis, pondrán**
- Conditional   **pondría, pondrías, pondría; pondríamos, pondríais, pondrían**

SUBJUNCTIVE
- Present   **ponga, pongas, ponga; pongamos, pongáis, pongan**
- Past   **pusiera/se, pusieras, pusiera; pusiéramos, pusierais, pusieran**

Tú **IMPERATIVE**   **pon**

PARTICIPLES
- Past   **puesto**

Querer

INDICATIVE
- Present   **quiero, quieres, quiere**; queremos, queréis, **quieren**
- Preterite   **quise, quisiste, quiso; quisimos, quisisteis, quisieron**
- Future   **querré, querrás, querrá; querremos, querréis, querrán**
- Conditional   **querría, querrías, querría; querríamos, querríais, querrían**

SUBJUNCTIVE
- Present   **quiera, quieras, quiera**; queramos, queráis, **quieran**
- Past   **quisiera/se, quisieras, quisiera; quisiéramos, quisierais, quisieran**

Reír (Sonreír)
(Although at first not apparent, these verbs, like *pedir,* are Class III radically changing verbs, *e > i/i*)

INDICATIVE

Present   **río, ríes, ríe**; reímos, reís, **ríen**
Preterite   reí, reíste, **rió < (ri-ió)**; reímos, reísteis, **rieron < (ri-ieron)**

SUBJUNCTIVE
Present   **ría, rías, ría; riamos, riáis, rían**
Past   **riera/se, rieras, riera; riéramos, rierais, rieran**

Saber

INDICATIVE
Present   **sé**, sabes, sabe; sabemos, sabéis, saben
Preterite   **supe, supiste, supo; supimos, supisteis, supieron**
Future   **sabré, sabrás, sabrá; sabremos, sabréis, sabrán**
Conditional   **sabría, sabrías, sabría; sabríamos, sabríais, sabrían**

SUBJUNCTIVE
Present   **sepa, sepas, sepa; sepamos, sepáis, sepan**
Past   **supiera/se, supieras, supiera; supiéramos, supierais, supieran**

Salir

INDICATIVE
Present   **salgo**, sales, sale; salimos, salís, salen
Future   **saldré, saldrás, saldrá; saldremos, saldréis, saldrán**
Conditional   **saldría, saldrías, saldría, saldríamos, saldríais, saldrían**

SUBJUNCTIVE
Present   **salga, salgas, salga; salgamos, salgáis, salgan**

Tú **IMPERATIVE**   **sal**

Sentir
(A model Class II, third conjugation radically changing verb, *e > ie/i*)

INDICATIVE
Present   **siento, sientes, siente**; sentimos, sentís, **sienten**
Preterite   sentí, sentiste, **sintió**; sentimos, sentisteis, **sintieron**

SUBJUNCTIVE
Present   **sienta, sientas, sienta; sintamos, sintáis, sientan**
Past   **sintiera/se, sintieras, sintiera; sintiéramos, sintierais, sintieran**

PARTICIPLES
Present (*-ndo*)   **sintiendo**

Ser

INDICATIVE
Present   **soy, eres, es; somos, sois, son**
Preterite   **fui, fuiste, fue; fuimos, fuisteis, fueron**

Imperfect **era, eras, era; éramos, erais, eran**

SUBJUNCTIVE
Present **sea, seas, sea; seamos, seáis, sean**
Past **fuera/se, fueras, fuera; fuéramos, fuerais, fueran**

Tú **IMPERATIVE** **sé**

Tener
(Model for all derivatives; *contener, retener, obtener*, etc)

INDICATIVE
Present **tengo, tienes, tiene**; tenemos, tenéis, **tienen**
Preterite **tuve, tuviste, tuvo; tuvimos, tuvisteis, tuvieron**
Future **tendré, tendrás, tendrá; tendremos, tendréis, tendrán**
Conditional **tendría, tendrías, tendría; tendríamos, tendríais, tendrían**

SUBJUNCTIVE
Present **tenga, tengas, tenga; tengamos, tengáis, tengan**
Past **tuviera/se, tuvieras, tuviera; tuviéramos, tuvierais, tuvieran**

Tú **IMPERATIVE** **ten**

Traer
(Model verb for all derivatives; *contraer, distraer, abstraer*, etc.)

INDICATIVE
Present **traigo**, traes, trae; traemos, traéis, traen
Preterite **traje, trajiste, trajo; trajimos, trajisteis, trajeron**

SUBJUNCTIVE
Present **traiga, traigas, traiga; traigamos, traigáis, traigan**
Past **trajera/se, trajeras, trajera; trajéramos, trajerais, trajeran**

PARTICIPLES
Present (*-ndo*) **trayendo**

Valer

INDICATIVE
Present **valgo**, vales, vale; valemos, valéis, valen
Future **valdré, valdrás, valdrá; valdremos, valdréis, valdrán**
Conditional **valdría, valdrías, valdría; valdríamos, valdríais, valdrían**

SUBJUNCTIVE
Present **valga, valgas, valga; valgamos, valgáis, valgan**

Venir

INDICATIVE
- Present: **vengo, vienes, viene**; venimos, venís, **vienen**
- Preterite: **vine, viniste, vino; vinimos, vinisteis, vinieron**
- Future: **vendré, vendrás, vendrá; vendremos, vendréis, vendrán**
- Conditional: **vendría, vendrías, vendría; vendríamos, vendríais, vendrían**

SUBJUNCTIVE
- Present: **venga, vengas, venga; vengamos, vengáis, vengan**
- Past: **viniera/se, vinieras, viniera; viniéramos, vinierais, vinieran**

Tú **IMPERATIVE**   **ven**

PARTICIPLES
- Present (-*ndo*): **viniendo**

Ver

INDICATIVE
- Present: **veo**, ves, ve; vemos, veis, ven
- Imperfect: **veía, veías, veía; veíamos, veíais, veían**

SUBJUNCTIVE
- Present: **vea, veas, vea; veamos, veáis, vean**

PARTICIPLES
- Past: **visto**

Volver
(A model Class I, second conjugation radically changing verb, *o* > *ue*)

INDICATIVE
- Present: **vuelvo, vuelves, vuelve**; volvemos, volvéis, **vuelven**

SUBJUNCTIVE
- Present: **vuelva, vuelvas, vuelva**; volvamos, volváis, **vuelvan**

PARTICIPLES
- Past: **vuelto**

Appendix IV
Spanish verbal types and uses

A. PRONOMINAL AND NON-PRONOMINAL VERBS

1. TRUE REFLEXIVE VERBS (NON-PRONOMINAL [S ≠ DO OR IO] AND PRONOMINAL [S= DO or IO], often called "verbs of daily routines." The list is by no means complete:

acostar "to put someone to bed"	acostarse "to go to bed'
afeitar "to shave" (someone else)	afeitarse "to shave"
arreglar "to arrange/fix something"	arreglarse "to get ready"
bañar "to bathe" (someone)	bañarse "to bathe"
cambiar de "to change"(opinion, etc.)	cambiarse de "to change" (clothes, etc.)
cepillar "to brush"	cepillarse "to brush (one's hair/teeth)"
despertar "to wake someone up"	despertarse "to wake up"
desvestir "to undress someone"	desvestirse "to get undressed"
duchar "to shower someone"	ducharse "to take a shower"
hacerle daño (a alguien) "to hurt someone"	hacerse daño "to hurt oneself"
lastimar "to injure someone"	lastimarse "to injure oneself"
lavar "to wash (something/someone)"	lavarse "to wash onself/one's hands, face, etc."
levantar "to lift, raise, get someone out of bed"	levantarse "to get up/out of bed"
maquillar "to put makeup on someone"	maquillarse "to put on one's own makeup"
peinar "to comb someone's hair"	peinarse "to comb one's own hair"
pintar "to paint"	pintar(se), see maquillar(se)
quemar "to burn something/someone"	quemarse "to burn oneself"
rascar "to scratch something/someone"	rascarse "to scratch oneself"
revelar "to reveal/to develop film"	revelarse "to undress" (for a medical exam)
romper "to break/tear something"	romperse "to break /tear" (a part of one's body)
secar "to dry something/someone"	secarse "to dry oneself (off)"
sentar "to seat someone"	sentarse "to sit down"
vestir "to dress someone"	vestirse "to get dressed"

2. PRONOMINAL VERBS EXPRESSING INNER LIFE OR CHANGE OF STATE

aburrir "to bore someone"	aburrirse "to get/become bored"
acordar "to agree to do something"	acordarse de "to remember"
ajustar "to adjust something"	ajustarse a "to adapt/adjust oneself"
alegrar "to make someone happy"	alegrarse de "to get/become happy"
animar "to cheer someone up"	animarse a "to cheer up/take heart"
asombrar "to astonish"	asombrarse "to be/become surprised"
asustar "to frighten/scare"	asustarse "to get/become frightened/scared"
calmar "to calm someone down"	calmarse "to calm down"
callar "to silence someone"	callarse "to become silent"
cansar "to tire "(someone)	cansarse "to get tired"
conducir "to conduct/drive a vehicle"	conducirse "to behave oneself"

decidir "to decide" (an issue)   decidirse a "to make up one's mind"
divertir "to amuse"   divertirse "to have a good time"
enfadar "to annoy"   enfadarse "to get/become annoyed"
enojar "to anger/make angry"   enojarse "to get/become angry"
entusiasmar "to excite/thrill"   entusiasmarse "to become excited"
escandalizar "to scandalize"   escandalizarse "to be/become shocked"
exasperar "to exasperate someone"   exasperarse "to get exasperated/impatient"
interesar "to interest someone"   interesarse "to become interested"
marear "to make someone dizzy"   marearse "to get/become dizzy/nauseated"
molestar "to bother/annoy"   molestarse "to become/get annoyed/angry"
ocupar "to occupy"   ocuparse de "to be busy with"
ofender "to offend/insult someone"   ofenderse "to take offense/be insulted"
preocupar "to worry someone"   preocuparse "to worry"
sentir "to sense, feel someone/something"   sentirse "to feel some way" (good, bad, sick)
sorprender "to surprise someone"   sorprenderse "to be surprised"
tranquilizar "to calm someone down"   tranquilizarse "to calm down/stop worrying"

3. VERBS OF MOTION (NON-PRONOMINAL VS. PRONOMINAL)

a. The following verbs are all transitive, whether used non-pronominally or pronominally:

abonar "to pay"   abonarse a "to subscribe to"
acercar "to bring items close together"   acercarse a "to approach, come close to"
alejar "to move items apart"   alejarse de "to move away, to distance oneself"
detener "to detain someone"   detenerse "to come to a stop"
bajar "to bring something down"   bajarse "to get off a conveyance, come down"
dirigir "to direct"   dirigirse a "to go to/address oneself to"
encontrar "to meet/find"   encontrarse "to be located/situated"
instalar "to install something"   instalarse "to move into a place"
meter "to put something into"   meterse "to become involved in something"
mover "to move something"   moverse "to move around"
parar "to stop"   pararse "to stand up" [Amer. sp.]
pasear "to walk (eg. the dog)   pasearse "to go for a walk/stroll"
reunir "to gather people or things"   reunirse con "to get together"
saltar "to jump"   saltarse "to jump" (energetically)
subir "to lift, go up with something"   subirse a "to climb, get on/into a vehicle"

b. The following verbs are all intransitive, used either non-pronominally or pronominally:

entrar a/en "to enter, go into"   entrarse a/en (regional variation on entrar)
ir "to go" (focus is on the destination)   irse "to leave" (no stated goal; focus is on the starting point)
quedar "to remain/be located/be left over"   quedarse "to remain, stay behind"
salir de "to leave/depart" (focus is on the destination)   salirse de (focus is on the starting point)
venir "to come"   venirse (regional variation)
volver "to return"   volverse "to turn around" / + *loco* "to go crazy"

4. VERBS ALWAYS USED PRONOMINALLY

abstenerse de "to abstain from"
acordarse de "to remember/bring to mind"
acostumbrarse a "to become accustomed to/get used to"
arrepentirse de "to repent (of one's sins)"
atreverse a "to dare"
ausentarse de "to not attend/absent oneself from"
burlarse de "to make fun of/poke fun at"
cerciorarse de "to make sure of"
darse cuenta de "to realize" (that something is the case)
desesperarse "to despair/give up hope"
desmayarse "to faint/pass out"
empeñarse en "to strive/devote efforts to"
enamorarse de "to fall in love with"
enterarse de "to find out about"
equivocarse (de) "to make a mistake"
fiarse de "to trust"
figurarse "to imagine something/figure something out"
fugarse "to escape"
inclinarse a "to be inclined"
jactarse de "to boast/brag"
portarse "to behave/conduct oneself"
quejarse de "to complain"
rebelarse "to rebel"
reírse de "to laugh at"
suicidarse "to commit suicide"
vangloriarse "to boast"

B. FREQUENTLY USED EXCLUSIVELY INTRANSITIVE VERBS

abogar
acaecer
acontecer
acudir
aterrizar
aullar
batallar
bostezar
chismear
coexistir
colaborar
comerciar
comparecer
concurrir
consistir
constar
conversar
convivir
cooperar
corresponder
degenerar
depender
durar
emigrar
estallar
estar
existir
fallecer
flotar
fluir
funcionar
gemir
germinar
gesticular
gotear
gravitar
gruñir
insistir
ladrar
limosnear
luchar
madrugar
maullar
militar
nadar
naufragar
palpitar
permanecer
persistir
prescindir
prevalecer
proceder
progresar
provenir
reaccionar
reaparecer
rebuznar
recurrir
relampaguear
relinchar
residir
resultar
rugir
ser
simpatizar
sobresalir
soler
sollozar
substituir
surgir
suspirar
traficar
triunfar
trotar
veranear
viajar
yacer

C. SPANISH VERBS WHOSE ENGLISH EQUIVALENTS REQUIRE A PREPOSITION

agradecer "to be thankful FOR"
aguardar "to wait FOR"
aprovechar "to take advantage OF"
buscar "to look FOR"
conseguir "to succeed IN"
escuchar "to listen TO"
esperar "to wait FOR"
mirar "to look AT"
pagar "to pay FOR"
pedir "to ask FOR"

D. SPANISH VERBS FOLLOWED BY A PREPOSITION BEFORE ANOTHER VERB OR A NOUN

Note: The notation, "+v" indicates an infinitive complement, "+n" represents a noun or possible other complement, and "+v/n" shows that either type of complement may be used. A considerable number of these verbs are pronominal. These are classified according to Paragraph A, (1-4) in this Appendix. If a significant change in meaning occurs between the pronominal verb and its non-pronominal counterpart, the verb is classified under Chapter 13.11.

1. The preposition is A:

Note: These verbs are especially problematic for the English speaker when a verbal complement follows, since in these cases, English places the infinitive (to + LV) directly after the conjugated verb, causing errors like, *Vino a ayudarnos.* > **Vino ayudarnos. (He came to help us.)*

abandonarse a +v/n (A-2)
acercarse a +v/n (A-3a)
acertar a +v
acostumbrarse a +v/n (A-2)
aguardar a +v/n
animar a +v/n
apostar a +n
aprender a +v
arriesgarse a +v (A-2)
ascender a +v/n
asomarse a +v/n (A-4)
aspirar a +v/n
atreverse a +v (A-4)
autorizar a +v
avenirse a +v/n
aventurarse a +v (A-4)
ayudar a +v
comenzar a +v
condenar a +n/v
consagrarse a +v/n (A-2)
contestar a +n
contribuir a +v/n
convidar a +v/n
correr a +v/n
dar(se) a +v/n (A-3a)
dedicarse a +v/n (A-2)
desafiar a +v/n
detenerse a +v (A-3a)
determinarse a +v (A-2)
dirigirse a + v/n (A-3a)
disponerse a +v (A-2)
echarse a +v (A-3 a)
empezar a +v

enseñar a + v
esforzarse a +v (A-2)
evitar a +v/n
exponerse a +v/n (A-3a)
faltar a + v/n
incitar a +v
inclinarse a +v (A-4)
inspirar a +n
invitar a +n/v
ir(se) a + v
jugar (a)
llegar a +v/n
meterse a +v/n (A-3a)
negarse a +v (Ch. 13.11)
obligarse a +v (A-2)
ofrecerse a +v/n (A-2)
oler a +n
oponerse a +v/n (A-2)
parecerse a +n (Ch. 13.11)
pasar a +v
persuadir(se) a +v (A-2)
ponerse a +v (Ch. 13.11)
prepararse a +v (A-1)
principiar a +v
probar a +v
rebajarse a +v (A-2)
reducirse a +v (A-2)
renunciar a +v/n
resignarse a +v/n (A-2)
resistir(se) a +v /n (A-2a)
resolver a +v
romper a +v
saber a +n

sentarse a +v (A-1)
subir(se) a +v (A-3b)

venir(se) a +v (A-3b)
volver a +v

2. The preposition is DE:

abusar de +n
acabar de +v
acordarse de +v/n (A-4)
admirarse de +n (A-4)
alegrarse de +v/n (A-2)
alejarse de +v/n (A-3 a)
apoderarse de +n (A-4)
arrepentirse de +v/n (A-4)
asombrarse de +v/n (A-2)
asustarse de +v/n (A-2)
avergonzarse de +v/n (A-2)
burlarse de +n (A-4)
cambiar de +n
cansarse de +v/n (A-2)
carecer de +n
cargar de +n
cesar de +v
cogerle (a uno) de +n
cuidar de +v
dejar de +v
depender de +v/n
despedirse de + v/n (Ch. 13.11)
disculparse de +v (A-2)

disfrutar de +v/n
enamorarse de +v/n (A-2)
encargarse de +v/n (A-2)
enterarse de +n (A-4)
equivocarse de +n (A-4)
extrañarse de +v/n (A-2)
felicitarse de +v/n (A-2)
gozar de +v/n
guardarse de +v/n (A-2)
jactarse de +v/n (A-4)
llenar de +n
maravillarse de +v/n (A-4)
mudarse de +n (A-3 a)
ocuparse de +v/n (A-2)
olvidarse de +v/n (A-4)
preciarse de +v/n (A-2)
reírse de +v/n (A-4)
servirse de + v/n (A-3a)
sorprenderse de +v/n (A-2)
tirar de +n
tratar de +v
tratarse de +n

3. The preposition is EN:

complacerse en +v/n (A-2)
confiar en +v/n
convenir en +v
convertirse en +n (A-3 a)
desembocar en +n
empeñarse en +v/n (A-2)
fijarse en +n (A-3a)
insistir en +v/n

molestarse en + v (A-2)
obstinarse en +v (A-4)
pensar en +n
quedar en +v
recrearse en +v/n (A-4)
reparar en +n
tardar en +v
vacilar en +v

4. The preposition is CON:

amenazar con +v/n
casarse con +n
conformarse con +v/n (A-4)
contar con +v/n
contentarse con +v/n (A-4)

cumplir con +n
entretenerse con +v/n (A-2)
incomodarse con +v/n (A-2)
reunirse con +n (A-3a)
soñar con +v/n

5. The preposition is POR:

declararse por +v/n (A-2)
estar por +v/n
luchar por +v/n
morirse por +v/n

optar por +v/n
preocuparse por +v/n (A-2)
quedarle (a uno)+algo+por+INF.
reventar por +v/n

6. Verbs taking various prepositions:

a. A number of intransitive pronominal variants of otherwise transitive verbs may be followed by different prepositional complements, such as:

> apurarse por/a +v/n (A-2)
> encontrarse con/a +n (A-3a)
> enfrentarse a/con +n (A-2)
> entusiasmarse (de/con/por) +n/v (A-2)
> interesarse por/en + n/v (A-2)
> meterse a/en +n/v (A-3a)
> ocuparse en/de +n/v (A-2)
> preocuparse por/de +n/v (A-2)
> sorprenderse de/con +n (A-2)

b. Some other verbs take different prepositional complements. Although the list is not complete, some of these are:

> consentir en/a +v/n
> consultar con/a +n
> dudar en/de + v/n
> entrar(se) en +n/a +n/v (A-3b)
> morir de + n; morirse de +n/por +v (A-2)
> salir(se) de +n/a+v (A-3b)

Glossary of Grammatical Terms
Items in bold have their individual entries.

ABSOLUTE SUPERLATIVE: A Spanish **adjective** form ending in *–ísimo* and expressing "of the highest category," without comparing the adjective to another. *Es inteligentísimo.* = *He's really/extremely/highly intelligent.*

ACTIONAL PASSIVE (See: *SER* PASSIVE)

ACTIONAL VERB: Any **verb** expressing observable action or movement rather than a mental/emotional state or state of being; *correr* = *to run*; *salir* = *to leave*; *pedir* = *to ask for*.

ACTIVE VOICE: The opposite of **passive voice**. An active sentence has a **subject** in the role of agent, a **verb**, and an **object**, the latter being the entity produced or impacted by the verb. *John visited his familia* = *Juan visitó a su familia*.

ADJECTIVAL CLAUSE: A **subordinate clause** that functions as **an adjective**, i.e., it modifies (says something about) a **noun** in the **main clause**. The noun is termed **the antecedent** of the adjective clause. *Tienen un perro que se les escapa a cada rato* = *They have a dog that runs off all the time.* See also **relative clause**.

ADJECTIVE: One of basic **parts of speech** in either language. Adjectives are components of the **nominal system,** and they serve to modify nouns; *a beautiful house/una casa bella; the last day/el último día*. Adjectives are of two basic types: **determiners** (also called **limiting adjectives**) and **descriptive adjectives**. The first example above shows a descriptive adjective, and these generally precede the noun in English, but follow in Spanish. Limiting adjectives (second example, above) usually precede the noun in both languages, and include **articles** (both **definite** [*el/the*] and **indefinite** [*un/a*]), **possessives** [*mi/my*], **demonstratives** [*este/this*], and others.

ADMIRATIVE: An emotional expression of admiration, such as, *¡Qué hombre!* = *What a man!*; *¡Cómo corre!* = *How he runs!*

ADVERB(IAL) CLAUSE: A **subordinate clause** functioning as an **adverb**, that is, it expresses such ideas concerning the verb as, "when?, where?, how?, under what conditions?" The adverbial clause is underlined in the example: *Estaré en el aeropuerto cuando llegue tu vuelo* = *I'll be at the airport when your flight arrives.*

AGENT: It is the actual performer of the action. The agent may be expressed or merely implied. In **active** transitive sentences, the agent corresponds to the **subject** as in the sentence, *La policía arrestó a la mujer* = *The police arrested the woman.* In a **true passive** sentence the agent, when expressed, appears as a prepositional phrase introduced with *by* in English and *por* in Spanish. The agent appears in parentheses in these examples: *The woman was arrested (by the police)* = *La mujer fue arrestada (por la policía)*.

AGREEMENT: A grammatical phenomenon operating on both **morphology** and **syntax**. It is a more important feature of Spanish than of English. At the morphological level, Spanish requires that its **nouns** and **adjectives** agree (match one another) with respect to **number** (always), *muchas ciudades grandes*, and **gender** (usually), *varios hombres ricos*, in accordance with specific rules. At the level of **syntax**, sentence **subjects** must agree with the **verbs** they govern with respect to **person** and **number**. For example, in the English present tense system, a third person singular subject (*he, she, it*) must take a verb form which ends in *–s*. *John goes home early*, not **John go home early*. In Spanish, each of the **persons** (*yo, tú, él, ella; nosotros, vosotros, ellos, ellas*) require a specific verbal ending. For example, the second person singular subject *tú* usually takes a verbal form ending in *–s*: *Tú tienes un gato*. However, the first person plural subject *nosotros* requires a verbal form in *–mos*; *Nosotros tenemos un gato*, not **Nosotros tiene un gato*, or any verbal form other than *tenemos*.

ALLOMORPH: Any one of the various ways a **morpheme** can manifest itself. For example, the morpheme /-s/ used to pluralize English nouns is realized in three possible ways, depending upon the **phonetic** features of the last sound of the singular. When you say *cats*, the final *–s* is pronounced [-s], but when you say *dogs*, you hear [-z]. These are but two of the three possible allomorphs of the morpheme /s/, the English pluralizing morpheme. Spanish *decir* has an array of allomorphs for its root morpheme: *dec-, dig-, dic-, dij-, dir-* and *dich-*.

AMBIGUITY: Any lack of clarity in an utterance where two or more meanings are possible. In normal speech, the context usually allows us to understand individual sentences without confusion. But in isolation, sentences are often ambiguous, for example, *su camisa* can mean, *his/her/your/their shirt* if context is lacking.

AMBIVALENT GENDER: Animate nouns such as those ending in *–ista* (*comunista*) may designate either males or females, depending only on the **article** used. Others such as *testigo* may be of either gender, as determined by the article.

ANALOGY: A subconscious tendency and regularizing force in speakers to bring into familiar and well established grammatical paradigms items which seem somehow "not to fit." For example, in Spanish, the second person singular verb form in all tenses but one ends in *–s*; so, *–s* is analogically supplied to the one exception (the **preterite**) in an attempt to make it match all other such forms in the language. This, however, produces a non-standard form: *tuviste* > **tuvistes*. If in English we have *sing, sang, sung* and *ring, rang, rung*, why not, *bring, *brang, *brung*?

ANIMATE: Referring to **nouns** or **pronouns** representing living beings rather than things: *people, men, women, Russians, coyotes/gente, hombres, mujeres, rusos, coyotes*.

ANTECEDENT: The **noun** modified (described) by an adjective (*una empresa grande*) or an adjectival clause (*una empresa que tuvo que despedir a muchos empleados*) In both cases, *empresa* is the antecedent.

APOCOPATION: The shortening of a word, usually for phonetically conditioned reasons. In Spanish, for example, certain **adjectives** are apocopated (lose their final *–o*) before **masculine, singular nouns**: *algún hombre, un centavo, primer día, tercer capítulo*, etc.

APODOSIS: The **clause** in a two-clause **conditional sentence** (often termed the "result clause" or the "conclusion") expressing the outcome of what is stated in the so-called "if-clause" or "hypothesis" (**protasis**). The apodosis is underlined in the examples: *If I had the money, I would give it to you* = *Si tuviera el dinero, te lo daría*.

APPARENT PASSIVE (See *ESTAR* PASSIVE)

APPARENT SUBJECT: In English sentences expressing the mere existence of people or things, the word *there* appears with the third persons (singular and plural) forms of *to be*. The word holds the subject position in the sentence, but has no real meaning: *There is/were/had been/will be + noun(s)*. The structure is termed "existential *there* + *to be*."

APPOSITION: Nouns and pronouns are in apposition when they occur together, one providing clarifying information about the other, for example, *my brother the lawyer/mi hermano el abogado; we atheists/nosotros los ateos; you leftists/ustedes los izquierdistas*.

ARTICLE: A type of **adjective,** often called a **limiting adjective** or a **determiner**, which always precedes the **noun,** and marks it in either of two ways. **Definite articles** show that the speaker and listener are both aware of the existence and identity of the noun referred to. English has but one definite article, *the*, while Spanish has four, each **inflected** for **gender** and **number**: *el, la, los, las*. **Indefinite articles** show that the noun exists, but remains unidentified. English uses *a* before consonants and *an* before vowels. Spanish has the usual fully inflected set, *un, una, unos, unas*.

ASPECT: A feature of the **verbal systems** of both languages involving the various points of view speakers can take in their expression of verbal states or actions. **Grammatical aspect**, sometimes called "viewpoint aspect" tells whether an event is **perfective** (completed) or **imperfective** (ongoing). The several contrasts between the Spanish

preterite and **imperfect** are largely matters of grammatical aspect, especially when adverbial phrases such as *ayer* vs. *todos los días* appear. **Lexical aspect** classifies verbal **predicates** according to three inherent **lexical /semantic** properties—**punctuality, dynamism** and **telicity**. These concepts in turn allow such predicates to be described as activities, states, accomplishments or achievements.

A-TEMPORAL VERBAL USAGE: The use of a verbal form generally thought of as expressing a particular time, for example, *had*, usually thought of as a past tense form, with some meaning other than past time. *I had a car last year* clearly uses *had* with past meaning. But in, *If I If had the money right now (but I don't)*, *had* refers to the present, and so used, it acquires a special meaing, that of counter-factuality, i.e., *right now, I don't have the money.*

ATONIC VOWEL: In words of two or more syllables, the unstressed vowels when the word is said. In, *a-MI-go,* the first and last vowels are atonic. In, *in-te-li-GEN-te,* all the vowels are atonic except the **tonic** one in the next-to-last syllable.

AUXILIARY VERB: Also called "helping verbs" because of their use in varying capacities with other verbs, auxiliaries are of two types, **primary** and **modal**. **Primary auxiliaries** have the purely grammatical function of expressing such concepts as person, tense and mood. They may also convey aspectual concepts like the **perfection** (completion) of acts (*have/haber*) or **progression** (*be/estar*). Some English primary auxiliaries show tense in certain structures: **present** (*do/does*) and **past tense** (did), and the **future** (will) and **conditional** (*would*). **Modal auxiliaries** carry real, lexical meaning, such as *ought to/deber; be able to/poder.*

BASE FORM (LEXICAL VERB): In English, the **infinitive** (*to go, to see, to have*), without the infinitive marker (**particle**) *to*. In, *You must leave now,* the base form/lexical verb *leave* appears rather than the infinitive (*to leave*).

CANONICAL POSITION: The syntactical position generally assumed by a particular grammatical item. For example, in the sentence, *We built a house,* the direct object, *house,* comes last in the subject + verb + direct object arrangement of items. In, *Conocemos a tus abuelos muy bien,* the direct object, *abuelos,* is in its canonical position, but in, *A tus abuelos, los conocemos muy bien,* it is not.

CASE: A feature of the **pronominal system** which determines the grammatical function and syntactical position of pronouns in a sentence. In English, for example, a pronoun can be a **subject**, **object** or a **possessive**: *he, him, his*. Spanish has four pronoun cases, 1) **nominative** (él), indicating the **subject**; 2) **accusative** (lo), expressing a **direct object**; 3) **dative** (le), designating an **indirect object** and 4) **genitive** (su/suyo), showing possession.

CLASSIFIED NOUN: A Spanish personal noun bearing a title and referred to rather than being directly addressed. The **definite article** must accompany the title under these conditions: *El Dr. Santana se encuentra en el aula 12A.* When Spanish refers to a non-personal entity, the item is differentiated from others of the same kind (classified) through the use of the **definite article**, e.g., *la calle 20; la Europa medieval.*

CLAUSE: A grouping of words in either language which must contain both a subject and a verb. Since Spanish **finite verbal forms** imply their **subjects**, a verb form alone can constitute a clause, for example, *dice/he says*; both fit the definition of a clause. On the other hand, *in the kitchen/en la cocina; before the wedding/antes de la boda* are not clauses since they contain neither subjects nor verbs. They are termed **phrases.** There are many types of clauses: **dependent** and **independent clauses, restrictive** and **non-restrictive clauses, nominal, adjectival,** and **adverbial clauses**.

CLITIC DOUBLING: The Spanish use of a **prepositional object pronoun** in conjunction with either a **direct or indirect object conjunctive pronoun** for purposes of emphasis or clarification. The direct and indirect object pronouns are often referred to as **(en)clitic pronouns** since they must appear with the verb. These, then, can be "doubled" (**reduplicated**) by the accompanying **prepositional object** construction: *A ella, la veo a* *menudo en mis clase, pero a él, no; Le di el mensaje a Rosa.*

CLOSE VOWEL (HIGH VOWEL): By definition, the Spanish vowels [i] and [u] produced when the surface of the tongue reaches its maximum closeness to the roof of the mouth, known as the palate. They are also referred to as "high vowels" because of the relatively elevated position the tongue assumes with respect to the palate.

COGNATE: Words in any two languages derived from a common source and often readily recognizable, for example, *unánime/unanimous*. Sometimes their commonality is less obvious as in the case of *ahorrar* (=*to save*), related to English *to hoard*. There are also "false cognates," similar words having different meanings: *embarazada* is not *embarrassed*, but *pregnant*.

COLLOQUIAL: Language usages belonging to the informal, spoken rather than the formal, written language.

COMPARATIVE DEGREE: One of the three degrees of comparison, the other two being the **positive** and **superlative degrees**. Both **adjectives** and **adverbs** are involved. In English, the comparative degree usually adds the suffix –*er* to the **positive degree**, e.g., *tall > taller, short > shorter, bright > brighter, fast > faster*, though there are many irregular forms. Spanish employs a **phrase** to form its comparative, e.g., *más alto, más corto, más listo, más rápido*, and like English also contains irregularities in its system.

COMPARISON OF EQUALITY: A type of comparative structure in which two items are compared showing that one is equal to the other in various ways. English uses the formula, *as...as*, while Spanish translates this with *tan(to)...como*. **Nouns, adjectives** and **adverbs** occur in these comparisons: *You have as much money as I (do) = Tú tienes tanto dinero como yo*, involves a noun. An adjective or adverb occur in the following: *Juan es tan alto/corre tan rápido como su hermano = John is as tall/runs as fast as his brother*.

COMPARISON OF INEQUALITY: A type of comparative structure in which two items are compared indicating that one has more/less of a certain quality than the other. With **adjectives and adverbs** Spanish says, *más/menos + adj./adv. + que: Él es más afortunado/corre más rápido que yo*. The English formula is, *adjective/adverb [comparative form] + than: He is shorter/reads slower than I (am/do)*. **Nouns and verbs** also appear in these structures: *Tiene más/menos dinero que yo = He has more/less money than I (do); Juan estudia más/menos que su hermano = John studies more/less than his brother*.

COMPLEMENTARY DISTRIBUTION: The term refers to the comparison of two different but related items, each one occurring in a distinct and separate environment from the other. For example, the spellings for the Spanish phoneme /k/ are in complementary distribution. They are *c* and *qu*. The former occurs only before the vowels, *a* (*casa*), *o* (*cosa*), *u* (*cuna*), or a consonant (*clase*), while the latter appears only before *e* (*queso*) and *i* (*quiso*). The term has multiple applications, not only **orthographic**, but phonetic, morphological and syntactical as well.

COMPLEX SENTENCE: A sentence composed of two **clauses**, one called the **main clause** and the other, the **subordinate clause (dependent clause)**. The subordinate clause may be introduced by **subordinating conjunctions** such as *antes de que, hasta que*, etc. and **relative pronouns** like *que, el que*, etc. In these examples, the main clause is underlined, while the subordinate one, using a relative pronoun, is in italics: We recognized the girl *who(m) we had seen on the plane* = Reconocimos a la chica *que habíamos visto en el avión*. In both cases, the subordinate clauses are **adjectival**.

COMPOUND SENTENCE: A sentence composed of two **clauses** which, if separated, could function as two complete and independent sentences. The clauses bear equal weight and are connected by a **coordinating conjunctions**, among which are, *and/ y* and *but/ pero*. *The house is white, and/but the roof is yellow = La casa es blanca, y/pero el techo es amarillo*.

CONCORDANCE (See AGREEMENT)

CONDITIONAL SENTENCE (See HYPOTHETICAL FUTURE, CONTRARY-to-FACT, NEUTRAL) CONDITIONAL TENSE: A tense that usually expresses the potential result if certain conditions are realized. English forms this tense using the **auxiliary** *would* + **lexical verb** (*would go*); Spanish adds the ending *–ía* to its **infinitive** (*iría*). The tense appears in the conclusion of **counter-factual conditional sentences** (*If I had the time, I would help you = Si tuviera el tiempo, te ayudaría/ayudaba*). Note that in colloquial speech the imperfect indicative often replaces the conditional in counter-factual expression. The conditional also functions also as a "future to the past" in such contexts as, *He said (that) he would visit us = Dijo que nos visitaría*. For its use as an expression of past probability or conjecture, see Chapter 8.10-13. For its English use in expressing repeated or habitual past actions, see Chapter 6.2.

CONJUGATION: A term applying to the Spanish verbal system. Every Spanish **infinitive** belongs to one of three possible conjugations: **first conjugation**, verbs ending in *–ar*, **second conjugation**, verbs ending in *–er* and **third conjugation**, verbs ending in *–ir*. To "conjugate" a verb refers to the act of generating all six of its possible forms in any given **tense**.

CONJUNCTIVE PRONOUN: Sometimes referred to as **(en)clitic** or "with-verb" **pronouns**, they encompass the **direct, indirect and reflexive object pronouns** of Spanish. Examples are *lo, le* and *se*, respectively. In English they are the **object(ive) pronouns**, used as **direct objects** (*I see her*), **indirect objects** (*I wrote (to) her*), **prepositional objects** (*They talk about her*) and **reflexives** (*She got herself up*). Spanish **syntax** requires that the conjunctive pronouns always directly precede or follow and attach to the verb, according to specific rules based on the verbal form involved. The English object(ive) pronouns routinely follow the verb.

CONTENT QUESTION: A question containing an **interrogative** word and soliciting information rather than a mere affirmation (*yes/sí*) or negation (*no/no*). *Why are you here?; Where has he gone? = ¿Por qué estás aquí?; ¿Adónde ha ido?*

CONTRACTION: Very characteristic of English, a fusion of two words, the element missing being represented in writing by an apostrophe ('). Some English examples are: *Mary is/has > Mary's, He did not > He didn't, I will > I'll*. Spanish has only two, *a + el > al* and *de + el > del*.

CORRELATIVE CONSTRUCTION: Paired constructions linking balanced words, phrases or clauses. English uses, *the more/less...the more/less...: The more/less he studies, the more/less he learns.* Spanish follows with, *cuanto (mientras) más/menos...(tanto) más/menos.... Cuanto (Mientras) más/menos estudia, (tanto) más/menos aprende.* A clausal example is, *He not only works but also studies = No solo trabaja sino que también estudia.*

CORRESPONDENCE OF TENSES (See SEQUENCE OF TENSES)

COUNT NOUN: Nouns having in common the fact that they may be counted 1, 2, 3, etc. Examples are: *houses/casas, children/niños, trees/árboles, problems/problemas*.

COUNTER-FACTUAL CONDITIONAL SENTENCE: Often called "unreal conditional sentences," they are composed of two clauses: **a hypothesis** is proposed in the **protasis** (***If*-clause**) and a conclusion to that hypothesis occurs in the **apodosis** (***then*-clause/conclusion**). The verb forms used in both clauses imply that neither clause expresses reality, and runs counter-to-fact. *If I had a lot of money (which I don't), I would move to Hawaii (but I can't) = Si tuviera mucho dinero (pero no lo tengo), me mudaría a Hawaii (pero no puedo hacerlo).*

DATIVE OF INTEREST: A term referring to the way Spanish uses its **indirect object**, expanding its definition to include "the affected or involved entity," the one who has "interests" in the outcome of the action or is affected by it. In, *El agente nos vendió la casa* the **indirect object**, *nos*, can best be described as the one affected by or interested in some way in the sale of the house. Furthermore, depending upon context, this "interest" may be of various types, for example, the Spanish sentence can have at least three different meanings: *The agent sold the house to/for/on us*,

the latter meaning we were caught unaware. *Se le murió el abuelo* = His grandfather died on him, shows the effect a sudden and unexpected death.
DECLARATIVE SENTENCE: A sentence in any tense which makes an affirmation, for example, *The group has left for the museum* = *El grupo ha salido para el museo.*

DEFECTIVE (INCOMPLETE) VERBS: A small group of Spanish verbs occurring only in certain forms, usually because of their meaning. For example, *acontecer* is used only in the third persons and refers to events, never people. *Concernir* is another such verb. Verbs that express natural phenomena are also defective (*nevar, llover, tronar*), but some grammarians refer to these as **uni-personal** verbs since they appear only in the third person singular form. Most of the English **modal auxiliaries** are defective: *must,* for example has but a single form.

DEFINITE ARTICLE: A special type of **determiner** or **limiting adjective** placed before **nouns** and indicating that the speaker and the listener are aware of both the existence and identity of the noun being mentioned. English has but one, *the,* while Spanish has four, *el, la, los, las,* each **inflected** for **gender** and **number**.

DEMONSTRATIVE ADJECTIVE: A special **determiner (limiting adjective)** used before **nouns** with three sets of words in Spanish (*este, ese, aquel*) and two in English (*this, that*). They are used to indicate relative proximity (closeness) to the speaker, either in space or in time. The Spanish demonstratives are all **inflected** for **gender** and **number**. English can pluralize each of its forms, *this > these/that >those*. Relative proximity is expressed as follows: *Este/Estos* = *This/These* indicate closeness to the speaker. *Ese/Esos* = *That/Those* show proximity to the addressee. Spanish uses its third set of demonstrative adjectives (*aquel/aquellos*) to designate considerable distance from both the speaker and the addressee. English has no special form, but can convey the last idea by, *that/those* + noun *yonder/over there*.

DEMONSTRATIVE PRONOUN: A **nominalized** form of the **demonstrative adjective** in which the **noun** in the **demonstrative adjective + noun** combination has been "swallowed up" by the adjective, thus converting it into a pronoun: *este libro > este/this book > this (one)*. In the recent past, Spanish marked its demonstrative pronouns with a graphic accent to distinguish them from the adjectives. The *Real Academia Española* now recommends this only in cases of possible ambiguity. English usually adds *one(s)* to the original adjective to accomplish the nominalization. As regards forms, the words themselves are identical to the demonstrative adjectives in both languages.

DESCRIPTIVE ADJECTIVE: Adjectives which in Spanish usually follow their **noun antecedents**, and describe the **noun** in such a way as to distinguish it from others. English routinely places such adjectives before the noun, thus producing a major contrast between the two languages: *una casa bella/a beautiful house* (there are ugly ones, too), *los exámenes difíciles/the hard exams* (there are easy ones, too).

DETERMINERS (LIMITING ADJECTIVES): Adjectives which are usually placed before their **noun antecedents**. Among them are the **articles**, both **definite** and **indefinite** (*el/the; un/a[an]*), **possessive adjectives** (unstressed forms), *mi/my,* **demonstrative adjectives** (*este/this*), adjectives expressing number or order (*dos/two; segundo/second*), etc.

DIMINUTIVE: The opposite of augmentative, and in Spanish, nouns formed by the addition of various suffixes to express the concepts of smallness or dearness. Examples are, *perrito, manitas, cuadernillo, boquilla, añitos,* derived from *perro, mano, cuaderno, boca, año,* respectively.

DIPHTHONGIZATION: A historical phonetic process by which a pure vowel, when stressed, converts to a diphthong, a vowel combination. Characteristic of Spanish are the dipthongization of *e > ie* (*pensar,* but *pienso*) and *o > ue* (*dormir,* but *duermo*).

DIRECT ADDRESS: Statements (affirmative or negative) or questions which are said to or asked of another person in a direct way, in other words, a quote: *The judge said, "There are no if's, and's or but's about it"* = *Dijo el juez, --No hay pero que valga.*

DIRECT OBJECT: In any sentence, the **noun** or **pronoun** acted upon or receiving the direct impact of the verb in the sentence. Here, the direct object nouns are underlined: *He ate an apple* = *Comió una manzana*; *John visited his relatives* = *Juan visitó a sus familiares*. Direct object pronouns occur in the following examples: *He visited them; Él los/les visitó.*

DIRECT OBJECT PRONOUN: The **pronoun** serving as the direct object in a sentence for reasons outlined in the previous entry. They are in Spanish, *me, te, lo/la/le; nos, os, los/las/les.* English has, *me, you, him, her, it; us, them.* In English **syntax** they always follow the verb, but as they belong to the **conjunctive pronoun** classification in Spanish, they either directly precede or follow and attach to the verb in accordance with specific rules based on the type of verbal form involved.

DISJUNCTIVE PRONOUN: These include the Spanish **subject** and **prepositional object** pronouns. The subject pronouns are, *I/yo, you/tú, he/él, she/ella, you/usted, it/*(no word); *we/nosotros-as, you* (pl.)*/vosotros-as, they/ellos-as, you* (pl.)*/ustedes.* The Spanish prepositional pronouns are identical to the subject pronouns except in the first and second persons singular, in which the forms are *mí* and *ti* (*...para mí/...de ti*). With the preposition *con*, the two forms become *conmigo* and *contigo*, respectively. The prepositional object pronouns may be **reflexive** (*Hablo de mí [mismo]* = *I speak about myself*) or **non reflexive** (*Hablo de él* = *I speak about him/it*). Note that the English prepositional object pronouns are the **object(ive) pronouns**.

DURATIVE EVENTS: A semantic property of lexical **aspect** which describes events that continue for a period of time. Verbs of this category may be either **stative** such *as ser, estar, querer, tener,* etc. with no specific initial or end-points, or events which have concrete ending points: *correr una milla; pintar un cuadro.*

DYNAMIC VERBS/ACTIONS: Verbs denoting an action or process as opposed to a state, for example, *correr, comer.*

ELLIPSIS: The permissible omission of some element in the second part of a sentence which has been expressed in the first. *He can lift one hundred pounds, but I can't.* Omitted after *can't,* but implied, is "*lift that much.*" A Spanish example: *Él puede levantar cien libras, pero yo no.*

(EN)CLITIC PRONOUN (See CONJUNCTIVE PRONOUN)

EPICENE GENDER: A **gender** assignment of any **noun** which has yet to be fully agreed upon. Some consider the word, *sartén,* to be **masculine**, others insist it is **feminine**. Some nouns of epicene gender have a slightly different meaning when masculine (*el mar/the sea*) and when feminine (*la mar/the sea* [poetic usage]).

***ESTAR* PASSIVE:** A Spanish **passive sentence** using *estar* + **past participle** rather than *ser*, and expressing the state of the subject rather than the action which occurred to it. In, *El caballo estaba atado a un poste*, no action is expressed, only the state in which the animal found itself.

EXISTENTIAL *HABER*: The use of this **verb**, not as an **auxiliary** in the formation of the **perfect tenses** (*Ya hemos comido*), but as an expression of mere existence: *Hay un problema; Hubo una explosion; Habrá una junta; Va a haber una guerra.* The English equivalent is, *There + to be: There's a problem; There was an explosion; There will be a meeting; There's going to be a war.*

FAMILIAR: A Spanish form of address (**register**) showing familiarity, even intimacy, with the addressee. Its **subject pronouns** are *tú* (singular) and *vosotros/-as* (plural), though *vos* is also used in many Latin American countries. English does not distinguish between **familiar** and **formal** address, and uses *you* for both.

FINITE VERB FORM: Any Spanish verbal form in any tense which expresses the grammatical characteristics of **person, number, tense and mood**. Examples are, *tiene, tuvieron, tendrás, tengáis.*

FORMAL: A Spanish form of address (**register**) indicating respect for the addressee, often on the basis of age differences, social standing, etc. Its **subject pronouns** are *usted(es)*.

GENDER: A distinction made in some languages, including Spanish, in which **inanimate** nouns are classified as either **masculine** or **feminine**. Sexual gender is in no way involved when the definition is restricted to non-living (**inanimate**) entities. The classification is arbitrary, based largely on the history of the word, its ending or other considerations. When **animate** beings are involved, sex and gender are readily equated.

GERUND: Another term for the **present participle**, the verbal form which ends in –*ndo* in Spanish, -*ing* in English.

HIGH VOWELS (See CLOSE VOWELS)

HOMOPHONIC NOUNS/WORDS: Spanish homophonic **nouns** are those of identical spelling and pronunciation, but which differ in meaning with a change of **gender:** *el capital* (money)/*la capital* (city). English has a huge number of homophonic words, most with different spellings, and they belong to virtually every grammatical category: *plane/plain, red/read; see/sea, sun/son*.

HYPERCORRECTION: A usage occurring because people attempt to speak properly, applying rules of language they understand incompletely. The so-called *dequeísmo* of some varieties of modern spoken Spanish is a case in point. The preposition *de* occurs in many Spanish constructions introducing **subordinate clauses**, for example, *antes de que, alegrarse de que,* etc. The *de* is often then generalized to all subordinators, producing such grammatical errors as, **Nos dijo de que saliéramos;*Sugieren de que vayamos por otra carretera*. In English, the suffix *–less* on *regardless* makes it a type of negative. But there is a prefix, *ir-*, that performs the same function in *irrespective*. This prefix is then transferred by speakers hoping to be totally correct to *regardless* producing **irregardless*.

HYPOTHETICAL FUTURE: A type of **conditional sentence** which expresses a hypothesis and a conclusion about the future, neither of which will probably ever be realized. *Si el año venidero eligieran Presidente a Santos, seguro que estallaría una guerra civil* = *If next year they were to elect Santos as President, you can bet a civil war would break out*. Spanish constructs all hypothetical future conditional sentences on the pattern shown above, while English employs a number of different structures.

IMPERATIVE (COMMANDS): The terms refers to any command, **affirmative** or **negative**, **direct** or **indirect**. Direct: *Come!, Don't come!/¡Venga!, ¡No venga!; ¡Ven!, ¡No vengáis;* Indirect: *Let/Have them come!/¡Que vengan!*

IMPERATIVE MOOD: An occasionally cited third **mood** of Spanish, along with the **indicative** and the **subjunctive**, which includes all the command forms in that language.

IMPERFECT INDICATIVE TENSE: One of the two Spanish **simple past tenses**, the other being the **preterite**, regularly formed using the endings –*aba* (*tomaba*) or –*ía* (*comía*). Only three verbs are irregular in this tense: *ir, ser, ver*. For the most part the imperfect indicative expresses past description or the habitual repetition of past actions.

IMPERFECTIVE ASPECT: That **aspect** of the Spanish **verbal system** which focuses on the middle portion of past actions or states without regard to the beginning, end or outcome of either.

IMPERSONAL EXPRESSION: An expression using English *it* + third person singular of *to be* + **adjective**, (in Spanish, third person singular *ser* + adjective), to express an idea which applies not to specific individuals, but to anyone who hears the message. *It is necessary…/Es necesario…; It has been routine/Ha sido rutinario*.

INANIMATE: Referring to things (**nouns**) which are not living, such as items, places, qualities, conditions. Examples are, *libros/books, el centro urbano/downtown, el amor/love, la enfermedad/sickness*.

INCEPTIVE (INCHOATIVE) VERB: A verb which, because of its meaning, stresses the beginning of an event: *We were startled/got scared* = *Nos asustamos; The car started up without any problem* = *Arrancó el carro sin problema*.

INDEFINITE ARTICLE: A type of **nominal (noun) determiner** which, although acknowledging the existence of the noun, does not specify its identity, unlike the **definite article**. English has two

Glossary of Grammatical Terms

allomorphs, *a* (used before consonants) and *an* (used before vowels). The plural of each is *some*. Spanish has the usual four-part set, **inflected** for both **gender** and **number**: *un, una, unos, unas*.

INDEFINITE SUBJECT: A sentence subject which is not an identifiable individual: *One never has time = Nunca se tiene/Uno nunca tiene tiempo; It's said that... / Se dice que......*

INDICATIVE MOOD: That **mood** of Spanish which, unlike the **subjunctive**, expresses what happened (*salió*) or was happening (*salía*) in the past, what is happening in the present or in a general sense (*sale*), what will occur in the future (*saldrá*), or would occur, certain conditions being met (*saldría*). Included under its rubric are three **simple tenses**, the **present**, the **preterite**, and the **imperfect**, and two so-called **synthetic tenses**, the **future** and the **conditional** tenses, and a full set of **perfect** and **progressive** tenses.

INDIRECT ADDRESS: Any utterance which is not a quote but rather a reported statement, usually framed as a subordinate clause. See the following contrastive examples: **Direct address**: *John said, "I think I'm having a heart attack." = Juan dijo, -- Creo que estoy sufriendo un ataque cardíaco.* **Indirect address**: *John said (that) he thought (that) he was having a heart attack = Juan dijo que creía que estaba sufriendo un ataque cardíaco."*

INDIRECT OBJECT: If present in a sentence, it represents the one who benefits from, receives or is in some way affected by the action producing or impacting the **direct object**, either expressed or implied. In, *John gave Susan a present*, the direct object is "a present"; "Susan" is the indirect object, that is, the beneficiary of the "present giving." English allows the sentence to be restructured, introducing the **preposition** *to* (sometimes *for*), which clearly mark indirect objects, *John gave a present to Susan*. In Spanish, indirect object nouns are always preceded by the **preposition** *a*, and often use a **redundant (reduplicated) indirect object pronoun**: *Le dimos un reloj de oro al jubilado.*

INDIRECT OBJECT PRONOUN: As **pronouns**, these substitute for **indirect object nouns** in both languages and perform the same grammatical function. They belong to the **conjunctive** set of Spanish **personal pronouns** and are, *me, te, le; nos, os, les*. In English they are identical to the **object(ive) pronouns** (*me, you, him, her, it; us, you, them*), and may or may not be preceded by the prepositions, *to* or *for*, depending upon the syntactical arrangement chosen.

INDIRECT QUESTION: A question embedded in a sentence, usually as a **subordinate noun clause**. *Nobody knows where he lives = Nadie sabe dónde vive*. Note that in English, the **syntax** of the direct **content question** (*Where does he live?*) is altered. In Spanish, the question word retains the orthographic accent used in the direct question, but the syntax remains unchanged.

INFINITIVE: The **verbal** form representing the name of the action or state of being involved, often called the **noun (nominal)** form of the verb. As it is never **inflected**, it cannot express **person, number, tense** or **mood**. The form always ends in *–r* in Spanish (*hablar, comer, vivir*), and in English is composed of *to* + the **base form/lexical verb** (*to speak, to eat, to live*).

INFLECTION: A feature of a language's **morphological system** indicating the use of different endings added to words to show their grammatical function. Compared with English, Spanish is a **highly inflected language** since in the **nominal system**, endings are added to mark **gender** and **number**. In its verbal system, the six forms of every **tense** take endings expressing **person, number, tense** and **mood**. English **nouns** are inflected only to distinguish **singular** from **plural**. In the **present tense**, verbs use the inflection *–s* to mark the third person singular form (*I go~He goes*). The regular **past tense** and **past participles** are regularly inflected with *–ed*, and the **present participle (gerund)** takes the inflection *–ing*.

INTENSIFIER: A word or phrase used to emphasize, stress, or clarify another word. English employs its **reflexives** ending in *-self*, while Spanish has *mismo* (*She did it herself = Ella misma lo hizo*). English can intensify elements by using heavy vocal stress (*They saw the play, not the film*). Spanish rarely uses this tactic, but rather rearranges a syntactical pattern, or more frequently adds a **redundant** (**reduplicated**) **phrase**, for example, *A mí me gustó la clase* = *I liked the class*.

INTERROGATIVE: A term referring to any type of question, whether answerable with a mere affirmation or negation (**yes/no question**) eg., *Do you need money?/¿Necesitas dinero?*, or with real information (**content question**), *What did he say?/¿Qué dijo?* With respect to content questions whose interrogative element is composed of more than one element, Spanish and English syntax differ: Spanish integrates (keeps together) the question elements (*¿De dónde es Usted?*) whereas English tends to separate them, placing the first Spanish element at the end of the question: *Where are you from?*

INTERTONIC VOWEL: The unstressed vowel occurring either before or after the stressed vowel in a word. In *veremos*, both the first *e* and the *o* are intertonic. Intertonic vowels are said in phonetics to be in the "weak position" and are often lost. In the formation of the Spanish **synthetic** future from the **periphrasis** *caber + (h)é*, the intertonic infinitive vowel is lost, producing the modern form, *cabré*. The process affects English, too, and is responsible for a number of hypercorrections, such as *athelete, in which the speaker supplies a supposed intertonic vowel which never existed.

INTRANSITIVE: In either language, a verb which does not take a **direct object** and is related only to a single noun, its subject. Examples are, *to leave/salir, to come/venir*. The most common of these can be found in Appendix IV.

INVERSION (subject/verb): The syntactical switch between a subject and a verb occurring when a statement converts into a question, for example: *You have a car > Have you a car?* = *Usted tiene un carro > ¿Tiene usted un carro?*. Keep in mind that in Spanish inversion is not a requirement to form questions: *¿Usted tiene un carro?*

INVOLVED ENTITY: (See DATIVE OF INTEREST)

IRREGULAR VERB: In either language, any verb which in any of its forms deviates from the usual (**regular**) **morphological** patters, that is, those patterns followed by the majority of verbs in the language. **Roots**, endings, or both may be involved. A verb can be slightly irregular; for example, *contar* has another form of its root, *cuent-*, or highly irregular, like *decir*, which has a variety of roots, *dig-, dec-, dic-, dij-, dir, dich-*. In English, verbal irregularities are generally confined to the **present, past,** and **past participle**, for example, *go, went* (not *goed), *gone* (not *goed).

LEXICAL VERB (See BASE FORM)

LEXICON: Taken as a whole, the entire collection of words available for use in any language. For example, it could be said that one language has more **adjectives** in its lexicon than another.

LIMITING ADJECTIVE (See DETERMINERS)

LOCATIVE: The term is used mainly to designate **adverbs** or **prepositional phrases** expressing physical location, such as, *here/aquí, inside (of) the country/dentro del país*, etc. Location in time can also be conveyed through the same means: *now/ahora, at eight o'clock/a las ocho*.

MAIN CLAUSE: Sometimes referred to as an **independent clause** or **matrix clause**, it is the clause expressing the main idea in a **complex sentence**, and makes sense by itself, without the information provided in the **subordinate clause** with which it is associated. The main clauses are underlined, as follows: *We met a man who had worked in Bolivia* = *Conocimos a un señor que había trabajado en Bolivia*.

MID-VOWELS (See SEMI-CLOSE VOWELS)

MODAL AUXILIARY (See AUXILIARY VERBS)

MOOD (See INDICATIVE MOOD, IMPERATIVE MOOD, SUBJUNCTIVE MOOD)

MOOD/TENSE/ASPECT MORPHEME: In **finite** Spanish verbs, the **morpheme** found between the **verbal root** and its **person/number morpheme**. It conveys all three grammatical concepts that its name implies. In the form *amáramos*, this morpheme is underlined.

MORPHEME: Any segment of a word that expresses a unit of **grammatical or lexical** meaning. In the Spanish verbal form *cantaban*, the segment, *cant-* is the **root morpheme** carrying the **lexical meaning**, *-aba-* is the **tense/mood/aspect morpheme**, showing that the verb is of the **first conjugation**, and in the **imperfect indicative tense** and the morpheme *–n* is the **person/number morpheme**, indicating that the verb is in a **third person plural** form. As can be seen, morphemes can convey both meaning and grammatical function.

NASAL: A phonetic term designating a group of sounds whose commonality is that they are produced by passing a stream of air through the nasal rather than the oral cavity. Examples are the sounds [m] and [n].

NEUTER ARTICLE: The Spanish word *lo*, used with **adjectves**, **adverbs** and certain **clauses**, which, unlike other **articles** that mark nouns in specific ways, designates entire concepts having no **gender** or **number**. Examples: *...lo feo de su aspecto, ...lo mucho que te quiero, ...lo que tenemos que hacer.*

NEUTRAL CONDITIONAL SENTENCE: In either language, a **conditional sentence** expressing possibilities without implying that what is said runs counter to reality, never occurred, or most probably will not occur. They refer to any time, past, present or future, as in the examples: *If he went, he for sure had a good time = Si fue, seguro que se divirtió mucho; If he knows something, he's not telling anyone = Si algo sabe, no se lo dice a nadie; If you come to the meeting tomorrow, you'll meet the professor = Si vienes mañana a la reunión, conocerás al profesor.* Only the **indicative tenses** occur in these sentences.

NOMINALIZATION: A linguistic maneuver through which a **part of speech** not normally viewed as a **noun** is converted into one. **Adjectives** are the part of speech most commonly nominalized. In a Spanish article + noun + adjective phrase (*el vestido azul*), the noun can be **suppressed**, and the result is a nominalization, (*el azul*), expressed in English as *the blue one*. Adjective phrases may be nominalized, *...la (chica) de los ojos verdes = ...the one with the green eyes.* **Demonstrative and possessive pronouns** are but nominalized forms of these two types of adjectives: *Ese (hombre) de los ojos azules, es el mío (= mi esposo).*

NON-COUNT NOUN: Sometimes called **mass nouns**, they are **nouns** which cannot be counted, 1, 2, 3. Examples are, *water/agua, sugar/azúcar, milk/leche, air/aire.*

NON-FINITE –ED CLAUSE: A descriptive **clause** using the **past participle** as an **adjective**, more common in the written than the spoken language: *Their studies finished, the students began looking for jobs = Terminados sus estudios, los estudiantes comenzaron a buscar trabajo.*

NON-FINITE –ING CLAUSE: A descriptive **clause** using the **present participle** *(-ing/-ndo)* adjectivally: *Knowing their cause was lost, they surrendered = Sabiendo que su causa estaba perdida, se rindieron.* Such clauses in Spanish can be overused and are probably generated under the influence of English. Stylistically it may be better to use a **finite verbal** construction: *Como sabían que su causa estaba perdida, se rindieron.* The same is true for the **non-finite –ed clauses** of the previous entry.

NON-FINITE VERB FORM: Any of three verbal forms which do not show the usual verbal categories of **person**, **number**, **tense** and **mood**. They are the **infinitive** (*to eat/comer*), the **present participle** or **gerund** (*eating/comiendo*) and the **past participle** (*eaten/comido*), but only when it functions as a verbal form (*han comido*) rather than as an **adjective** where it is subject to **inflection** for **person** and **number**, as in *...unas manzanas comidas por los puercos.*

NON-RESTRICTIVE CLAUSE: A adjectival (relative) **clause** used parenthetically to modify a **noun**, and providing no information clarifying or contrasting that noun with any other possible one. Both languages routinely sets such clauses off using commas. *Mi tía, que ya tiene muchos años, va a vivir con mi madre = My aunt, who now is quite elderly, is going to live with my mother.*

NOUN (NOMINAL) CLAUSE: A **clause** functioning as a **noun** or noun phrase due to the fact that it answers the question, *What?/¿Qué?* The noun clauses are underlined in the examples: *¿Qué recomienda el médico? > El médico recomienda <u>que nos mudemos a otra ciudad</u>* = *What does the doctor recommend? > The doctor recommends <u>that we move to another city</u>.* ; *¿Qué dijo el policía? > El policía dijo <u>que ha habido un accidente en el autopista</u>* = *What did the cop say? > The cop said <u>that there's been an accident on the freeway</u>.* ; *¿Qué te gustó de esa película? > Me gustó <u>que no muestra mucha violencia</u>* = *What did you like about that movie? > I liked <u>that it does not show too much violence</u>.*

NUMBER: The distinction between **singular and plural** in both languages and a feature of both the **nominal system** (*cat/gato, cats/gatos*) and the **verbal system**: singular, *I have/tengo* vs. plural, *we have/tenemos.*

OBJECT(IVE) PRONOUN: The English **pronouns** serving as **direct objects, indirect objects,** and **prepositional objects.** They are in the **singular,** *me, you, him, her, it,* and in the **plural,** *us, you (all)* and *them.* In the example following, *them* appears in all three object(ive) roles: *We met them, gave them the money, and forgot about them.*

ORTHOGRAPHY: In either language, anything related to the writing system, including correct spelling, capitalization, punctuation, and graphic (written) accent use.

PARADIGM: A discernible pattern followed by Spanish **verbal forms** in their various tenses, especially apparent in **regular** verbs. For example, the **present indicative** paradigm for a regular Spanish verb of the **first conjugation** is: *hablo, hablas, habla; hablamos, habláis, hablan.* All regular *–ar* verbs follow this paradign. Other grammatical categories have paradigms, for example the English **object(ive) pronouns** (*me, you, him, her, it; we, you, them*).

PARTICLE: A word, often a preposition or a pronoun, which has a specialized function. For example, the different prepositions added to the verb *to give* (*give in, give out, give up*) are called particles since they cause the verb to have vastly different meanings when appended to it. Similarly, the Spanish pronoun *se* when used with verbs like *enojarse, ponerse, enfermarse,* cause the verb to express a change of state, often sudden and complete.

PARTITIVE: A way of expressing parts of a whole rather than the whole itself, for example, *a little water/poca agua, a lot of water/mucha agua, a few friends/unos cuantos amigos.*

PARTS OF SPEECH: A traditional and very old system of reducing the basic components of language to their most elemental essentials. Generally, eight or more are listed and defined:

    1. ADJECTIVE: A word which modifies (describes or classifies a **noun**), such as *beautiful,* in *the beautiful house/la casa bella.* English adjectives routinely precede the nouns they modify, while in Spanish they may precede or follow. Adjectives are classified as either **limiting (determiners)** or **descriptive.**

    2. ADVERB: A word used to modify a **verb** (*He ran <u>quickly</u>/Corrió <u>rápidamente</u>*), an **adjective** (*She's <u>highly</u> competent/Es <u>sumamente</u> capaz*) or another **adverb** (*He speaks <u>very</u> slowly/Habla <u>muy</u> lento/lentamente*).

    3. CONJUNCTION: A word used to connect two elements, such as the word *y/and* in *tú <u>y</u> yo/you <u>and</u> I*). When **clauses** are involved, conjunctions are of two types: **coordinating,** if the clauses have approximately equal weight (*She said something, <u>but</u> he didn't say anything* = *Ella dijo algo, <u>pero</u> él no dijo nada*) and **subordinating** which connect a **main clause** to a **subordinate clause,** as in, *They told us (<u>that</u>) they had ten children* = *Nos dijeron <u>que</u> tenían diez hijos.* The most common coordinating conjunctions are *and/y, but/pero* and *or/o,* while the most frequent subordinating one is *that* (often suppressed)/*que.*

    4. INTERJECTION: A word injected into a sentence, expressing such emotions as pain or surprise (*ouch!/¡ay!*). Some are classified as expletives, somewhat taboo outbursts of cursing, rage, disappointment, disgust, etc.

5. NOUN: A word which names a person, place, thing, quality, condition, etc., as in these examples: *John/Juan, France/Francia, house/casa, goodness/la bondad, poverty/la pobreza.* Nouns are the center of any language's **nominal system**, and **articles (definite** and **indefinite), adjectives (descriptive** and **limiting)**, as well as **possessive** and **demonstrate adjectives** function in association with them as secondary components of the system.

6. PARTICIPLE: These are of two types in both languages, **the present participle** (-*ing/-ndo*) and the **past participle** (usually ending in –*ed* in English and –*do* in Spanish), although numerous exceptions can be cited. Participles are "hybrid forms," functioning as **verbs** or **adjectives**. In the case of the past participle, *closed/cerrado*, its verbal role is apparent in the **perfect tenses** (*They had closed the door = Habían cerrado la puerta*). Its adjectival use is manifest in the **phrase** *a closed door = una puerta cerrada*).

7. PREPOSITION: In either language a word (usually short) which relates one linguistic element to a noun or pronoun to convey such concepts as location (*on~in/en*), destination (*to/a*), intended recipient (*for/para*) possession (*of/de*), etc.: ... *in Mexico/ ...en México, ...to the coast/...a la costa, ... for us/...para nosotros, ...of/from/about our problem/...de nuestro problema.*

8. PRONOUN: A word which substitutes for a noun when the context allows its meaning to be clear. *His boss left for the airport. He was in a big rush. = Su patrón salió para el aeropuerto. (Él) estaba muy apurado.* Pronouns are of numerous types, **personal** (*yo/I*), **indefinite** (*someone/alguien*), **possessive** (*yours/el suyo*), **demonstrative** (*that one/ese*).

9. VERB: A word expressing an action (*run/correr*), state of being (*to be/ser~estar~ haber*), or mental state (*to know/saber~conocer*).

PASSIVE VOICE: A way of expressing an idea by making the sentence **subject** the sentence **object** as well. In, *The employees were fired = Los empleados fueron despedidos*, the "employees" are the grammatical subject of the sentence, and also the object (receivers of the action of firing). These examples demonstrate the **true passive** composed of a **subject** + a form of *to be/ser* + **a past participle**. The actual doer of the action, either expressed or implied, is called **the agent**, and if stated, is introduced with *by/por (...by their boss/... por su patón)* in a prepositional phrase. Both languages have various ways of expressing passive ideas.

PAST (PASSIVE) PARTICIPLE: (See: **Parts of Speech**)

PAST TENSE FAMILY OF VERBS: Spanish verb **tenses** generally associated with the expression of past time in any context. In the **indicative mood**, they are the **preterite** (*hablé*), the **imperfect** (*hablaba*) and the **conditional** (*hablaría*). The **pluperfect (past perfect)** is also included (*había hablado*). In the subjunctive, they are the **past subjunctive** (*hablara/-se*) and the **pluperfect subjunctive** (*hubiera/-se hablado*).

PAST SUBJUNCTIVE: The term used in this text for the tense often called the imperfect subjunctive. It is the form that ends in either –*ra* (*tuviera*) or –*se* (*tuviese*) and is derived, without exception, from the third person plural, preterite form (*tuvieron > tuvie-ra/-se*).

PEDADOGY: A term referring to the teaching of any academic discipline, including languages, encompassing such issues as the writing of teaching materials, methodology, etc. The present text has been written with the teacher and his/her pedagogical needs in mind.

PEJORATIVE (DISPECTIVE): A usage implying disrespect or contempt for someone or something. In many varieties of Spanish, the use of the **definite article** with a first name can produce the affect: *La María* [implied is that she is a bad person] *anda diciendo cosas de ti*. A **demonstrative adjective** following a noun can be dispective: *el hombre ese*. English can use the adjectives *little* and *old* without their literal meanings to produce pejorative expressions: *...that little liar, ...old man Roberts*.

PERFECT INFINITIVE: The **infinitive** from which the **perfect tenses** are derived. It is formed with the **auxiliary** (*have/haber*) + **past participle** (*to have spoken/haber hablado*).

PERFECT PROGRESSIVE INFINITIVE: The **infinitive** upon which the **perfect progressive tenses** are based. It is formed with the **auxiliary** *have/haber*) + **auxiliary past participle** *been/estado* + **gerund/present participle** (*to have been speaking/haber estado hablando*).

PERFECT TENSE: Any tense formed with the **auxiliary** *have/haber* + **past participle** (*They had lived/habían vivido*), and expressing the completion of an action prior to another time, be it **past** (*habían hablado*), **present** (*han comido*), or **future** (*habrán salido*).

PERFECTIVE ASPECT: Unlike the **imperfective aspect**, it focuses upon such features of an event as its beginning (*La conocí = I met her*), the event as a whole with a beginning, middle and end (*Leímos various libros = We read several books*) or just the end of an event, usually with a result implied (*No pude abrir la caja = I couldn't open the box* (implied is, "I tried but failed"). The term also applies to changes of state (*En ese momento, se sintió muy enojada*).

PERIPHRASIS: A way of expressing an idea using, in contrast to just one word, any group of words to state the same idea. For example, the **future**, *estaremos*, can be rendered with a periphrasis composed of *ir a* + **infinitive** (*vamos a estar*). Likewise, the **conditional** *estaríamos* is, periphrastically, *íbamos a estar*. The one-word future and conditional forms (*iré/iría*) are referred to as **synthetic** forms, generated historically by a fusion of verbal forms.

PERSON: A feature of both the **pronominal** and **verbal systems** of both languages distinguishing those involved in a speech act under three categories, both **singular and plural**. The **first person** represents the speaker, the **second person**, the person spoken to and the **third person**, the person or thing spoken about. The subject pronouns illustrate this pattern: first person singular (*I/yo*), plural (*we/nosotros-as*), second person singular (*you/tú*), plural (*vosotros-as*), third person singular (*he~she~it/él~ella*), plural (*they/ellos-as*). With only one exception, the English third person singular present tense form ends in *–s* (*live > lives*). Otherwise, English **verbs** are not marked for person, but all Spanish verbal forms are, through the use of **inflectional** endings.

PERSON/NUMBER MORPHEME: In Spanish verbs, the last **morpheme** in the form, carrying the concepts of **person and number**. Four out of six of them remain constant across the entire verbal system, *-s* (*iba-s*) marking the second person singular, *-mos* (*íba-mos*) for the first person plural, *-is* (*iba-is*) for the second person plural, and *–n* (*iba-n*) for the third person plural.

PERSONAL ACCUSATIVE: Sometimes called "the personal *a*," it is a feature of Spanish grammar in which the **preposition** *a* (no translation in English) usually precedes any **animate noun** or personal referent used as a **direct object**. Examples are, *Nadie vio al ladrón; No tengo a nadie; ¿A quiénes quieres invitar?*

PERSONAL PRONOUN: Any **pronoun** referring to people or things. They are classified in English as **subject** (*I, she, they*) or **object(ive)** (*me, her, them*) pronouns. Spanish places them under two major headings, **the disjunctive pronouns**, **subject** (*yo, tú...*) and **prepositional** (*mí, ti...*), and the **conjunctive pronouns**, which include **direct objects** (*lo, la*), **indirect objects** (*le*), and **reflexive objects** (*se*).

PHRASAL VERB (TWO-WORD VERB): A large and productive class of English verbs composed of a normal **verb** followed by a **preposition**. The combination can have an array of different meanings, for example, *to hand in, to hand out, to hand over, to hand down*. Spanish has no similar system.

PHRASE: Often introduced by **a preposition**, phrases function in various ways: **adverbially** to express location (*on the corner/en la esquina*), time (*at eight o'clock/a las ocho*), destination (*to church/a la iglesia*), manner (*with enthusiasm/con entusiasmo*), and as **adjectives** (*The house under construction.../La casa en construcción...*). The Academy provides an concise definition of the term: *Conjunto de palabras que basta para formar sentido, especialmente cuando no llega a constituir oración.* A word is in order concerning the Spanish **cognate** of this term. *Frase* is often used to translate English *sentence*, but in strictly grammatical parlance, *frase* means *phrase* while *oración* is preferred for *sentence*.

POSITIVE DEGREE: The base (uninflected) form of an **adjective** (*tall/alto*) or **adverb** (*slow/lento*) used without comparing its accompanying **noun** to another. There are two other **degrees of comparison**, **the comparative** (*taller/más alto*) and **the superlative** (*the tallest/el más alto*).

POSSESSIVE ADJECTIVE: A special set of **adjectives** indicating who possesses what, for example, *my book/mi libro, your class/tu clase, their friends/sus amigos*. Spanish has another group of these, the **stressed (postposed) possessive adjectives**, where the possessive adjective follows the **noun**: *el libro mío, la clase tuya, los amigos suyos~...de ellos*.

POSSESSIVE PRONOUN: A special set of **pronouns** in which both the possessor and the possessed entity are combined. For example, *my book*, using a **possessive adjective**, becomes *mine*, *their friends* becomes *theirs*. The original **noun** has been "swallowed up" in the possessive pronoun. Spanish does this using its **postposed** set of **possessive adjectives** with **the article** retained to imply **the noun,** which has been **suppressed**, for instance, *el mío*, originally *el* + noun + *mío*.

POSTPOSITIONING: The act of syntactically placing one item after another. Spanish **descriptive adjectives** are usually postpositioned with respect to the **nouns** they modify (*la ciudad vieja*), while in English, they are **prepositioned** (*the old city*).

POTENTIAL (See CONDITIONAL)

PREDICATE: That portion of a sentence which says (predicates) something about the **subject** of the sentence. It includes the verb and the rest of the utterance, if any. In, *The students met with their professor for the first time last Tuesday,* the predicate is the entire sentence, minus the **subject,** *the students*.

PREDICATE ADJECTIVE: An adjective used after forms of *to be/ser~estar*. *He is tall = Es/Está alto*. In Spanish the subject's inherent characteristics are described using *ser*, while with *estar*, a reaction to the subject´s appearance (it has changed) is stressed.

PREDICATE NOUN: A noun following a form of *to be/ser* (only) and identifying the subject. *Ese señor es mi professor de química = That man is my chemistry professor; Juan será el decano = John is going to be the dean*.

PREPOSITIONAL PRONOUN: Pronouns governed by **prepositions**, for example, *for me/para mí, about us/de nosotros, with them/con ellos*. In English, they are the **object(ive) pronouns**, also used as **direct** and **indirect object pronouns**. In Spanish, the prepositional pronouns are the same as the **subject pronouns**, except in two cases, the **first** and **second persons**, **singular**, *mí* and *ti*.

PREPOSITIONING (See POSTPOSITIONING)

PRESENT PARTICIPLE (GERUND): The **verbal form** ending in *–ing* in English, *-ndo* in Spanish. With the **auxiliary** verb *to be/estar*, it forms the **progressive tenses**, *He was eating = El estaba comiendo*. Independently used, it usually functions as an **adverb**: *I hurt my eyes* [how?] *(by) watching television = Me lastimé los ojos viendo la tele*.

PRESENT TENSE FAMILY: Spanish **tenses** generally expressing actions that occur in present time. In the **indicative**, they are the **present perfect** (*ha salido*), the **present progressive** (*está saliendo*) and the **simple present** (*sale*). The **future** (*saldrá*) is often included in the family. In the **subjunctive**, the present tense family includes the **present perfect subjunctive** (*haya salido*), the **present progressive subjunctive** (*esté saliendo*) and the **simple present subjunctive** (*salga*).

PRETERITE TENSE: A Spanish **past tense** (like the **imperfect**) having many formal irregularities, and expressing past actions as completed. Some exemplary forms are, *hablé, tuviste, comió, hicimos, salisteis, fueron*.

PRIMARY AUXILIARY: Auxiliary verbs that, unlike **modal auxiliaries**, have no true **lexical** meaning, but rather convey strictly grammatical concepts such as tense, person and number. Some English primary auxiliary verbs (*do/does, did; don't/dosen't, didn't*) carry the concept of tense (present or past) in certain structures. The **perfect** (*to have gone/haber ido*) and the **progressives tenses** (*to be working/estar trabajando*) use primary auxiliaries

PRINCIPLE PARTS OF THE ENGLISH VERB: A traditional way of listing English verbs according to their forms, 1) **present**, 2) **past** and 3) **past participle**. A **regular** verb, for example, *to work*, would appear listed as, *work/worked/worked*. In the case of *to see (see/saw/seen)*, however, the verb is irregular as it does not follow the regular pattern (**paradigm**) outlined above.

PROGRESSIVE INFINITIVE: The infinitive from which **the progressive tenses** are derived. In English, *to be* + *–ing (to be eating)* and in Spanish, *estar* + *-ndo (estar comiendo)*.

PROGRESSIVE TENSE: A family of **tenses** expressing actions in progress. They use forms of *to be* + *-ing* in English (*We are/will be/were working*) and in Spanish, *estar* + *-ndo (Estamos/Estaremos/Estábamos trabajando)*.

PRONOMINAL REDUPLICATION / REDUNCANCY:
A feature of Spanish in which a grammatical item is repeated using another structure. It occurs for purposes of emphasizing or clarifying the item which, in other contexts, could stand on its own. In, *Le prepararon una linda carta de recomendación a Esteban*, *a Esteban* repeats *le* and stresses that *he*, not another person, was recommended.

PRONOMINAL USAGE: Any Spanish usage of a **conjunctive pronoun** with a verb: *Me necesitan; No nos quisieron saludar; ¡Vístete!* In such settings, the pronoun may be repeated in a prepositional construction, called pronominal reduplication, for purposes of emphasis or clarification: *A él le gusta mucho, pero a ella no; A mi perro no lo encuentro en ninguna parte*.

PRONOMINAL VERB: Spanish **verbs** always used with a **conjunctive pronoun** to convey their intended meaning. Prime examples are the **reflexive verbs**, (*bañarse, vestirse, acostarse, suicidarse*) where the **subject** and **object** are the same individual: (*Yo = me) bañé, (Tú = te) vestías, (Ellos = se) van a acostar, (Ella = se) suicidó*. There are pronominal verbs that are not truly reflexive, but rather express "inner life" or changes of physical, mental or emotional states of being, for example, *enfermarse, volverse loco, enojarse*.

PROSODIC (SUPRASEGMENTAL) FEATURES: Features of the spoken language extending over more than one successive minimal element, such as stress, rhythm and intonation.

PROTASIS: In any **conditional sentence**, the **clause** expressing the hypothesis, usually introduced by *if* in English, *si* in Spanish. The protasis, also called the "if-clause" or "hypothesis," is underlined in the examples: <u>*If I knew her name*</u>, *I would look it up in the telephone book* = <u>*Si supiera su nombre*</u>, *lo buscaría en la guía de teléfonos*.

PUNCTUAL ASPECT: A temporal property describing events that are not conceived of as lasting in time. Examples are, *to realize/darse cuenta, to find/encontrar, to enter/entrar, to leave/salir, to fall down/caerse, to get angry/enojarse, to get sick/enfermarse*.

RADICAL (See ROOT; STEM)

RADICALLY-CHANGING (STEM-CHANGING) VERB: A closed set of Spanish verbs characterized by changes in either the *–e-* or the *–o-* in their infinitive **roots** when the verbs assume their various forms. Specific rules govern the behavior of such verbs. The *–e-* may become the **dipthong** *-ie-* or be **raised** to *–i-* in the forms; for example, *mentir* has two other roots, *mient-* and *mint-*. Likewise, *morir* has two other root forms, *muer-* and *mur-*. *Pensar* and *volver*, however, have only one other root form apiece, *piens-* and *vuelv-*.

RECIPROCAL: In either language, actions individuals do to one other, for example, *They kissed (each other)* = *Se besaron*.

REFLEXIVE: A grammatical structure broadly indicating that the **subject** and the **object** (either **direct or indirect**) are the same entity. In, *El hombre se afeitó*, the subject (*el hombre*) performs an action on himself (*se*), the **direct object**. Similarly in, *El hombre se afeitó la barba*, *la barba* is **the direct object**, and *se* is here the **indirect object**, showing that the shaving of the beard was to the benefit of the subject and not another person. Reflexive verbs are differentiated from others by the appendage of *–se* to their **infinitives**, (*bañar* > *bañarse*). They belong to a larger verbal category called **pronominal** verbs.

REFLEXIVE PRONOUN: A set of **pronouns** which, when accompanied by a sentence **subject** either expressed or implied, show that the **subject** and the **object** are the same entity. English has reflexive pronouns ending in *–self* (*himself, ourselves*), while Spanish uses its **conjunctive pronouns**. In the **third person, singular** and **plural**, that pronoun becomes *se* (*Yo me acosté; Él se acostó*). The **paradigm** for the Spanish reflexive pronouns is, *me, te, se; nos, os, se*.

REGISTER: A general term designating how languages clarify the relationship between the speaker and the addressee. Spanish forms of **direct address** are of either the **familiar** register (*tú/vosotros-as*) or the **formal** one (*usted/ustedes*). Register in Spanish affects not only the words used for the addressee, but the accompanying verb forms and other grammatical items as well. Register is not an issue in English grammar; *you* works for virtually all addressees.

REGULAR VERB: Any English verb whose **past tense** and **past participle** forms are identical, both ending in *–ed*: present tense *walk* uses *walked* for its past and past participle. Spanish verbs are classified as regular if, 1) their patterns represent those of the majority of verbs of their **conjugation**, and 2) if their roots have but one form, and their endings match those of the majority of Spanish verbs of their **conjugation**. *Hablar, comer, vivir* are model regular verbs since they meet both specifications.

RELATIVE CLAUSE: A **subordinate adjective clause** providing information concerning the **antecedent** in the **main clause** through the use of a **relative pronoun**: *I've written to the person (that/who(m)) you have already interviewed.* = *Le he escrito a la persona a quien ya has entrevistado.*

RELATIVE PRONOUN: A type of **pronoun** occurring in **subordinate adjective clauses** and relating that clause to an **antecedent** in the **main clause**. These pronouns may identify people (*que/quien* =*that/who(m)*), express possession (*cuyo/whose*), show **nominalization** (*el que/the one who (that)*), etc. Comparative examples of their use follow: *The woman who(m) he married is a blonde* = *La mujer con quien se casó es rubia*; *The author whose article you read teaches at Dartmouth* = *El autor cuyo artículo leíste da clases en Dartmouth*; *He knows the one who brought them* = *Él conoce al que los trajo*.

REPETITIVE ACTIONS: From the view-point of **grammatical aspect**, these are actions depicted as occurring more than once, for example, *Mi abuelo fumaba puros* = *My grandfather would/used to smoke cigars*. **Lexical aspect** would focus on verbs called semelfactive; their innate meaning implies repetition, for example, *martillar/to hammer*.

RESTRICTIVE CLAUSE: An **adjective clause (relative clause)** modifying its **antecedent** in such a way as to provide essential information, thus differentiating it from possible others. They are used to prevent confusion. In, *La niña que tiene ocho años...* = *The girl who is eight...* the reference is specifically to the eight-year old girl and not to any other younger or older girl.

RHIZOTONIC: Applied specifically to Spanish verbs, the term designates the stressed root of a verbal form. For instance, the **radically-changing verbs** *pensar, dormir* and *pedir* have as their rhizotonic roots the forms *piens-, duerm-,* and *pid-,* respectively. The **strong preterites** have rhizotonic forms in their first and third persons, singular: *traj-e/traj-o, pud-e/pud-o, dij-e/dij-o*.

ROMANCE LANGUAGES: Not because they are "the languages of love," these languages are so called because they derive from Latin, the language spread throughout the Roman Empire. They include Spanish, Portuguese, French, Italian and Romanian, among other minor ones.

ROOT MORPHEME: This **morpheme**, also called the **radical** or the **stem,** is that part of a Spanish verbal form which carries the **lexical** meaning. In **regular verbs**, for example, *hablar, comer* and *vivir*, it is the same for all possible forms of the verb, that is, *habl-, com-,* and *viv-,* respectively. In **irregular verbs**, it may have two forms, (*caer* has *ca-* and *caig-*), or more. *Decir* has as its possible roots, *dec-, dig-, dic-, dij-, dir-* and *dich-.*

RULES OF GRAMMAR: These are of three different types. 1) <u>**Descriptive rules**</u> are those based upon how the language works, taken from careful observation. For example, the Spanish second person singular verbal form ends in *–s* across the tenses with one exception, that of the preterite (*viniste,* not **vinistes*). 2) <u>**Prescriptive rules**</u> are those based on what the experts suggest or even demand as good usage to produce the best language possible. We are taught to say *traje,* not **truje, había dos,* not **habían dos.* In English, **ain't* is considered "bad grammar" as is "**We don't want none."* 3) <u>**Conventional rules**</u> are established by group decisions on the part of experts and generally affect such features of language as **orthography** (spelling, punctuation, written accent use, etc.). For example, a convention of Spanish orthography is to spell the sound [k] as follows when it occurs before the five vowels or any consonant: *ca, co, cu, que, qui, c +* consonant as in *casa, cosa, cuna, queso, quiso, clase.* Italian has another spelling convention for the orthography representing the sound [k].

SE **PASSIVE:** A Spanish construction using the pronoun *se* to produce a sentence which, in English, translates using a **true passive structure**. The Spanish structure can be analyzed in several ways, but it is not a real passive. The "unfortunate" name comes strictly from how English chooses to translate the idea. Examples are: *Se robó mi carro* = *My car was stolen; Se hicieron varias preguntas* = *Several questions were asked; Se nos alimentó bien* = *We were well fed.*

SEMANTICS: That field of linguistic study concerned mainly with how words, phrases, etc. derive their meaning. Idiomatic usages (eg., *nothing at all*) are of interest, as well as slang and meaning change occurring over time.

SEMI-CLOSE VOWELS (MID-VOWELS): By definition, the Spanish vowels [e] and [o] in whose production the level of the tongue reaches a level mid-way between the tongue's surface and the roof of the mouth, the palate.

SEQUENCE/CORRESPONDENCE OF TENSES: Applicable more to Spanish than to English, it involves the time relationships between the events described by the verbs in **main clauses** and those in **subordinate clauses**. It is governed by norms which, in either present or past time sequences, describe how verbal forms in subordinate clauses express times prior to, simultaneous with or subsequent to time expressed in the main clause. Two parallel examples follow and in both, the subordinate verb expresses a time subsequent to that of the main verb: *Nuestros padres <u>esperaban</u> que <u>nos divirtiéramos</u> en la playa; Nuestros padres <u>esperan</u> que <u>nos divirtamos</u> en la playa.*

SER **PASSIVE:** A type of passive sentence which, like all passives, has the **subject** of the sentence and the **object** as the same entity. Its English formation is, **subject** + form of *to be,* + **past participle** (*The packages will be sent tomorrow*). The Spanish version is virtually identical: **subject** + form of *ser* (never *estar*) + **past participle** *(Los paquetes serán enviados mañana).* The actual doer of the action **(the agent)** may be only implied, as in the examples, but if expressed, appears in a prepositional phrase (*by the manager/por el gerente*). The passive is not used in Spanish as much as in English. Spanish will use the active voice where the passive agent becomes the active subject (*El gerente va a enviar los paquetes mañana*).

SIBILANT: Any one of a number of sounds accompanied by an audible hissing. The sounds [s] and [z] are examples.

STATIVE VERB: Any verb which, rather than expressing an action, denotes a state of being (*ser~estar/to be*), possession (*tener/to have*), mental state (*querer*/to want), ability (*poder*/to be able) or the like.

STEM (See: ROOT; RADICAL)

STEM-CHANGING VERB (See RADICALLY-CHANGING VERB)

STRONG PAST PARTICIPLE: An alternate Spanish **past participial** form differing from the regular form in *–do* by the fact that it is stressed on its *root*. Traditionally, *elegido* had as its strong alternate, *electo*, and *absorbido* had *absorto*. The regular, unstressed (**weak**) form was usually found as a verb (*Han elegido a un Papa nuevo*), while the strong form occurred as an **adjective** (*Es el Papa electo*). The Academy states that in the present-day language only three verbs have dual past participles and that for each, the forms may be used interchangeably as verbs or as adjectives. These three verbs are, *imprimir* (*imprimido/impreso*), *freír* (*freído/frito*) and *proveer* (*proveído/provisto*).

STRONG PRETERITE: A sizeable group of Spanish verbs whose **first** and **third person, singular** forms in the **preterite** are stressed on the **root (rhizotonic)**, not the ending. In the examples the underline shows that vocal stress falls on the root in each form: *hic-e/hiz-o; pud-e/pud-o; traj-e/traj-o*. Not only are the roots of these verbs **irregular**, their endings are also. Compare *hablé/habló, viví/vivió* with the strong forms above.

SUBJECT: The Academy gives the following definition: *Función oracional desempeñada por un sustantivo, un pronombre o un sintagma nominal en concordancia obligada de persona y de número con el verbo*. In, *Es posible que no sepan lo que hicimos*, the underlined element is "*un sintagma nominal*." Another suitable definition is, A syntactic element usually seen as representing someone or something of which something is said or predicated and which includes the agent in a basic **transtitive** construction.

SUBJECT PRONOUN: A **paradigm** of **pronouns** representing the actor in the sentence. *I, you, he, she, it; we, they* discovered the treasure; *yo, tú, él, ella; nosotros-as, vosotros-as, ellos-as* + correct verbal form + sentence remainder. Note that the Spanish subject pronouns are usually omitted, except for purposes of emphasis, contrast, or clarification (*Ella se marcha, pero nosotros vamos a quedarnos en casa*).

SUBJUNCTIVE MOOD: One of the three **moods** of both languages—the others being **the indicative** and **the imperative**—and often showing that an action exists at the time only in the mind of the subject, not in his/her experienced reality (*Quiero que vengan bien preparados*). It may also express things that are doubted or denied (*No creo que vengan bien preparados*) or reacted to or commented upon (*Es una pena que no vengan bien preparados*). **Morphologically**, it occurs in Spanish as two **simple tenses**, the **present and past subjunctives** (*tenga* and *tuviera/tuviese*, respectively), and in **the perfect and progressive tenses**. In English, it is the **base (lexical) form** of the verb, and if negative, that form is preceded by *not* (*have/not have*). Subjunctive forms generally occur in **subordinate clauses**. Three Spanish sentence examples and one in English follow: *No quiero que ella tenga más hijos; Busco a una ayudante que no tenga hijos; Estaré feliz cuando mi hija tenga hijos*; The doctor recommends that she *have/not have* more children.

SUBORDINATE (DEPENDENT) CLAUSE: A **clause** connected to a **main clause**, but incomplete in its meaning without being subordinated (connected) to the main clause by a **subordinating conjunction** or **relative pronoun**. There are three basic types in each language: 1) **the subordinate noun clause** (They insist *that we leave at once* = *Insisten en que salgamos en seguida*), 2) **the subordinate adverbial clause** (I'll be at home *when you call* = *Estaré en casa cuando (tú) llames*) and 3) **the subordinate adjective clause** (We need someone *who knows Hebrew* = *Necesitamos a alguien que sepa hebreo*).

SUPERLATIVE DEGREE: The last **degree of comparison** of **adjectives** and **adverbs** (the first being the **positive degree** (*alto*/tall) and the second the **comparative degree** (*taller/más alto*), and denoting the highest degree or quality of the entity discussed with respect to all other entities in its class. The English forms add the suffix *–est*, while Spanish employs a phrase composed of, **definite article** + (**noun**) + *más/menos* + **a positive degree**

form **adjective** or **adverb**, (*the tallest (mountain)/la (montaña) más alta*). The **suppression** of the noun in such structures produces a **nominalization** (*the tallest one/la más alta*).

SUPPLETIVE FORM: A verbal form in no way resembling the infinitive from which it is derived. All present and past tense forms of English *to be* are suppletive (*am, are, is; was, were*), but the participles, *being* and *been*, are not. The Spanish preterite forms of *ir* and *ser*, which are identical, are suppletive (*fui, fuiste, fue*, etc.).

SUPPRESSION: Always taking place only in clear contexts, it is the elimination of an item to avoid **redundancy**. In these examples, **the noun** can be suppressed, and a **nominalization** results: *el estudiante más listo/the smartest student > el más listo/the smartest one*. Unlike Spanish, English routinely uses the device with **verbs:** *I know she has once or twice, but I never thought she would again.* The verb, whatever is might be, has been suppressed, but is implied by the **auxiliaries**.

SYNTAX: That division of linguistic science concerned with the order of the elements composing an utterance and the relationships between those elements. Compared with English, Spanish has a flexible syntax, meaning that Spanish has more options than does English for arranging words in its sentences. For example, Spanish can say, *Juan vendió la casa, Vendió la casa Juan, La casa, la vendió Juan*, etc. Syntactically speaking, English always places its **object(ive) pronouns** after the verb (*Her parents raised her well*), while Spanish, with exceptions governed by syntactical rules, places such pronouns before the verb: *La criaron bien sus padres.*

SYNTHETIC FUTURE/CONDITIONAL: The Spanish formation of the **future** and **conditional tenses** through the fusion of words, a process that occurred over time. In Old Spanish, the future was expressed **periphrastically** by using the **present** of *haber + de + infinitive, hemos de ganar*. Over time, the forms of *haber* became **postposed** to the **infinitive**, producing the synthesis, *ganaremos*. Likewise with the conditional: the **imperfect** of *haber + de + infinitive* (*habíamos de ganar > ganaríamos*). In the modern language, both tenses can be rendered **synthetically** (*ganaremos/ganaríamos*) or **periphrastically** (*vamos a ganar/íbamos a ganar*).

TELICITY: A semantic feature of **lexical** aspect focusing on whether events have concrete or abstract beginnings and endings. With telic events, the initial and final points are concrete (*beber una cerveza*), while with atelic events, these points are abstract (*leer la Biblia*).

TEMPORAL: An **adverbial** usage referring to time, for example, *when/cuando, then/entonces, afterwards /después*, or a phrase so used, *at eight o'clock/a las ocho, around nine o'clock/a eso de/por las nueve*. Temporal adverbial constructions sometimes occur as conjunctions, subordinating one clause to another, eg., *No te voy a pagar hasta que termines el proyecto.*

TENSES: The linguistic expression of relative times through the use of various verbal forms designating and differentiating the basic **temporal** concepts of past, present, and future. English has a rather simple tense system, while Spanish uses a highly **inflected** one, with endings that communicate **person, number, aspect, tense,** and **mood.**

The Simple Tenses are expressed in a single word. English has two, the **present** (*see*) and the **past** (*saw*). Spanish has five, three in the **indicative,** the **present** (*veo*), the **preterite** (*vi*) and the **imperfect** (*veía*), and two in the **subjunctive**, the present (*vea*) and the **past** (*viera/-se*). Some authorities include the **future** (*veré*) and **conditional** (*vería*) among the simple tenses of the indicative.

The Compound Tenses: Unlike the simple tenses, which use but one word, compound tenses are composed of two or more. They are the **perfect tenses** (*have + past participle/haber + past participle*), the **progressive tenses** (*be + -ing/estar + -ndo*), and **the perfect progressive tenses** (*have + been + -ing/haber + estado + -ndo*). Examples of each follow: perfect tense: *They had left/habían salido;* progressive tense: *We will be travelling/Estaremos viajando;* perfect progressive tense: *I have been working/He estado trabajando.* The English **future and conditional** tenses are not included among the compound tenses since the **auxiliaries** *will/would* must occur with the **lexical verb** to form of these two-word tenses.

TERMINAL INTONATION (RISING/FALLING): In the oral rendition of any utterance, it is the rising or falling tone of voice which, especially in Spanish, distinguishes **yes/no questions** from **affirmative and negative statements**, there being no change in syntax. *Sabes* and *No sabes* (with falling intonation) are statements, but although in writing their question forms are marked ¿?, in speech a rising intonation accompanies them, *¿sabes?* , *¿No sabes?* in order that they be perceived audibly as questions.

TONIC VOWEL: The vowel in any word receiving more vocal stress than the other vowels. **Atonic vowels** are the unstressed vowels. The tonic vowels are underlined in these examples: *construcción, animal; construction, animal.*

TOPICALIZATION: A Spanish discourse device in which a **syntactical** arrangement of items placed at the front of the sentence causes those items to be the true topic of the sentence, i.e, what the sentence is about. The non-topicalized **indirect object** in, *Nunca les escribo a mis parientes* becomes topicalized in, *A mis parientes, nunca les escribo.*

TRANSITIVE: Traditionally, any verb in either language which can, because of its meaning, take a **direct object** (either **noun** or **pronoun**), for example, *to love/amar, to study/estudiar, to see/ver*. Sentence examples follow: *They love their professor = Aman a su professor; We study Russian = Estudiamos ruso; Nadie la quiere ver = Nobody wants to see her.*

TRUE PASSIVE: (See: *SER* PASSIVE)

UNIPERSONAL VERB: Spanish verbs generally referring to natural phenomena and therefore occurring only in the third person singular. Examples are, *tronar > truena, llover > llueve, atardecer > atardece.*

UNREAL COMPARISON: An expression introduced by...*como si* = ...*as If (though)* implying that what is said is not true or real, but occurs only as a point of comparison, for example, *Anda como si estuviera borracho = He walks as if (though) he were drunk.*

VELAR EXTENSION: A phonetic phenomenon affecting certain Spanish verbal forms of the **present indicative** and **present subjunctive** in which the sound [g] is appended to the **root** before endings are added. For example, the root *ten-* of *tener,* is extended through the addition of –g- before -o can be added to form the **first person singular present indicative** form (*tengo*) and all forms of the **present subjunctive** (*tenga, tengamos, tengan,* etc.)

VERBAL NOUNS: A Spanish **noun** derived from a **verb**. Most of these are masculine in gender, for example, *alcanzar > el alcance, cerrar > el cierre.* An older term is "postverbal."

VERBID (See: Non-Finite Verbal Forms)

VERIFICATION TAG: A language device by which one "tags" either an affirmative or negative statement, requesting the listener confirm or deny the veracity of the original utterance. The Spanish system is simple; *Tu hermano vivía en Barcelona, ¿no?/¿verdad?* The English structure is rather more complex, requiring the original noun to convert to a pronoun, the tag to be negative if the original sentence is affirmative (and the reverse), and recalling the verb through an **auxiliary**: *Your brother was living in Barcelona, wasn't he?*

VOICE: The term used for the potential choice speakers have to render thoughts either **actively** or **passively.** In **active voice** sentences, the **subject** performs the action on an entity (**object**) other than him/her/itself. *The waiter broke the plate = El mesero quebró el plato.* In the **passive voice** version, the grammatical subject and object become the same entity (*The plate was broken [by the waiter] = El plato fue quebrado [por el mesero]*). The real performer of the action may be only implied, or expressed in a prepositional phrase (in brackets) by a word called the **agent**.

VOICED CONSONANT: A consonant sound accompanied by an audible vibration of the vocal chords. Examples are, [b], [d], [g], [z].

VOICELESS CONSONANT: A consonant sound absent the vibration of the vocal chords. One perceives only a sound produced by air under pressure: [p], [t], [k], [s].

VOWEL RAISING: A phonetic change undergone by the semi-close vowels (mid vowels) [e] and [o] when the tongue rises in the mouth to such a degree as to change the quality of the vowel into the close vowels (high vowels), [i] and [u], respectively. Another root of *mentir* is *mint-* where the vowel *-e-* is raised to *-i-*. Likewise, in *dormir*, the root *dorm-* can "morph" into *durm-* through the vowel raising process.

WEAK PAST PARTICIPLE: Any Spanish **past participle** regularly formed through the addition of *-do* to the **root**: *hablado, comido, vivido*.

WEAK PRETERITE: Spanish **regular preterite** verbal forms always stressed on their endings: *hablé, com-iste, viv-ió, sent-imos, abr-isteis, trat-aron*.

YES/NO **QUESTION:** A question, affirmative or negative, answerable with a simple *yes/sí* or *no/no*, for example: *Do you/Don't you know her name?* = *¿Sabes /¿No sabes/ su nombre?*

Y-EXTENSION (YOD EXTENSION); -*UIR* VERBS: Spanish verbs ending in *–uir* insert *–y-* between the **root** and certain endings, for example, *incluyo, incluyes, incluya, incluyan, incluyendo*. However, the *–y-* occurring in many forms of verbs ending in a vowel + *-er* or *-ir* (*leer/oír*), for example, *leyeron, leyendo; oyó, oyera* is not yod extension. It is simply the application of a Spanish orthographic rule stating that an unaccented *–i-* between vowels must be written as *–y-* (**le-ió > leyó; *o-ieron > oyeron*).

Bibliography

Academia mexicana de la lengua. *Web.* 24 Nov. 2012. http:/www.academia.org.ma/index2.php
Alcina Franch, Juan and José Manuel Blecua. *Gramática española*. 8th. Barcelona: Editorial Ariel, S.A., 1991.
Alonso, Amado. *Estudios lingüísticos; temas hispanoamericanos*. 3rd. Madrid: Gredos, 1967.
Azevedo, Milton M. *Introducción a la lingüística española*. Englewood Cliffs, NJ: Prentice Hall, 1992.
Ballesteros, S. *Manual práctico de ortografía, redacción y gramática*. México: Editores Mexicanos Unidos, 1978.
Bello, Andés and Rufino Cuervo. *Gramática de la lengua castellana*. Buenos Aires: Editorial Sopen Argentina, 1958.
Besser, Pam. *A Basic Handbook of Writing Skills*. Mountain View, CA: Mayfield Publishing Co., 1994.
Bolinger, Dwight. *English Prosodic Stress and Spanish Sentence Order*. Vol. 37. Hispania, 1954.
Bull, William E. *Spanish for Teachers: Applied Linguistics*. New York, NY: The Ronald Press, 1965.
—. *The Visual Grammar of Spanish*. Berkeley, CA: Regents of the University of California and Houghton Mifflin, 1972.
—. *Time, Tense and the Verb*. Berkeley, CA: University of California Press,1968.
Butt, John and Carmen Benjamin. *A New Reference Grammar of Modern Spanish* New York, NY: McGraw-Hill, 2004.
Casares, Ángel L. and Marshal Morris, *El tapiz por el revés*. San Juan, PR: Academia Puertorriqueña de la lengua Española, 1986.
Celce-Murcia, Marianne and Elite Olshtain. *Discourse and Context in Language Teaching: A Guide for Language Teachers*. New York, NY: Cambridge University Press, 2000.
Collins Spanish Dictionary. 4th ed. London: Collins, 1999.
Corder, S. P. *The Significance of Learners' Errors*. Vol. 5. International Review of Applied Linguistics, 1967.
Cotton, Eleanor Greet, and John M. Sharp. *Spanish in the Americas*. Washington, D.C. Georgetown University Press, 1988.
Diccionario básico del español de México. México, D.F.: El Colegio de México, 1986.
Diccionario México. Tercera edición, nueva versión. México, D.F.: Herrero Hermanos Sucs., S.A., 1994.
Fowler, H. Ramsey, Jane E. Aaron and Kay Limburg. *The Little, Brown Handbook*. 5th. ed. New York, NY: Harper Collins, 1992.
Fuentes, Juan Luis. *Ortografía, reglas y ejercicios*. México, D.F.: Ediciones Larousse S.A. de C.V., 1988.
García-Pelayo y Gross, Ramón and Micheline Durand. *Larousse de la conjugación*. México, D.F.: Ediciones Larousse, 1982.
Gili Gaya, Samuel. *Curso superior de sintaxis española*. 3ra edición. Barcelona: Bibliograf, S.A., 1980.
Gordon, Ronni and David Stillman. *The Ultimate Spanish Review and Practice with CD-ROM*. Ultimate Review and Reference Series, Amazon.com, 2005.
Hacker, Diana. *The Bedford Handbook for Writers*. Boston, MA: Bedford Books of St. Martin's Press, 1991.
Heffernan, James A.W. and John E. Lincoln. *Writing, A College Handbook*. 4th edition. New York, NY: W.W. Morton & Co., 1994.
Hill, Sam. *Contrastive English-Spanish Grammatical Structures*. Lanham, MD: University Press of America, 1985.
Hill, Sam, and William P. Bradford. *Bilingual Grammar of English-Spanish Syntax, A Manual with Exercises*. Lanham, MD: University Press of America, 1991.
—. *Bilingual Grammar of English-Spanish Syntax, Revised Edition*. Lanham (New York, Oxford), MD: University Press of America, 2000.
Hodges, John C., Winifred Bryan Horner, Susanne Strobeck Webb and Robert Keith Miller. *Harbrace College Handbook*. 12th ed. Fort Worth, TX: Harcourt, 1994.
Kenyon, John S. and Thomas A. Knott. *A Pronouncing Dictionary of American English*. Springfield, MA: G & C Merriam Co.

King, Larry D. and Margarita Suñer. *Gramática española: Análisis lingüístico y práctica*. 3rd ed. New York, NY: McGraw-Hill, 2004.

Klein, Philip W. *Enfoque lingüístico al idioma español*. Nueva York, NY: Peter Lang, 1992.

Koike, D. *Transfer of Pragmatic Competence and Suggestions in Spanish Foreign Language Learning*. Speech Acts Across Cultures. Edited by Susan Gass and Joyce New. Berlin: Mouton de Gruyter, 1995.

Krashen, S. D. *The Input Hypotheses: Issues and Implications*. New York, NY: Longman, 1985.

Lado, Robert. *Linguistics Across Cultures*. Ann Arbor, MI: University of Michigan Press, 1957.

Larousse, Conjugación: lengua española, Larousse, México, 2007

Leech, Geoffrey, and Jan Svartvik. *A Communicative Grammar of English*. London: Longman Group Ltd., 1975.

Legget, Glenn, C. David Mead and Melinda G. Kramer. *Prentice Hall Handbook for Writers*. 11th ed. Englewood Cliffs, NJ: Prentice, 1991.

Long, Michael. *Focus on Form: A Design Feature in Language Teaching Methodology*. Foreign Language Research in Cross-Cultural Perspective. Edited by K. Bot, R. Ginsberg and C. Kramsch. Amsterdam: John Benjamins, 1991.

—. *The Role of the Linguistic Environment in Second Language Acquisition*. Handbook of Second Language Acquisition. Edited by William Ritchie and Tej Bahtia. San Diego, CA: Academic Press, 1996.

Long, Ralph B. and Dorothy R. Long. *The System of English Grammar*. Glenview, IL: Scott, Foresman and Company, 1971.

Lunsford, Andrea and Robert Connors. *The St. Martin's Handbook*. 3rd. ed. NewYork, NY: St. Martin's, 1995.

Marcella, Frank. *Modern English*. Englewood Cliffs, NJ: Prentice-Hall, 1972.

Marchante Cueca, María Pilar. "Los adverbios de modalidad. Los adverbios de duda: *quizá(s), tal vez, a lo mejor.*" RedEle 4 Web. 18 Nov 2012. Prod. http://www.education .gob.es/dctm/redele/Material-RedEle/Revista/2005_04/2005_redEdELE_4_08Marchante.pdf?documentId=. 2005.

Marius, Richard and Harvey S. Wiener. *The McGraw-Hill College Handbook*. 4th ed. New York, NY: McGraw-Hill, 1994.

Martínez de Sousa, José. *Diccionario de ortografía*. Madrid: Ediciones Generales Anaya, 1985.

—. *Diccionario general del periodismo*. Madrid: Paraninfo, S.A., 1981.

Matthews, Peter. *The Concise Oxford Dictionary of Linguistics*. New York, NY: Oxford University Press, 1997.

Mayberry, M. *Mood selection in Temporal Clauses in Spanish: A Descriptive Analysis*. Unpublished Master's Report, University of Texas at Austin, 2000

McArthur, Tom and Beryl Atkins. *Dictionary of English Phrasal Verbs and their Idioms*. London and Glasgow: Collins, 1974.

Mejías-Bikandi, E. "Assertion and Speaker's Intention: A pragmatically Based Account of Mood in Spanish." *Hispania* 77 (1994): 892-902.

__. "Pragmatic Presupposition and Old Information in the Use of the Subjunctive Mood in Spanish." *Hispania* 81 (1998): 941-948.

Merriam Webster's Collegiate Dictionary. 10th ed. Springfield, MA: Merriam-Webster, 1994.

Moliner, María. *Diccionario del uso del español*. Madrid: Editorial Gredos, 1986.

Morales Pettorino, Felix *et al*. *Diccionario ejemplificado de chilenismos*. 2 vols. Valparaíso, 1984 y 1985.

Mulderig, Gerald P. and Elsbree Langdon. *The Heath Handbook of Composition*. 13th ed. Lexington, KY: Heath, 1995.

Nash, Rose, ed. *Readings in Spanish-English Contrastive Linguistics*. Vol. 1. San Juan, PR: Inter American University Press, 1973.

Nash, Rose, and Domitila Belaval, *Readings in Spanish-English Contrastive Linguistics*. Vol. 2. San Juan, PR: Inter American University Press, 1980.

__. *Readings in Spanish-English Contrastive Linguistics*. Vol. 3. San Juan, PR: Inter   American University Press, 1982.

Navas Jaén and Pilorge, P. Y. "Romancero y cancionero de Jaén." *BLO* 2 (2012): 129-151

Olsen, Michael. "The Complementizer Particle *si* in Guayaquileño Spanish." *Hispanic Linguistics Symposium, Bloomington IN, October 2010.*
Ortiz, Martha D. "El voseo en El Salvador." (MA Thesis, San Jose State University) 2000.
Parker, F. and K. Riley. *Linguistics for Non-Linguists: A Primer with Exercises.* Boston, MA: Allyn Bacon, 2005.
Quilis Morales, Antonio, Manuel Esgueva, María Luz Gutiérrez, and Pilar Ruiz-Va. *Gramática española.* 2da ed. Madrid: Editoral Centro de Estudios Ramón Areces, S.A., 1993.
Quirk, Randolph, Sidney Greenbaum, Geoffrey Leec and Jan Svartvik. *A Grammar of Contemporary English.* New York, NY: Harcourt Brace Jovanovich, Inc., 1972.
Real Academia Española and Asociación de Academias de la Lengua Española. *Nueva gramática de la lengua española.* 1st ed. in Print. 2010.
Real Academia Española. *Diccionario de la lengua española.* 21ra edición. Madrid: Espasa Calpe, S.A., 1992.
—. *Diccionario Panhispánico de Dudas.* 1st. ed. Web, 5 Jan. 2012.
—. *Esbozo de una nueva gramática de la lengua española.* Madrid: Espasa Calpe, 1979.
—. *Gramática de la lengua española.* Madrid: Espasa Calpe, S.A., 1931.
Rivera-Mills, Susana V. "Selected Proceedings of the 13th Hispanic Linguistics Symposium, Somerville, MA: Cascadilla Proceedings Projectwevill." Edited by Luis A Ortiz-López. 2011: 94-106.
Rivera Rubero, Pura A. *La comunicación en el contexto empresorial.* Hato Rey, PR: Publicaciones Puertorriqueñas, 1998.
Rivers, Wilga M., Milton M. Azevedo and William H. Heflin, Jr. *Teaching Spanish, A Practical Guide.* Lincolnwood, IL: National Textbook Co., 1989.
Rutten, N.C.M.A. *Inversión en oraciones interrogativas españolas.* Utrecht University, MA Thesis, 1995.
Santamaría, Andrés, Augustino Cuartas, Joaquín Mangada and José Martínez de Sousa. *Diccionario de incorrecciones, peculiaridades y curiosidades del lenguaje.* Madrid: Paraninfo, S.A., 1987.
Santamaría, Francisco J. *Diccionario de mejicanismos.* México: Porrúa, 1978.
Schmidt, R. *The Role of Consciousness in Second Language Learning.* Vol. 11. Applied Linguistics, 1990.
Seco, Manuel. *Diccionario de dudas y dificultades de la lengua española.* Novena edición renovada. Madrid: Espasa Calpe, S.A., 1991.
—. *Gramática escencial del español.* Madrid: Espasa Calpe, S.A., 1986.
—. *Manual de gramática española.* 2 vols. Madrid: Aguilar, 1982.
Simon and Schuster's International Diccionary, English/Spanish, Spanish/English. New York, NY: Macmillan.
Slabakova, Roumyana, Sylvia Motrul and Philippe Prévost. *Inquiries in Linguistic Development in Honor of Lydia White.* Philadelphia, PA: John Benjamins, 2006.
Solé, Yolanda R. and Carlos A. Solé. *Modern Spanish Syntax.* Lexington, KY: D.C. Heath, 1977.
Stockwell, Robert P., Donald Bowen and John W. Martin. *The Grammatical Structures of English and Spanish.* Chicago, IL: University of Chicago Press, 1965.
Terrell, Tracy and Maruxa Salgués de Cargill. *Lingüística aplicada a la enseñanza del español a angloparlantes.* New York, NY: John Wiley & Sons, 1979.
Teschner, Richard V. *Cubre: Curso breve de gramática española.* 2da edición. New York, NY: McGraw-Hill Companies, 1998.
The American Heritage Larousse Spanish Dictionary. Boston, MA: Houghton Mifflin Co., 1986.
Torrego, E. *On Inversion in Spanish and Some of its Effects.* Vols. 15, No. 1. Linguistic Inquiry, 1984.
Troyka, Lynn Quitman. *Simon and Schuster Handbook for Writers.* 3rd ed. Englewood Cliffs, NJ: Prentice, 1993.
Vendler, Zeno. "Verbs and Times." *The Philosophical Review* 66.2 (1957): 143-160.
Watkins, Floyd C. and William B. Dillingham. *Practical English Handbook.* 9th ed. Boston, MA: Houghton, 1992.
Webster's Unabridged Dictionary of the English Language. New York, NY: Gramercy Books, 1994.
Whitley, Stanley M. *Spanish/English Contrasts.* 2nd ed. Washington, DC: Georgetown University Press, 2002.

Zagona, K. "The Syntax of Spanish." (Cambridge University Press) 2002.
Zamora Vicente, Alonso. *Dialectología española*. 2da ed. Madrid: Gredos, 1979

Index

A
a little (See partitive)
a lot (of) (See partitive)
a, an indefinite articles (E/S) 19.14
absolute superlative (S) 25.4
accomplishments, lexical aspect (S) 6.6
accusative, personal
    confusion with indirect objects (S) 27.5
    definition of (S) 22.16
    for identification of a direct object (S) 27.5
    for personifications 22.17
    in pronominal reduplication (S) 22.18
    in verb + noun constructions (S) 18.7
    omission of (S) 22.17
    with *¿quién(es)?* (S) 22.16, 23.2
    with indefinite pronouns (S) 27.5
    with non-specific human entities (S) 27.5
    with personal relative pronouns (S) 22.16, 26.5-10
    with *querer* 22.17
    with *tener* 22.17
achievements, lexical aspect (S) 6.6
activities, lexical aspect (S) 6.6
adjective clauses, relative
    donde, (S) 26.5; (S/E) 26.12
    English adjective (relative) clauses (E) 26.14
    list of relative pronouns (S/E) 26.6
    non-restrictive clause, relative pronouns (E/S) 26.6-13
    relative pronouns (S/E) 26.2, 26.6-13
    restrictive vs non-restrictive (E/S) 26.5
adjective clauses, subordinate
    antecedent of (E/S) 7.3
    mood selection (E/S) 7.19-20
    sequence of tenses in (E/S) 7.15
adjectives
    admirative expressions (E/S) 23.5
    adverbial use of (E/S) 22.5
    agreement (gender/number) (S) 20.1
    apocopation of (S) 20.2
    as adverb (See adverbial use)
    classification in Spanish (S) 20.2-4
    composed of verb + preposition (E) 9.7
    gran(de) (S) 20.10
    in admirative expressions (E/S) 23.5-6
    in predicate (*ser/estar* +) (S/E) 10.4
    interrogative (S) 23.3
    number of forms (S/E) 20.1
    of nationality (S) 20.4
    past participle as (S) 4.15; 16.7-8
    phrasal-verbal (E) 9.7
    position of; English vs. Spanish (E/S) 20.5
    quantifying (See limiting adjectives) (S/E) 20.6
    verb + preposition formation (E) 9.7
    with *be/tener*; *make/dar* (S/E) 12.67
    with *ser* and *estar* (S/E) 10.4
adjectives, comparative forms
    absolute superlative (S) 25.4
    degrees (gradations) of comparison (E/S) 25.1
    English regular forms 25.2-3
    formation/morphology (E/S) 25.2
adjectives, demonstrative (E/S) 21.4
    English and Spanish sets (E/S) 21.4
    nominalization of (E/S) 21.5
adjectives, descriptive
    characteristics of (S/E) 20.7
    meaning change and positioning (E/S) 20.9
    position (in general) (S) 20.7
    pre-positioned with nouns (S) 20.8; (E) 20.5
adjectives, limiting (determiners) (S) 20.6
    characteristics (S) 20.6
    position (S) 20.6
adjectives, nominalization of (S/E) 20.11
    abstract, *lo* + adjective (S/E) 20.12
    English reference (E) 20.11
    English, *one(s)* (E) 20.11
adjectives, possessive (E/S) 21.1
    ambiguity resolution in (S) 21.2
    inter-lingual difficulties with (S/E) 21.2
    stressed and unstressed forms (S) 21.2
adverbial clauses
    adverb of extent (S) 7.26
    adverbial clause defined (E/S) 7.4
    adverbials always + subjunctive (S) 7.21
    adverbs of concession (S) 7.23
    adverbs of manner (S) 7.24
    adverbs of time (S) 7.22
    donde (S) 7.25
    mood selection in (E/S) 7.21-7.26
    sequence of tenses in (E/S) 7.1
    subordination of (E/S) 26.2, 26.4
adverbs
    abstract nominalization with *lo* (S/E) 20.12
    accompaniment (E/S) 22.14
    adjectives used as (E/S) 22.5
    admirative, *lo/qué* + (S) 23.6

affirmative/negative (E/S) 27.2
algo 27.5
as coordinating conjunctions (S/E) 26.1
as subordinating conjunctions (E/S) 26.2, 26.4
comparative forms (See adjectives)
compound temporal adverbs (E/S) 27.5
con, de = with 22.13
English idioms, *in, on, at* 22.11
formation of (E/S) 22.4
in correlative constructions (E/S) 25.9
lo + adverb (E/S) 20.12
of manner with *alguno/ninguno* (E/S) 27.5
of time (temporal) (E/S) 22.9
pero vs. *sino (que)/but* (E/S) 26.1
superlative forms (See adjectives)
temporal (of time) (E/S) 27.2
 de, por = in 22.12
adverbs of location (locative)
at = en 22.9
in = en 22.7
in, on, at, to vs. *en* 22.6
location phrase (E) vs. clause (S) 22.14
on = en 22.8
to = en 22.10
adverbs vs. prepositions
differing usages (E/S) 22.3
identical usages (E/S) 22.2
list of (E/S) 22.1
affirmative and negative words (see chapter 27)
grammatical functions (E/S) 27.1
references (E/S) 27.2
rules for negation (S) 27.3; (E) 27.4
agent (in passives) (S/E) 16.5
agreement (gender and number) (See adjectives and articles)
agreement (subject/verb) (E) 2.1-3; (S) 3.1
al + INF (E/S) 15.2
algunos/-as (E/S) 27.5
allomorph (E) 2.7; (S) 4.1
ambiguity
avoidance of (S/E) 11.13
in passives (S/E)) 16.8
with indirect object pronouns (S/E) 11.10
with *se* as an indirect object (S/E) 11.11
andar + *-ndo* (S) 3.5
antecedent
lo as (S) 7.20
of adjective clause (E/S) 7.3, 7.19
apodosis (E/S) 17.1
apposition (E/S) 19.12
aquel vs. *ese* (See demonstratives)

articles, definite
different usages of (E/S) 19.12
identical usage of (E/S) 19.11
in nominalizations (E/S) 20.11-12
phonetics of *the* (E) 19.10
with possessions/bodily parts (S/E) 19.12-13
articles, indefinite (E/S) 19.14
English allomorphs of (E) 19.14
English, *some* (E) 19.14
neuter *lo* (S) 19.10, 20.12, 23.6
with nouns of nationality/profession (E/S) 19.14
as ... as (See comparison of equality)
as if /as though (See unreal comparison)
aspect
aspect in English 6.1
aspect; grammatical vs. lexical (E/S) 6.1
aspect; point of view (S) 6.1
lexical vs. aspectual contrasts (E/S) 6.7
past time; preterite/imperfect (S) 6.1
asterisk, use (See Introduction)
at (locative preposition) (E/S) 22.9, 22.11
auxiliary verbs
contraction of (E) 2.5, 24.3
general description (E) 2.5
modals auxiliaries (*See* that heading)
primary (non-modal) auxiliaries (E) 2.5

B
be
as aux. & non-aux. (E) 2.5
irregular forms (E) 2.4
subjunctive (E) 2.4; 7.4
with *-ing* (E) 2.4, 3.5; (E/S) 15.1
British spelling (E) 2.6
British usages (E) 5.10, 8.22, 11.12, 23.11

C
can (See modal auxiliaries)
clause (see adjective, adverbial and noun).
identification clause vs. phrase (E/S) 22.14
location clause vs. phrase (E/S) 22.14
subordinate/dependent (E/S) 7.1
cognates 9.4
commands (*See* imperatives)
como si (S/E) 17.4
comparative forms
comparative degree forms (E/S) 25.2-3
positive degree forms (E/S) 25.1-2
superlative degree forms (E/S) 25.3
comparison of equality (S) 25.8

expressing only extent (E/S) 25.8
    with adjectives/adverbs (E/S) 25.8
    with/without nouns (E/S) 25.8
comparison of inequality (E/S) 25.5
    connectives with clauses (S) 25.5
    prepositions *de/que* in (S) 25.5
comparison, superlative degree (E/S) 25.1
    adjective phrase in (E/S) 25.6
    adjective position in (E/S) 25.6
    in/on vs. *de* (E/S) 26.6
    nominalization in (S) 25.3; (E/S) 25.3, 25.6
    of two entities (E) 25.6
    with modified adverbs (E/S) 25.7
complements (S/E)
    adverbial 1.3
    direct object 1.3
    indirect object 1.3
    prepositional 1.3
complex sentence (S/E) 26.1
composite verbs (S) 4.8-9
compound adjectives (E) 9.7
compound nouns (E) 9.8
compound sentences (E/S) 26.1
con > *conmigo,* etc. (S) 11.3
conditional sentences
    components of (E/S) 17.1, 17.3
    contrary-to-fact past (E/S) 17.3
    contrary-to-fact present (E/S) 17.3
    hypothetical future (E/S) 17.3
    neutral conditionals (E/S) 17.2
conditional tense
    formation (S) 4.13
    future to past time (S/E) 7.18
    past probability (S) 5.5, 8.10-11
    substitute for *-ra* form (S) 17.3
conjunctions
    coordinating (E/S) 26.1
    for adjective clauses (E/S) 26.2
    for adverbial clauses (E/S) 26.2
    for noun clauses (E/S) 26.2
    pero vs. *sino* (S) 26.1
    subordinating (E/S) 26.2
conjunctive pronouns (E/S) 11.1
    positioning (E/S) 11.4-5
connectors (See Chapter 18)
consonant substitution (in verbs) (S) 4.8-11
continuous aspect (See progressive)
contractions, English
    mandatory (E) 5.10, 23.11
    optional (E) 5.2-4, 5.8
    problematic (E) 24.4

    restrictions (E) 24.2
contractions, in general
    classifications of (E) 24.3
    English 24.2
    Spanish 24.1
correlative constructions (E/S) 25.9
correspondence/sequence of tenses (S) 7.15-18
could (E/S) 8.6-8; 8.12; 8.20
count nouns (E/S) 19.20
cual(es), relative clauses (S/E) 26.9
cuyo/-a, -os, -as (E/S) 26.13

D

dar + noun constructions (S/E) 12.7
dative (*See* involved entity) (E/S) 11.10
de
    pariphrastic possession (S) 19.15
    preposition of possession (S) 19.15
deber vs. *deber de* (S/E) 8.9
declarative (affirmative) sentences (E/S) 5.2-5, 5.7
defective verbs (E/S) 4.16
definite article (*See* articles)
demonstratives (See adjectives/pronouns)
    adjectives (E/S) 21.4
    pronouns (E/S) 21.5
description, past (E) 6.2
descriptive adjectives (*See* adjectives)
determiners (*See* adjectives, limiting)
diphthongization, in verbs (S) 4.2-4
direct object (*See* complements)
    conjunctive pronouns (S/E) 11.4-8; (S) 11.11
    personal (See accusative)
    pronominal reduplication of (S) 11.14
do (primary aux.) (E) 2.5, 5.3-4, 23.7, 23.11
double negatives (E/S) 27.3
durative aspect (S) 6.5-6
dynamism, lexical aspect (S) 6.6

E

each other (E/S) 13.13
el cual (See *cual*) (S/E) 26.10
ellipsis
    in compound sentences (E) 23.8
    in response, yes-no questions (E/S) 23.7
    of infinitive (E/S) 23.9
ello/eso (S) 11.3
emphasis
    prepositional object pronouns (S) 11.11-14
    pronominal reduplication (S) 11.14
    pronouns with reflexive verbs (E) 13.6
    sentences with (S) 11.14

word order expressing (S/E) 1.6
en = English *in, on, at, to* (S/E) 22.6-10
ese vs. *aquel* (S/E) 21.4-5
estar
    estar/ser + predicate adjective (S/E) 10.4
    exclusive uses of (S/E) 10.3
    expressing perfective aspect (S) 10.1
    in interrogative structures (S/E) 10.5
    passive (S) 10.1; (S/E) 16.7-8
    uses shared with *ser* (S/E) 10.1
    with predicate adjectives (S/E) 10.4
este (S/E) 21.4-5
existential *haber* = *there...to be* (E/S) 10.6-8

F

faltar/hacerle falta a uno (S/E) 12.1-3
few (E/S) 19.21
finite verbs (*See* verb conjugations) (S) 3.2
for (See por vs para) (S/E) 22.20-21
formal vs. familiar (S) 11.2
future
    hypothetical (S/E) 17.3
    of probability (S) 5.5; (S/E) 8.10-11
    perfect (S/E) 3.4
    present progressive as (E/S) 15.1
    reference in adverb clauses (E/S) 7.22

G

gender
    adjectives, (S) 20.1-4
    articles (S) 19.10; 19.14
    nouns (see nouns)
    personal pronouns (S/E) 11.2-3, 11.6-8
    pronouns (S) 21.3; 21.5; 27.5
Germanic language (E) 1.1
gerund/present participle (E) 2.4-5; (S) 3.5-6, 4.15;
    (E/S) 5.1, 5.3-5, 15.1-7
get (E/S) 13.9
grammatical nomenclature (E/S) 3.9, Appendix II,
    Glossary
gustar (S/E) 12.1-3
    English literal translations of (S/E) 12.1
    English normal translations of (S/E) 12.2
    list of *gustar*-like verbs (S/E) 12.1
    pronominal reduplication in (S) 12.3
    structural analysis (S/E) 12.3
    syntactic structures with (S/E) 12.1-3

H

haber
    auxiliary, primary (S) 3.4-5
    existential *haber* = *there...to be* (E/S) 10.6-8
    obligation (S/E) 8.23-4
habitual events, past (E) 6.2
hacer
    for time duration (S/E) 12.4
    in weather expressions (S/E) 12.5
have
    auxiliary, primary (E) 2.5; (E/S) 8.22, 23.10-11
hay vs. *there is/are* (S/E) 10.8
how (admirative) (E/S) 23.5-6

I

if clauses (hypothesis) (E/S) 17.1
imperatives (See Chapter 14)
    affirmative, attenuated (E) 14.2-3; (S) 14.4
    affirmative, direct (E) 14.2-3; (S) 14.6
    conjunctive pronoun position with (S) 14.7
    in general, direct & softened (E/S) 14.1
    indirect (E) 14.8; (S) 14.9
    negative, attenuated (E) 14.2-3; (S) 14.4
    negative, direct (E) 14.2-3; (S) 14.6
    requests and criticisms (S) 14.5
imperfect indicative
    description of (S) 6.2
    in contrary-to-fact present conditionals (S)
        17.3
    requests and criticisms (S) 14.5
    vs. preterite, contrast (S/E) 6.1-2, 6.4
imperfect subjunctive (See past subjunctive)
impersonal constructions
    general (E/S) 13.14-15
    obligation (S/E) 8.24
    reflexive (E/S) 13.16
    se in unplanned occurrences (S/E) 13.17
implied subjects (See null subjects)
in (E) 22.2; 22.11
indefinite pronoun (S/E) 27.1-2, 27.5
indefinite subject (E/S) 13.14-15
indicative mood (S) 3.1, 3.3-5, 7.5-6, 7.11-13
indirect object (*See* complements) (E/S) 1.3
infinitive (S) 3.2
    dependent (S) 11.4
    nominal form (E/S) 15.4
    perceived actions (E/S) 15.6
    substitute for subjunctive (S) 7.7
    verbs taking vs. *-ing* (E) 15.3
inflection (S) 3.2, 19.10, 19.14, 20.1-4, 21.1, 21.4
intensifiers (E/S) 13.6; (S) 11.13
interrogatives
    ¿*(a)quién(es)?* vs. *who(m)?* (E/S) 23.1-2
    ¿*cuál?* vs. ¿*qué?* (S/E) 23.3-4

Index

in content question (E/S) 5.2-5, 5.11
integrated vs. separable (S/E) 23.1
intonation (yes-no questions) (E/S) 5.6, 5.9-10
yes-no questions, affirmative (E/S) 5.2, 5.9
yes-no questions, negative (E/S) 5.2, 5.10
involved entity (S/E) 11.10
-ísimo absolute superlative (S) 25.4
it (E/S) 11.2-3, 11.6-8
its vs. *it's* (E) 24.4

K
know how = *saber* (E/S) 8.5-6

L
Latin (S) 1.1
leísmo (S) 11.8
less vs. *fewer* (E) 19.21
less, the (E/S) 25.9
lexical verb (base form) (E) 2.1
little, a (E/S) 19.21
lo (article) (S) 19.10; (S/E) 20.12
lo + ADJ/ADV
    admirative (S/E) 23.6
    nominalization (S/E) 20.12
lo cual (S/E) 26.11
lo que (S/E) 7.20
location/locative
    phrases vs. clauses (E/S) 22.14
    prepositions of (E/S) 22.6-10
loísmo (S) 11.7-8

M
main clause verbs (governing noun clauses)
    of belief/knowledge (S) 7.6, 7.11
    of comment/reaction (S) 7.6, 7.10
    of communication (S) 7.6, 7.12
    of doubt/denial (S) 7.6, 7.9
    of influence/volition (S/E) 7.6-8
    of perception/sensation (S) 7.6, 7.13
many (E/S) 19.21
más (comparative) (S) 25.2-3
más de/que (S) 25.5
mass/non-count nouns (E/S) 19.20-21
may (E/S) 8.7, 8.12-13, 8.15
mayor (S) 25.2-3
mejor (S) 25.2-3
menor (comparative) (S) 25.2-3
might (E/S) 8.12-13
mismo, -a, -os, -as/-self
    as intensifiers (S) 13.6
    with reflexive pronouns (E) 13.6

modal auxiliaries, English (by meaning) (E/S) 8.3
    ability, physical and/or mental 8.4-6
    conjecture/probability (8.10-11)
    determination/refusal (8.16)
    inevitability (8.18)
    obligation, 8.20-22
    opinion, solicitation of (8.19)
    permission (8.7)
    possibility (8.12-13)
    repeated/habitual actions (8.17)
    requests (8.8)
    supposition (8.14)
    wishes (8.15)
modal auxiliaries, English (general)
    listing (E) 2.5
    multiple meanings (E) 8.1
    syntax of (E) 8.1-2
    vs. primary auxiliaries (E) 8.1
modal auxiliaries, Spanish
    compared with English (8.1)
    deber vs. *deber de* (8.9)
    doubt/possibility (non-verbal) (E/S) 7.9, 8.13
    future/conditional, probability (E/S) 5.5, 8.11
    obligation, impersonal (8.24)
    obligation, personal (8.23)
    poder vs. *saber* (E/S) 8.5-6
mood (S) 3,1; (See indicative; subjunctive)
    adjective clauses (S) 7.19-20
    adverbial clauses (S) 7.22-26
    decir, insistir, sentir + noun clause (S) 7.14
    either mood (S) 7.5
    indicative tenses, dependent clauses (S) 7.5
    noun clauses, research on (S) 7.5
    reflecting futurity (S) 7.5
    simple tenses, subjunctive (S) 7.5
    subjunctive tenses, dependent clauses (S) 7.5
more (comparative) (E) 25.2; (S/E) 25.5
more, the (E/S) 25.9
morpheme (S) 3.2
much (E/S) 19.21
mucho/-a (E/S) 19.21
muchos/-as (E/S) 19.21
must (E/S) 8.10-11, 8.18, 8.22

N
negated antecedent (S) 7.19
negation, rules for (E) 27.4; (S) 27.3
negative question (E/S) 5.2, 5.5
neither ... nor (E/S) 27.2; (E) 23.8
    nor (in negative ellipsis) (E) 23.8
ningún/ninguno (S/E) 27.2, 27.5

no one/nothing (E/S) 27.2
nominalization
    lo used in (S/E) 20.12
    of adjectives (S/E) 20.11
    of demonstratives (E/S) 21.5
    of possessives (S/E) 21.1, 21.3
    of relative pronouns (S/E) 26.10-11
    of verbs (E/S) 15.4
non-finite verb (S) 3.2
non-personal verb (S) 4.16
not
    in British tags 23.11
    in English contractions 24.3
    in statements/questions (E/S) 5.2-5, 5.8, 5.11
noun clauses (S)
noun, count vs. non-count (E/S) 19.20
noun, infinitive as (E/S) 15.4
noun, phrasal-verbal (E) 9.8
nouns, gender
    artificial gender (S) 19.4
    epicene gender (S) 19.5
    gender categories 19.2
    homophonic nouns (S/E) 19.6
    in general (E/S) 19.1
    natural gender (E/S) 19.3
    phonetic factors in (S) 19.7
nouns, number (E/S) 19.8
null (implied) subject (S) 1.4
number
    adjectives (S) 20.1-4
    articles (E/S) 19.10, 19.14
    nouns (See nouns, number)
    personal pronouns (S/E) 11.2-3, 11.6-12

O
object
    direct (S) 1.3, 11.4, 11.13-14; (S/E) 11.6-8
    indirect (S) 1.3, 11.4, 11.13-14; (S/E) 11.9-10; (E) 11.12
    indirect + direct (S) 11.11
    personal accusative (See accusative)
    prepositional (S) 11.1, 11.13-14; (S/E) 11.3
    reflexive (E/S) 11.3, 13.6, 13.8, 13.13
obligation (E) 8.20-22; (S) 8.9, 8.23-4
of (periphrastic possession) (E) 19.17
on (locative preposition) (E/S) 22.8, 22.11
one(s) (E) 13.14
ought (to) (E) 8.20

P
para vs por (See *por vs para*)

participle, past/perfect
    as adjective (S) 4.15
    as verb (S) 4.15
    in passive sentences (E) 16.2-3; (S) 16.5-16.8
    irregular (S) Appendix III
    vs. English present participle (S/E) 15.17
participle, present (gerund)
    adverbial usage of (S) 15.1
    as adjective (E) 15.5-7
    dependent (S) 11.4
    English verbs taking (E) 15.3
    in progressive tenses (S/E) 15.1
    of *ir* and *venir* (S/E) 15.1
    perceived actions (S/E) 15.6
    vs. Spanish adjective clause (E/S) 15.5
    vs. Spanish infinitive (S/E) 15.2
    vs. Spanish past participle (S/E) 15.7
particles (E) 9.2; (S) 13.9
partitive constructions (E/S) 19.20-21
    count and non-count nouns (E/S) 19.20
    English and Spanish systems (E/S) 19.21
parts of speech (See Glossary)
pasiva-refleja (See *se* passive)
passive voice: Chapter 16
    analysis (E/S) 16.1
    description of (E/S) 16.1
    English constructions (E) 16.23
    estar-passive (apparent passive) (S) 16.7-8
    frequency of passive structures (E/S) 16.4, 16.12
    indirect objects in passives (E) 16.3; (S) 16.11
    passive voice (E) vs. active voice (S) 16.12
    se-passive (S/E) 11.13, 16.9-11
    ser passive (actional "true" passive) (S/E) 16.5-6
    types of passive sentences (S) 16.4
past subjunctive (imperfect subjunctive)
    contrary-to-fact conditionals (S) 17.3
    requests and criticisms (S) 14.5
    sequence of tenses (S) 7.18
past, regular (E) 2.8
perceived actions (E/S) 15.6
perfect tenses, formation/uses (S/E) 3.4
periphrasis (S) 4.13; (S/E) 15.1
periphrastic possession (S) 19.15; (E) 19.17
permission, modal of (E/S) 8.7
personal accusative (See accusative)
phonic intensification (See vocal stress)
phrasal verbs
    adjectives based upon (E) 9.7
    contrastive analysis of (E/S) 9.6
    definition (E) 9.1-2

  nouns based upon (E) 9.8
  phrasal-prepositional verbs (E) 9.5
  Spanish speakers and (E/S) 9.4
  syntax of (E) 9.3
plural (*See* topic in Chapters 19, 20 and 21)
poco -a, -os, -as (S) 19.21
por vs. *para* (S/E) 22.19-21
por, idiomatic (S) 22.20
possession/possessives
  adjectives of (E/S) 21.1
  agreement differences (E/S) 21.2
  expression of (S) 19.14-15; (E) 19.16
  nominalization of (E/S) 19.18
  periphrastic (E) 19.17
  pronouns of (E/S) 21.3
  questions concerning (S) 19.15; (E) 19.17
  structures related to (E/S) 19.19
possibility/probability
  future/conditional of (S) 5.5, 8.11
  modals of (E/S) 8.10-12
pre-positioned adjectives (S) 20.6
predicate adjective (with *ser/estar*) (S/E) 10.4
predicate noun (with *ser*) (S) 10.1-2
predication, elements of (E/S) 1.1-3
prepositions
  con, de vs. *with* (S/E) 22.13
  de vs. *que* (S) 25.5
  de vs. *with/in* (identification) (S/E) 22.13
  de, por vs. *in* (S/E) 22.12
  English idioms with *in, on, at* 22.11
  in vs. *de, por* + time (E/S) 22.12
  in, on, at, to vs. *en* (E/S) 22.6-10
  in/on vs. *de*, superlatives (E/S) 26.6
  phrase vs. adjective clause, identification (E/S) 22.14
  phrase vs. adjective clause, location (E/S) 22.14
prepositional pronouns, (E/S) 11.1, 11.3
  repetition of (S/E) 22.15
  vs. adverbs (S/E) 22.1, 22.3
present indicative (S) 4.7-9
  future meaning (S) 15.1
  pronunciation, 3rd singular (E) 2.7
  vs. present progressive (S) 15.1
present participle (gerund/*-ndo*) (S) 4.15
  as adjective (E) 15.5
  vs. infinitive (E/S) 15.2
  with postures/positions (E) 15.7
  with verbs of perception (E/S) 15.6
present perfect (*pretérito perfecto*) (S) 3.4, 3.9
preterite tense

  description of (S) 6.3
  strong forms (S) 4.12
  weak forms (S) 3.3
preterite-imperfect contrast (S/E) 6.1
  grammatical aspect (S) 6.1-5
  lexical aspect (S) 6.1, 6.6-7
probability/possibility (See possibility/probability)
progressive aspect (S/E) 3.5
  imperfect vs preterite progressives (E/S) 6.5
  perfect progressives (S) 3.5
  present progressive, time reference (E/S) 15.1
progressive tenses (S) 3.5
pronouns
  classifications (E/S) 11.1
  conjunctive (position with verb) (S) 11.4; (E) 11.5
  conjunctive/"with-verb"/(en)clitic (S) 11.1, 11.14-15
  demonstrative (E/S) 21.5
  direct object (S/E) 11.6-8
  disjunctive (S) 11.1-3
  double objects (IO+DO) (S/E) 11.11-12
  in topicalization (S) 11.14
  indefinite (S/E) 27.1-2, 27.5
  indirect object (S/E) 11.1, 11.9-12
  indirect object, ambiguity in (S/E) 11.10-11
  indirect object, as "involved entity" (S/E) 11.10
  indirect object, English structures (E) 11.9, 11.12
  indirect object, with *gustar, etc.* (S) 12.1-3
  interrogative (E/S) 23.1-4
  it, Spanish equivalents (E/S) 11.2, 11.6-8
  object(ive) (E) 11.1
  possessive (E/S) 21.3
  prepositional objects (E/S) 11.1-3
  prepositional objects, in pronominal reduplication (S) 11.13
  prepositional objects, non-reflexive vs. reflexive forms (S/E) 11.3
  pronominal reflexive usages (S) 13.4
  pronominal usages (S) 11.4, 11.6-11
  relative (S) 26.6-13; (E) 26.14
  subject (S/E) 11.1-2
pronunciation rules
  English *–ed* (E) 2.8
  English final *–s* (E) 2.7, 19.9
protasis (E/S) 17.1
punctuality, lexical aspect (S) 6.6

Q

quantifier (S) 20.6; (E/S) 19.21
que
- *¡qué!* (admirative) (S/E) 23.5-6
- *¿qué?* vs. *¿cuál(es)?* (S/E) 23.3-4
- relative pronoun (S/E) 26.6-7
- subordinating conjunction (S) 26.2

querer (negative, preterite) (S/E) 6.7; (E/S) 8.16
questions (basic)
- content (E/S) 5.2, 5.11
- elliptical responses to (E) 23.7
- in admirative expression (E/S) 26.3
- yes-no, affirmative/negative (E/S) 5.2, 5.9-10

quien(es) (relative) (S/E) 26.8

R

radically-changing (stem-changing) verbs
- Class I (S) 4.3
- Class II (S) 4.4
- Class III rules (S) 4.5
- defined (S) 4.2
- two special cases (S) 4.6

reciprocal constructions & ambiguity (S/E) 13.13
redundant constructions (S) 11.11, 11.13
reduplication, pronominal (S) 11.13-14
- prepositional pronouns in (S) 11.13
- with D.O. nouns & pronouns (S) 11.13
- with I.O. nouns & pronouns (S) 11.11, 11.13

reflexive pronouns
- as D.O. (S/E) 13.4-5
- as I.O. (S/E) 13.4-5, 13.8
- as intensifiers (E) 13.6
- in unplanned occurrences (S) 13.17
- non-personal subject (S) 13.14
- passive substitute (S/E) 16.9-11

relative words
- between clauses (E/S) 26.6+
- suppression of (E/S) 26.2-3; (E) 26.14

repetition of events, past (E) 6.2
requests and criticisms (S/E) 14.5
Romance language (S) 1.1

S

saber vs. *poder* (S/E 8.5-6)
se
- causeless events (S/E) 13.16
- in unexpected occurrences (S) 13.17
- indefinite (non-personal subject) (S) 13.14
- passive substitute (S/E) 16.9-11
- reciprocal (S/E) 13.13
- reflexive pronoun (S/E) 13.4-5, 13.8
- substitute for indirect object *le(s)* (S) 11.11
- syntactic peculiarity of (S) 13.15

se-passive (passive *se*) (S) 16.9-11
seguir + *-ndo* (S) 3.5
self, -selves (E) 11.3; (E/S) 13.6
sentence
- constituents of (E/S) 1.2-3
- structural formulas and legend (E/S) 5.2-11
- verb phrase (E/S) 5.6
- verbal remainder (E/S) 5.6

sentence types
- affirmative statement (E/S) 5.2-7
- compound vs. complex (E/S) 26.1
- content question (E/S) 5.2-5.6, 5.11
- contraction, *aux* and *not* (E) 5.8
- emphatic (S/E) 1.6
- negative statement (E/S) 5.2-5.6, 5.8
- yes-no question, affirmative/negative (E/S) 5.2-5.6, 5.9-10

ser
- as a copula + predicate noun (S) 10.1
- in interrogative structures (S/E) 10.5
- with predicate adjectives (S/E) 10.4

ser/estar
- exclusive uses of each (S/E) 10.2-3
- passive (with past participle) (S) 10.1, (S) 16.5-6
- perfective/imperfective aspect (S) 10.1
- shared usages (S/E) 10.1
- with predicate adjectives (S/E) 10.4

shall/should (E/S) 8.19
should (E/S) 8.14, 8.20
si clauses (S/E) See Chapter 17
sí, prepositional pronoun (S/E) 11.3
statements, affirmative/negative (E/S) 5.2-8
states, lexical aspect (S) 6.6
stem-changing verbs (See radically-changing verbs)
stress, word (S) 19.8
stressed/unstressed vowel (S) 4.2-6, 19.8
subject
- change of/no change of (S) 7.6
- indefinite (non-personal) (E/S) 13.14
- optional vs. mandatory (S/E) 11.2
- subject/verb inversion (S) 5.3

subjunctive
- as commands (S) 7.5
- forms, present/past (S) 3.6
- in adjective clauses (S) 7.19-20
- in adverbial clauses (S) 7.21-25
- in conditional sentences (S) 7.5; (S/E) 17.3
- in English 7.4, 7.8

    in noun clauses (S) 7.2, 7.6-10, 7.14
    in noun clauses, English equivalents 7.8
    in unreal comparison (S/E) 17.4
    infinitive as substitute for (S) 7.7
    sequence (correspondence) of tenses (S) 7.15-18
    use in subordinate clause (S/E) 7.1-4
superlative (E/S) 25.3
    absolute (E/S) 25.4

T
tag questions (S/E) 23.10-11
telicity, lexical aspect (S) 6.6
tener
    + noun constructions (S/E) 12.6
    model irregular verb (S) 4.17
    with personal accusative (S) 22.17
tenses (*See* individual listings)
    basic tenses of each family (E/S) 5.1
    definition of (S) 3.1
    families of (E/S) 5.1
    sequence (correspondence) of (S) 7.15-18
    terminology of (E/S) 3.9; Appendix II
that relative clause (E/S) 26.2, 26.14
theme morpheme (S) 3.2
there...to be (existential) (E/S) 10.6-8
these/those (E/S) 21.4-5
this/that (E/S) 21.4-5
time-duration with *hacer* (E/S) 12.4
tú/usted > *vosotros/ustedes* (S/E) 11.2
two-word verbs (phrasal verbs) (E/S) 9.1-6

U
un, uno/-a, unos/-as (S/E) 19.14
unreal comparison (S/E) 17.4
usted/tú (S/E) 11.2

V
velar-extension (in verbs) (S) 4,9
venir + *-ndo* (S) 3.5
verb + preposition constructions (S/E) 18.1-8
    verb + preposition + noun/pronoun
        constructions (S/E) 18.6-8
    verb + preposition + verb constructions (S/E)
        18.4-5
verbal nomenclature (S/E) 3.9; Appendix II
verbal periphrasis (S) 4.13; (S/E) 15.1
verbal system, observations (S) 3.6
verbs, English only (*See* verbs, English regular; irregular)
    composite (*See* phrasal verbs)
    morphology (E) 2.3-4

    multi-word (*See* phrasal verbs)
    number of forms (E) 2.1-4
    orthographic changes (E) 2.6
    phrasal (E) 9.1-9.4
    phrasal-prepositional (E) 9.5
    pronunciation of inflections (E) 2.7-8
    reflexive (E) 13.6-7
    two-part (*See* phrasal verbs)
    two-word (*See* phrasal verbs)
    with infinitive and/or present participle (E)
        15.3
verbs, in general
    auxiliary (*See* auxiliary verbs)
    comparison of systems (E) 2.1; (S) 3.1
    English, irregular (E) 2.3-4, Appendix I
    English, regular (E) 2.2
    intransitive (S/E) 13.1
    nominalization of (S/E) 15.4
    number in (S) 3.1
    pronominal usages (S) 13.3
    Spanish, irregular (S) Chapter 4; Appendix III
    Spanish, regular (S) 3.2-5
    terminology (E/S) 3.9; Appendix II
    transitive, with animate or inanimate DO
        (S/E) 13.2
    verb phrase (E/S) 5.6
    verbal remainder (E/S) 5.6
verbs, reflexive ("truly" pronominal) (S) 13.4
    change of meaning (S/E) 13.11
    exclusively pronominal (S/E) 13.12
    of "inner life"/change of state (S/E) 13.9
    of motion (S/E) 13.10
    of observable actions (S/E) 13.5
    reflexive pronouns (S/E) 13.6
    Spanish/English correspondence (E/S) 13.7
    with direct and indirect objects (S) 13.5
    with reflexive and non-reflexive objects (S)
        13.5
    with Spanish indirect objects (E/S) 13.8
verbs, Spanish only (*See* Spanish regular; irregular)
    consonant substitution (S) 4.8
    defective (S/E) 4.6
    future/conditional irregularities (S) 4.13
    gustar and related verbs (S/E) 12.1-3
    imperfect-preterite contrast (*See* Chapter 6)
    inceptive (inchoative) reflexive (S/E) 13.9
    morphemes of (S) 3.2-3
    motion/attraction (S) 18.4
    non-finite forms (S) 3.2
    number of forms (S) 3.2

orthographic changes in (S) 3.7-8
past participles (S) 4.15
reflexive pronominal (S/E) 13.4-5, 13.8-11
strong (irregular) preterite (S) 4.12
suppletive forms (E) 2.4; (S) 4.14
tenses; simple, perfect, progressive (S) 3.3-5
uni-personal/non-personal (S/E) 4.16
velar extension (S) 4.9
vowel changes in radical/root/stem (S) 4.2-6
y-extension (S) 4.10-11
verification tags (S) 23.10; (E) 23.11
verification tags (See: tag questions)
vocal stress (E/S) 1.6; (S) 4.2-6
volition/influence (S/E) 7.7-8
vos (S) 3.1
vosotros/vosotras vs. *ustedes* (S) 3.1
vowel diphthongization (S) 4.2-4, 4.6
vowel raising (S) 4.5

W

weather expressions (E/S) 12.5
what (a) admirative (E) 23.5
what/which
    interrogative (E/S) 23.3-4
    relative (E/S) 26.14
who/whom
    interrogative (E/S) 23.1-2
    relative (E/S) 26.14
whose
    interrogative (E) 19.17; (S) 19.15
    relative (S/E) 26.13
will/would (E) 2.5, 6.2, 8.7-8, 8.16-17
wishes (E/S) 8.15
word order
    adjectives, descriptive/limiting (S/E) 20.6-9
    basic English 1.2-3, 5.6; (S/E) 1.5
    basic Spanish 1.4, 5.6; (S/E) 1.5; (S) 11.13-14
    conjunctive pronouns & verb (S/E) 11.4-5
    direct and indirect object interchange (S) 1.6
    emphatic (S/E) 1.6
    negative words (S/E) 27.1-4
    passive voice (S/E) 16.5, 16.7
    pronominal reduplication (S) 11.13
    subject (S) 1.4
    topicalization (S) 11.14
would (See *will/would*)
    past description vs. conditionality (S) 6.2

Y

y-extension (S) 4.10
yes-no questions (E/S) 5.6; 5.9-10
yod-extension (S) 4.11
you
    generic (E) 3.1
    indefinite subject (E/S) 13-14
    Spanish equivalents (E) 3.1

About the Authors

Sam Hill, now in his 13th year of retirement from California State University, Sacramento, received his B.A. in Secondary Education from Arizona State University (Tempe) in 1963 with a major in Spanish and minors in English and Russian. A Woodrow Wilson fellowship for graduate study at Stanford University led to a M.A. in Spanish Peninsular Literature (1964) and a Ph.D. in Spanish Historical Linguistics with a minor concentration in Portuguese (1970). While at Sacramento State, Professor Hill taught a wide range of courses, including ESL, beginning and intermediate Spanish and Portuguese, upper division courses in Spanish Grammar and Phonetics, and graduate seminars in Historical Spanish Linguistics and Comparative Grammars. He was also active in his Department's now highly successful Three-Summer M.A. Travel Study program in Spain, Mexico, Peru and Guatemala. He also enjoyed productive sabbatical leaves in Brazil (1980) and Puerto Rico (1991). Dr. Hill is the main author of the first two editions of this text (1991 and 2000) and in retirement continues to travel extensively.

María Mayberry, Associate Professor of Spanish, now in her eighth year teaching at California State University, Sacramento, is a native of Monterrey, Mexico. She studied in Mexico at Instituto Tecnológico y de Estudios Superiores de Monterrey, where she received the degree of *Licenciada en Ciencias de la Comunicación* in 1981. After studying ESL classes and completing and AA in Computer Programming at San Antonio College, she moved to Austin, Texas, where she received her B.A. degree with a Major in Spanish and a Minor in History, an MA and Ph.D. degrees in Spanish linguistics and Second Language Acquisition from the University of Texas at Austin. She teaches beginning Spanish as well as courses in Spanish Grammar, Phonetics and graduate seminars in Applied Linguistics and Contrastive Grammatical Structures of Spanish and English. Her research focuses on understanding the difficulties faced by adult second language learners when processing speech. Her commitment to teaching and researching Spanish as a second/foreign language is rooted in her own experiences as an adult language learner. Prof. Mayberry joined the Foreign Language Department at CSUS in Fall 2006 with six years of experience teaching Spanish at the University of Texas at Austin. She was awarded a sabbatical leave for the spring 2014 semester.

Edward Baranowski is a Professor of Spanish at California State University Sacramento. He received his PhD in Hispanic Linguistics from the University of Wisconsin, and since his arrival at CSUS in 2002 has taught all levels of Spanish language, Advanced Grammar, Spanish Phonetics, Introduction to Language and Linguistics, and graduate seminars in Dialectology, the History of the Spanish Language, Contrastive Grammatical Structures of Spanish and English, and Applied Spanish Linguistics. His area of expertise is Spanish Historical Linguistics, and in addition to publishing articles in this field, he has also contributed transcriptions of colonial texts to the *Cíbola* and *Cordiam* projects. In an administrative capacity, he has served as director of the department's Three-Summer M.A. Travel Study program in Guatemala, Mexico, Peru and Spain, and in 2011-2012 was also director of the California State University International Program in Spain.

IN MEMORIAM:

Professor William P. Bradford, co-author of the first two editions of this text, and a valued confidant and colleague, passed away in July of 2007 after a brief illness. His insightful and continuous contributions to the text during its years of evolution and classroom testing are noted with gratitude and affection.